The Coins of the English East India Company. Presidency Series

By

Dr. Paul Stevens

Honorary Research Associate, Heberden Coin Room, Ashmolean Museum, Oxford University

SPINK

The Coins of the English East India Company.
Presidency Series

Copyright © 2017
Paul J.E. Stevens

Hardback edition: ISBN 978-1-907427-69-5
Paperback edition: ISBN 978-1-907427-72-5

Published by Spink & Son Ltd
69, Southampton Row
Bloomsbury
London WC1B 4ET
www.Spink.com

Printed and bound in Malta
by Gutenberg Press

Contents

Acknowledgements

Many people have contributed to this book over the last 25-35 years that I have been collecting the information. Many of those people are mentioned in the main body of the work but I would particularly like to thank the following people for help over the course of many years. Shailen Bhandare has been a constant source of inspiration and has drawn most of the Persian legends. Equally, Stan Goron has helped me in many ways to keep going with the work.

Bob Johnston has provided a huge amount of information, which has kept arriving by post and Email for nearly 15 years. He has helped to check the book and made many useful suggestions. Without him this work would have missed many important facts and contained many more mistakes.

Hemanth Chopra has been particularly helpful with the coinage of the Madras Presidency, identifying many new varieties and correcting some of my numerous early mistakes.

Information about new coins was contributed by: David Fore, Paul Withers, Thomas Curtis of AH Baldwin, Hillel Kaslove, Jan Lingen, Farokh Todywalla, Keith Wilford, Peter Thompson, Randy Weir, Peter Mitchell and Graham Byfield of AH Baldwin, Howard & Francis Simmons, Jonathan Morris, Manoranjan Mahapatra (points raised on the internet website of the South Asia Coin Group), Prashant Kulkarni, Barry Tabor, Heinz Bons, Suresh Kawale and probably many others, to whom I can only apologise for not naming them. My thanks also go to Spink & Son for allowing me to use some of the illustrations from Pridmore's works, and Edward Baldwin for allowing me to use pictures from Baldwin's auction catalogues.

Finally, I would like to thank Emma Howard of Spink who organised all the printing and distribution of the book.

Preface

Major Pridmore's catalogue of the coins of the Indian Presidencies[1] is the most complete reference work about the coins of the EIC Presidency series. The present work started with an idea to update Pridmore's catalogue with a list of those coins that had been newly identified since that catalogue was written, and came from Ken Wiggins. Ken enlisted Bob Puddester and, later, me to help compile the new catalogue. It soon became apparent that the work presented an opportunity to add more than just a list of new coins, and that we could use it to explore some of the areas where new information had come to light about certain coinages and mints, or where a new interpretation could be made from existing knowledge.

---

[1] Pridmore F (1975), The Coins of the British Commonweath of Nations to the end of the reign of George VI 1952. Part 4 India. Volume 1 East India Company Presidency Series c1642-1835. Spink & Son Ltd

Ken's untimely death, shortly after the completion of the first draft of Madras, in July 2000, threw us into some confusion. Ken's vast knowledge, in particular of the Moghul-style issues, left a great gap in our ability to continue. Bob eventually decided, after much thought and due to pressure of other projects, that he could not continue, and so it was left to me to try to find a way forwards and, at least, to preserve the work that we had done already. Nevertheless, Ken and Bob contributed significantly and I would like to acknowledge that fact here,

By 2012 I had completed the work on the coins of the Bengal Presidency and this has been published[2] (referred to herein as Stevens, Bengal). In that book I added a catalogue of the coins referred to in each chapter of the book. Several people have commented that they found this hard to use because they had to skip around the book to find the relevant entries so I determined in the next volume (Bombay) to put the catalogue together in a single chapter. However, I became bogged down in the research needed to complete the text part of the Bombay volume and a number of people have commented that they really only use the catalogue, so I have eventually decided that I would publish a catalogue of all three Presidencies together. This has meant taking the Bengal work and reassembling it into one section. I have used the same catalogue numbers as in Stevens, Bengal, and added new entries and made some corrections. Bengal is followed by new catalogues of Bombay and then Madras.

Conventions and Abbreviations

The edges of the coins are sometimes abbreviated: P = plain; SG = straight grained; GL = grained left; GR = grained right.

As far as the weight is concerned, the official weight is shown, if known, and also the actual weight of known specimens. If only one value is shown for this latter weight, then only one specimen has been measured, if a range is shown, then more than one specimen has been recorded.

The diameter values represent the smallest and largest diameters measured on one or more specimens.

The values shown are estimates for a coin of that type in average condition. For instance crudely made hammered coins will mainly be found in about VF condition whilst machine made coins will usually be found in EF or better.

AH	*Anno Hijri*
AD	*Anno Domini*
CNG	Classical Numismatic Group (of USA)
ClassNG	Classical Numismatic Gallery (of India)
EIC	(English) East India Company
IOR	India Office Records (held in the British Library)
JONS	Journal of the Oriental Numismatic Society

---

[2] Stevens PJE (2012), The Coins of the Bengal Presidency, AH Baldwin & Sons Ltd

ONSNL	Oriental Numismatic Society's News Letter
RY	Regnal Year
SCMB	Seaby's Coin and Medal Bulletin
SNC	Spink's Numismatic Circular
XRF	X-ray Fluorescence

Photographs and Pictures

As many coins and features as possible are illustrated. Sometimes line drawings are used instead of photographs especially when no very clear coin is available, or when the entire design needs to be shown, but is never present on a single coin. In fact most of the Persian legends on the coins are shown in this way.

Since, in my view, the importance of illustrations is to reveal the features of the coins, and since actual-size photographs often do not show sufficient detail, all of the pictures are enlarged unless otherwise stated. The actual size of the coin is shown by the diameters listed in the catalogue and by the circles shown (dashed circles indicate estimated diameters). Where a diameter (or any other measurement) is estimated, this is indicated by ~, as ~25 meaning approximately 25.

For each coin type, photos are shown with the obverse on your left as you look at the page, and the reverse on your right. This differs from Pridmore, who chose the same approach as this for South Indian and European-style coins, but for Moghul-style coins he put the obverse on the right and reverse on the left. This seems a little confusing, and the approach therefore is standardised for all coins.

The Arrival of the English in India[3]

Throughout the sixteenth century the English sought to emulate both the Portuguese with their monopoly of trade with the east, and the Spanish with their control of the gold and silver of South America. Initially they chose not to challenge directly these monopolies by force, but to find a new way to achieve a similar endpoint. Thus the century saw an extensive search for the North West Passage to the Indies and the "discovery" of Labrador and the colonisation of Virginia. The sixteenth century also saw the beginnings of the formation of companies holding monopolies of trade between England and certain other markets, and it was a company of this type, formed on 31st December 1600, that was granted a charter for the exclusive right to trade with the East Indies. The first two voyages did not go to India but to the islands of the East Indies, but the third expedition in 1607, was sent to explore the opportunities for trade in the Arabian Sea and specifically to call, *inter alia*, at Surat in Gujerat on the west coast of India. One of the ships of the small fleet of this third voyage, commanded by a captain Hawkins, eventually reached Surat on 28th August 1608.

However, they were not the first Englishmen to visit India. This achievement is

---

[3] Taken verbatim from Stevens, Bengal

attributed to a certain Mr. Stevens, who had joined a party of Portuguese to visit the famous Jesuit establishment in Goa during the 1570s. Hawkins, though, considered himself far more than a mere visitor, and styled himself 'the King of England's Embassador' and in this capacity he found himself faced with tremendous odds in trying to establish a factory at Surat. Not the least of these difficulties came from the Portuguese, who rightly recognised the danger to their monopoly, and twice tried to assassinate him before he finally determined to travel overland to the Moghul court at Agra and gain permission from the Emperor himself. However, although Hawkins managed to ingratiate himself with the Emperor Jahangir, his ambition to establish a trading post at Surat was eventually thwarted by a combination of the Portuguese Jesuits and Mukarrab Khan, the official in charge of the ports of Gujerat.

The English continued to try to establish themselves in Surat but, up until 1635, the Portuguese continued to challenge these attempts both by undermining the English representations to the local Indian Powers, and by directly engaging the English ships in pitched battle. Initially the English could only base themselves near to Surat at a place named Swalley Hole, but the twelfth voyage, commanded by Thomas Best, arrived at Surat in 1612 and finally succeeded in obtaining the necessary permission to establish a factory, possibly because the Moghuls were beginning to realise that the English were seriously capable of challenging Portuguese naval power. In 1635 the Portuguese and the English signed, in Goa, a treaty that gave the English access to Portuguese trading posts all around the Arabian Sea, including the posts along the west coast of India. One of the islands controlled by the Portuguese was Bombay, and this island was ceded to Charles II as part of the dowry for his marriage to the Portuguese princess, Catherine of Braganza in 1661. Charles then leased Bombay to the East India Company in 1668

Meanwhile, two Dutchmen with experience of trading in the East had arrived in London in 1609 and offered to lead a voyage to the east, or Coromandel, coast and to explore trade between there and Siam and Bantam. Floris and Antheuniss, the two Dutchmen, sailed from England in January 1611 and by August they had arrived on the east coast of India and visited the ports of Masulipatam and Petapoli in Golconda. Whilst the local trade with Siam did not live up to expectations in the longer term, Masulipatam became established as a factory of the EIC on and off for many years. In the 1630s the headquarters of the English was moved from Masulipatam to Armagon and then back again, as the English tried to deal with the various vicissitudes facing them such as famine, the animosity of the Dutch, and local wars between Golconda and its neighbours. In 1639, the English agent at Armagon, Francis Day, sailed down the coast visiting the Portuguese fort of San Thome and then on to a small fishing village called Madraspatam. Here he negotiated with the local *naik*, the right to build a fort on a piece of land measuring about one square mile, and whence he determined to remove the Armagon agency. Quite why he chose this spot is a matter of speculation, but it is of interest to record that the main reason for the establishment of the great city of Madras upon its present site, may well have been its proximity to San Thome, wherein is reputed to have lived Francis Day's mistress!

Further up the east coast, in the Bay of Bengal, Antheuniss had made contact with Bengal in the 1620s but it was not until the 1640s and 1650s that serious trade began. Factories were established in various places including Hoogli, Patna and Dacca, and by 1681 the area was afforded the status of a separate Presidency. However, Calcutta was not then the major factory. This did not happen until after the farcical affair of the attempted invasion of Moghul India (with a standing army of perhaps 100,000 men) by a British army of 308 men. After various skirmishes, and the effective annihilation of the British infantry, the arrival of a British fleet allowed a truce agreeable to both sides to be reached. Part of the agreement allowed Job Charnock, the leader of the British forces, to select a site for a factory and he eventually chose a place near a village called Kalighat, later modified to Kalikata and then Calcutta.

Bengal Presidency Calcutta Mint Early Years 1757-1760

Summary[1]

In 1756, the Nawab of Bengal attacked and captured Calcutta, whereupon the British sent an army and fleet to recapture the town, which they did in January 1757. Following this, they obliged the Nawab to grant them the right to establish a mint and they began to strike coins, at first showing the mint name 'Alinagar Kalkata, 'Alinagar being the name given to the town by the Nawab. However, later in the year, following the battle of Plassey, the new Nawab allowed the East India Company (herinafter EIC) to strike coins with the mint name, Kalkata. Coins with this mint name were struck in years 4, 5 and 6 of 'Alamgir II, but the shroffs imposed a heavy *batta* on them and it proved impossible to get them into circulation. At the very end of 1760, the EIC requested, and obtained, permission to strike coins with the mint name Murshidabad, in Calcutta. These new coins were first issued in the name of 'Alamgir II, AH 1174, RY 6. The Calcutta authorities also decided to begin minting silver coins with the mint name, Arcot, in Calcutta and applied to Madras for the dies.

The only copper coins issued were those struck for the use of the workers employed in repairing and expanding the town's fortifications.

---

[1] Stevens Bengal

Gold Mohur – 'Alamgir II – 'Alinagar Kalkata – 1757

In April 1757 the EIC was given permission to strike gold and silver coins, although no mention of gold actually being struck has been found in the records.

See Photo for rupee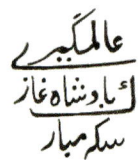

sikka mubārak bādshāh ghāzī 'ālamgīr [AH] (= the auspicious coin of the victorious Emperor, 'Alamgir [AH])

See Photo for rupee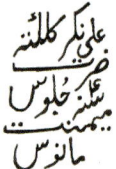

zarb 'alīnagar kalkata sanah [RY] julūs maimanat mānūs (= Struck at 'Alinagar Calcutta in the [RY] year of tranquil prosperity)

Official Weight (g)	11.08
Actual Weight (g)	?
Actual Diameter (mm)	~25
Metal	Gold

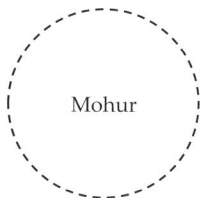

Mohur

Catalogue

Cat No.	Pr. No.	AH	RY	Comments	Value ($)
1.1	1	?	4	Reported in SCMB 1949 p. 372. Described as: unique gold mohur of 'Alamgir II regn. Year 4 with mint name 'Alinagar Calcutta. From a talk presented by Dr. R.B. Whitehead	NV

Silver Rupee *et infra* – 'Alinagar Kalkata – 1757

In early July 1757, 4000 rupees were struck with the mint name 'Alinagar Kalkata.

1.2

sikka mubārak bādshāh ghāzī 'ālamgīr [AH] (= the auspicious coin of the victorious Emperor, 'Alamgir [AH])

zarb 'alīnagar kalkata sanah [RY] julūs maimanat mānūs (= Struck at 'Alinagar Calcutta in the [RY] year of tranquil prosperity)

Silver Rupee *et infra* – 'Alinagar Kalkata – 1757 (cont)

	Rupee	Half Rupee
Official Weight (g)	11.64	5.82
Actual Weight (g)	11.61	?
Actual Diameter (mm)	~25	21
Metal	Silver	

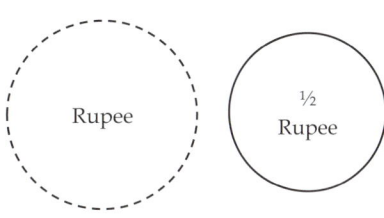

Catalogue

Cat No.	Pr. No.	Denom	AH	RY	Comments	Value ($)
1.2	2	Rupee	xxxx	4	Ref: Ashmolean Museum	NV
1.3	-	Half Rupee	xxxx	4	Ref: Baldwin (2001), sale 25 (Wiggins), lot 613	5,000

Gold Mohur *et infra* – 'Alamgir II – Kalkata – 1757 to 1760

In October 1757 gold was sent to the mint to be coined into mohurs. There is no indication, in the records, of fractions being struck and the whereabouts of the half and quarter in the Caldecott sale (JB Caldecott, Sotheby, 11th June 1912) is not known.

1.5

sikka mubārak bādshāh ghāzī 'ālamgīr [AH]
(= the auspicious coin of the victorious Emperor, 'Alamgir [AH])

zarb kalkata sanah [RY] julūs maimanat mānūs (= Struck at Calcutta in the [RY] year of tranquil prosperity)

	Mohur	Half Mohur	Quarter Mohur
Official Weight (g)	11.08	5.54	2.77
Actual Weight (g)	?	?	?
Actual Diameter (mm)	~25	~21	~16

Gold Mohur *et infra* – 'Alamgir II – Kalkata – 1757 to 1760 (cont)

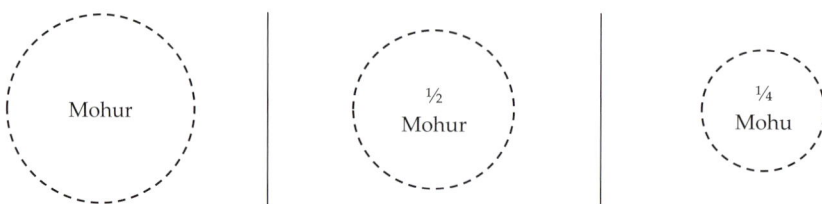

Mohur	½ Mohur	¼ Mohu

Catalogue

Cat No.	Pr. No.	Denom	AH	RY	Comments	Value ($)
1.4	-	Mohur	?	4	See Stevens, Bengal p. 7. No specimens known	NV
1.5	3	"	1171	5		10,000
1.6	4	"	1174	6		10,000
1.7	5	Half Mohur	[xxxx]	[x]	Not examined by Pridmore. Caldecott Sale (1912), Lot 77	NV
1.8	6	Quarter Mohur	[xxxx]	[x]	Not examined by Pridmore. Caldecott Sale (1912), Lot 77	NV

Silver Rupee *et infra* – 'Alamgir II – Kalkata – 1757 to 1760

On 28th July 1757, permission was given to strike coins with the mint name Kalkata. The smaller denominations (eighth and sixteenth) claimed to be Calcutta mint and not showing the mint name, are usually indistinguishable from Murshidabad. The listing for these smaller coins is based on Pridmore, but these coins might equally well be Murshidabad issues.

1.9

sikka mubārak bādshāh ghāzī 'ālamgīr [AH] (= the auspicious coin of the victorious Emperor, 'Alamgir [AH])

zarb kalkata sanah [RY] julūs maimanat mānūs (= Struck at Calcutta in the [RY] year of tranquil prosperity)

Silver Rupee *et infra* – 'Alamgir II – Kalkata – 1757 to 1760 (cont)

	Rupee	Half Rupee	Quarter Rupee	Eighth Rupee	Sixteenth Rupee
Official Weight (g)	11.64	5.82	2.91	1.45	0.73
Actual Weight (g)	11.29-11.63	5.84	?	?	?
Actual Diam (mm)	22.2-24.0	18.5-19.3	~14	~10	~7
Metal	Silver				

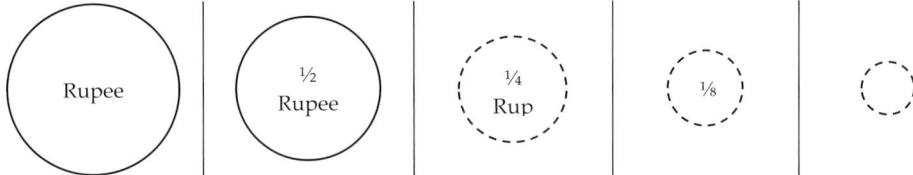

Catalogue

Cat No.	Pr. No.	Denom	AH	RY	Comments	Value ($)
1.9	-	Rupee	1171	4	Ref: Johnston, also Singapore/HK sale 28 (1999), lot 1002, also Baldwin sale 28 (2001), lot 1343	2,000
1.10	7	"	1171	5		1,800
1.11	8	"	1172	5		1,800
1.12	-	"	xxxx	6	Ref: Baldwin (2001), sale 25 (Wiggins), lot 614	1,000
1.13	9	Half Rupee	xxxx	4		5,000
1.14	10	Quarter Rupee	xxxx	4	See photo in Pridmore (Pr. 10)	3,000
1.15	11	Eighth Rupee	xxxx	4	Recorded from Pridmore, but his photo does not show the mint name. These may be Murshidabad mint issues	NV
1.16	12	"	xxxx	5		NV
1.17	13	Sixteenth Rupee	xxxx	5	Recorded from Pridmore. He shows no photo, and refers to NC 1903, No. 5, where the coin described could be Murshidabad or Calcutta	NV

Silver Rupee – 'Alamgir II – Murshidabad – 1761

Permission to strike rupees at Calcutta, with the mint name Murshidabad, was received right at the end of 1760. These coins probably would have been struck early in 1761, before coins with the name of Shah 'Alam II were authorised in July. The coins would have to be dated 1174 with RY 6. If the AH is not visible then the coins cannot be considered to belong to the EIC

Silver Rupee – 'Alamgir II – Murshidabad – 1761 (cont)

1.18

 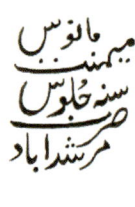

sikka mubārak bādshāh ghāzī 'alamgīr 1174 (= the auspicious coin of the victorious Emperor, 'Alamgir 1174)

zarb murshīdābād sanah 6 julūs maimanat mānūs (= Struck at Murshidabad in the 6th year of his reign of tranquil prosperity).

Actual Weight (g)	11.68
Actual Diameter (mm)	23.2-23.7
Metal	Silver

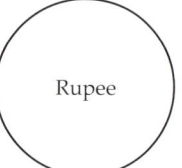

Rupee

Catalogue

Cat No.	Pr. No.	Denom	AH	RY	Comments	Value ($)
1.18	-	Rupee	1174	6	Only one specimen known at present	1,000

Copper Monetary Tickets – 1757

In October 1757, the mint master was instructed to produce copper tickets for the use of the labourers rebuilding the fortifications of the city.

1.19

A circle divided by a cross. In each of the four compartments is one of the letters: V E I C (Vnited East India Company)

A large script numeral 1 (or 6 or 3 or 2) within a raised circle.

Copper Monetary Tickets – 1757 (cont)

	Anna	Six Pice	Three Pice	Two Pice
Actual Weight (g)	28.6-29.2	14.58	?	4.65
Actual Diam (mm)	Varies. See table below	22.0	~18	~15
Metal	Copper			

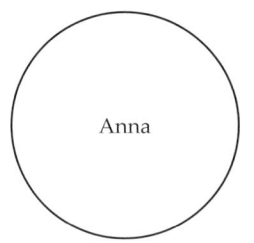
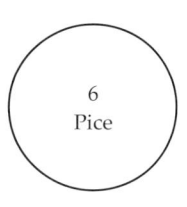

Catalogue

Cat No.	Pr. No.	Denom	Obv	Actual Diam (mm)	Comments	Value ($)
1.19	186	Anna	A	33.2	BM	NV
1.20	-	"	B	25-27	Ref: Rhodes	8,000
1.21	-	"	C	"	Ref: Rhodes	8,000
1.22	187	Six Pice	-	-	BM	NV
1.23	-	Three Pice	-	-	None found although a pencil drawing exists in an old copy of Thurston[2].	NV
1.24	-	Two Pice	-	-	Ref: Rhodes. Personal comm, June 2006. Published by Kathotia IK (2006), JONS 188, p. 23. See below for photo	3,000

Obverse Varieties for Anna

C in balemark	The C in the balemark may be leaning backwards or be straight.
Letters in Balemark	The letters in the balemark may be arranged normally or in mirror image.

	A	B	C
C in balemark	Leans backwards	Straight	Leans backwards
Letters in Balemark	Normal	Normal	Mirror image

---

[2] Thurston E (1890), Catalogue of the Coins in the Madras Museum. Superintendent, Government Press, Madras.

Copper Monetary Tickets – 1757 (cont)

C leans backwards

C stands straight

Normal letters

Letters mirror image

Other Denominations

Two pice denomination

*Scan from copy of Thurston
showing 3 pice denomination
added in pencil (the 9 is an
upside-down 6)*

Bengal Presidency Calcutta Mint 1761-1790

Summary

By the beginning of 1761, the Calcutta authorities had established a working mint, and had attempted, unsuccessfully, to get the public to accept coins with the mint name Kalkata. They therefore had forced the Nawab to allow them to strike coins with the mint name Murshidabad in their mint at Calcutta. They began to do this from the beginning of 1761, issuing coins in the name of 'Alamgir II and, in the middle of 1761, followed this with coins in the name of Shah 'Alam II. In addition, they had begun to strike Arcot rupees and, for several years Arcot rupees represented the major output of the Calcutta mint. Having finally sorted out the types of rupees that would be most useful, the Calcutta authorities faced another challenge with the silver coinage, namely the scarcity of silver available to produce such a coinage. The reason for this scarcity is complicated and multifactorial, but it meant the authorities were unable to obtain sufficient silver to meet the currency demands of Bengal, and Robert Clive, the Governor, attempted to solve the problem by creating a bi-metallic currency, issuing gold coins with a fixed value relative to silver and with disastrous results for the Bengal economy. A subsequent gold coinage proved more successful and continued, on and off, until 1788.

The second major challenge facing the Calcutta authorities was the *batta* system. Throughout India *batta* was charged by the shroffs on exchanging low weight/fineness coins for those of better quality. This also applied in Bengal but here there was an additional local custom of *batta*. Newly produced silver coins were called "*sicca*" and had a premium of 15% or 16% added to them when they were issued from the mint. When coins were issued with the next RY, the *batta* on the coins of the previous RY was reduced to 12% or 13%, i.e. they suddenly became worth 3% less than they had been, even though usually they were not very worn and contained the same amount of silver. Worse still, coins that were two or more years old were reduced to "sonauts" with the premium being reduced to 10% or 11%, that is 4% or 5% worse than *sicca*. Both these forms of *batta* allowed the shroffs to make large profits at the expense of the poorer people and were considered, particularly by the authorities in England, to be especially iniquitous. Many attempts, therefore, were made to remove the practice and reduce the opportunities to charge *batta* on exchanging coins from one mint for those from another.

All of these problems were exacerbated by the extension of the Company's power in Bengal. In 1765 the EIC was granted the *Diwani* (tax collecting rights) of Bengal, Bihar and Orissa. This, theoretically, meant that all of the mints of this area, which were: Murshidabad, Patna and Dacca, as well as Calcutta, now came under their control. In practice, the mints continued under the control of the Nawab and his native officers at least until 1769, when the EIC began to exert more direct control. Despite this, in theory at least, the coins issued from all the mints in Bengal, Bihar and Orissa should be considered as EIC issues from 1765.

In about 1770, with the issue of the RY 11 rupees, all four mints in the Presidency were instructed to strike identical coins, that is the Murshidabad *sicca*, and this was the first serious attempt to try to address the problem of *batta*. In the following year an attempt was made to stop the other type of *batta*, which was charged on older Murshidabad rupees, by instructing the shroffs not to charge this exaction on RY 11 coins once the RY 12 coins were issued. Both these efforts had limited success and very few Murshidabad style coins were issued in RY 13 and 14 (with the RY 12), with the mints of Patna and Dacca being closed. When RY 15 coins were issued, the RY 12 coins were immediately reduced in value by the shroffs, and the authorities had to find another way to address this issue. This time they issued coins in RY 16, 17 and 18, all showing the fixed RY of 15. Finally, in 1777, the Murshidabad mint was closed and the fixed RY of 19 was introduced, with coins being issued from only the Calcutta mint. However, the problem of *batta* was not finally solved until the introduction of the milled silver coinage in the early 1790s (see later). RY 19 remained on the silver and gold coins right up until 1835, with the silver rupee becoming known as the 19 sun *sicca*.

Silver Rupee – Kalkata – 1761 to 1763

Eighth rupees are recorded in various other sources, but all the photos seen could equally well be Murshidabad coins, and probably are. Only nazarana rupees seem to have been struck for presentation to the Emperor. It is possible that a RY 2 coin was struck, though none is known.

2.2

sikka zad bar haft kishwar sāya fazl ilāh hāmī dīn muhammad shāh ʿālam bādshāh [AH] (= Defender of the religion of Muhammad, Shah ʿAlam Emperor, Shadow of the divine favour, put his stamp on the seven climes, [AH])	*zarb kalkata sanah [RY] julūs maimanat mānūs* (= Struck at Calcutta in the [RY] year of tranquil prosperity)

Official Weight (g)	11.64
Actual Weight (g)	?
Actual Diameter (mm)	~25
Metal	Silver

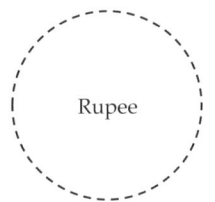

Rupee

Catalogue

Cat No.	Pr. No.	Denom	AH	RY	Comments	Value ($)
2.1	-	Rupee	1175	3	**Nazarana.** Ref: Baldwin (2001), sale 25 (Wiggins), lot 618	10,000
2.2	14	"	1176	4	**Nazarana.** See Pridmore for picture, which may have been taken from Marsden (1825), Oriental Coins, Plate 44, No 937	NV

11

Gold Mohur – Calcutta/Murshidabad – 1761 to 1765

It is not possible to determine if the coins were struck at Calcutta or Murshidabad. It seems likely that other fractions such as quarters and eighths would have been struck, as well as the fractions recorded below.

2.3

sikka zad bar haft kishwar sāya fazl ilāh hāmī dīn muhammad shāh 'ālam bādshāh [AH] (= Defender of the religion of Muhammad, Shah 'Alam Emperor, Shadow of the divine favour, put his stamp on the seven climes, [AH])

zarb murshīdābād sanah [RY] julūs maimanat mānūs (= Struck at Murshidabad in the [RY] year of his reign of tranquil prosperity.)

	Mohur	1/16 Mohur	1/64 Mohur
Official Weight (g)	11.64	0.73	0.181
Actual Weight (g)	?	0.8	0.170
Actual Diameter (mm)	~25	~9	5
Metal	Gold		

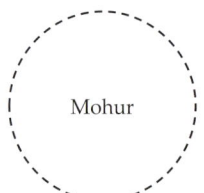

Mohur   ¹⁄₁₆   ¹⁄₆₄

Gold Mohur – Calcutta/Murshidabad – 1761 to 1765 (cont)

Catalogue

Cat No.	Pr. No.	Denom	AH	RY	Comments	Value ($)
2.3	-	Mohur	1176	3	Ref: Kulkarni	10,000
2.4	-	"	1177	5	Recorded from KM 663	10,000
2.4c	-	Half Mohur	1176	4	Ref: Baldwin	6,000
2.5	-	1/16 Mohur	xxxx	x	Ref: Bons. Mint name not visible, so not certainly from Murshidabad.	5,000
2.6	-	1/64 Mohur	xxxx	5	0.170g. Reported by Kulkarni (Numismatic Digest, vol 27-28, pp. 117-118). Second specimen reported by Rhodes in Sept.2006 from Gautam Dalmiya	2,000

1/64 Mohur

Gold Mohur *et infra* – Calcutta/Murshidabad – 1766 to 1768

Issued from the mints of Calcutta, Murshidabad and Patna. The C on the reverse may be the Calcutta mintmark but see Stevens, Bengal pp. 32-33.

2.7

   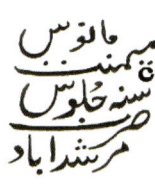

sikka zad bar haft kishwar sāya fazl ilāh hāmī dīn muhammad shāh 'ālam bādshāh [AH] (= Defender of the religion of Muhammad, Shah 'Alam Emperor, Shadow of the divine favour, put his stamp on the seven climes, [AH])
NB Colour added to photos

zarb murshīdābād sanah [RY] julūs maimanat mānūs C (= Struck at Murshidabad in the [RY] year of his reign of tranquil prosperity. C)

Gold Mohur *et infra* – Calcutta/Murshidabad – 1766 to 1768 (cont)

	Mohur	½ Mohur	¼ Mohur	⅛ Mohur
Official Weight (g)	11.64	5.82	2.91	1.45
Actual Weight (g)	?	?	2.90	?
Pridmore Diam (mm)	19.4	15.5	11.9-12.5	~11.5
Metal	Gold			

 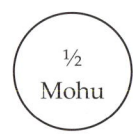 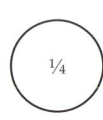 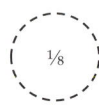

Catalogue

Cat No.	Pr. No.	Denom	AH	RY	Comments	Value ($)
2.7	15	Mohur	1180	8		10,000
2.8	16	Half Mohur	xxxx	7		8,000
2.8c	-	Quarter Mohur	xxxx	7	ClassNG (2012), sale 7, lot 322	3,000
2.9	-	Eighth Mohur	xxxx	7	Rhodes from Gautam Dalmiya. No C visible but probably off flan	2,000

Quarter mohur   *Eighth mohur*

Gold Mohur *et infra* – Calcutta/Murshidabad – 1769 to 1788

2.17

 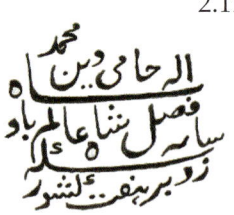    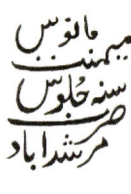

sikka zad bar haft kishwar sāya fazl ilāh hāmī dīn muhammad shāh ʿālam bādshāh [AH]
(= Defender of the religion of Muhammad, Shah ʿAlam Emperor, Shadow of the divine favour, put his stamp on the seven climes, [AH])

zarb murshīdābād sanah [RY] julūs maimanat mānūs (= Struck at Murshidabad in the [RY] year of his reign of tranquil prosperity.)

Gold Mohur *et infra* – Calcutta/Murshidabad – 1769 to 1788 (cont)

	Mohur	Half Mohur	Quarter Mohur	Eighth Mohur	Sixteenth Mohur
Official Weight (g)	12.36	6.18	3.09	1.54	0.77
Actual Weight (g)	12.16-12.36	6.15	?	1.48-1.54	0.71-0.77
Actual Diam (mm)	22.1-25.0	~18	~14	12.2-13.9	9.0-12.7
Metal	Gold				

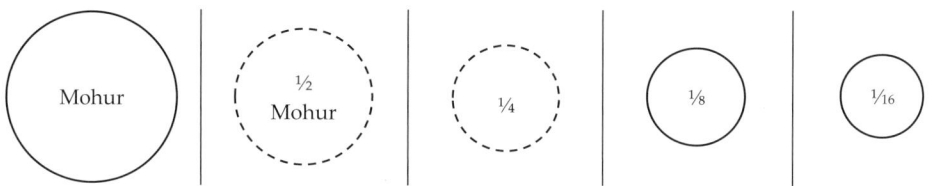

Catalogue

Cat No.	Pr. No.	Denom	AH	RY	Comments	Value ($)
2.10	17	Mohur	1182	10		2,000
2.11	18	"	1183	10		2,000
2.12	19	"	1183	11		2,000
2.12c	-	"	1184	10	Ref: Stacks	2,000
2.13	20	"	1184	11		2,000
2.14	21	"	1184	11	Proof. BM	NV
2.15	22	"	1185	12		2,000
2.16	23	"	1186	12		2,000
2.17	-	"	1187	12		2,000
2.18	25	"	1188	12	Mule with old rev. die	5,000
2.19	27	"	1189	12	Mule with old rev. die. See Baldwin (2006), sale 47 (Stiller), lot 806	5,000
2.19c	-	"	1190	12	Mule with old rev. die. Ref: Baldwin	5,000
2.20	24	"	1187	15		2,000
2.21	26	"	1188	15		2,000
2.22	28	"	1189	15		2,000
2.23	29	"	1190	15		2,000
2.24	30	"	1194	19	Date confirmed	3,000
2.25	31	"	1195	19		2,000
2.26	32	"	1196	19		2,000
2.27	33	"	1197	19		2,000

Listing continued on next page

Gold Mohur *et infra* – Calcutta/Murshidabad – 1769 to 1788 (cont)

Catalogue (cont)

Cat No.	Pr. No.	Denom	AH	RY	Comments	Value ($)
2.28	34	Mohur	1198	19		2,000
2.29	35	"	1199	19		2,000
2.30	36	"	1200	19		2,000
2.31	37	"	1201	19		2,000
2.32	38	"	1202	19	See also Glendining's sale October 1988 for coin struck on larger flan	2,000
2.33	39	Half Mohur	1182	10		2,000
2.34	40	"	1182	10	Silver proof	5,000
2.34c	-	"	1183	10	Ref: Album (2012), sale 13, lot 1398	2,000
2.35	41	"	1183	11		2,000
2.36	-	"	1200	19	Ref: Baldwin (2000), sale 22 (Wheeler) lot 131	2,000
2.37	42	Quarter Mohur	1182	10		1,000
2.38	43	"	1182	10	Silver proof	3,000
2.39	44	"	1202	19		1,000
2.40	45	"	1203	19		1,000
2.41	46	Eighth Mohur	1182	10		800
2.42	47	"	1182	10	Silver Proof. BM	2,000
2.43	48	"	1183	10		800
2.44	49	"	1183	10	Silver Proof	2,000
2.45	50	"	xxxx	15		800
2.46	-	"	1200	19	Smithsonian Institution. Reported by Kaslove	1,000
2.47	51	"	1202	19		800
2.48	52	"	1203	19		800
2.49	53	Sixteenth Mohur	1182	10		700
2.50	54	"	1182	10	Silver Proof. BM	1,000
2.51	55	"	1183	10		700
2.52	56	"	1183	10	Silver Proof	1,000
2.53	57	"	xxxx	15	BM	700
2.54	58	"	1202	19	Also exists struck from 1/8 Mohur dies. Ref: Kaslove & Glendining sale Oct 1988 lot 493	700
2.55	59	"	1203	19		700

Silver Rupee *et infra* – Calcutta – RY 2 of Shah 'Alam II

Probably issued from the Calcutta mint as an early or trial piece before a decision was made to copy the Murshidabad *sicca* as closely as possible (see Stevens, Bengal pp. 46-48). NB reverse inscription

2.56

sikka zad bar haft kishwar sāya fazl ilāh hāmī dīn muhammad shāh 'ālam bādshāh [AH] (= Defender of the religion of Muhammad, Shah 'Alam Emperor, Shadow of the divine favour, put his stamp on the seven climes, [AH])

zarb mubarak murshīdābād sanah 2 julūs maimanat mānūs (= Struck at auspicious Murshidabad in the 2nd year of tranquil prosperity)

Actual Weight (g)	11.63
Actual Diameter (mm)	26.7-27.0
Metal	Silver

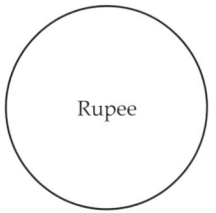

Rupee

Catalogue

Cat No.	Pr. No.	Denom	AH	RY	Comments	Value ($)
2.56	-	Rupee	1174	2	Probably the first issue of the Murshidabad *sicca* from the Calcutta mint in the name of Shah 'Alam II. Only one known at present	3,000

17

Silver Rupee *et infra* – Calcutta/Murshidabad, 1761 to 1771

Distinguished from the next type by the presence of a sun mark on the obverse. Coins of this type were struck at both Calcutta and Murshidabad and cannot be distinguished from each other

2.78

sikka zad bar haft kishwar sāya fazl ilāh hāmī dīn muhammad shāh ʿālam bādshāh [AH] (= Defender of the religion of Muhammad, Shah ʿAlam Emperor, Shadow of the divine favour, put his stamp on the seven climes, [AH])	*zarb murshīdābād sanah [RY] julūs maimanat mānūs* (= Struck at Murshidabad in the [RY] year of his reign of tranquil prosperity.)

	Rupee	**Half Rupee**	**Quarter Rupee**	**Eighth Rupee**	**Sixteenth Rupee**
Official Weight (g)	11.64	5.82	2.91	1.46	0.73
Actual Weight (g)	11.50-11.65	5.71	2.80-2.87	1.32-1.46	0.70-0.73
Actual Diam (mm)	22.0-23.6	17.8-19.5	13.0-15.3	11.4-11.8	8.4-9.8
Metal	Silver				

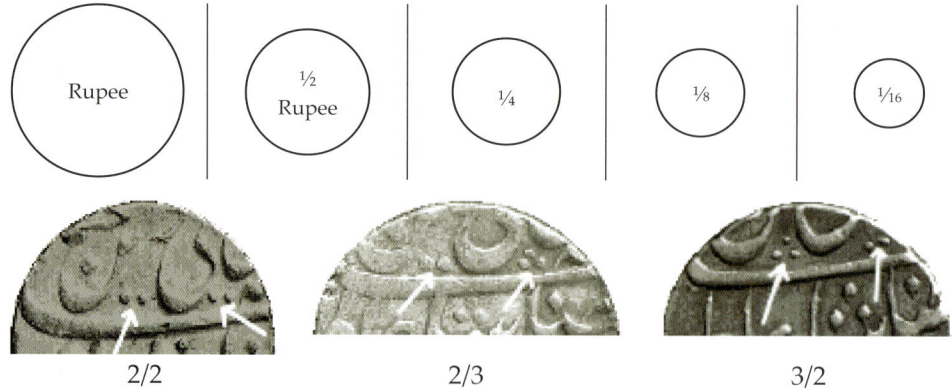

2/2   2/3   3/2

Dot patterns in top line of obverse of rupee

Silver Rupee *et infra* – Calcutta/Murshidabad, 1761 to 1771 (cont)

Catalogue

Cat No.	Pr. No.	Denom	AH	RY	Dots	Comments	Value ($)
2.57	-	Rupee	1174	2	3/2	Ref: Rhodes. Also may occur with dots 2/3 but dots	250
2.58	-	"	1175	2	3/2	not clear & AH not visible	250
2.58a	-	"	1175	3	?	**Nazarana.** Berlin museum.	5,000
2.59	-		1175	3	2/2	Ref: Rhodes	150
2.60	-	"	1175	3	3/2	Ref: Rhodes	150
2.61	-	"	1176	3	?	Ref: Rhodes	150
2.62	-	"	1176	4	?	**Nazarana.** Obv may be same die as Calcutta Nazarana. Ref: Kaslove, Rhodes – See NS.XXI by E.V.Zambaur	5,000
2.63	-		1176	4	2/2	Ref: Rhodes	150
2.64	-		1176	4	3/2	Ref: Rhodes	150
2.65	-	"	1177	4	?	Ref: Rhodes	150
2.66	-	"	1177	5	2/3	Ref: Rhodes	150
2.67	-	"	1178	5	2/3	Ref: Rhodes	150
2.68	-	"	1179	5	2/3	Baldwin (2006), sale 47 (Stiller), lot 810. Incorrect mix of AH & RY	500
2.69	-	"	1178	6	2/3	**Nazarana.** Ref: Kaslove	5,000
2.70	-	"	1179	6	2/3	Ref: Rhodes	150
2.71	87	"	1179	7	2/3		150
2.72	88	"	1180	7	2/3		150
2.73	-	"	1180	8		**Nazarana.** Ref: Mitchiner M1896. Also SNC Sept 1979	5,000
2.74	89	"	1180	8	2/3		150
2.75	90	"	1181	8	2/3	Ref: Rhodes. Also occurs with dots 0/3	150
2.76	-	"	1181	9	?	**Nazarana.** Ref: Kaslove. See Skelton[3]. Berlin museum (for AH) ex P.P. Adler	5,000
2.77	91	"	1181	9	2/3		150
2.78	92	"	1182	9	2/3	Ref: Rhodes	150
2.79	343	"	1182	10	2/3	**Nazarana**	5,000
2.80	93	"	1182	10	2/3		150
2.81	94	"	1183	10	2/3		150

Listing continued on next page

---

[3] Skelton HP (1862) New Illustrated Manual of the Current Gold and silver Coins of all Civilized Nations of the Globe Giving their Weight, Standard, & Value, Together with the Systems of Money, Weights, & Measures and Statistics, Commercial Geography, & Industry of the Different Countries, James Hagger, London.

Silver Rupee *et infra* – Calcutta/Murshidabad, 1761 to 1771 (cont)

Catalogue

Cat No.	Pr. No.	Denom	AH	RY	Comments	Value ($)
2.82	-	Half Rupee	1176	3	Ref: Rhodes	150
2.83	-	"	xxxx	7	Ref: Chopra	150
2.84	96	"	1181	8	Ref: Rhodes. See also Mitchiner 1897c	150
2.84a			1181	9	Berlin museum. Ex P.P. Adler	300
2.85	-	1/4 Rupee		3	Ref: Rhodes	100
2.86	-	"		4	Ref: Rhodes	100
2.87	-	"		5	Ref: Rhodes	100
2.88	-	"		6	Ref: Rhodes	100
2.89	-	"	1179	7	Ref: HK/Singapore (2003), sale 36, lot 458. Hijri date not usually visible	100
2.90	-	"	118x	8	Ref: Johnston	100
2.91	-	"	xxxx	9	**Nazarana**. Ref: Kaslove. See Skelton[102]	5,000
2.92	97	"	1181	9	Also Berlin museum. Ex P.P. Adler (see this coin for AH)	100
2.93	-	1/8 Rupee	1175	2	Ref: Noble Sale 48 (1995), Lot 2123.	120
2.94	-	"	xxxx	3	Ref: Rhodes	120
2.95	-	"	xxxx	4	Ref: Baldwin (2006), sale 47 (Stiller), lot 805.	120
2.96	-	"	xxxx	4	Struck on a broad flan from smaller dies. Wt. 1.46g. Ref: Baldwin (2006), sale 47 (Stiller), lot 804.	800
2.97	-	"	117x	5	Ref: Chopra	120
2.98	-	"		6	Ref: Rhodes	120
2.99	-	"	1179	7	Ref: Weir	120
2.100	98	"	118[x]	7	Ref: HK/Singapore (2002), sale 34, lot 578	120
2.101	99	"	xxxx	8		120
2.102	100	"	1182	9	Ref: Ravi Shankar Sharma. See also Berlin museum (dated AH 118x). ex P.P. Adler	120
2.103	-	1/16 Rupee	xxxx	2	Ref: Rhodes	120
2.104	-	"	xxxx	3	Ref: Rhodes	120
2.105	-	"	xxxx	5	Ref: Rhodes	120
2.106	-	"	xxxx	6	Ref: Rhodes	120
2.107	-	"	xxxx	7	Ref: Rhodes	120
2.108	-	"	xxxx	8	Ref: Rhodes	120
2.109	101	"	xxxx	9		120
2.109a	-	1/32 Rupee	xxxx	9	Berlin museum. Ex Guthrie (0.365g)	NV

Silver Rupee *et infra* – Calcutta/Murshidabad, 1771 to 1777

Distinguished from the previous type by the presence of a crescent/moon mark on the obverse. Coins of years 11 & 12 were issued from all four mints of Calcutta, Murshidabad, Patna and Dacca. There may be a secret dot system to distinguish the coins from the different mints, but this is rather speculative at present (see Stevens, Bengal pp. 71-72). Year 15 coins were issued from Murshidabad and Calcutta but appear to be identical.

2.116

sikka zad bar haft kishwar sāya fazl ilāh hāmī dīn muhammad shāh ʿālam bādshāh [AH] (= Defender of the religion of Muhammad, Shah ʿAlam Emperor, Shadow of the divine favour, put his stamp on the seven climes, [AH])	*zarb murshīdābād sanah [RY] julūs maimanat mānūs* (= Struck at Murshidabad in the [RY] year of his reign of tranquil prosperity.)

	Rupee	**Half Rupee**	**Quarter Rupee**	**Eighth Rupee**	**Sixteenth Rupee**	**1/32 Rupee**
Official Weight (g)	11.64	5.82	2.91	1.46	0.73	0.37
Actual Weight (g)	11.36-11.65	5.70-5.78	2.77-2.88	1.39-1.47	0.72-0.73	?
Actual Diam (mm)	21.4-25.5	17.4-19.3	13.8-14.6	10.8-12.9	8.6-10.7	~7-8
Metal	Silver					

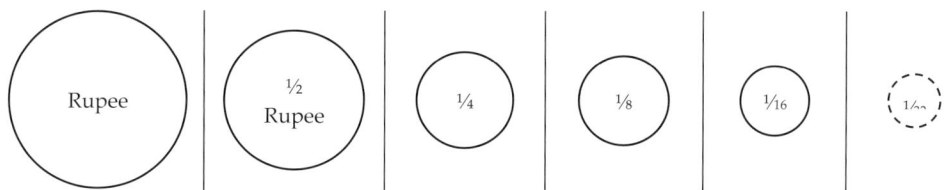

21

Silver Rupee *et infra* – Calcutta/Murshidabad, 1771 to 1777 (cont)

Catalogue

Cat No.	Pr. No.	Denom	AH	RY	Dots	Comments	Value ($)
2.110	-	Rupee	1182	10	?	Ref: Rhodes	150
2.110c			1182	10		Nazarana. Berlin museum. Ex P.P. Adler	5,000
2.111	95	"	1183	10	5/3		150
2.112	-	"	1184	10	?	Ref: Rhodes	150
2.113	-	"	1183	11	?	**Nazarana.** Ref: Bons	5,000
2.114	109	"	1183	11	?		150
2.115	-	"	1184	11	?	**Nazarana.** Ref: Pridmore (1978), SNC, LXXXVI, p. 68. Also Kaslove	5,000
2.116	110	"	1184	11	5/0		150
2.117	110	"	1184	11	4/3		150
2.118	110	"	1184	11	5/3	Ref: Johnston	150
2.119	111	"	1184	11		**Proof.** BM	NV
2.120	-	"	1185	11	5/0	Ref: Kaslove, also Tandon	150
2.121	-		1185	11	4/3		150
2.122	-		1185	11	5/3		150
2.123	-	"	1187	11	4/3?	Ref: Senior. AH not certain.	150
2.124	-	"	1185	12	5/0	**Nazarana.** Ref: Kaslove. Also Album (2009), Sale 7, lot 653. Plain flower & no dots to right of RY	5,000
2.125	-	"	1165	12	4/3	Error date. Ref: Kaslove; also Rhodes from a collection in Calcutta	800
2.126	112	"	1185	12	4/3		150
2.126c	-	"	1185	12	5/3	Ref: Baldwin	150
2.127	113	"	1186	12	5/0	Plain flower & no dots to right of RY	150
2.128	113	"	1186	12	4/3	Ref: Kaslove, also. Johnston	150
2.129	113	"	1186	12	5/3		150
2.130	114	"	1187	12	5/0	Plain flower & no dots to right of RY	150
2.131	115	"	1188	12	4/3		150
2.132	116	"	1189	12	?	Mule of Obverse with earlier reverse	150
2.133	344	"	1185	13	4/3	**Nazarana.** Ref: Pridmore (1978), SNC, LXXXVI, p. 68. Kaslove, personal communication. Baldwin (2006), sale 47 (Stiller), lot 836	5,000
2.134	-	"	1188	15	4/3	**Nazarana.** Ref: Pridmore (1978), SNC, LXXXVI, p. 68. Baldwin (2001), sale 25 (Wiggins), lot 620. See also Album (2008), sale 5, lot 489	5,000

Listing continued on next page. For dot positions see at end of listing.

Silver Rupee *et infra* – Calcutta/Murshidabad, 1771 to 1777 (cont)

Catalogue (cont)

Cat No.	Pr. No.	Denom	AH	RY	Dots	Comments	Value ($)
2.135	-	Rupee	1188	15	4/3	Ref: Johnston	150
2.136	117	"	1189	15	4/3		150
2.137	118	"	1190	15	4/3		150
2.138	-	Half Rupee	118x	10	-	Ref: Wilkes (2009), list 5, lot 298	200
2.139	119	"	1184	11	-		200
2.140	120	"	1184	11	-	Proof. BM	NV
2.141	121	"	1186	12	-		200
2.142	-	"	1189	15	-	Ref: Johnston	200
2.143	-	"	1190	15	-		200
2.144	-	Quarter Rupee	xxxx	10	-	HK/Singapore (2003), sale 36, lot 459. Could be star or crescent mm. Kaslove has one with crescent	300
2.145	122	"	xxxx	11	-		300
2.146	123	"	xxxx	11	-	Proof. BM	NV
2.147	124	"	xxxx	12	-		300
2.148	125	"	xxxx	15	-		300
2.149	-	Eighth Rupee	xxxx	10	-	HK/Singapore (2003), sale 36, lot 459	200
2.150	126	"	xxxx	11	-		100
2.151	127	"	xxxx	11	-	Proof. BM	NV
2.152	128	"	1186	12	-	Very rare with AH date visible	100
2.153	128	"	1188	12	-	Ref: Johnston. Very rare with AH date visible	100
2.154	128	"	xxxx	15	-		100
2.155	129	"	118x	15	-	Finer Style. Ref: Baldwin (2001), sale 25 (Wiggins), lot 621	250

Listing continued on next page

2.113

Nazarana rupee AH 1183, RY 11. Struck from special dies with fine engraving

Silver Rupee *et infra* – Calcutta/Murshidabad, 1771 to 1777 (cont)

Catalogue

Cat No.	Pr. No.	Denom	AH	RY	Comments	Value ($)
2.156	102	1/16 Rupee	118x	10		100
2.157	130	"	1184	11	Ref: Rhodes	100
2.158	131	"	xxxx	11	Proof. BM	100
2.159	132	"	1186	12	Ref: Rhodes Very rare with AH date	100
2.160	133	"	xxxx	15		100
2.161	-	1/32 Rupee	xxxx	11	Ref: Baldwin (2001), sale 25 (Wiggins), lot 624	800
2.162	-		xxxx	15	**Nazarana**. Ref: Baldwin (2001), sale 25 (Wiggins), lot 622	2,000
2.163	-	1/64 Rupee	xxxx	12	Ref: Kaslove but not certain of mint & date. From Wiggins sale. A sixty-fourth rupee dated RY 15 has been reported (Chopra) but the mint is not certain	NV

Dots on Obverse and Reverse of Rupees

Obverse dots	There may be four or five dots in the loop of *fazl*
Reverse dots	There may be three dots or none above the start of the word *julus*

4 dots on obverse   *5 dots on obverse*   *3 dots on reverse*   *No dots on reverse*

Rupee 5/0 with plain flower.

Silver Rupee *et infra* – Calcutta – 19 Sun *Sicca* Coinage

In May 1777, an order was made that coins would be issued from only one mint of the Presidency, Calcutta. This introduced the perpetual 19 sun *sicca* coins. However, the Hijri date continued to change each year as can be seen from the listing below.

2.181

sikka zad bar haft kishwar sāya fazl ilāh hāmī dīn muhammad shāh 'ālam bādshāh [AH] (= Defender of the religion of Muhammad, Shah 'Alam Emperor, Shadow of the divine favour, put his stamp on the seven climes, [AH])

zarb murshīdābād sanah 19 julūs maimanat mānūs (= Struck at Murshidabad in the 19th year of his reign of tranquil prosperity)

	Rupee	Half Rupee	Quarter Rupee	Eighth Rupee	Sixteenth Rupee	1/32 Rupee
Official Weight (g)	11.64	5.82	2.91	1.46	0.73	0.37
Actual Weight (g)	11.48-11.59	5.64-5.80	2.56-2.87	1.44-1.46	0.70-0.73	?
Actual Diam (mm)	21.0-27.0	17.9-19.7	14.8-16.5	11.3-13.1	9.5-10.9	~9
Metal	Silver					

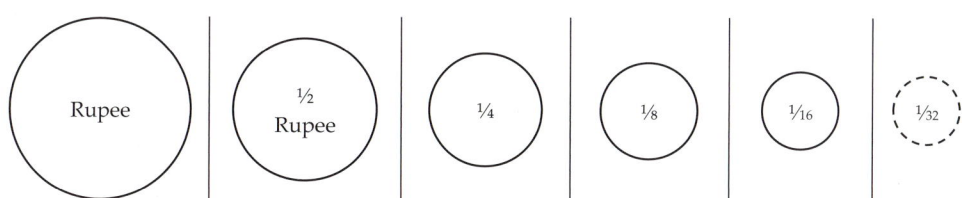

Silver Rupee *et infra* – Calcutta – 19 Sun *Sicca* Coinage (cont)

Catalogue

Cat No.	Pr. No.	Denom	AH	RY	Comments	Value ($)
2.165	345	Rupee	1190	19	Nazarana	5,000
2.166	135A	"	1190	"		500
2.167	135B	"	1191	"		150
2.168	136	"	1192	"		150
2.169	137	"	1193	"		150
2.170	138	"	1194	"		150
2.171	139	"	1195	"		150
2.172	140	"	1196	"		150
2.173	141	"	1197	"		150
2.174	142	"	1198	"		150
2.175	143	"	1199	"		150
2.176	-	"	1200	"	Ref: Johnston	150
2.177	144	"	1201	"		150
2.178	145	"	1202	"		150
2.179	146	"	1203	"		150
2.180	-	"	1204	"	Ref: Baldwin (2001), sale 25 (Wiggins), lot 628	150
2.181	147	"	1205	"		150
2.182	148	"	120x	12	Mule. Old rev die re-used.	500
2.183	-	Copper trial	xxxx	19	Ref: Baldwin (2010), sale 68, lot 4262. Wt = 9.66g	2,000
2.184	149	1/2 Rupee	1193	19	Ref: HK/Singapore (2003), sale 36, lot 463	200
2.185	149	"	1194	"	Ref: as previous	200
2.186	149	"	1196	"	Ref: Thompson	200
2.187	-	"	1200	"	Ref: Rhodes	200
2.188	150	1/4 Rupee	119x	19		200
2.189	151	1/8 Rupee	1190	19	Ref: Rhodes	200
2.190	-	"	1198	"	Ref: Rhodes	200
2.191	-	"	xx99	"	Ref: Johnston	200
2.192	-	"	1205	"	Ref: Rhodes	200
2.193	429	"	xxxx	"	Finer style than usual. See Baldwin (2001), sale 25 (Wiggins), lot 646	500
2.194	152	1/16 Rupee	xxxx	19		200
2.195	-	1/32 Rupee	xxxx	19	Ref: HK/Singapore (2003), sale 36, lot 464	200

Silver Rupee *et infra* – Calcutta – 19 Sun *Sicca* Coinage (cont)

2.183

Copper trial. Probably produced when testing new machinery (see Stevens, Bengal chapter 4)

Silver Rupee – Arcot – In the Name of 'Alamgir II

Issued from several mints including Madras, Calcutta and Murshidabad

2.196

  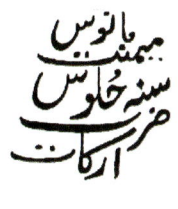

sikka mubārak bādshāh ghāzī 'ālamgīr [AH] (= the auspicious coin of the victorious Emperor, 'Alamgir [AH])	*zarb arkāt sanah 6 julūs maimanat mānūs* (= Struck at Arcot in the 6th year of his reign of tranquil prosperity.)

Official Weight (g)	11.43
Actual Weight (g)	10.64-11.49
Actual Diameter (mm)	20.0-25.0
Metal	Silver

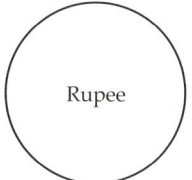

Rupee

Catalogue

Cat No.	Pr. No.	Denomination	AH	RY	Comments	Value ($)
2.196	Madras 140	Rupee	1172	6	Issued from Calcutta mint from 1761 to 1776. Also from Madras (cat no 2.63) and Murshidabad (not recorded separately). AH almost never visible.	80

Copper Single & Half Annas – 1760s & 1770s

No entries found in the records about the dates of issue of these coins

2.197

shāh 'alam bādshāh ghāzī [AH] (= Shah 'Alam Victorious Emperor [AH])

zarb kalkata maimanat 1 ana (= Struck at prosperous Calcutta, the value of 1 anna)

	Anna	Half Anna
Official Weight (g)	28.89	14.45
Actual Weight (g)	27.05-28.78	14.47
Actual Diam (mm)	25.0-28.5	22.3-23.0
Metal	Copper	

Anna

½ Anna

Catalogue

Cat No.	Pr. No.	Denom	AH	Comments	Value ($)
2.197	188	Anna	1177	Specimens with clear dates are very rare	1,500
2.198	189	"	1188		1,500
2.199	190	Half Anna	1188		2,500

2.199

Half anna appears to say "aph ana" (half anna) on reverse

Bengal Presidency Pulta Mint (Princep's Coinage)

Summary

In 1780, an entrepreneur named John Prinsep discovered copper mines in Bihar and applied for permission to begin mining copper. Soon afterwards he had the idea that he could use the copper to produce a new copper coinage for the Bengal Presidency. The authorities in Calcutta granted the necessary permission for him to mine the copper and produce the coinage, which he began to do in 1781. His minting process was entirely new to India in that he introduced machinery including laminating or rolling machines and fly-presses. The authorities in London did not agree that Prinsep (or anyone else for that matter) should have been allowed these mining and coining rights and instructed Calcutta to end the contract. However the terms of the contract allowed Prinsep the right of an extension for an extra 27 years following the successful completion of the first three years. London's instructions arrived 12 days too late to cancel the contract, and Prinsep asked for it to be extended for the extra 27 years. Eventually the dispute was settled with Prinsep agreeing to stop his coinage, and receiving a large sum of money to compensate him for all his costs. Following this, Prinsep offered to work as mint master at Calcutta for no salary, and produce a silver and gold coinage for the EIC using his machinery, but despite the quality of the gold and silver patterns that he produced, his offer was rejected.

Silver Patterns. Double Rupee *et infra* 1784

   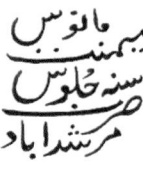

3.1

sikka zad bar haft kishwar sāya fazl ilāh hāmī dīn muhammad shāh 'ālam bādshāh 1198 (= Defender of the religion of Muhammad, Shah 'Alam Emperor, Shadow of the divine favour, put his stamp on the seven climes, 1198). All within a border of pellets

zarb murshīdābād sanah 26 julūs maimanat mānūs (= Struck at Murshidabad in the 26 year of his reign of tranquil prosperity). Within a raised, toothed rim.

	Double Rupee	Rupee	Half Rupee	Quarter Rupee	Eighth Rupee
Pridmore Weight (g)	23.53	11.66	?	2.99	?
Pridmore Diam (mm)	34.5	28.5	~21	17	~14
Metal	Silver				
Edge	Varies. See below				

Prinsep's pattern silver coins. Rupee (3.2) & quarter rupee (3.4)

Silver Patterns. Double Rupee *et infra* 1784 (cont)

Catalogue

Cat No.	Pr. No.	Denom	Edge	Comments	Value ($)
3.1	346	Double Rupee	* UNITED * EAST *INDIA * COMPANY * 1784		10,000
3.2	347	Rupee	"		NV
3.3	348	Half Rupee	Decoration of dots and three strokes repeated	See Pridmore sale, part II, lot 675, for the half rupee of this series	7000
3.4	349	Quarter Rupee	"		NV
3.5	350	Eighth Rupee	"		NV

Copper Pattern Quarter Anna – 1194 (1780)

3.6

shāh 'ālam bādshāh 1194 (= Shah
'Alam Emperor 1194)
Within a broad, raised, toothed rim.

*ẓarb murshīdābād sanah 22 julūs maimanat
mānūs* (= Struck at Murshidabad in the 22nd
year of his reign). Within a broad, raised,
toothed rim.

Pridmore Weight (g)	8.73
Pridmore Diam (mm)	23.3
Metal	Copper
Edge	Plain

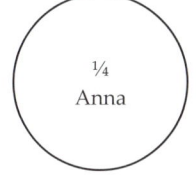

¼
Anna

Catalogue

Cat No.	Pr. No.	Comment	Value ($)
3.6	351		2,000

Copper Pattern Half Anna – 1195 (1780/81)

 3.7

shāh 'ālam bādshāh 1195 (= Shah 'Alam Emperor 1195.) No diacritical mark under the B of *bādshāh*. Within a broad, raised, toothed rim.

sanah 22 julūs (= in the 22nd year of his reign.) Within a broad, raised, toothed rim.

Actual Weight (g)	14.19
Actual Diam (mm)	27
Metal	Copper
Edge	Plain?

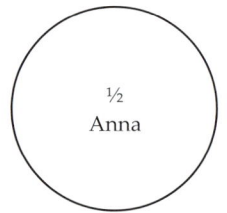

½ Anna

Catalogue

Cat No.	Pr. No.	Comment	Value ($)
3.7	-	See Wodak E, (1958), SNC, LLXVI, p. 62, Fig 2	2,000

Copper Pattern Quarter Anna – 1195 (1780/81) – Type 1

 3.8

shāh 'ālam bādshāh 1195 (= Shah 'Alam Emperor 1195). Within a broad, raised, toothed rim.

sanah 22 julūs (= in the 22nd year of his reign). Within a broad, raised, toothed rim.

Copper Pattern Quarter Anna – 1195 (1780/81) – Type 1 (cont)

Pridmore Weight (g)	7.19
Pridmore Diam (mm)	21.5
Metal	Copper
Edge	Plain

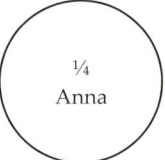

Catalogue

Cat No.	Pr. No.	Comment	Value ($)
3.8	352	Two distinct styles – as above photo, and as lot 677 in Pr sale	2,000
3.9	352	(Weir)	2,000

3.9

Photo from Pridmore sale (colour added)

Copper Pattern Quarter Anna – 1195 (1780/81) – Type 2

3.10

 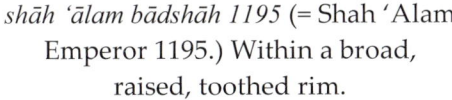

shāh ʿālam bādshāh 1195 (= Shah ʿAlam Emperor 1195.) Within a broad, raised, toothed rim.

sanah 22 julūs (= in the 22nd year of his reign.) Within a broad, raised, toothed rim.

Actual Weight (g)	11.79
Actual Diam (mm)	24.3-24.6
Metal	Copper/Dull grey. White metal?
Edge	SG with raised centre line

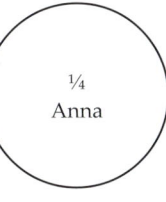

Copper Pattern Quarter Anna – 1195 (1780/81) – Type 2 (cont)

Catalogue

Cat No.	Pr. No.	Comment	Value ($)
3.10	-	Ref: CNG (2005), sale 66, lot 2065, also Fore. Also reported in tin	2,000

Copper Pattern Sixteenth Anna – 1195 (1780/81) – Type 1

3.11

shāh 'ālam bādshāh 1195 (= Shah 'Alam Emperor 1195). Within a beaded rim.

sanah 22 julūs (= in the 22nd year of his reign). Within a beaded rim.
NB single cluster of dots below legend

Actual Weight (g)	2.73
Actual Diam (mm)	15.3-15.6
Metal	Copper
Edge	Plain

¹⁄₁₆ Ann

Catalogue

Cat No.	Pr. No.	Comment	Value ($)
3.11	-	Stevens collection	1000

Copper Pattern Sixteenth Anna – 1195 (1780/81) – Type 2

3.12

shāh 'ālam bādshāh 1195 (= Shah 'Alam Emperor 1195). Within a beaded rim.

sanah 22 julūs (= in the 22nd year of his reign). Within a beaded rim.
NB 2 rosettes below legend

Photo black and white

Copper Pattern Sixteenth Anna – 1195 (1780/81) – Type 2 (cont)

Actual Weight (g)	2.08 (32.13 grains)	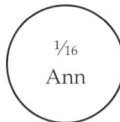
Actual Diameter (mm)	15.6	
Metal	Copper	¹⁄₁₆ Ann
Edge	Plain	

Catalogue

Cat No.	Pr. No.	Comment	Value ($)
3.12	-	See Pridmore sale (1982), lot 678	800

Copper Half Anna *et infra* – Currency Issues

3.23

shāh 'ālam bādshāh 1195 (= Shah 'Alam Emperor AH 1195). Within a raised, toothed rim.

sanah 22 julūs (= In the 22nd year of his reign). Within a raised, toothed rim. NB stars below legend

	Half Anna	Quarter Anna	Eighth Anna	Sixteenth Anna
Official Weight (g)	14.54	7.27	3.64	1.81
Actual Weight (g)	12.56-16.25	5.85-7.47	2.77-4.25	1.60-2.07
Actual Diam (mm)	25.5-29.7	21.5-24.6	17.5-19.5	14.0-16.5
Metal	Copper			
Edge	Plain			

The low weight coins within the ranges shown above tend to be rather worn

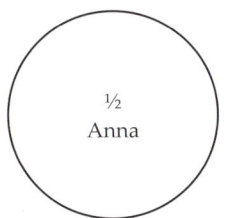 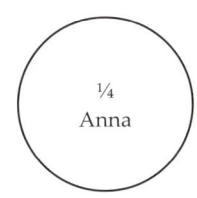 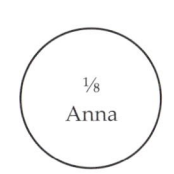 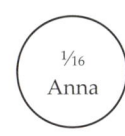

½ Anna   ¼ Anna   ⅛ Anna   ¹⁄₁₆ Anna

Copper Half Anna *et infra* – Currency Issues (cont)

Catalogue

Cat No.	Pr. No.	Denom	Status	Axis	Actual Diam (mm)	Comment	Value ($)
3.13	191	Half Anna	Currency	↑↓	29.0		80
3.14	-	"	Currency	↑↓	28.0	28mm. Ref: SNC April 1980.	80
3.15	192	"	Currency	↑↑	26.0	Ref: Weir	80
3.16	192	"	Currency	↑↓	26.0	Ref: Weir	80
3.17	192	"	Currency	↑↓	26.3	Flowery shaped device instead of stars. Wt = 13.05, Ref: Weir	80
3.18	193	"	Proof	↑↓	28.8	Ref: BM. 14.33g	NV
3.19	194	Quarter Anna	Currency	↑↓	23.7	size and position of stars can vary – a study would reveal several varieties	70
3.20	194	"	Currency	↑↑	23.7	Ref: Weir	70
3.21	194	"	Currency	↑←	23.7		70
3.22	195	"	Currency	↑↓	22.8		70
3.23	196	"	Proof	↑↓	24.6		500
3.24	197	Eighth Anna	Currency		19.6		60
3.25	198	"	Currency	↑↓	18.3		60
3.26	199	"	Proof	↑↓	20.8	Ref: BM. 3.82g	400
3.27	200	Sixteenth Anna	Currency	↑↓	15.8	3 varieties of star (Weir)	50
3.28	201	"	Currency	↑↓	14.5		50
3.29	202	"	Proof		16.4		300

Half anna 3.13

Eighth anna 3.24

Sixteenth anna 3.27

Bengal Presidency Calcutta Mint 1790-c1800

Summary

In 1789, a major report about the coinage of the Bengal Presidency concluded that the problems of *batta* as well as counterfeiting, filing, drilling etc, could be overcome by the introduction of coin production following the "European" method. John Prinsep, of course, had already done this but most of his machinery and skilled employees had been rejected by the Calcutta authorities and little capability was available to achieve the objective. Fortunately, the Calcutta mint master had employed Prinsep's foreman and his assistant, the latter of whom was to make a significant contribution to the construction and operation of the new mint. Nevertheless, although milled gold coins were produced reasonably quickly, milled silver coins proved more difficult and were not produced in Calcutta until 1793. Even then, the production of silver blanks continued to be undertaken manually and it was not until 1802 that this part of the process was executed with machinery.

Machine-made copper coins were first produced in 1795, although these first heavy coins proved too expensive, and in 1796 lighter copper coins were produced.

Gold Mohur – Shah 'Alam II – 1790

First issued at the end of August 1790, see Stevens, Bengal pp. 146-147. Differs from the next type in not having the extra tiny dot in the top line of the obverse.

  4.1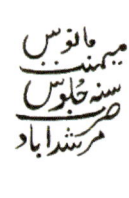

sikka zad bar haft kishwar sāya fazl ilāh hāmī dīn muhammad shāh 'ālam bādshāh 1202 (= Defender of the religion of Muhammad, Shah 'Alam Emperor, Shadow of the divine favour, put his stamp on the seven climes, 1202	*zarb murshīdābād sanah 19 julūs maimanat mānūs* (= Struck at Murshidabad in the 19th year of his reign of tranquil prosperity).

Official Weight (g)	12.36
Actual Weight (g)	12.29
Actual Diameter (mm)	25.5-26.2
Metal	Gold
Edge	Grained Right

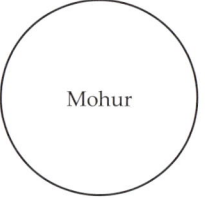

Mohur

Catalogue

Cat No.	Pr. No.	Comments	Value ($)
4.1	61		2000
4.2	-	Copper trial pieces (see Stevens, Bengal p. 146). No specimens discovered	NV

No extra dot in top line   *Extra dot in top line*

Gold Mohur *et infra* – Shah 'Alam II – 1793-1818

Distinguished from the previous type by the presence of the extra dot in the top line of the obverse.

Design for Mohur and Half Mohur

 4.3

| *sikka zad bar haft kishwar sāya fazl ilāh hāmī dīn muhammad shāh 'ālam bādshāh 1202* (= Defender of the religion of Muhammad, Shah 'Alam Emperor, Shadow of the divine favour, put his stamp on the seven climes, 1202 | *zarb murshīdābād sanah 19 julūs maimanat mānūs* (= Struck at Murshidabad in the 19th year of his reign of tranquil prosperity). |

Design for Quarter Mohur

 4.7

| *1204 sikka shāh 'ālam bādshāh ghāzī* (= 1204, Coin of Shah 'Alam the victorious Emperor) | *zarb murshīdābād sanah 19* (= Struck at Murshidabad in year 19) |

	Mohur	Half Mohur	Quarter Mohur
Official Weight (g)	12.36	6.18	3.09
Actual Weight (g)	12.34	6.15	3.09
Actual Diameter (mm)	26.5-26.9	21.6-21.8	16.7-17.0
Metal	Gold		
Edge	Grained Right		

Gold Mohur *et infra* – Shah 'Alam II – 1793-1818 (cont)

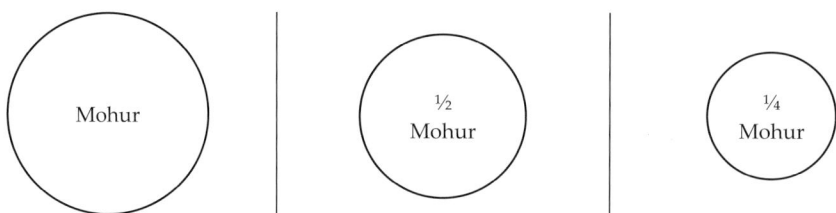

Catalogue

Cat No.	Pr. No.	Denom	Status	Comments	Value ($)
4.3	62	Mohur	Currency		2,000
4.4	65	"	Proof		NV
4.5	63	Half Mohur	Currency		1,500
4.6	66	"	Proof		NV
4.7	64	Quarter Mohur	Currency		1,000
4.8	67	"	Proof		NV

Mint Marks on Gold & Silver Coins

Machine-struck gold and silver coins were issued from several mints during the period 1790-1835. The mint of issue may be identied by a variety of secret marks and I have followed Pridmore in the attributions of the marks except for the rupees and mohurs of Patna and Dacca (see Stevens, Bengal for discussion of this subject).

Calcutta, Murshidabad, Patna and Dacca

For the single & half mohur/rupee, the mints are identified by the presence or absence of a tiny dot in the three decorative dot groups on the obverse

For the quarter mohur/rupee, the mints are identified by the presence or absence of a tiny dot in the decorative dot groups on the reverse.

Mohur/Rupee & Half Mohut/Rupee

Calcutta – No dot in the 3 circles

Murshidabad – dot in centre circle

Patna – dot in right circle

Dacca – dot in left-hand circle

Quarter Mohur/Rupee

Calcutta – Dot in centre circle

Murshidabad – no dot

Patna – dot in left group

Dacca – dot in right-hand group

Mint Marks on Gold & Silver Coins (cont)

Farrukhabad Silver struck at Calcutta, Farrukhabad, Benares & Saugor

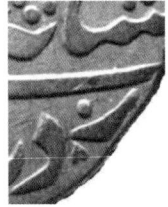  

Calcutta rupee and half, obverse. Inverted V

Calcutta rupee and half, reverse. No dot in circle

Calcutta quarter rupee obverse. Inverted V. No dot on reverse, as rupee

Farrukhabad, rupee and half rupee: extra dot on obverse
No dot on reverse

Farrukhabad, quarter rupee: dot in centre of circle on reverse. No inverted V on obverse

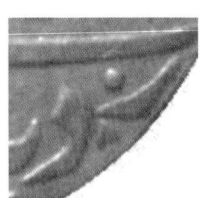 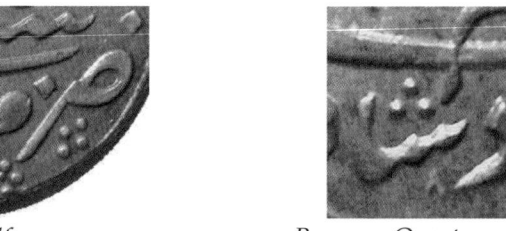

Benares, Rupee & half rupee.
Inverted V on obverse
Bead in centre of circle of dots on reverse

Benares, Quarter rupee.
Inverted V on obverse
Reverse as rupee

Saugor mint – No secret marks

Silver Rupee – Wide Rim Type – 1792

Pridmore assigned this type with wide rims and AH dates to trials in 1790. However, see Stevens, Bengal, pp. 157-158[4] for a discussion about assigning it to a later date (1792).

4.9

sikka zad bar haft kishwar sāya fazl ilāh hāmī dīn muhammad shāh 'ālam bādshāh 1202
(= Defender of the religion of Muhammad, Shah 'Alam Emperor, Shadow of the divine favour, put his stamp on the seven climes, 1202)

zarb murshīdābād sanah 19 julūs maimanat mānūs (= Struck at Murshidabad in the 19th year of his reign of tranquil prosperity).

Official Weight (g)	11.64
Actual Weight (g)	11.63
Actual Diameter (mm)	29.5-29.8
Metal	Silver
Edge	Grained Right

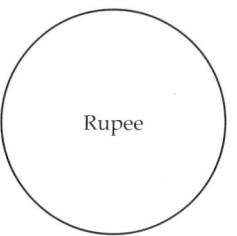

Rupee

Catalogue

Cat No.	Pr. No.	Status	Comments	Value ($)
4.9	153	Currency		2,000
4.10	-	Proof	Ref: Baldwin (2000), sale 22 (Wheeler), lot 161. Could this just be a well-struck piece?	NV

---

[4] Stevens PJE (2012), The Coins of the Bengal Presidency, AH Baldwin & Sons Ltd

Silver Rupee – 1793 to 1794

The earliest milled rupee, issued for circulation, has the date AH 1202 on the obv.

4.11

sikka zad bar haft kishwar sāya fazl ilāh hāmī dīn muhammad shāh 'ālam bādshāh 1202 (= Defender of the religion of Muhammad, Shah 'Alam Emperor, Shadow of the divine favour, put his stamp on the seven climes, 1202)	*zarb murshīdābād sanah 19 julūs maimanat mānūs* (= Struck at Murshidabad in the 19th year of his reign of tranquil prosperity).

Official Weight (g)	11.64
Actual Weight (g)	11.63
Actual Diameter (mm)	28.8-29.4
Metal	Silver
Edge	Grained Right

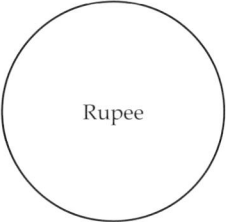

Rupee

Catalogue

Cat No.	Pr. No.	Comments	Value ($)
4.11	154	With AH date and no dots in circles on obverse. See p. 41 for picture of the secret marks	500

Silver Pattern Rupee et infra – 1794 to 1818

Patterns for silver coins issued from 1794 to 1818 (although they could also have been patterns for the gold coins). The date when they were struck is not known. The designs are the same as the currency issues, but without any of the round dots. The straight-edged dots appear on the reverse of the single and half size pieces.

Rupee & Half Rupee Patterns

4.12

sikka zad bar haft kishwar sāya fazl ilāh hāmī dīn muhammad shāh 'ālam bādshāh
(= Defender of the religion of Muhammad, Shah 'Alam Emperor, Shadow of the divine favour, put his stamp on the seven climes)

zarb murshīdābād sanah 19 julūs maimanat mānūs (= Struck at Murshidabad in the 19th year of his reign of tranquil prosperity).

4.14

Half rupee pattern

45

Silver Pattern Rupee *et infra* – 1794 to 1818 (cont)

Quarter Rupee Pattern

4.16

1204 sikka shāh ʿālam bādshāh (= AH 1204 Coin of Shah ʿAlam Emperor)	*zarb murshīdābād sanah 19* (= Struck at Murshidabad in the 19th year)

	Rupee	Half Rupee	Quarter Rupee
Actual Weight (g)	12.45	6.23	3.07
Actual Diameter (mm)	Varies. See table below		
Metal	Silver		
Edge	Varies. See table below		

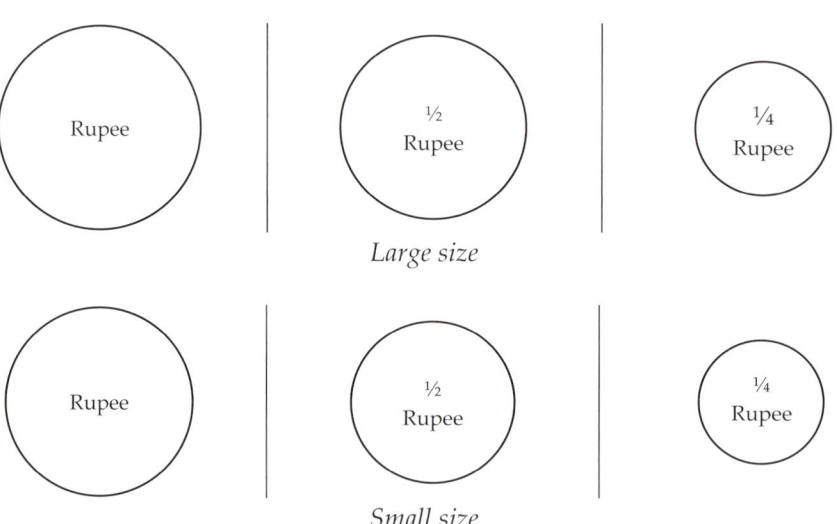

Large size

Small size

Silver Pattern Rupee *et infra* – 1793 to 1818 (cont)

Catalogue

Cat No.	Pr. No.	Denom	Status	Diam (mm)	Edge	Comments	Value ($)
4.12	355	Rupee	Pattern	27.0	P		2,000
4.13	358	"	Pattern	25.0	GL		2,000
4.14	356	Half Rupee	Pattern	24.3	P		1,500
4.15	359	"	Pattern	21.4	GL		1,500
4.16	357	Quarter Rupee	Pattern	17.7	P		1,200
4.17	360	"	Pattern	16.3	GL		1,200

Silver Rupee *et infra* – 1793 to 1818

No AH date on the obverse of the rupee and half. The quarter rupee has the fixed AH date 1204. The secret marks for Calcutta are the same as on the gold coins (p. 41)

Rupee & Half Rupee

4.18

sikka zad bar haft kishwar sāya fazl ilāh hāmī dīn muhammad shāh ʿālam bādshāh
(= Defender of the religion of Muhammad, Shah ʿAlam Emperor, Shadow of the divine favour, put his stamp on the seven climes)

zarb murshīdābād sanah 19 julūs maimanat mānūs (= Struck at Murshidabad in the 19th year of his reign of tranquil prosperity).

Silver Rupee *et infra* – 1793 to 1818 (cont)

Quarter Rupee

4.22

 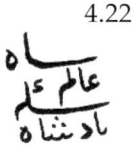  

1204 sikka shāh 'ālam bādshāh (= AH 1204 Coin of Shah 'Alam Emperor)

zarb murshīdābād sanah 19 (= Struck at Murshidabad in the 19th year)

	Rupee	Half Rupee	Quarter Rupee
Official Weight (g)	11.64	5.82	2.91
Actual Weight (g)	11.61-11.64	5.74-5.82	2.88-2.91
Actual Diameter (mm)	26.6-26.9	21.8-22.2	16.8-17.1
Metal	Silver		
Edge	Grained right		

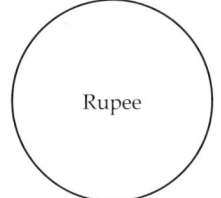 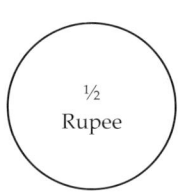 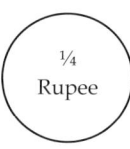

Catalogue

Cat No.	Pr. No.	Denom	Status	Edge	Comments	Value ($)
4.18	157	Rupee	Currency	GR		200
4.19	160	"	Proof	GR		2,000
4.20	158	Half Rupee	Currency	GR		150
4.21	161	"	Proof	GR		1,500
4.22	159	Quarter Rupee	Currency	GR	Occurs with large and small AH dates	100
4.24	162	"	Proof	GR		1,000

All of the currency coins occur with varying-sized numeral 19 on the reverse

Copper Weight for Rupee 1793 to 1818

4.25

An oval circle containing the legend. The weight above and the weight units below.
179
Min. weight
Old Cal. Rup
oblique milled
grs
Star countermark next to weight numerals.

Blank

Official Weight (g)	11.59g (179 grains)	
Actual Weight (g)	11.49	
Actual Diameter (mm)	26.5	
Metal	Copper	
Edge	Plain	

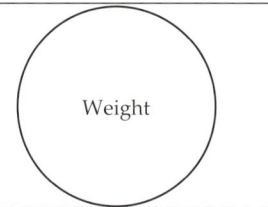

Catalogue

Cat No.	Pr. No.	Comments	Value ($)
4.25	-		200

Copper Quarter & Eighth Anna Patterns (Pice & Half Pice)

Patterns shown to the Calcutta Council in November 1795 when it was agreed that the inscriptions should be changed. No examples of these patterns have been discovered and their weight and size are not known, although they probably weighed the same as the 1795 coins issued for circulation (11.64g & 5.85g).

A Persian inscription: *ek pau anna*
(= quarter of an anna)
Quarter anna

A Persian inscription: *nīm pau anna*
(= half a quarter of an anna)
Eighth anna

Catalogue

Cat No.	Pr. No.	Denomination	Comments	Value ($)
4.26	-	Quarter Anna	None known	NV
4.27	-	Eighth Anna	None known	NV

Copper Pice & Half Pice 1795/96

4.29

The value in three languages: Bengali: e*k pai sikka*. Persian: *yek pai sikka*. Hindi: e*k pai sikka*. (Translation of all languages = One pai sikka).

sanah julūs 37 shāh ʻālam bādshāh (= in the 37th year of the Emperor Shah ʻAlam)

Official Weight (g)	Varies. See below
Actual Weight (g)	"
Actual Diam (mm)	"
Metal	Copper
Edge	Plain

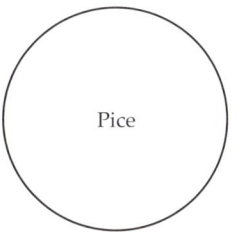

Pice

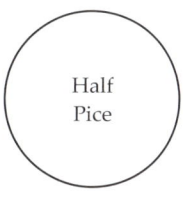

Half Pice

Catalogue

Cat No.	Pr. No.	Denom	Date Issued	Status	Official wt (g)	Actual wt (g)	Actual Diam (mm)	Comments	Value ($)
4.28	203	Pice	1795	Currency	11.64	11.66	?		500
4.29	204	"	1796	"	8.73	8.06-8.91	27.6-30.1		50
4.30	211	Half Pice	1795	Currency	5.82	5.83	25.2-25.4	Obverse legend: Half Pie sicca in 3 languages	500
4.31	212	"	1796	"	4.36	4.14-4.8	23.1-23.5	Ref: Kaslove, Johnston	80

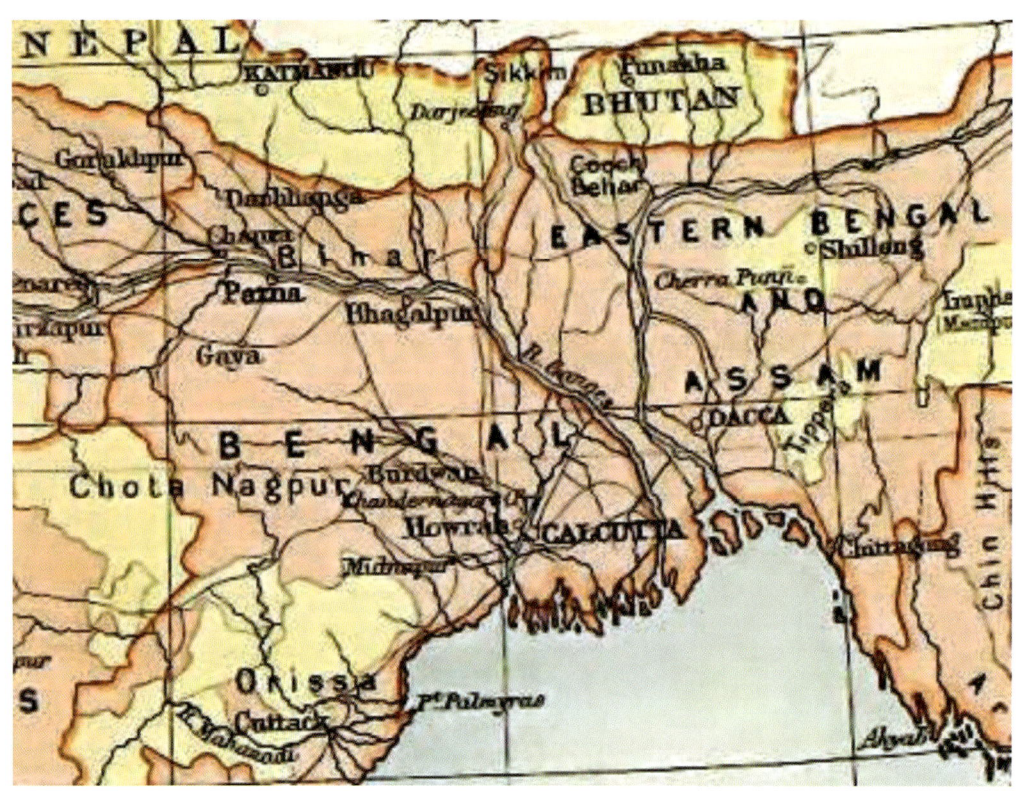

Bengal Presidency Other Mints in Bengal, Bihar & Orissa

Summary[5]

The mints, other than Calcutta that initially operated in the Bengal Presidency, were Murshidabad, Patna and Dacca. There was a mint at Monghyr, but further research has led to the conclusion that it was closed before the British acquired control. A copper pattern was prepared at Cuttack and sent to Calcutta, but never issued as currency.

The mint at Murshidabad issued gold and silver hammered coins that are indistinguishable from those issued from the Calcutta mint, and they are catalogued under the latter mint. Arcot rupees were also issued. This mint was closed in 1777, and re-opened in 1792 to issue the new milled coinage. It was finally closed in June 1795.

Patna and Dacca each issued gold and silver hammered coins with their own mint names ('Azimabad and Jahangirnagar respectively). However, in 1770/71 they were instructed to issue coins that were identical to those of Calcutta and Murshidabad, which they did for a limited time until they were closed, in about 1773/74.

Dacca was briefly re-opened in 1782, but the death of the mint master there, meant that only a few specimen coins were produced, and the mint never went into full production. These coins have not been identified but probably had the mint name Jahangirnagar.

Like Murshidabad, Patna and Dacca were re-opened in 1792, to help with the milled coinage and they both closed at about the end of 1795.

The milled coins contain secret marks to indicate the mint of origin, so that any problems with weight or fineness could be traced back to their source (see p. 41).

Tripura and Garhwal were occupied by the British in 1761 and 1815 respectively and a small number of coins were issued from these places whilst under British control.

---

[5] Stevens PJE (2012), The Coins of the Bengal Presidency, AH Baldwin & Sons Ltd

Bengal Presidency Murshidabad Mint

Murshidabad – Gold Mohur *et infra* –1765 to 1768

The first gold coins issued from the Murshidabad mint, under the authority of the British, were issued in 1765 in an attempt to fill the gap left by the scarcity of silver coins. The Calcutta coins are reputed to be those marked with the letter C, but the identity of the Murshidabad coins is not known

Catalogue

Cat No.	Pr. No.	Denomination	AH	RY	Comments	Value ($)
5.1	-	Mohur	?	?	Fractions may also have been struck	NR

Murshidabad – Silver Rupee *et infra* – 1765 to 1777

See Calcutta mint catalogue . There is no known way of distinguishing Calcutta coins from those struck at Murshidabad. They are, therefore, only catalogued under Calcutta.

Murshidabad – Arcot Rupee – 1765 to 1777

Arcot rupees were struck at Murshidabad from time to time. They were presumably identical to those struck at Calcutta and are, therefore, only catalogued under Calcutta.

Murshidabad – Gold Mohur *et infra* – 1794

A very small number of gold coins were issued from the Murshidabad mint in 1794. They are identified from the secret marks shown below and on p. 41.

5.2

sikka zad bar haft kishwar sāya fazl ilāh hāmī dīn muhammad shāh 'ālam bādshāh 1202
(= Defender of the religion of Muhammad, Shah 'Alam Emperor, Shadow of the divine favour, put his stamp on the seven climes, 1202)

zarb murshīdābād sanah 19 julūs maimanat mānūs (= Struck at Murshidabad in the 19th year of his reign of tranquil prosperity).

Murshidabad – Gold Mohur *et infra* – 1794 (cont)

	Mohur	Half Mohur	Quarter Mohur
Official Weight (g)	12.36	6.18	3.09
Actual Weight (g)	12.28-12.30	?	3.09-3.11
Actual Diameter (mm)	26.0-27.4	~22	16.3-17.8
Metal	Gold		
Edge	Grained Right		

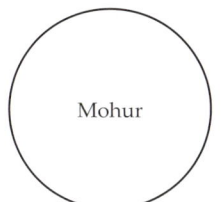  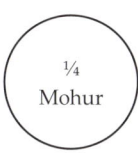

Catalogue

Cat No.	Pr. No.	Denom	AH Date	Comments	Value ($)
5.2	71	Mohur	1202	Seems to occur with and without the tiny extra dot in the top line. See Stevens, Bengal p. 219	2500
5.2c	71	"	1202	Wider rim (see also Patna gold). Ref: Johnston	5000
5.3	72	Half Mohur	1202		2000
5.4	73	Quarter Mohur	1204		1500

Mint Marks

Single & Half Mohur/Rupee

Murshidabad – dot in centre circle

For the single & half mohur/ rupee the mint is identified by the presence or absence of a tiny dot in the 3 decorative dot groups on the obverse

Quarter Mohur/Rupee

Murshidabad – no dot

For the quarter mohur/rupee the mints are identified by the presence or absence of a tiny dot in the decorative dot groups on the reverse.

Quarter mohur. NB only 2 groups of dots visible at bottom right of reverse rather than normal 3 groups

Murshidabad – Milled Coinages – Silver Rupee – 1793

The first milled silver rupees issued from the Murshidabad mint had the AH date 1202 on the obverse

5.5

sikka zad bar haft kishwar sāya fazl ilāh hāmī dīn muhammad shāh 'ālam bādshāh 1202 (= Defender of the religion of Muhammad, Shah 'Alam Emperor, Shadow of the divine favour, put his stamp on the seven climes, 1202)	*Z arb murshīdābād sanah 19 julūs maimanat mānūs* (= Struck at Murshidabad in the 19th year of his reign of tranquil prosperity).

Official Weight (g)	11.64
Actual Weight (g)	11.64-11.68
Actual Diameter (mm)	29.4-30.1
Metal	Silver
Edge	Grained Right

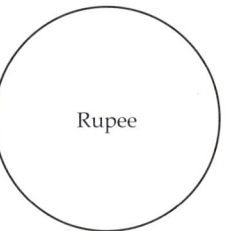

Rupee

Catalogue

Cat No.	Pr. No.	AH date	Comments	Value ($)
5.5	156	1202	Dot in centre circle on obverse. See above	1,000

Murshidabad – Rupee *et infra* – 1794 to 1795

Later milled rupees issued from Murshidabad did not have the AH date on the obverse. The secret marks are the same as those on the gold coins (see p. 41).

5.6

sikka zad bar haft kishwar sāya fazl ilāh hāmī dīn muhammad shāh ʿālam bādshāh (= Defender of the religion of Muhammad, Shah ʿAlam Emperor, Shadow of the divine favour, put his stamp on the seven climes)

zarb murshīdābād sanah 19 julūs maimanat mānūs (= Struck at Murshidabad in the 19th year of his reign of tranquil prosperity).

	Rupee	Half Rupee	Quarter Rupee
Official Weight (g)	11.64	5.82	2.91
Actual Weight (g)	11.61-11.64	5.74-5.82	2.88-2.91
Actual Diameter (mm)	26.6-26.9	21.8-22.2	16.8-17.1
Metal	Silver		
Edge	Grained Right		

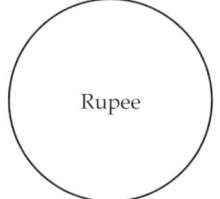

Rupee

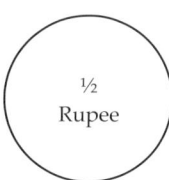

½ Rupee

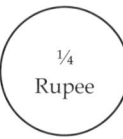

¼ Rupee

Murshidabad – Rupee *et infra* – 1794 to 1795 (cont)

Catalogue

Cat No.	Pr. No.	Denom	AH	Comment	Value ($)
5.6	166	Rupee	None	Dot in centre circle on obverse	250
5.7	167	Half Rupee	None	Not seen by Pridmore. See Falcke G., (1997), ONS 151, p14. Also Baldwin (2006), sale 47 (Stiller), lot 829	750
5.8	168	Quarter Rupee	1204	Baldwin (2001), sale 25 (Wiggins), lot 639. No dot in any of the groups in the reverse	750

5.8

Quarter rupee

Bengal Presidency Patna Mint

Patna – Gold Mohur *et infra* –1765 to 1768

The first gold coins issued from the Patna mint, under the authority of the British, were minted in 1765 in an attempt to fill the gap left by the scarcity of silver coins (see Stevens, Bengal, pp. 32-33). The Calcutta coins are reputed to be those marked with the letter C, but the identity of the Patna coins is not known.

Catalogue

Cat No.	Pr. No.	Denomination	AH	RY	Comments	Value ($)
5.9	-	Mohur	?	?	Fractions may also have been struck	NV

Patna – Gold Mohur *et infra* – 1768 to 1769

5.10

 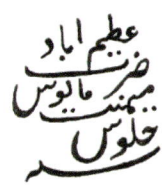

| *sikka zad bar haft kishwar sāya fazl ilāh hāmī dīn muhammad shāh ʿālam bādshāh [AH]* (= Defender of the religion of Muhammad, Shah ʿAlam Emperor, Shadow of the divine favour, put his stamp on the seven climes, [AH]) | *zarb ʿazīmābād sanah [RY] julūs maimanat mānūs* (= Struck at ʿAzimabad in the [RY] year of his reign of tranquil prosperity). |

	Mohur	Eighth Mohur
Actual Weight (g)	11.04	1.38
Actual Diam (mm)	~21	9.6-9.9
Metal	Gold	

 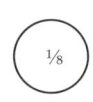

Patna – Gold Mohur *et infra* – 1768 to 1769 (cont)

Catalogue

Cat No.	Pr. No.	Denomination	AH	RY	Comments	Value ($)
5.10	-	Mohur	-	10	Reported by an Indian numismatist also Baldwin (2011), New York sale XXV, lot 436	10,000
5.11	-	Eighth Mohur	-	10	Stevens collection	7,000

5.11

Eighth mohur

Patna – Gold Mohur *et infra* – 1769 to 1770

The intermediate style of gold coin was issued from the Patna mint in RY 10 & 11 of Shah 'Alam. The coins had some characteristics of the Murshidabad sicca, but retained the mint name, 'Azimabad (see Stevens, Bengal pp. 190-191). Note heavier weight

5.12

   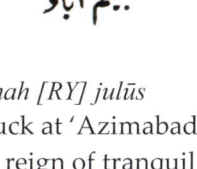

sikka zad bar haft kishwar sāya fazl ilāh hāmī dīn muhammad shāh 'ālam bādshāh [AH] (= Defender of the religion of Muhammad, Shah 'Alam Emperor, Shadow of the divine favour, put his stamp on the seven climes, [AH])

zarb 'azīmābād sanah [RY] julūs maimanat mānūs (= Struck at 'Azimabad in the [RY] year of his reign of tranquil prosperity).

	Mohur	Quarter Mohur	Sixteenth Mohur
Actual Weight (g)	12.33	3.1	0.77 (from Pr)
Actual Diameter (mm)	22.8-23.1	~15	12 (from Pr)
Metal	Gold		

Patna – Gold Mohur *et infra* – 1769 to 1770 (cont)

Mohur

¼ Mohur

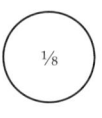

⅛

Catalogue

Cat No.	Pr. No.	Denomination	AH	RY	Comments	Value ($)
5.11c	-	Mohur	1182	10	Ref: Kawale	15,000
5.12	-	"	1183	10	Stevens collection	15,000
5.13	-	Quarter Mohur		11	Vienna museum reported by Bhandare, (2010), JONS, 205, p. 31	NV
5.14	60	Sixteenth Mohur	1182	10	BM	NV

Patna – Silver Rupee – 1765 to 1769

5.16

sikka zad bar haft kishwar sāya fazl ilāh hāmī dīn muhammad shāh ʿālam bādshāh
(= Defender of the religion of Muhammad, Shah ʿAlam Emperor, Shadow of the divine favour, put his stamp on the seven climes, [AH])

zarb ʿazīmābād sanah [RY] julus maimanat mānūs (= Struck at ʿAzimabad in the [RY] year of his reign of tranquil prosperity).

	Rupee	Half Rupee	Quarter Rupee	Eighth Rupee	Sixteenth Rupee
Actual Weight (g)	11.29-11.54	5.52-5.74	?	1.42	0.74
Actual Diam (mm)	23.1-25.0	17.5-19.4	~15	11.3-11.5	9.0-9.5
Metal	Silver				

Patna – Silver Rupee – 1765 to 1769 (cont)

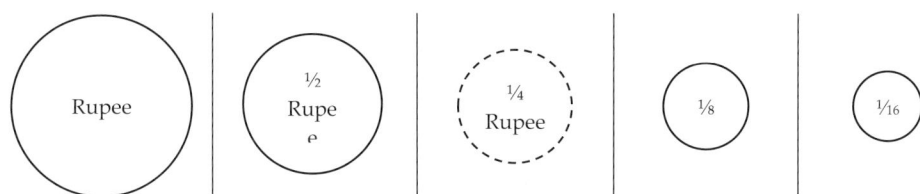

Catalogue

Cat No.	Pr. No.	Denomination	AH	RY	Comments	Value ($)
5.15	-	Rupee	xxxx	6	Ref: Baldwin (2001), sale 25 (Wiggins), lot 593. May be pre-British	150
5.16	104	"	1179	7		200
5.17	105	"	1180	8		200
5.18	-	"	1181	8	Ref: Baldwin (2002), sale 31, lot 704	200
5.19	106	"	1181	9		200
5.20	107	"	1182	9		200
5.21	108	"	1182	10	See also Mitchiner 1897	200
5.21c	-	Half Rupee	xxxx	8	Ref: Rhodes	NV
5.22	-	"	xxxx	9	Ref: Rhodes, 2006	800
5.23	-	"	xxxx	10	Ref: Rhodes, Sept 2006	800
5.24	-	Quarter Rupee	xxxx	xx	Ref: Rhodes	NV
5.25	-	Eighth Rupee	xxxx	xx	Ref: Chopra	NV
5.26	-	Sixteenth Rupee	xxxx	5	Ref: Todywalla sale 26, lot 230	150

Eighth and sixteenth rupees

Patna – Silver Rupee – 1769 to 1770

Like the gold coins, the intermediate style of silver coins was issued in RY 10 & 11. The coins had the moon on the obverse and the flower on the reverse, in imitation of Murshidabad siccas, but retained the mint name 'Azimabad.

5.28

sikka zad bar haft kishwar sāya fazl ilāh hāmī dīn muhammad shāh 'ālam bādshāh (= Defender of the religion of Muhammad, Shah 'Alam Emperor, Shadow of the divine favour, put his stamp on the seven climes, [AH])

zarb 'azīmābād sanah [RY] julūs maimanat mānūs (= Struck at 'Azimabad in the [RY] year of his reign of tranquil prosperity).

Actual Weight (g)	11.50-11.58
Actual Diameter (mm)	24.0-25.5
Metal	Silver
Edge	Plain

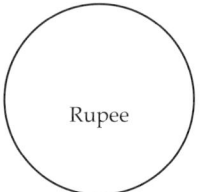

Rupee

Catalogue

Cat No.	Pr. No.	AH	RY	Comments	Value ($)
5.27	-	1183	10		1,500
5.27a	-	1183	11	**Nazarana.** Ashmolean museum	NV
5.28	134	1183	11		1,000

5.27a

Nazarana rupee dated AH 1183, RY 11

Patna – Silver Rupee – 1770 to 1772

The Patna mint struck Murshidabad style coins between 1770 and its closure in 1772/73. Secret mint marks may have been put on the coins, but even if this was so, which marks might represent Patna is not known. The coins are all catalogued under Calcutta (see Stevens, Bengal, chapter 2 pp. 71-72 & 93-99 for more detailed discussion,)

Patna – Gold Mohur *et infra* – 1795 to 1796

Pridmore assigned coins with this secret mark (dot in right-hand circle) to the Dacca mint but see Stevens, Bengal pp. 217-219 for the reasons for changing this.

5.30

sikka zad bar haft kishwar sāya fazl ilāh hāmī dīn muhammad shāh 'ālam bādshāh
(= Defender of the religion of Muhammad, Shah 'Alam Emperor, Shadow of the divine favour, put his stamp on the seven climes, 1202)

zarb murshīdābād sanah 19 julūs maimanat mānūs (= Struck at Murshidabad in the 19th year of his reign of tranquil prosperity).

	Mohur	Half Mohur	Quarter Mohur
Official Weight (g)	12.36	6.2	3.1
Actual Weight (g)	12.35	?	?
Actual Diameter (mm)	27.1-27.5	~22	~17
Metal	Gold		
Edge	Grained Right		

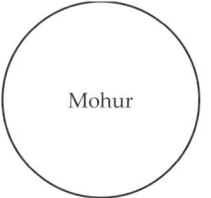  

Patna – Gold Mohur *et infra* – 1795 to 1796 (cont)

Catalogue

Cat No.	Pr. No.	Denom	AH	RY	Comment	Value ($)
5.29	68	Mohur	1202	19	Ref: Baldwin (2000), sale 22 (Wheeler), lot 135. Normal border	7,000
5.30	-	"	1202	19	Ref: Baldwin (2000), sale 22 (Wheeler), lot 137. Wider rim and smaller design	7,000
5.31	69	Half Mohur	1202	19	Ref: Baldwin (2000), sale 22 (Wheeler), lot 136	4,000
5.32	70	Quarter Mohur	1204	19	None traced	NV

Mint Marks

Single & Half Mohur/Rupee

Patna – dot in right circle

For the single and half mohur/rupee, the mint is identified by the presence or absence of a tiny dot in the three decorative dot groups on the obverse

Quarter Mohur/Rupee

Patna – dot in left group

For the quarter mohur/rupee, the mint is identified by the presence or absence of a tiny dot in the decorative dot groups on the reverse.

Patna – Silver Rupee 1793

The first milled silver coins issued from the Patna mint have the AH date, 1202, on the obverse. Pridmore assigned the coins with this secret mark (dot in right-hand circle) to the Dacca mint, but see Stevens, Bengal pp. 217-219 for the reasons for changing this.

5.33

sikka zad bar haft kishwar sāya fazl ilāh hāmī dīn muhammad shāh ʿālam bādshāh 1202
(= Defender of the religion of Muhammad, Shah ʿAlam Emperor, Shadow of the divine favour, put his stamp on the seven climes, 1202)

zarb murshīdābād sanah 19 julūs maimanat mānūs (= Struck at Murshidabad in the 19th year of his reign of tranquil prosperity).

Official Weight (g)	11.64
Actual Weight (g)	11.63
Actual Diameter (mm)	29.3-29.6
Metal	Silver
Edge	Grained Right

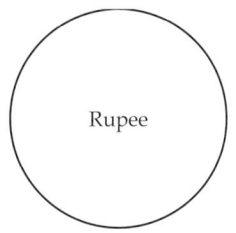

Rupee

Catalogue

Cat No.	Pr. No.	Comments	Value ($)
5.33	155	Dot in right circle on obverse	1,000

Patna – Silver Rupee – 1794 to 1796

Later silver coins did not have the AH date on the obverse except the quarter rupee. Pridmore assigned the coins with this secret mark to the Dacca mint but see Stevens, Bengal pp. 217-219 for the reasons for changing this.

 5.34

sikka zad bar haft kishwar sāya fazl ilāh hāmī dīn muhammad shāh 'ālam bādshāh
(= Defender of the religion of Muhammad, Shah 'Alam Emperor, Shadow of the divine favour, put his stamp on the seven climes)

zarb murshīdābād sanah 19 julūs maimanat mānūs (= Struck at Murshidabad in the 19th year of his reign of tranquil prosperity).

	Rupee	Half Rupee	Quarter Rupee
Official Weight (g)	11.64	5.82	2.91
Actual Weight (g)	11.48-11.58	?	?
Actual Diameter (mm)	26.3-27.1	~22	~17
Metal	Silver		
Edge	Grained Right		

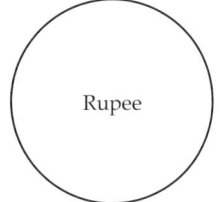

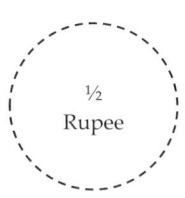

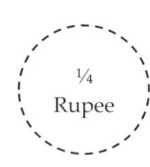

Catalogue

Cat No.	Pr. No.	Denomination	AH	Comments	Value ($)
5.34	163	Rupee	None	Dot in right circle on obverse	800
5.35	164	Half Rupee	None		600
5.36	165	Quarter Rupee	1204	Dot in left group on reverse	400

Patna – Copper Pice – Shah 'Alam II – 1794

The Patna assay master produced copper coins as a trial in 1794, but the identity is not known. He may well have used the existing rupee dies (see Stevens, Bengal pp. 220-222).

5.37

Possible design for Blake's copper coins struck at Patna

Catalogue

Cat No.	Pr. No.	Denom	RY	Struck AD	Comment	Value ($)
5.37	-	Pice	19?	1794	Blake (mint master) made a trial of 10 maunds of copper – probably about 2500 copper coins in 1794	NV

Bengal Presidency Dacca Mint

Dacca – Gold Mohur – 1769 to 1773

Design not known. May be same as rupee but in gold

Catalogue

Cat No.	Pr. No.	Comment	Value ($)
5.38	-	None traced. Ref: Pridmore p. 234	NV

Dacca – Silver Rupee *et infra* – 1765 to 1769

A half rupee probably exists but has not yet been discovered

5.40

sikka zad bar haft kishwar sāya fazl ilāh hāmī dīn muhammad shāh 'ālam bādshāh [AH] (= Defender of the religion of Muhammad, Shah 'Alam Emperor, Shadow of the divine favour, put his stamp on the seven climes, [AH])

zarb jahangirnagar sanah [RY] sicca [mubarak] julūs maimanat mānūs (= The [auspicious] coin struck at Jahangirnagar in the [RY] year of his reign of tranquil prosperity).

	Rupee	¼ Rupee	⅛ Rupee	¹⁄₁₆ Rupee
Actual Weight (g)	11.60	2.87	?	0.70
Actual Diam (mm)	20.6-21.3	14.0-14.5	~11	8.6-9.4
Metal	Silver			

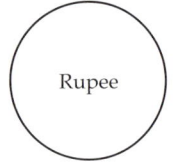 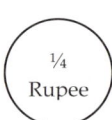 

Full-flan striking of rupee

Dacca – Silver Rupee *et infra* – 1765 to 1769 (cont)

Catalogue

Cat No.	Pr. No.	Denom	AH	RY	Comment	Value ($)
5.39	-	Rupee	-	6	Ref: Rhodes	3,000
5.39c	-	"	1180	8	Ref: Ravi Shankar Sharma	3,000
5.40	-	"	1181	9		3,000
5.41	-	"	1182	10	Ref: Baldwin (2002), sale 31, lot 710. Baldwin (2003), sale 33, lot 1007	3,000
5.42	-	Quarter Rupee	[xxxx]	7		2,000
5.43	-	"	[xxxx]	8	Ref: HK/Singapore (2003), sale 36, lot 467	2,000
5.44	-	"	[xxxx]	10	Ref: HK/Singapore (2002), sale 35, lot 703	2,000
5.45	-	Eighth Rupee	117x	6	Ref: Rhodes (2006)	1,500
5.46	-	"	[xxxx]	8	Ref: HK/Singapore (2003), sale 36, lot 467	1,500
5.47	-	"	[xxxx]	9	Ref: Rhodes also Ashmolean museum	1,500
5.48	-	Sixteenth Rupee	[xxxx]	7	Ref: HK/Singapore (2003), sale 36, lot 467	1,000
5.49	-	"	[xxxx]	8	Ref: HK/Singapore (2002), sale 35, lot 703	1,000

5.43

Quarter rupee

5.48

Sixteenth rupee

Dacca – Silver Rupee – Shah 'Alam – 1769/70

As with Patna, Dacca appears to have changed the style of the rupee to look more like that of Murshidabad, before finally starting to produce more precise copies of the Murshidabad sicca. Only coins of RY 10 are known and they show half a sun and a moon on the obverse and a flower on the reverse, but retain the mint name Jahangirnagar. A nazarana rupee in the BM shows just a moon on the obverse, more like the Murshidabad coins.

Dacca – Silver Rupee – Shah 'Alam – 1769/70 (cont)

5.50

sikka zad bar haft kishwar sāya fazl ilāh hāmī dīn muhammad shāh 'ālam bādshāh [AH] (= Defender of the religion of Muhammad, Shah 'Alam Emperor, Shadow of the divine favour, put his stamp on the seven climes, [AH])	*zarb jahangirnagar sanah [RY] julūs maimanat mānūs* (= Struck at Jahangirnagar in the [RY] year of his reign of tranquil prosperity).

Actual Weight (g)	11.57
Actual Diameter (mm)	21.2-21.6
Metal	Silver
Edge	Plain

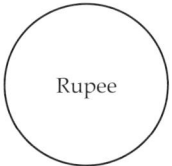

Rupee

Catalogue

Cat No.	Pr. No.	AH	RY	Comment	Value ($)
5.50	-	1183	10	Different style from previous type	5,000
5.51	103	1183	10	**Nazarana**. BM. Moon on obverse	NV

5.51

Nazarana rupee

Dacca – Silver Rupee – 1770 to 1772

The Dacca mint struck Murshidabad style coins between 1770 and its closure in 1773/74. Secret mint marks may have been put on the coins, but even if this was so, which marks might represent Dacca is not known. The coins are all catalogued under Calcutta (see Stevens, Bengal pp. 71-72 & pp. 93-99 for more detailed discussion)

Dacca – Gold Mohur – Shah 'Alam II – 1782

The Dacca mint was briefly re-opened in 1782 and a few gold coins were produced. They probably had the mint name Jahangirnagar and the fixed RY 19. Other than that, the design and dates are not known. See Stevens, Bengal, pp. 202-206

Catalogue

Cat No.	Pr. No.	Denom	AH	RY	Comment	Value ($)
5.52	-	Mohur	1198?	19?	Dacca briefly re-opened in 1782 but no coins known.	NV

Dacca – Silver Rupee – Shah 'Alam II – 1782

As with the gold, the design and dates are not known. They probably have the mint name Jahangirnagar and the fixed RY19.

Catalogue

Cat No.	Pr. No.	Denom	AH	RY	Comment	Value ($)
5.53	-	Rupee	1198?	19?	Dacca briefly re-opened in 1782 but no coins known.	NV

Dacca – Milled Gold Mohur *et infra* – 1794 to 1796

Pridmore assigned mohurs with this secret mark (dot in left-hand circle) to the Patna mint but see Stevens, Bengal pp. 217-219 for reasons for changing this.

5.54

sikka zad bar haft kishwar sāya fazl ilāh hāmī dīn muhammad shāh 'ālam bādshāh 1202
(= Defender of the religion of Muhammad, Shah 'Alam Emperor, Shadow of the divine favour, put his stamp on the seven climes, 1202)

zarb murshīdābād sanah 19 julūs maimanat mānūs (= Struck at Murshidabad in the 19th year of his reign of tranquil prosperity).

Dacca – Milled Gold Mohur *et infra* – 1794 to 1796 (cont)

	Mohur	Half Mohur	Quarter Mohur
Official Weight (g)	12.36	6.18	3.09
Actual Weight (g)	?	?	?
Actual Diameter (mm)	~26.7	~21.7	~16.8
Metal	Gold		
Edge	Grained Right		

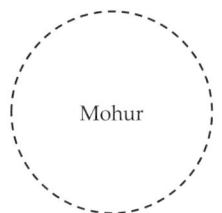

Mohur

½ Mohur

¼ Mohur

Catalogue

Cat No.	Pr. No.	Denom	Comment	Value ($)
5.54	74	Mohur	Baldwin (2000), sale 22 (Wheeler), lot 143? Dot not clear	10,000
5.55	75	Half Mohur	None traced	NV
5.56	76	Quarter Mohur	None traced	NV

Mint Marks

Single & Half Mohur/Rupee

Dacca – dot in left-hand circle

For the single and half mohur/rupee, the mint is identified by the presence or absence of a tiny dot in the three decorative dot groups on the obverse

Quarter Mohur/Rupee

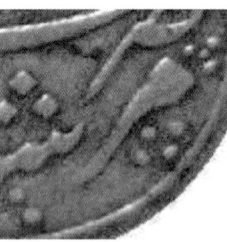

Dacca – dot in right-hand group

For the quarter mohur/rupee, the mint is identified by the presence or absence of a tiny dot in the decorative dot groups on the reverse.

Dacca – Milled Silver Rupee *et infra* – 1794 to 1796

Pridmore assigned rupees with this secret mark (dot in left-hand circle) to the Patna mint but see Stevens Bengal pp. 217-219 for reasons for changing this. NB no AH date

5.57

sikka zad bar haft kishwar sāya fazl ilāh hāmī dīn muhammad shāh 'ālam bādshāh
(= Defender of the religion of Muhammad, Shah 'Alam Emperor, Shadow of the divine favour, put his stamp on the seven climes)

zarb murshīdābād sanah 19 julūs maimanat mānūs (= Struck at Murshidabad in the 19th year of his reign of tranquil prosperity).

	Rupee	Half Rupee	Quarter Rupee
Official Weight (g)	11.64	5.82	2.91
Actual Weight (g)	11.40-11.50	5.66	2.84-2.87
Actual Diameter (mm)	25.9-26.8	21.6-22.1	16.6-17.5
Metal	Silver		
Edge	Grained Right		

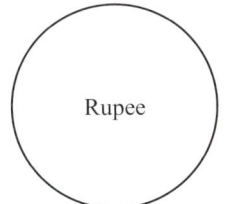 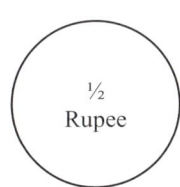 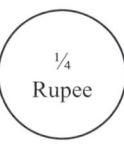

Catalogue

Cat No.	Pr. No.	Denom	AH	Comments	Value ($)
5.57	169	Rupee	None	Dot in left circle on obverse	1,000
5.58	170	Half Rupee	None		800
5.59	171	Quarter Rupee	1204	Dot in right group on reverse	600

Monghyr Mint

In 1761 the Nawab of Bengal, Mir Kasim Ali Khan, moved his capital from Murshidabad to Monghyr. He built himself a palace and reorganised his army along European lines and ran the Government of Bengal from there in a way that appears to have been approved of by his subjects. However, he soon fell out with the British at Calcutta who had begun abusing their ability to avoid paying taxes and resented the fact that the Nawab took steps to try to stop the practice. A British army was sent to Monghyr and captured the fort in October 1763[6]. Thenceforth, the town became part of British India and, for many years, continued to contain an arsenal but no regular garrison.

There has been some debate about whether or not the British issued coins from the Monghyr mint after they captured the fort. Extremely rare mohurs and rupees exist dated 1176 ry 4 with the mint name Monghyr but no other coins are known from this mint. The Hijri year 1176 finished on the 11th of July 1763, before the British captured the place. These coins would, therefore, have been issued by the Nawab from his mint at Monghyr. Only coins dated 1177 or later would have been issued by the British and none of these is known. The records held in the British Library have not yielded any evidence for the British issuing coins from Monghyr but at least one entry suggests that the mint was still open at the start of November 1763, although it could be referring to coins issued earlier. The letter is dated 1st November 1763, when the Calcutta mint master wrote[7]:

… the strictest care has been ever had to keep the Calcutta rupee up to the same weight and fineness as what are coined at Moorshedabad and Mongheer…

and, in 1775, Monghyr rupees were still available in the bazaar[8]:

…You will please further to inform the Board that the sicca rupees which are seen in the weekly state of the Treasury are Mongheer siccas…

Gold mohur dated 1176 RY 4, with mint name Monghyr

---

[6] Bengal Public Consultations. IOR P/1/36, 17th October 1763, pp. 314/315. Letter from Major Adams to the President at Calcutta, dated 11th October 1763.

[7] Bengal Public Consultations. IOR P/1/36, p. 389. 21st November 1763. Letter from Anselm Beaumont (mint master) to Bengal Council) dated 21st November 1763.

[8] Bengal Consultations. IOL P/2/10, 15 June 1775, p. 282. Letter from the Sub-Treasurer.

Cuttack Mint

The possibility of a pattern coin having been struck at Cuttack by a representative of the EIC was first reported by Thurston in 1893[9] but seems to have been subsequently largely overlooked, although it is discussed by Garg[10].

In May 1804, the Commissioner for Cuttack, George Harcourt, wrote to Calcutta about the lack of small value coin in the province. With his letter, he enclosed a specimen of a copper coin that he had had prepared by local craftsmen, and requested that the Cacutta mint might strike fifty thousand rupees worth of such a coin[11]:

I request you will be pleased to make known to his Excellency the Most Noble the Governor General in Council that a considerable inconvenience is at present experienced in the province of Cuttack from the want of some current coin of small value. At this time cowries are the only currency in Cuttack, and they are extremely inconvenient to the merchants and inhabitants, and particularly so to the troops stationed in the province, and the pilgrims resorting to the temple at Juggernaut.

Should his Excellency the most Noble the Governor General be pleased to order a copper coinage for the use of the province of Cuttack, I take the liberty of submitting a coin, the standard value of which should be fixed with view of indemnifying Government in the expense of coinage, and which should also tend to retain it in the province.

With a view to ensure the ready reception of this coin, it is proposed that the face should bear the figure of Juggernaut and on the reverse the value of the coin might be denoted in the Persian and Oriah language together with the year of coinage.

From the want of proper artists in Cuttack, the enclosed specimen is badly executed. Should his Excellency be pleased to approve of the above suggestions, I have the honor to request that His Excellency will permit the coinage for the present to be executed in Calcutta, to the amount of fifty thousand rupees, which I have reason to hope will, for the present, answer every object expected to be derived from this arrangement.

The letter was forwarded to the Mint Committee, who felt that they needed a number of questions answered before they could agree to undertake such a coinage[12]. However, within a month, in June 1804, the Accountant General was ordered to send as many pice as could be found in the Calcutta mint, to Cuttack[13]. These were loaded

---

[9] Thurston E (1893), Note on the History of the East India Company Coinage from 1753 to 1835, Journal of the Asiatic Society of Bengal, vol LXII, part 1, No. 1, 1893.

[10] Garg (2010), Draft of PhD thesis.

[11] Bengal Revenue Consultations (Opium etc). P/89/35. 10th May 1804, No. 2. Letter from George Harcourt (Commissioner for Cuttack), dated 8th May 1804.

[12] Bengal Revenue Consultations (Opium etc). P/89/35. 17th May 1804, No. 1. Letter from the Mint Committee to Government, dated 16th May 1804.

[13] Bengal Revenue Consultations (Opium etc). P/89/35. 28th June 1804, No. 1. Letter to the Accountant General dated 23rd June 1804.

aboard the ship "Scourge" and sent to Cuttack on 16th August[14]. A further 30,000 rupees-worth of pice were sent in 1813[15].

The specimen referred to in the above extract has not been traced, although it may exist in a museum in India.

Copper Pice? – 1804	
Figure of Juggernaut	Value in Persian & Oriah and date

Catalogue

Cat No.	Pr. No.	Comments	Value ($)
5.60	-		NV

---

[14] Bengal Revenue Consultations (Opium etc). P/89/35. 16th August 1804, No. 1. Letter from sub-treasurer dated 9th August 1804.

[15] Bengal Public Consultations. P/8/14. 11th February 1813. No. 39. Letter from the Accountant General to Calcutta Government, dated 9th January 1813.

    Bengal Public Consultations. P/8/14. 26th February 1813. No. 32. Letter from Davidson (Calcutta mint master) dated 23rd February 1813.

Tripura Mint

Rhodes and Bose published a rupee apparently issued under the authority of the East India Company in 1761[16]. A British force was sent to Tripura in February 1761, and obliged the king to grant the area of Chakla Roshanabad to the Company. The rupee described by Rhodes and Bose (see below) was probably issued as part of this action and is, presumably, a presentation piece.

Silver Rupee – AH 1175 (=AD 1761)

5.61

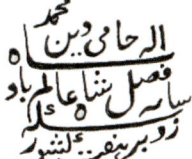

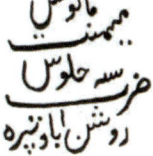

sikka zad bar haft kishwar sāya fazl ilāh hāmī dīn muhammad shāh 'ālam bādshāh [AH]
(= Defender of the religion of Muhammad, Shah 'Alam Emperor, Shadow of the divine favour, put his stamp on the seven climes, [AH])

zarb rūshanābād tiprah sanah 3 julūs maimanat mānūs (= Struck at Roshanabad Tripura in the 3rd year of his reign of tranquil prosperity).

Actual Weight (g)	11.49
Actual Diameter (mm)	~30
Metal	Silver
Edge	Plain

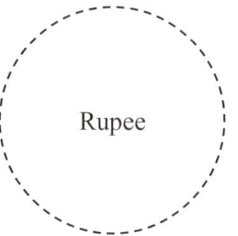

Catalogue

Cat No.	KM	RB	Comments	Value ($)
5.61	511	248	Only one known at present, in the Ashmolean museum, Oxford	NV

---

[16] Rhodes NG & Bose SK (2002), The Coinage of Tripura. Kolkata.

Garhwal Mint

Rhodes published a copper takka apparently issued from a local mint in Garhwal[17]. The coin is in the collection of the American Numismatic Society (ANS 86.449/1921.54.835). The following account is a brief summary of Rhodes' paper.

Following the war with Nepal, in 1815 Garhwal was divided between a native ruler and direct British control, and in 1816 the border was further clarified ensuring that, *inter alia*, the copper mines of Garhwal were within British jurisdiction. Copper coins had been produced when Garhwal had been under the rule of the Nepalese, but it had been thought that this activitiy had ceased when the British acquired control. However the coin published by Rhodes and shown below suggests that some minting activity continued for a short while after the British conquest. The coin was probably produced in 1815.

Copper Takka – Samvat 1872

5.62

mulk (angrez) kampanī bahādur (= the dominion of the victorious (East India) Company)	*zarb srīnagar sambat 1872…* (= struck at Srinagar, sambat year 1872…)

Actual Weight (g)	4.29	
Actual Diameter (mm)	~20-21	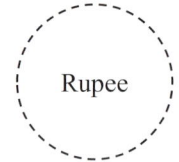
Metal	Copper	Rupee
Edge	Plain	

Catalogue

Cat No.	Pr. No.	Comments	Value ($)
5.62	-		NV

---

[17] Rhodes NG (2001), A Garhwal takka struck in the name of the East India Company, ONS Newsletter, 166, pp. 17-18.

Rhodes NG (2003), A Note on the copper mint in Garhwal, ONS Newsletter 177, p. 20.

Bengal Presidency Calcutta Mint C1800-c1830

Summary[18]

The gold and silver coins produced between 1800 and 1818 continued in the same style as those discussed previously. As well as these, in 1817 the Calcutta mint began to produce Farrukhabad rupees for use in the Ceded and Conquered territories (see later), and in 1818 changes were made to the weight and fineness of both the gold and silver Calcutta sicca coins, and the edges were changed to straight milling. However, the reduction in the fineness of gold was not popular and in 1825 the gold standard was increased and the new coins were given an edge with the milling grained to the left.

Copper coins were produced in ever increasing numbers and this, together with the new gold and silver coins and the expansion of British power across northern India, put an increasing strain on the mint. By 1820, a review of mint capacity revealed that a new approach would be needed to meet the ever increasing currency demands. A decision was taken to obtain a complete new mint from England and Captain Forbes was sent there to ensure that it would meet local requirements. In the meantime, minor improvements were made to the existing mint, which continued in operation until about 1831/32.

---

[18] Stevens PJE (2012), The Coins of the Bengal Presidency, AH Baldwin & Sons Ltd

Gold Mohur *et infra* – Shah 'Alam II – 1819

In 1819, the fineness of the coins was reduced and the weight increased so that the coins contained the same amount of gold. The edges are straight-grained.

Design for Mohur and Half Mohur

6.1

sikka zad bar haft kishwar sāya fazl ilāh hāmī dīn muhammad shāh 'ālam bādshāh 1202 (= Defender of the religion of Muhammad, Shah 'Alam Emperor, Shadow of the divine favour, put his stamp on the seven climes, 1202)

zarb murshīdābād sanah 19 julūs maimanat mānūs (= Struck at Murshidabad in the 19th year of his reign of tranquil prosperity).

Design for Quarter Mohur

6.5

 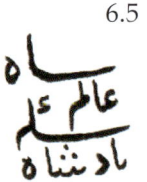  

1204 sikka shāh 'ālam bādshāh ghāzī (= 1204, coin of Shah 'Alam the victorious Emperor)

zarb murshīdābād sanah 19 (= Struck at Murshidabad in year 19)

	Mohur	Half Mohur	Quarter Mohur
Official Weight (g)	13.26	6.63	3.31
Actual Weight (g)	13.28	6.64	3.31
Actual Diameter (mm)	28.3-28.8	23.2-23.4	18.0-18.1
Metal	Gold (91.7%)		
Edge	Straight Grained		

Gold Mohur *et infra* – Shah 'Alam II – 1819 (cont)

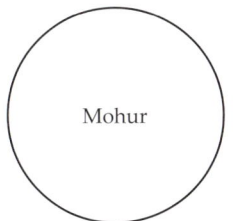
Mohur

½ Mohur

¼ Mohur

Catalogue

Cat No.	Pr. No.	Denomination	Status	Comments	Value ($)
6.1	77	Mohur	Currency		1,500
6.2	78	"	Proof		5,000
6.3	79	Half Mohur	Currency		1,000
6.4	80	"	Proof		3,000
6.5	81	Quarter Mohur	Currency		800
6.6	82	"	Proof		2,000

Gold Mohur – Shah 'Alam II – 1825 to 1830

In 1825, the fineness of the gold coins was increased to that of the coins issued before 1818. The weight was accordingly reduced and the coins given an edge grained-left.

6.7

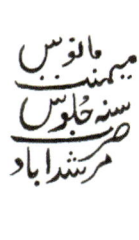

sikka zad bar haft kishwar sāya fazl ilāh hāmī dīn muhammad shāh 'ālam bādshāh 1202
(= Defender of the religion of Muhammad, Shah 'Alam Emperor, Shadow of the divine favour, put his stamp on the seven climes, 1202)

zarb murshīdābād sanah 19 julūs maimanat mānūs (= Struck at Murshidabad in the 19th year of his reign of tranquil prosperity).

Gold Mohur – Shah 'Alam II – 1825 to 1830 (cont)

Official Weight (g)	12.36
Actual Weight (g)	12.37
Actual Diameter (mm)	26.6-26.8
Metal	Gold (99.2%)
Edge	Grained Left

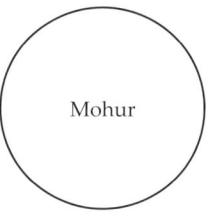

Mohur

Catalogue

Cat No.	Pr. No.	Comments	Value ($)
6.7	83	A silver trial? Has been reported (Todywalla sale 49, lot 214) but I'm not sure of the authenticity	1,500
6.8	-	Copper trial striking. Possibly for new steam-driven machinery? Ref: Baldwin (2010), sale 68, lot 4263	1,000

6.8

Copper trial striking

Silver Pattern Rupee 1818

A pattern probably struck in 1818 exemplifying a coin with European-style emblems.

6.9

Arms of the Company within a plain circle, surrounded by the legend.
AUSPICIO . REGIS . ET . SENATUS . ANGLIÆ *
(= Under the auspices of the King and parliament of England). All within a raised, toothed border.

The legend in English and Persian: *zarb Kalcutta* (= Struck at Calcutta):
CALCUTTA
RUPEE
ضرب كلكته
All within an open wreath of palm branches. Surrounded by a raised, toothed rim.

Silver Pattern Rupee 1818 (cont)

Pridmore Weight (g)	11.65	
Pridmore Diameter (mm)	28.7	
Metal	Silver	
Edge	Straight Grained	

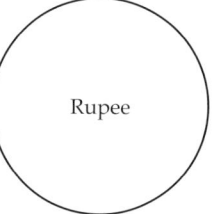
Rupee

Catalogue

Cat No.	Pr. No.	Comments	Value ($)
6.9	361		25,000

Rupee – Initial Issue of 1819 – Mint Name Murshidabad

In 1819, new silver coins of lower standard and higher weight were issued. They have straight-grained edges. The early issues lack the star below *bād* of *bādshāh*.

6.10

sikka zad bar haft kishwar sāya fazl ilāh hāmī dīn muhammad shāh ʿālam bādshāh
(= Defender of the religion of Muhammad, Shah ʿAlam Emperor, Shadow of the divine favour, put his stamp on the seven climes)

zarb murshīdābād sanah 19 julūs maimanat mānūs (= Struck at Murshidabad in the 19th year of his reign of tranquil prosperity).

Official Weight (g)	12.43	
Actual Weight (g)	12.40	
Actual Diameter (mm)	28.8-28.9	
Metal	Silver (91.7%)	
Edge	Straight Grained	

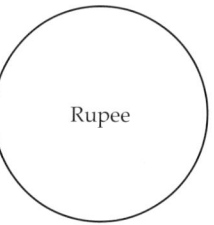
Rupee

Catalogue

Cat No.	Pr. No.	Comments	Value ($)
6.10	-		750

Rupee *et infra* 1819 to 1829 – Mint Name: Murshidabad

6.13

*sikka zad bar haft kishwar sāya fazl ilāh hāmī
dīn muhammad shāh 'ālam bādshāh*
(= Defender of the religion of Muhammad,
Shah 'Alam Emperor, Shadow of the
divine favour, put his stamp on the seven
climes)

*zarb murshīdābād sanah 19 julūs
maimanat mānūs* (= Struck at
Murshidabad in the 19th year of his
reign of tranquil prosperity).

	Rupee	Half Rupee	Quarter Rupee
Official Weight (g)	12.43	6.21	3.11
Actual Weight (g)	12.27-12.44	6.09-6.20	3.11-3.13
Actual Diameter (mm)	26.5-26.8	23.8-24.0	18.7-19.1
Metal	Silver		
Edge	Straight grained		

6.16

Quarter rupee, dated AH 1204

Rupee *et infra* 1819 to 1829 – Mint Name: Murshidabad (cont)

Catalogue

Cat No.	Pr. No.	Denom	Comments	Value ($)
6.11	172	Rupee		100
6.12	-	Trial Striking?	Overstruck on an Ottoman Mahmud II silver 5-Qurush. Ref: HK/Singapore (1997), Sale 25, Lot 673	NV
6.13	176	Rupee	Tiny letter S on rev	250
-	-	"	Unusual, crude style. Probably a contemparary forgery. Edge grained left. Baldwin (2001), sale 25 (Wiggins), lot 645.	NV
6.15	173	Half Rupee		90
6.16	174	Quarter Rupee		80
6.17	175	"	No dot privy mark. Comes with tall and short date (R. Weir)	100
-	-	"	Dated 1404 & low weight. Forgery. Ref: Wiggins, ONS No. 161, 1999, p. 20.	NV
-	-	"	Plain edge. Ref: Mitchiner , M1910. Not sure of status. Could be a forgery?	NV

  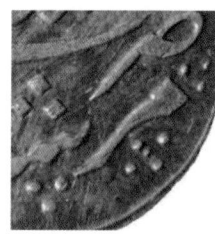 

No S   *S at top left hand of reverse of rupee*   *Dot in centre group*   *No dot privy mark on quarter rupee*

6.12

Overstruck on an Ottoman Mahmud II silver 5 qurush

Copper Weight for Rupee 1819 to 1829

6.20

Within an oval circle:
Min. wt.
new Cal. Rup.
straight-milled
and plain edged
Above is the weight:
190
With the units below:
grs

An oval circle containing the legend

Blank

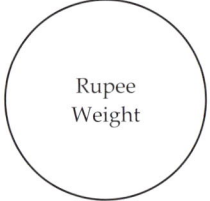

Rupee
Weight

Official Weight (g)	12.31 (190 grains)
Actual Weight (g)	12.26
Actual Diameter (mm)	26.5
Metal	Copper
Edge	Plain

Catalogue

Cat No.	Pr. No.	Comments	Value ($)
6.20	-		100

Rupee – 1817 to 1819 – Mint Name: Farrukhabad

Struck at the mints of Farrukhabad and Calcutta. The mints are identified by tiny privy marks (see p. 42 the different marks).

6.21

sikka zad bar haft kishwar sāya fazl ilāh hāmī dīn muhammad shāh 'ālam bādshāh
(= Defender of the religion of Muhammad, Shah 'Alam Emperor, Shadow of the divine favour, put his stamp on the seven climes)

zarb farruckābād sanah 45 julūs maimanat mānūs (= Struck at Farrukhabad in the 45th year of his reign of tranquil prosperity).

Rupee – 1817 to 1819 – Mint Name: Farrukhabad (cont)

Official Weight (g)	11.21
Actual Weight (g)	11.1-11.2
Actual Diameter (mm)	~25.5
Metal	Silver
Edge	Grained Right

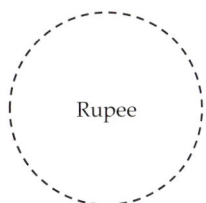

Catalogue

Cat No.	Pr. No.	Comments	Value ($)
6.21	317		500

Privy Marks

Calcutta rupee and half, obverse. Inverted V   *Calcutta rupee and half, reverse. No dot in circle*   *Calcutta quarter rupe,. obverse. Inverted V. No dot on reverse, as rupee*

Rupee *et infra* – 1820 to 1831 – Mint Name: Farrukhabad

This issue differs from previous one because of the increased weight. Struck at Farrukhabad, Calcutta, Benares and Saugor (see p. 42 for the secret marks).

6.22

   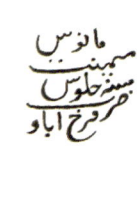

sikka zad bar haft kishwar sāya fazl ilāh hāmī dīn muhammad shāh 'ālam bādshāh (= Defender of the religion of Muhammad, Shah 'Alam Emperor, Shadow of the divine favour, put his stamp on the seven climes)

zarb farruckābād sanah 45 julūs maimanat mānūs (= Struck at Farrukhabad in the 45th year of his reign of tranquil prosperity).

Rupee *et infra* – 1820 to 1831 – Mint Name: Farrukhabad (cont)

	Rupee	Half Rupee	Quarter Rupee
Official Weight (g)	11.68	5.84	2.92
Actual Weight (g)	11.41-11.57	5.78	2.91
Actual Diameter (mm)	25.4-26.3	21	15.6-16.9
Metal	Silver		
Edge	Straight Grained		

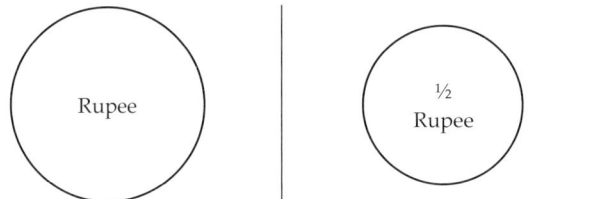

Catalogue

Cat No.	Pr. No.	Denom	Comments	Value ($)
6.22	320	Rupee		150
6.23	321	Half Rupee		120
6.24	322	Quarter Rupee		80

6.24

Quarter rupee

Copper Pice 1800 to 1829

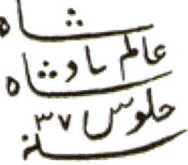

6.27

sanah julūs 37 shāh ʿālam bādshāh (= in the 37th year of the Emperor Shah ʿAlam)

The value in three languages: Bengali: *ek pai sikka*. Persian: *yek pai sikka*. Hindi: *ek pai sikka*. (Translation of all languages = One pai sikka). Within a plain, raised rim.

Official Weight (g)	Varies. See below
Actual Weight (g)	″
Actual Diameter (mm)	″
Metal	Copper
Edge	Plain

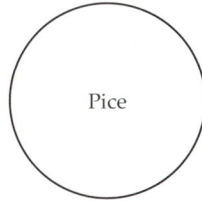

Cat. No. 6.26

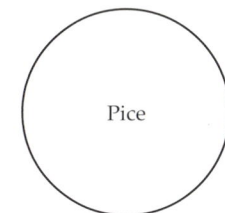

Cat. No. 6.27

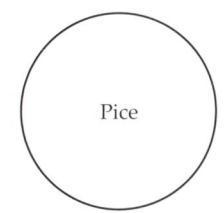

Cat. No. 6.28 & 6.29

Copper Pice 1800 to 1829 (cont)

Catalogue

Cat No.	Pr. No.	Denom	Date Issued	Status	Official wt (g)	Actual wt (g)	Actual Diam (mm)	Comments	Value ($)
6.26	205	Pice	1809	"	6.54	6.57	25.8-25.9		100
6.27	206	"	1817	"	6.47	6.06	27.2-27.5	Round flans	100
6.28	207	"	1829	"	"	6.10-6.43	25.9-26.3	Very neat flans	60
6.29	208	"		Proof	"				500

Example of Cat. No. 6.26

Copper Square Pattern/Trial Pice 1807

The legend of these coins is not known, but likely to be the same as the round copper pice, and struck on a square flan (see Stevens, Bengal pp. 262-264).

Catalogue

Cat No.	Pr. No.	Comments	Value ($)
6.30	-	No examples known. See Stevens, Bengal for more information about these trial pieces	NV

Bengal Presidency Benares Mint

Summary

The activity of the Benares mint can usefully be divided into five periods for the purpose of this summary. Firstly, from 1775 to 1805 the mint was farmed to local contractors, and there was little direct involvement of British officials, although in the early 1790s, the British Resident had nominal control. The coins produced during this period consisted of gold mohurs, silver rupees and fractions of both of these, and also crude copper pice. In the early 1800s, complaints from a particular native official within the mint, concerning malpractices of the most senior native officials (the darogah and the assay master), meant that the management controls were reviewed and, in 1803, a European mint/assay master was appointed, although he did not take effective action until the end of 1804. This introduced the second phase of mint operations.

This second phase fell into the period c1805 to 1812, when the mint was directly under the control of a European mint/assay master, although the style of the silver coins produced did not change significantly. Copper coins were sent from Calcutta rather than produced locally, and very few gold coins were produced. By 1812, the desire to improve the coins, particularly the rupee, led to a distinct change in style, but the old hammered method of coin production continued. This constitutes the third period, with only silver coins being produced.

The fourth period began with the introduction of machinery into the Benares mint, providing the ability to produce milled coins, starting in 1815, although the methods used still included manual production of the blanks. Rupees with the mint name Benares continued to be produced, and machine-struck trisuli pice also began to be manufactured. Farrukhabad rupees were also struck during this period.

The final period, from about 1820 until the mint closed in 1830, saw the introduction of yet more machinery and the cessation of the issue of the Benares rupee, leaving the Farrukhabad rupee as the only precious metal output of the mint. Throughout the fourth and fifth periods, Benares continued to produce copper trisuli pice.

Gold Mohur *et infra* –Shah 'Alam II – 1776 to 1812

Gold coins were produced in small numbers for most years. The legend for RY17/24 differs from that of other years. See page 106 for differentiating marks.

 7.23

sikka zad bar haft kishwar sāya fazl ilāh hāmī dīn muhammad shāh 'ālam bādshāh [AH date] (= Defender of the religion of Muhammad, Shah 'Alam Emperor, Shadow of the divine favour, put his stamp on the seven climes, [AH date])	*zarb muhammadābād benāres sanah [RY] julūs maimanat mānūs* (= Struck at Muhammadabad Benares in the [RY] year of his reign of tranquil prosperity).

	Mohur	Half Mohur	Quarter Mohur	Eighth Mohur
Official Weight (g)	10.88	5.44	2.72	1.36
Actual Weight (g)	10.86-10.89	5.42		1.6 but includes mount
Actual Diam (mm)	20.9-22.3	14.5-15.0	~12.5	~11
Metal	Gold			

Gold Mohur *et infra* – Shah 'Alam II – 1776 to 1812

Catalogue

Cat No.	Pr. No.	Denom	AH	RY	Differ. Marks	Comment	Value ($)
7.1	-	Mohur	xxxx	17	?	None known. Stevens pp. 306-307	NV
7.2	-	"	1192	18	B	Ref: Johnston	2,000
7.3	-	"	xxxx	19	?	None known. Stevens pp. 306-307	NV
7.4	-	"	xxxx	20	?	None known. Stevens pp. 306-307	NV
7.5	-	"	1193	21	?	G. Byfield at Sovereign Rarities	2000
7.6	-	"	xxxx	22	?	None known. Stevens pp. 306-307	NV
7.7	-	"	xxxx	23	?	None known but see Stevens, Bengal pp. 306-307	NV
7.8	-	"	xxxx	24	None	Ref: Senior (1993), ONSNL 137. Legend arranged differently from later dated coins	3,000
7.9	-	"	xxxx	25	?	None known but see Stevens, Bengal pp. 306-307	NV
7.10	-	"	1199	17/26	D	Ref: Johnston, also Baldwin (2008), sale 54 (Diana), lot 52	1,500
7.11	-	"	1199	17/27	D	Normal engraving. No barbels on fish	1,500
7.12	-	"	1199	17/27	None	Fish with barbels. No differ. marks	1,500
7.13	-	"	xxxx	[17/]28		None known but see Stevens, Bengal pp. 306-307	NV
7.14	-	"	1201	17/29	A	Ref: DNW (2002), sale 55, lot 1572	1,500
7.15	-	"	1202	17/29	A	Ref: Stevens collection	1,500
7.16	-	"	1202	30	D	Ref: Baldwin (2003), sale 35, lot 1704.	1,500
7.17	-	"	1202	31	D	Ref: Johnston, also Baldwin (2005), sale 43, lot 2959 for coin with complete AH date	1,500
7.18	-	"	1203	31	D	Ref: Baldwin (2005), sale 40, lot 985	1,500
7.19	-	"	1203	32	D	Ref: Baldwin (2004), sale 37, lot1532	1,500
7.20	-	"	1204	32	D	Ref: Baldwin (2003), sale 35, lot 1706	1,500
7.21	-	"	1209	36	D	Ref: Johnston	1,500
7.22	217	"	1209	37	D		1,500
7.23	218	"	1213	41	D	Ref: Johnston	1,500
7.24	-	Half Mohur	1xxx	32	D	Ref: Johnston. Possibility that this is a cut-down mohur, but edge looks normal.	3,000

Listing continued on next page

Gold Mohur *et infra* – Shah 'Alam II – 1776 to 1812 (cont)

Catalogue (cont)

Cat No.	Pr. No.	Denom	AH	RY	Differ. Marks	Comment	Value ($)
7.24b	-	Quarter Mohur	xxxx	26	?	Ref: Zubair Khan. Authenticity has been questioned	NV
7.24a	-	Eighth Mohur	xxxx	25	?	Berlin Museum. Ex Guthrie collection. Same type as RY 24 mohur.	NV

Eighth Mohur

Normal style · *RY 24 style. shāh 'ālam bādshāh ghāzī sikka mubārak* · *Fish with barbels (RY 27)*

Silver Rupee *et infra* – 1776 to 1812

The set of marks identified by Pridmore as 'darogah's' marks are named here 'differentiating' marks (see p. 106 for a list).

7.27

sikka zad bar haft kishwar sāya fazl ilāh hāmī dīn muhammad shāh 'ālam bādshāh [AH] (= Defender of the religion of Muhammad, Shah 'Alam Emperor, Shadow of the divine favour, put his stamp on the seven climes, [AH])

zarb muhammadābād benāres sanah [RY] julūs maimanat mānūs (= Struck at Muhammadabad Benares in the 17/[RY] year of his reign of tranquil prosperity).

Silver Rupee *et infra* – 1776 to 1812 (cont)

	Rupee	Half Rupee	Quarter Rupee	Eighth Rupee	1/16 Rupee
Official Weight (g)	11.33	5.66	2.83	1.42	0.71
Actual Weight (g)	10.85-11.37	5.40-5.65	2.63-2.82	1.30-1.42	0.68-0.71
Actual Diam (mm)	21.3-24.9	18.1-21.5	14.8-17.8	12.6-14.8	9.7-12.4
Metal	Silver				

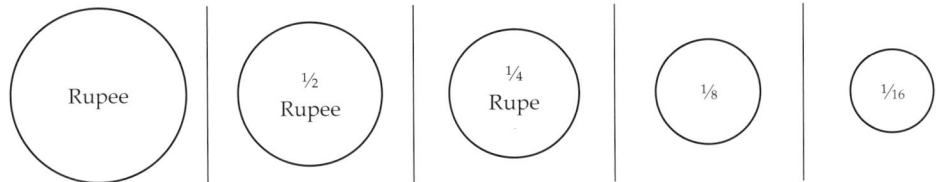

Catalogue

Cat No.	Pr. No.	Denom	AH	RY	Differ. Mark	Comments	Value ($)
7.25	219	Rupee	1190	17	A		150
7.26	220	"	1191	17	A		150
7.27	-	"	1191	17	B		150
7.28	221	"	1192	17	A		150
7.29		"	1192	17	B		150
(7.30)	-	"	xxxx	18	?	None known but see Stevens, Bengal p. 311. Probably does not exist.	NV
(7.31)	-	"	xxxx	19	?	None known but see Stevens, Bengal p. 311. Probably does not exist.	NV
7.32	-	"	1192	20	A	This and all later coins have dual RY eg 17/20	150
7.33	222	"	1193	20	A		100
7.34	223	"	1193	21	A		100
7.35	-	"	1194	21	A	Ref: Johnston from Mitchiner No 1933	100
7.36	224	"	1194	22	A		100
(7.36a)	-	"	1194	22		Ref: Indian hoard. Described has having ⚓'both sides'	NV
7.37	-	"	1195	22	A	Baldwin (2002), sale 31, lot 720	100
(7.37a)	-	"	1195	22		Ref: Indian hoard. Described has having an extra symbol ⚓	NV
7.38	225	"	1195	23	C		100
7.39	-	"	1195	23	A	Ref: Johnston, also Tandon (2008), JONS 194, p37	100

Cat No.s with brackets probably do not exist. Listing continued on next page

Silver Rupee *et infra* – 1776 to 1812 (cont)

Catalogue

Cat No.	Pr. No.	Denom	AH	RY	Differ. Mark	Comments	Value ($)
7.40	226	Rupee	1196	24	A		100
7.41	227	"	1197	25	D		100
7.42	-	"	1198	25	D		100
7.43	228	"	1198	26	D		100
7.44	229	"	1199	26	D		100
7.45	230	"	1199	27	D		100
7.46	-	"	1199	27	E	Ref: Johnston	100
7.46c	-	"	1199	27	F	Ref: Johnston	100
7.47	231	"	1200	27	E		100
7.48	-	"	120x	27	F		100
7.49	-	"	1201	28	A	Ref: Johnston	100
7.50	-	"	1201	28	G	Ref: Johnston	100
7.51	233	"	1201	29	A	Full die impression	1,000
7.52	232	"	1202	28	A		100
7.53	234	"	1202	29	A		100
7.54	235	"	1202	30	D		100
(7.55)	-	"	1202	31	D	Ref: HK/Singapore (2003), sale 36, lot 450 but no photo. May be 1203	100
7.56	236	"	1203	30	D		100
7.57	237	"	1203	31	D		100
(7.58)	-	"	1203	31	H	May be mark D	100
7.59	238	"	1204	32	D		100
7.60	-	"	1205	32	D		100
7.61	239	"	1205	33	D		100
7.62	240	"	1206	33	D		100
7.63	242	"	1206	34	D		100
7.64	243	"	1207	34	D		100
7.65	244	"	1207	35	D		100
7.66	245	"	1207	35	D	Full die impression	1,000
7.67	246	"	1208	35	D		100
7.68	247	"	1208	36	D		100
7.69	248	"	1209	36	D		100
7.70	249	"	1209	37	D		100

Cat No.s with brackets probably do not exist. Listing continued on next page

Silver Rupee *et infra* – 1776 to 1812 (cont)

Catalogue (cont)

Cat No.	Pr. No.	Denom	AH	RY	Differ. Mark	Comments	Value ($)
7.71	250	Rupee	1210	37	D		100
(7.71a)	-	"	1210	37	↓	Ref: Indian hoard. Described has having an extra symbol and legend in 2 lines	NV
7.72	251	"	1210	38	D		100
7.73	252	"	1211	38	D		100
7.74	253	"	1211	39	D		100
7.74c	-	"	1211	40	D	Mule	100
7.76	254	"	1212	39	D		100
7.77	255	"	1212	40	D		100
7.78	241	"	1213	33	D	Mule	250
7.79	256	"	1213	40	D		100
7.80	257	"	1213	41	D		100
7.81	258	"	1214	41	D		100
7.82	259	"	1214	42	D		100
7.82a	-	"	1214	42	I	Ref: Indian coin hoard	100
7.83	260	"	1215	42	D		100
7.84	261	"	1215	43	I		100
7.85	262	"	1216	43	I		100
7.86	263	"	1216	44	I		100
7.87	264	"	1217	44	J		100
7.88	265	"	1217	45	J		100
7.89	266	"	1217	45	J	Full die impression. Diam 29.5mm	1,000
(7.89a)	-	"	1218	43	J?	Ref: Indian coin hoard	100
7.90	267	"	1218	45	J		100
7.91	268	"	1218	46	J		100
7.92	-	"	1218	46	J	Full die impression. Ref: Fitzwilliam Museum. Diam 34.0mm	NV
7.93	269	"	1219	46	J		100
7.94	-	"	1219	47	J		100
7.94c	-	"	1219	47	K	Ref: Johnston	100
7.95	270	"	1219	47	K	Full die impression. Diam 33.3mm	1,000
7.96	271	"	1219	47	L		100
(7.96a)	-	"	1219	47		Ref: Indian coin hoard. Described as having ♆ both sides	NV

Cat No.s with brackets probably do not exist. Listing continued on next page

Silver Rupee *et infra* – 1776 to 1812 (cont)

Catalogue (cont)

Cat No.	Pr. No.	Denom	AH	RY	Differ. Mark	Comments	Value ($)
7.97	272	Rupee	1220	47	L		100
7.98	-	"	1220	48	L		100
7.99	273	"	1220	48	M		100
7.100	274	"	1221	48	M		100
(7.100a)	-	"	1221	48	M	Ref: Indian coin hoard. Described as having a legend in 2 lines	NV
7.101	275	"	1221	49	N		100
(7.101a)	-	"	1221	49	None	Ref: Indian coin hoard	100
7.102	276	"	1222	49	N		100
(7.102a)	-	"	1222	49	N	Ref: Indian coin hoard. Described as having a legend in 2 lines	100
7.103	277	"	1223	49	N		100
7.103c	-	"	1224	49	N	No barbels. Ref: Johnston	100
7.104	278	"	1224	49	N	With barbels. Fish have barbels from this date forwards	100
7.105	279	"	1225	49	N		100
7.106	280	"	1226	49	N		100
7.107	-	"	1227	49	N	Copper forgeries exist	100
7.108	-	Half Rupee	1196	17/24	A	Ref: Johnston	750
7.109	281	"	xxxx	31		Ref: Ashmolean Museum	NV
7.110		"	1214	41	D	Ref: HK/Singapore (2003), sale 36, lot 452	750
7.111		"	12xx	47	L	Ref: Album (2006), list 218, lot 50809	750
7.112		"	12xx	48	L	Ref: Baldwin (2001), sale 25 (Wiggins), lot 598	750
7.113		"	1224	49	N	Ref: HK/Singapore (2003), sale 36, lot 453. No barbels on fish	750
7.114		"	1226	49	N	barbels on fish (after 1224). Ref: Johnston	750

Cat No.s with brackets probably do not exist. Listing continued on next page

Full flan striking of rupee dated AH 1219, RY 47

Silver Rupee *et infra* – 1776 to 1812 (cont)

Catalogue (cont)

Cat No.	Pr. No.	Denom	AH	RY	Differ. Mark	Comments	Value ($)
7.115	282	Quarter Rupee	1191	17	A	Baldwin (2003), sale 33, lot 1011	500
7.116		″	119x	22	A	Baldwin (2001), sale 25, lot 599	500
7.117		″	1199	26	D	Baldwin (2001), sale 25, lot 600. Johnston	500
7.118		″	1212	40	D	Ref: HK/Sing (2003), sale 36, lot 454	500
7.119		″	121x	42	D	Baldwin (2001), sale 25, lot 601	500
7.120		″	xxxx	43	I	Baldwin (2001), sale 25, lot 602	500
7.121		″	xxxx	46	J	Baldwin (2006), sale 47 (Stiller), lot 841	500
7.121c		″	1219	47	K or L	Johnston	500
7.122		″	xxxx	49	N	Fish without barbels (before 1225). Baldwin (2006), sale 47, lot 841	500
7.123	-	″	xxxx	49	N	Fish with barbels (1225 or later). Ref: Baldwin (2001), sale 25 (Wiggins), lot 603	500
7.124	283	Eighth Rupee	xxxx	24	A	Ref: Baldwin (2001), sale 25 (Wiggins), lot 604	500
7.125		″	11xx	27	E	Ref: Thompson. Also HK/Sing (2003), sale 36, lot 455 also Johnston	500
7.126		″	xxxx	28	G	Ref: Weir, Also HK/Sing (2009), sale 46, lot 1122	500
7.127		″	1203	30	D	Johnston. Also Baldwin (2006), sale 47 (Stiller), lot 843	500
7.128		″	xxxx	41	D	Baldwin (2010), sale 65, lot 1699	500
7.129		″	xxxx	43	?	Ref: Weir	500
7.130		″	xxxx	46	?	Ref: Weir	500
7.131		″	xxxx	47	L	Ref: Johnston	500
7.132		″	xxxx	48	L	Baldwin (2006), sale 47 (Stiller), lot 844	500
7.133		″	xxxx	49	N	Baldwin (2001), sale 25, lot 605	500
7.134	284	Sixteenth Rupee	xxxx	21	?	Baldwin (2000), sale 22, lot 182	500
7.134c		″	xxxx	27	?	Ref: Johnston	500
7.135		″	xxxx	49	N	HK/Sing (2003), sale 36, lot 455	500

Silver Rupee *et infra* – 1776 to 1812 (cont)

Differentiating Marks

Mark A

Mark B

Mark C

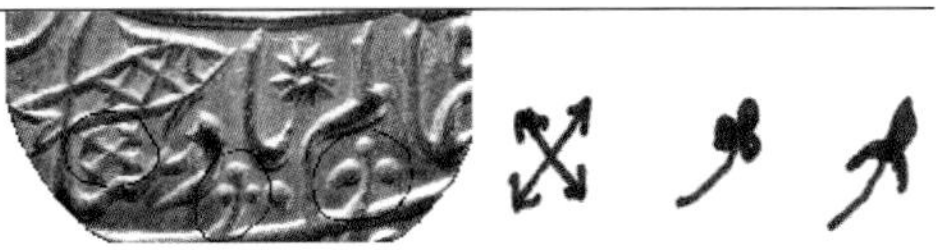

Mark D

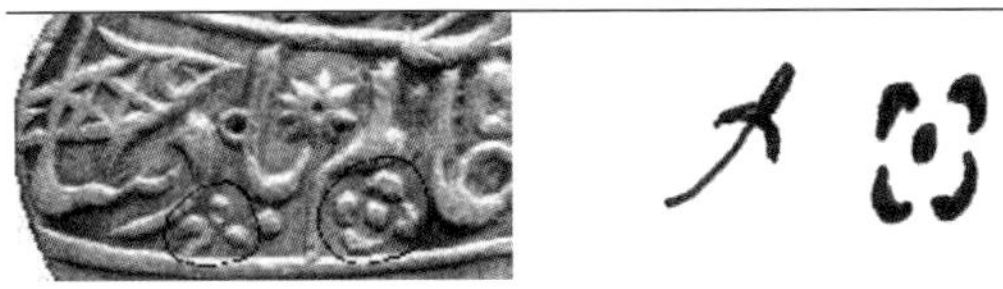

Mark E

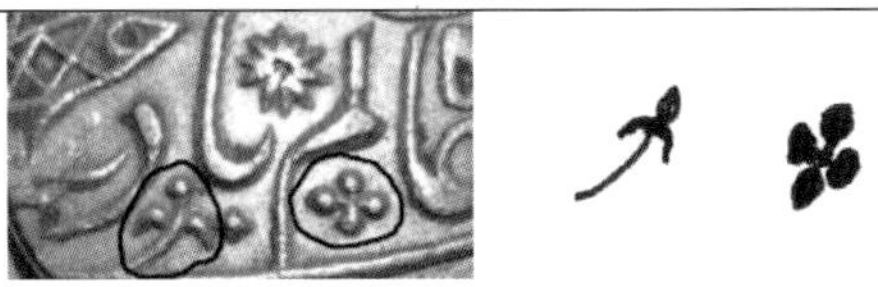

Mark F

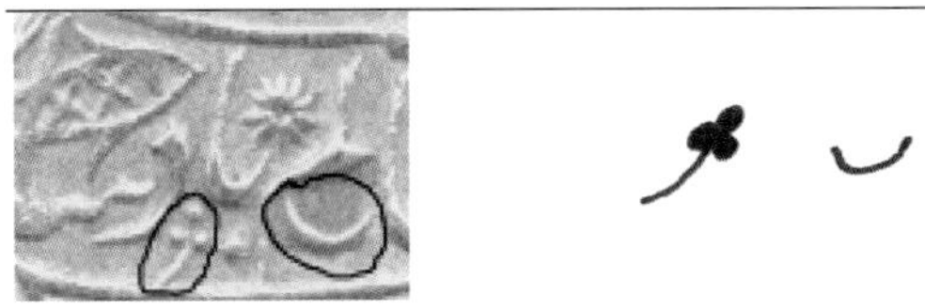

Mark G

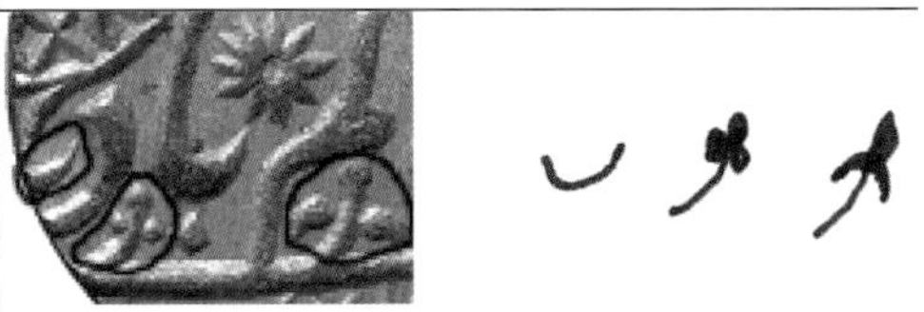

Mark H (left symbol not certain)

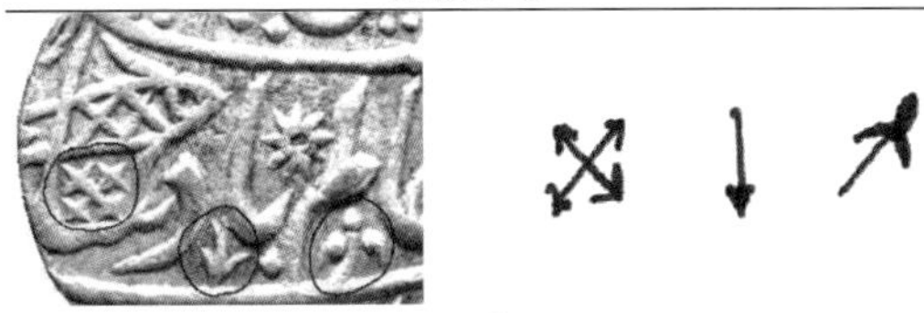

Mark I

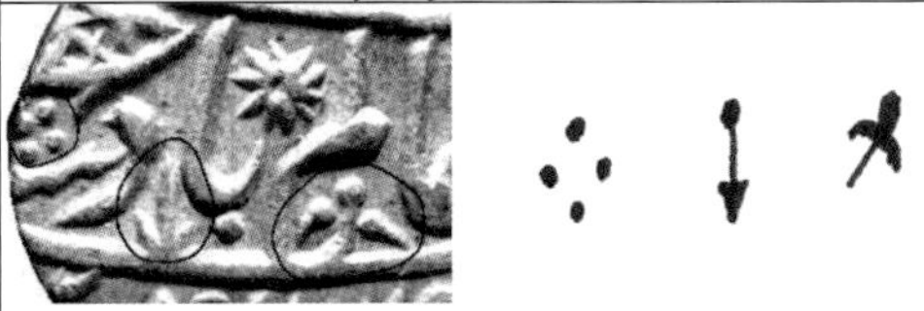

Mark J

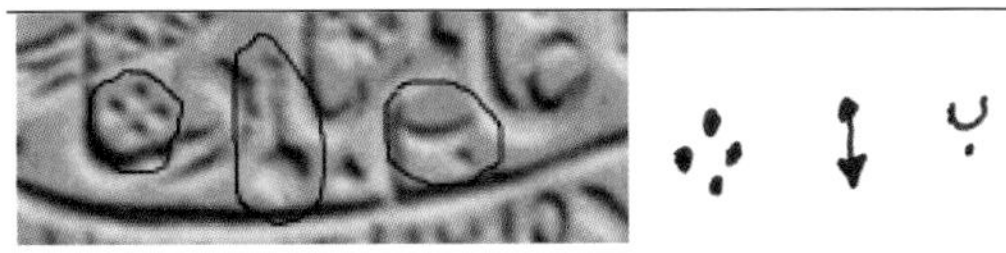

Mark K

Mark L

Mark M

Mark N

Silver Rupee – Transitional Type – 1812

This type may have been produced during the period 1810-1812, when the mint was being investigated by the Board of Commissions of the Ceded and Conquered territories (see Stevens, Bengal p. 347). However, a number of authorities have suggested that this may be a contemporary forgery.

7.136

sikka zad bar haft kishwar sāya fazl ilāh hāmī dīn muhammad shāh 'ālam bādshāh [AH] (= Defender of the religion of Muhammad, Shah 'Alam Emperor, Shadow of the divine favour, put his stamp on the seven climes, [AH])

zarb muhammadābād benāres sanah 17/[RY] julūs maimanat mānūs (= Struck at Muhammadabad Benares in the 17/[RY] year of his reign of tranquil prosperity).

Official Weight (g)	11.33
Actual Weight (g)	10.82
Actual Diameter (mm)	26.1-26.6
Metal	Silver

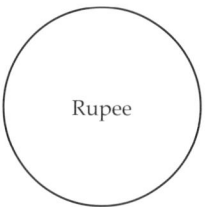

Rupee

Catalogue

Cat No.	Pr. No.	AH	RY	AD issued	Comment	Value ($)
7.136	-	1230	49	1812	Ref: Baldwin (2001), sale 25 (Wiggins), lot 608	1,000

Silver Rupee *et infra* – 1812 to 1815

No differentiating marks on obverse.

7.137

sikka zad bar haft kishwar sāya fazl ilāh hāmī dīn muhammad shāh 'ālam bādshāh [AH] (= Defender of the religion of Muhammad, Shah 'Alam Emperor, Shadow of the divine favour, put his stamp on the seven climes, [AH])

zarb muhammadābād benāres sanah 17/[RY] julūs maimanat mānūs (= Struck at Muhammadabad Benares in the 17/[RY] year of his reign of tranquil prosperity).

	Rupee	Half Rupee	Quarter Rupee
Official Weight (g)	11.33	5.66	2.83
Actual Weight (g)	11.26-11.32	5.67	2.79-2.81
Actual Diameter (mm)	21.9-24.0	21.8-22.7	15.0-17.7
Metal	Silver		

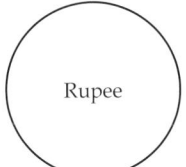 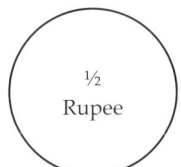 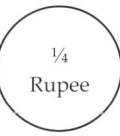

Rupee ½ Rupee ¼ Rupee

Catalogue

Cat No.	Pr. No.	Denom	AH	RY	Comment	Value ($)
7.137	-	Rupee	1227	49	Ref: Baldwin (2001), sale 25 (Wiggins), lot 607	300
7.138	285	"	1228	49	also comes on larger flan (Weir)	150
7.139	286	"	1229	49	Also comes on larger flan (Indian coin hoard)	100
7.140	287	Half Rupee	1229	49		350
7.141	288	Quarter Rupee	1229	49		350

Silver Patterns for Rupee *et infra* – 1815

 7.142

sikka zad bar haft kishwar sāya fazl ilāh hāmī dīn muhammad shāh 'ālam bādshāh 1229
(= Defender of the religion of Muhammad, Shah 'Alam Emperor, Shadow of the divine favour, put his stamp on the seven climes, 1229)

zarb muhammadābād benāres sanah 17/[RY] julūs maimanat mānūs (= Struck at Muhammadabad Benares in the 17th/49th year of his reign of tranquil prosperity).

	Rupee	Half Rupee	Quarter Rupee
Actual Weight (g)	11.33	5.68	2.84-2.85
Actual Diameter (mm)	27.3-27.5	18.4-19.0	16.6-19.2
Metal	Silver		
Edge	Grained Left		

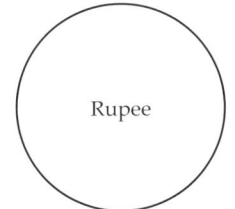 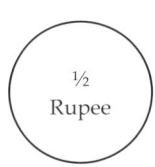 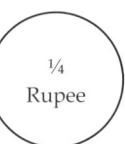

Catalogue

Cat No.	Pr. No.	Denom	AH	RY	Issued AD	Comments	Value ($)
7.142	291	Rupee	1229	17/49	1815		2,000
7.143	292	Half Rupee	"	"	"	Unfinished pattern.	2,500
7.144	293	Quarter Rupee	"	"	"	Unfinished pattern.	1,500

Silver Patterns for Rupee *et infra* – 1815 (cont)

7.143

Half rupee

7.144

Quarter rupee

Silver Rupee *et infra* – 1815 to 1820

7.145

sikka zad bar haft kishwar sāya fazl ilāh hāmī dīn 110hah110mad 110hah 'ālam bādshāh [AH] (= Defender of the religion of Muhammad, Shah 'Alam Emperor, Shadow of the divine favour, put his stamp on the seven climes, [AH])

zarb muhammadābād benāres sanah 17/49 julūs maimanat mānūs (= Struck at Muhammadabad Benares in the 17/49 year of his reign of tranquil prosperity).

	Rupee	Half Rupee	Quarter Rupee
Official Weight (g)	11.33	5.66	2.83
Actual Weight (g)	11.41	5.68	2.83-2.85
Actual Diameter (mm)	26.1-26.4	18.4-19.0	16.6-19.2
Metal	Silver		
Edge	Grained Right		

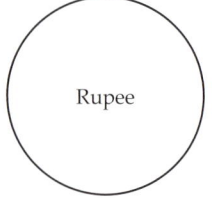

Rupee

Half Rupee

Quarter Rupee

Silver Rupee *et infra* – 1815 to 1820 (cont)

Catalogue

Cat No.	Pr. No.	Denom	AH	RY	AD Issued	Comment	Value ($)
7.145	289	Rupee	1229	17/49	1815-20		150
7.146	-	"	1230	17/49	"	Some doubt about the existence of this coin	NV
7.147	290	Half Rupee	1229	"	"		100
7.148	-	Quarter Rupee	1229	"	"		750

sikka Shah 'ālam bādshāh 1229

zarb benāres sanah 17/49

Quarter rupee. 7.148

Silver Farrukhabad Rupee *et infra* – 1820 to 1830

Also issued from the mints of Calcutta and Farrukhabad (see Stevens, Bengal pp. 295-297 & 461-662)

7.149

sikka zad bar haft kishwar sāya fazl ilāh hāmī dīn muhammad shah 'ālam bādshāh [AH] (= Defender of the religion of Muhammad, Shah 'Alam Emperor, Shadow of the divine favour, put his stamp on the seven climes, [AH])

zarb farruckābād sanah 45 julūs maimanat mānūs (= Struck at Farrukhabad in the 45 year of his reign of tranquil prosperity.)

	Rupee	Half Rupee	Quarter Rupee
Official Weight (g)	11.68	5.84	2.92
Actual Weight (g)	11.61	?	2.91
Actual Diameter (mm)	24.5-25.0	?	15.6-16.9
Metal	Silver		
Edge	Straight Grained		

Silver Farrukhabad Rupee *et infra* – 1820 to 1830 (cont)

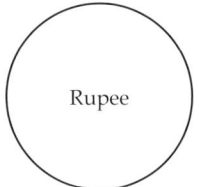

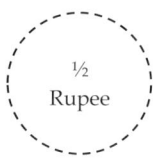

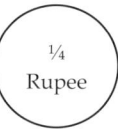

Catalogue

Cat No.	Pr. No.	Denom	Comment	Value ($)
7.149	323	Rupee		150
7.150	324	Half Rupee		300
7.151	324A	Quarter Rupee	Dated AH 1204 on obverse	250

Privy Marks

Rupee & half rupee.
Inverted V on obverse
Bead in centre of circle of dots on reverse

Quarter rupee.
Inverted V on obverse
Reverse as rupee

Silver Trial for Grained Edge on Farrukhabad Rupee 1822

7.152

Legend within a plain raised rim:
New
Milling
1822

namūnah zarb benāres (= Pattern struck at Benares). Within a plain, raised rim.

Silver Trial for Grained Edge on Farrukhabad Rupee 1822 (cont)

Actual Weight (g)	11.66
Diameter (mm) from Pridmore	25.4
Metal	Silver
Edge	Straight Grained

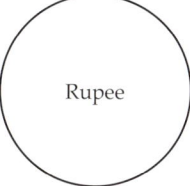

Rupee

Catalogue

Cat No.	Pr. No.	Comments	Value ($)
7.152	362	Recorded from Pridmore	NV

Copper Pice – 1776 to 1806

My thanks to Robert Johnston who provided much of the information for this listing, including the photos for the obverse and reverse varieties. Differentiating marks also appear on many of the known specimens and, where visible, appear to match the marks recorded on the silver coins. Because the coins are very crude and only parts of the design on obverse and reverse are visible, fewer of the marks are usually visible, so these have been recorded differently from those on the silver coins. They occur on the obverse in the middle of the word 'Alam.

7.165

fulūs shāh 'ālam (= Money of Shah 'Alam).	*zarb benāres 48* (= Struck at Benares [year] 48)

Official Weight (g)	10.64-11.96
Actual Weight (g)	11.39-12.05
Actual Diameter (mm)	15.7-22.5
Metal	Copper

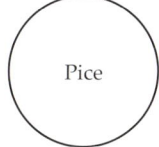

Pice

Copper Pice – 1776 to 1806 (cont)

Catalogue

Cat No.	Pr. No.	Obv	Rev	AH	RY	Differ. Marks	Comment	Value ($)
7.153	294	A	I		17	A		100
7.154	-	A	II		17	B		100
7.155	-	A	II		18	B	Ref: Johnston	100
7.156	295	A	II		19	B		100
7.157	-	A	II?		20	?	None known but see Stevens, Bengal pp. 322-323	NR
7.158	-	A	II?		21	?	*ibid*	NR
7.159	-	A	II?		22	?	*Ibid.* Wt. reduced until 1786.	NR
7.160	-	A	II?		23	?	None known but see Stevens Bengal pp. 322-323	NR
7.161	-	A	II?		24	?	*ibid*	NR
7.162	-	A	II?		25	?	*ibid*	NR
7.163	-	A	II?		26	?	*ibid*	NR
7.164	-	A	III	12xx	27	C	Wt. restored to 10.06g from 8.97g in 1786. Ref: Noble (1995), Sale 48, lot 2147	100
7.165	296	A	III		28	C		100
7.165b	-	A	III	120x	28	D		100
7.165a		B	III	1201	xx	D	No fish on obverse. Ref: Stevens collection	100
7.166	-	B	III	1203	30	E	Ref: Noble (1995), Sale 48, lot 2147, also Johnston	100
7.167	297	B	III		35	E		100
7.168	-	B	III		36	E	Ref: Baldwin (2001), sale 25 (Wiggins), lot 650.	100
7.169	-	B	III		38	E	Ref: Johnston	100
7.170	-	B	III		39		Pr. Sale, lot 650	100
7.171	-	B	III		41	E	Ref: Baldwin (2001), sale 25 (Wiggins), lot 650.	100
7.171c	-	B	III		42	E	Ref: Johnston	100
7.172	-	B	III		45	F	Ref: Baldwin (2001), sale 25 (Wiggins), lot 650.	100
7.173	-	B	III	[1]219	46	?	Ref: Johnston	100
7.174	298	B	III	[12]22	49	G	Ref: Bons. Arrow symbol instead of star in *seen* of *benares*	100

Copper Pice – 1776 to 1806 (cont)

Differentiating Marks

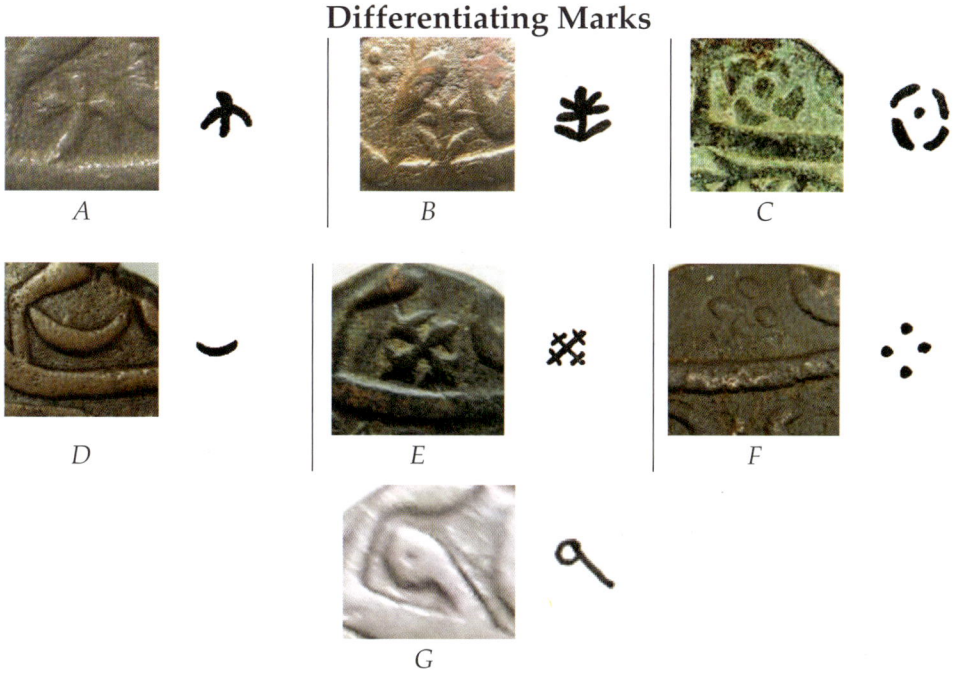

Obverse Varieties

Trident	There may or may not be a trident

	A	B
Trident	Absent	Present

Obverse A. No trident   *Obverse B. Trident present*

7.165a. Pice, AH 1201, no fish

Copper Pice – 1776 to 1806 (cont)

Reverse Varieties

Muhammadabad	The word *muhammadābād* may appear in the top line, or may be replaced by an ornament
RY	The RY date may be to the right of *julūs*, in the *sīn* of *benāres* or above the *sīn* of *benāres*
Trident	A trident may be present or absent
Star	There may be a star in the *sīn* of *benāres*

	I	II	III
Muhammadabad	Top Line	Top Line	Replaced by ornament
RY	Right of *julūs*	In *sīn* of *benāres*	Above *sīn* of *benāres*
Trident	Absent	Absent	Present
Star	None	None	In *seen* of *benāres*

Reverse I.	*Reverse II*	*Reverse III.*

Copper Pattern Double Pice *et infra* 1806

Prepared by Yeld in the Benares mint

7.175

fulūs shāh 'ālam (= Money of Shah 'Alam).   *zarb benāres 48* (= Struck at Benares [year] 48)

	Double Pice	Pice	Half Pice	Quarter Pice
Pridmore Wt (g)	15.55	7.78	3.89	1.94
Diam (mm) from Pridmore	30.5	?	?	16.0
Metal	Copper			
Edge	Plain			

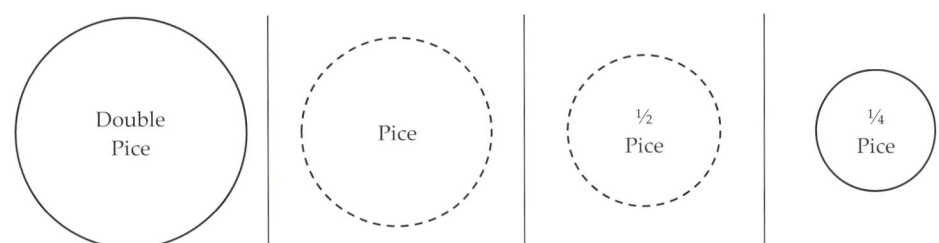

Catalogue

Cat No.	Pr. No.	Denom	Comment	Value ($)
7.175	299	Double Pice		7,000
7.176	300	Pice	None traced	NV
7.177	301	Half Pice	None traced	NV
7.178	302	Quarter Pice		5,000

Copper Pattern Double Pice *et infra* 1806 (cont)

7.178

Quarter pice pattern

Copper Double Pice *et infra* 1807 to 1809

Struck at Calcutta for use in Benares. None of the coins got into circulation at Benares, although the pice were exported by shroffs from Benares for circulation in Bihar.

7.180

sanah julūs 37 shāh 'ālam bādshāh (= In the 37th year of the Emperor Shah 'Alam)

Persian: *do pai sikka.*
Hindi: *do pai sikka.*
(Translation = Two pai sikka)

	Double Pice	Pice	Half Pice
Official Weight (g)	12.46	6.23	3.11
Actual Weight (g)	13.12-14.46	7.29	3.02-3.09
Actual Diameter (mm)	29.5	24.7	17.5
Metal	Copper		
Edge	Plain		

Copper Double Pice *et infra* 1807 to 1809 (cont)

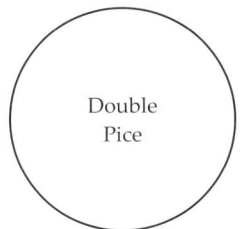

Double Pice

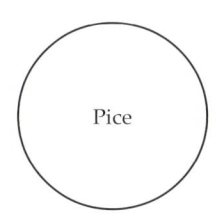

Pice

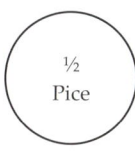

½ Pice

Catalogue

Cat No.	Pr. No.	Denomination	Status	Comment	Value ($)
7.179	303	Double Pice	Currency		500
7.180	304	"	Proof	Struck from rusty dies. Wt = 14.21?	1,000
7.181	305	Pice	Currency		400
7.182	306	"	Proof		800
7.183	307	Half Pice	Currency		300
7.184	308	"	Proof		600

Copper Pattern Pice 1813

7.185

 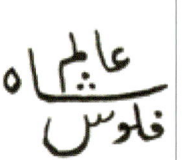 

fulūs shāh 'ālam (= Money of Shah 'Alam). *zarb benāres sanah 49* (= Struck at Benares in [year] 49)

Copper Pattern Pice 1813 (cont)		
	Double Pice	Pice
Actual Weight (g)	12.95	6.49
Pridmore Diameter (mm)	27.0	~20
Metal	Copper	
Edge	Plain	

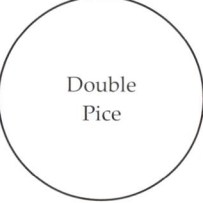
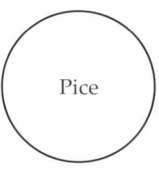

Catalogue

Cat No.	Pr. No.	Denomination	Comment	Value ($)
7.185	308A	Double Pice		7,000
7.185a	-	Pice	Stevens Collection	5,000

Copper Currency Pice – 1815 to 1829

Many contemporary forgeries of these coins exist. Most, if not all, light weight coins are contemporary forgeries.

7.186

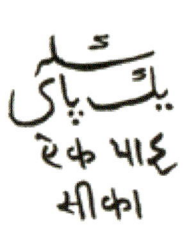

sanah julūs 37 shāh 'ālam bādshāh (= in the 37th year of the Emperor Shah 'Alam). Trisul

Persian: yek pai sikka.
Hindi: yek pai sikka. (Translation = One pai sikka). Trisul

Official Weight (g)	6.23
Actual Weight (g)	3.03-6.76
Actual Diameter (mm)	Varies. See table below
Metal	Copper
Edge	Plain

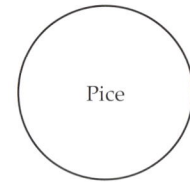

7.192

Coin countermarked with the letter E within a circle

Copper Currency Pice – 1815 to 1829 (cont)

Catalogue

Cat No.	Pr. No.	Status	Actual Diam (mm)	Comments	Value ($)
7.186	309	Currency	23.2-25.1	Many different styles.	50
7.187	309	"	"	Type with raised rim	100
7.188	310	"	20.5-23.2	Neater engraving with plain circle around design. The circle is only clear on those struck off-centre	50
7.189	311	"	26.5	As previous but larger flan	50
7.190	312	"	21.5-24.8	Cross-bar on Rev trisul. Exists with small flan and small letters	50
7.191	313	Proof	23.0-24.0	Proof of previous coin	500
7.192	-	Token?	25.6-26.3	Countermarked with letter E	200

1st type with thicker letters. 7.186   *1st type with raised rim. 7.187*

2nd type with neater engraving. 7.188   *2nd type struck off-centre, showing the circle surrounding the legend. 7.188*

Cross-bar on trisul

Mints of the Bengal Presidency

Bengal Presidency Mints in the Ceded & Conquered Provinces

Summary

The Nawab Vizier of Awadh, Sadat 'Ali, was forced into a treaty to cede various of his territories to the East India Company, a treaty which was signed on the 10th November 1801. The territory was divided into seven districts: Gorakhpur, Allahabad, Cawnpur, Farrukhabad (actually ceded by the Nawab of Farrukhabad), Etawah, Bareilly and Moradabad. On the removal of the Nawab's officers in 1802, the Governor General, Lord Mornington (afterwards Marquis of Wellesley), created a Board of Commission to determine how the new territories should be run. This was led by the Governor General's brother, Henry Wellesley, whose appointment was not approved by the Court of Directors in London. Henry Wellesley consequently resigned in 1803 and the Board was dissolved with the Collectors of each district being placed immediately under the control of the Board of Revenue [19].

At about the same time, General Lake was engaged in the second Maratha war, which led to him capturing, *inter alia*, Dehli on the 11th September 1803 and Agra on the 18th October.

These territories became known as the Ceded and Conquered Provinces and they brought with them the working mints of Allahabad, Bareilly, Farrukhabad, Saharanpur, Dehli, Agra and possibly Najibabad and Hathras (but see later).

By these means therefore, the East India Company acquired at least six and possibly more working mints, which therefore fall into the category 'transitional mints', that is mints that were kept operational for some time after they fell into British hands, but whose output continued in the native style. After due consideration, the mints at Allahabad, Bareilly, Saharanpur and Najibabad and

---

[19] Misra B B, The Central Administration of the East India Company 1773-1834. Manchester University Press, 1959, pp. 200-201.

Hathras (if they existed) were closed in 1805 and a new mint was built at Farrukhabad to produce a new style of copper and silver coin. This mint was closed in 1824

The mint at Dehli was kept in operation for a considerable number of years to supply coins for payment of the Emperor and was not closed until 1857/58, whilst that at Agra was probably closed at the same time as most of the other mints, in 1805, although no record of this has been found.

Further mints were acquired after the third Maratha war in 1818 and these included Saugor and Sohagpur. Sohagpur was closed quite quickly but Saugor was kept open for quite a few years (see Stevens, Bengal p. 479 *et seq.*). At about this time, consideration was given to opening a mint at Ajmir, but this never happened. A new mint was built at Saugor to supply Farrukhabad rupees to the Central Provinces. This mint was eventually closed in 1835.

Agra – Silver Rupee

Agra was renamed Akbarabad soon after the start of the reign of Shah Jahan I, famous for building the Taj Mahal, hence the mint name on the coins.

Agra was captured by the British on 18th October 1803 during the second Maratha war. Thus, coins struck there after this date must have been issued under the authority of the British. These include silver rupees and copper pice.

8.1

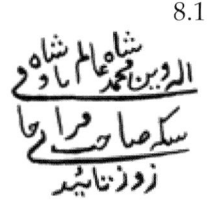

| legend that probably reads: *sikka zad sāhib-i qirān (a)z ta'yid ilāh hāmī dīn muhammad shāh 'ālam bādshāh [AH]* (= Struck coin like the second Lord of conjunctions, by the help of God, Defender of the faith of Muhammad, the Emperor Shah 'Alam [AH]). | *zarb mustaqir al-khilafa akbarābād sanah [RY] maimanat mānūs* (= struck at the seat of the Caliphate, Akbarabad, in the [RY] of tranquil prosperity |

Actual Weight (g)	10.99-11.05
Actual Diameter (mm)	19.5-20.8
Metal	Silver

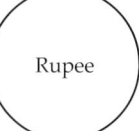

Rupee

Catalogue

Cat No.	Pr. No.	AH	RY	Comment	Value ($)
8.1	-	1219	47	Ref: Lingen	250
8.2	-	1220	47	Ref: Lingen.	250

Agra – Copper Pice, Shah Alam II

8.3

Shah Alam legend with AH date

A Persian legend, possibly as below, with flintlock pistol pointing left

Actual Weight (g)	?
Actual Diameter (mm)	~19
Metal	Copper

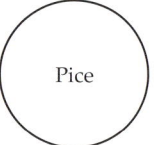

Pice

Catalogue

Cat No.	Pr. No.	AH	RY	Comment	Value ($)
8.2c	-	1217	xx	Ref: Steve Album	350
8.2e	-	xxxx	47	Ref: Jinendra Shah	350

Agra – Copper Pice, Muhammad Akbar II

8.3

sikka mubārak bādshāh ghāzī muhammad akbar (= The auspicious coin of the victorious Emperor Muhammad Akbar)

zarb akbarābād sanah [RY] julūs (= Struck at Akbarabad in the [RY] year). A flintlock pistol clearly visible

Actual Weight (g)	5.74
Actual Diameter (mm)	18.2-20.9
Metal	Copper
Edge	Plain

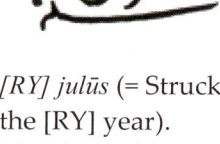

Pice

Catalogue

Cat No.	Pr. No.	AH	RY	Comment	Value ($)
8.3	-	1222	1	Ref: Khan	350

126

Allahabad – Silver 'Lucknow' Rupee

Allahabad was transferred to the British from the Nawab Vizier of Awadh in 1801 (AH 1216)[20].

In September 1803 the mint committee sent an account of the coins produced since the mint had been occupied by the British. This showed two types of rupee to have been produced: The 'Lucknow' rupee and the 'Shumshari' rupee.

The design of the Allahabad 'Lucknow' rupee is not known. It is possible that they are direct copies of the rupee struck at Lucknow itself, although this seems unlikely. Those rupees have the mint name *Muhammadabad Benares*.

Rupee of Muhammadabad Benares with no AH date

Usual rupee of Muhammadabad Benares with AH date 1218

Actual Weight (g)	Probably ~11.2
Actual Diameter (mm)	Probably ~22
Metal	Silver

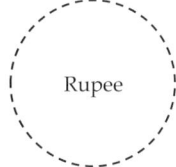

Catalogue

Cat No.	Pr. No.	AH	RY	Obv	Rev	Comments	Value ($)
8.4	-	1217	26			Records indicate these dates could exist, but since the design is not known, this remains speculation. An eighth rupee might also exist. See Lucknow museum catalogue No. 4855	NV
8.5	-	1218	26				NV
8.6	-	1219	26				NV

---

[20] Wiggins K W, (1996). Acquisition of Indian Mints by E.I.CO. Numismatic Panorama. New Dehli:

Allahabad – Silver 'Shumshari' Rupee

 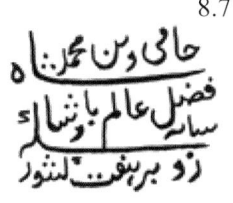 8.7

sikka zad bar haft kishwar sāya fazl ilāh hāmī dīn muhammad shāh 'ālam bādshāh [AH] (= Defender of the religion of Muhammad, Shah Alam Emperor, Shadow of the divine favour, put his stamp on the seven climes, [AH]) NB Ball & sword	*zarb allāhābād sanah 26 julūs maimanat mānūs* (=struck at Allahabad in the 26th year of his reign of tranquil prosperity)

Actual Weight (g)	11.17-11.19
Actual Diameter (mm)	21.0-22.0
Metal	Silver

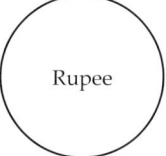

Rupee

Catalogue

Cat No.	Pr. No.	AH	RY	Comments	Value ($)
8.7	-	1216	26		250
8.8	-	1217	26	The only known example of this date has the letter A on the reverse.	2,000

Shumshari rupee, 1217/26 with letter A on reverse
The letter A may refer to the Collector, Richard Ahmuty

Bareilly – Silver Rupee – 1802 to 1805

This mint was acquired by the EIC in 1801

8.14

sikka zad sāhib-i qirān (a)z ta'yid ilāh hāmī dīn muhammad shāh 'ālam bādshāh [AH] (= Struck coin like the Lord of the second conjunction, by the help of God, Defender of the faith of Muhammad, the Emperor Shah 'Alam [AH]) | *zarb qita bareilī sanah 37 julūs maimanat mānūs* (= struck at the district of Bareilly in the 37th year of tranquil prosperity)

Actual Weight (g)	10.99-11.11
Actual Diameter (mm)	20.4-22.5
Metal	Silver

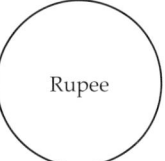

Rupee

Catalogue

Cat No.	AH	RY	Rev	Comments	Value ($)
8.9	1216	37	I	KM 52.1. Probably the first in the British series.	200
8.10	1216	37	II	KM 52.2	150
8.11	1216	37	III	KM 52.3	150
8.12	1217	37	III	KM 52.3	150
8.13	1218	37	III	Ref: Noble (1995), sale 48, lot 2173	150
8.14	1219	37	III		150
8.15	1220	37	III	Ref: Noble (1995), sale 48, lot 2174	150

Bareilly – Silver Rupee – 1802 to 1805

Reverse Varieties

Letter	There are different Persian letters in the *sīn* of *julūs*

	I	II	III
Letter	*alif*	*he*	*wa*

Rev. 1 – alif   *Rev II – he*   *Rev III – wa*

Rupee 1216/37

Rupee 1217/37

Although the British had effective control of the mint at Dehli from 1803, it remained nominally under the authority of the Moghul Emperor, and it is therefore debatable as to whether or not it falls into the definition of a transitional mint.

Dehli – Shah 'Alam II – Gold – Nazarana Mohur Type 1

Clearly differentiated from next type by the floral borders.

8.17

sikka zad sāhib-i qirān (a)z ta'yid ilāh hāmī dīn muhammad shāh 'ālam bādshāh [AH] (= Struck coin like the the second Lord of conjunctions by the help of God, Defender of the faith of Muhammad, the Emperor Shah 'Alam [AH]).
Surrounded by a floral border.

zarb dār al-khilāfa shāhjahānābād [RY] julūs maimanat mānūs (= Struck at the seat of the Caliphate, Shahjahanabad, in the [RY] year of his reign of tranquil prosperity).
Surrounded by a floral border.

Actual Weight (g)	10.55
Actual Diameter (mm)	27.4-28.2
Metal	Gold
Edge	Plain

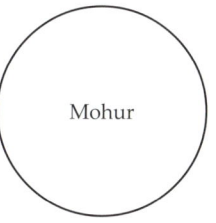

Mohur

Catalogue

Cat No.	KM	AH	RY	Comment	Value ($)
8.16	722	1219	47		25,000
8.17		1220	48	Ref: Baldwin, New York (2011), sale XXV, lot 473	25,000
8.18		1221	48		25,000
8.19		1221	49		25,000

Dehli – Shah 'Alam II – Gold – Nazarana Mohur Type 2

Distinguished from previous type by the beaded borders

8.20

sikka zad sāhib-i qirān (a)z ta'yid ilāh hāmī dīn muhammad shāh 'ālam bādshāh [AH] (= Struck coin like the the second Lord of conjunctions by the help of God, Defender of the faith of Muhammad, the Emperor Shah 'Alam [AH]).
Surrounded by a beaded border.

zarb dār al-khilāfa shāhjahānābād [RY] julūs maimanat mānūs (= Struck at the seat of the Caliphate, Shahjahanabad, in the [RY] year of his reign of tranquil prosperity).
Surrounded by a beaded border.

Colour added to photos

Actual Weight (g)	?
Actual Diameter (mm)	~35
Metal	Gold
Edge	Plain

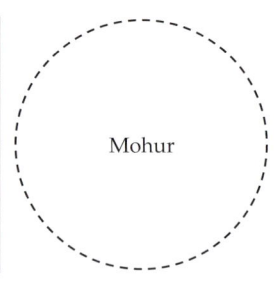

Mohur

Catalogue

Cat No.	KM	Denomination	AH	RY	Comment	Value ($)
8.20	721	Mohur	1218	46		15,000

Dehli – Shah Alam II – Silver Nazarana Rupee

8.22

sikka zad sāhib-i qirān (a)z ta'yid ilāh hāmī dīn muhammad shāh ʻālam bādshāh [AH] (= Struck coin like the the second Lord of conjunctions by the help of God, Defender of the faith of Muhammad, the Emperor Shah ʻAlam [AH])
Surrounded by a beaded border

zarb dār al-khilāfa shāhjahānābād [RY] julūs maimanat mānūs (= Struck at the seat of the Caliphate, Shahjahanabad, in the [RY] year of his reign of tranquil prosperity)
Surrounded by a beaded border

Actual Weight (g)	11.4
Actual Diameter (mm)	~27
Metal	Silver
Edge	Plain

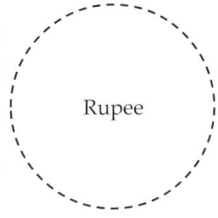
Rupee

Catalogue

Cat No.	KM	Denomination	AH	RY	Comment	Value ($)
8.21	B719	Nazarana Rupee	1218	46		5,000
8.22	C719	"	1221	49	Assigned to Muhammad Akbar by KM	5,000

Dehli – Shah 'Alam II – Rupee – Lion & Umbrella

8.23

sikka zad sāhib-i qirān (a)z ta'yid ilāh hāmī dīn muhammad shāh 'ālam bādshāh [AH] (= Struck coin like the the second Lord of conjunctions by the help of God, Defender of the faith of Muhammad, the Emperor Shah 'Alam [AH])

zarb dār al-khilāfa shāhjahānābād [RY] julūs maimanat mānūs (= Struck at the seat of the Caliphate, Shahjahanabad, in the [RY] year of his reign of tranquil prosperity)

Actual Weight (g)	11.17
Actual Diameter (mm)	26.0-26.7
Metal	Silver
Edge	Plain

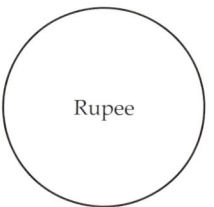

Rupee

Catalogue

Cat No.	KM	AH	RY	Comment	Value ($)
8.23	712	1218	46	Baldwin (2001), sale 25 (Wiggins), lot 501	2,000

Dehli – Shah 'Alam II – Rupee – Flower & Umbrella

8.24

sikka zad sāhib-i qirān (a)z ta'yid ilāh hāmī dīn muhammad shāh 'ālam bādshāh [AH] (= Struck coin like the the second Lord of conjunctions by the help of God, Defender of the faith of Muhammad, the Emperor Shah 'Alam [AH])

zarb dār al-khilāfa shāhjahānābād [RY] julūs maimanat mānūs (= Struck at the seat of the Caliphate, Shahjahanabad, in the [RY] year of his reign of tranquil prosperity)

	Rupee	Half Rupee	Quarter Rupee
Actual Weight (g)	11.17-11.44	5.72	2.86
Actual Diameter (mm)	24.3-25.5	~20	~17
Metal	Silver		
Edge	Plain		

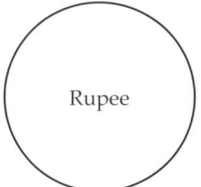 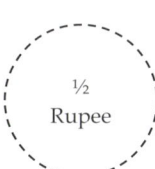 

Catalogue

Cat No.	KM	Denomination	AH	RY	Comment	Value ($)
8.24	713	Rupee	1218	46	Baldwin (2001), sale 25 (Wiggins), lot 501	1,000
8.25			1219	46	Ref: KM	1,000
8.26			1221	49	Baldwin (2001), sale 25 (Wiggins), lot 502	1,000
8.27	707	Half Rupee	1221	49	Ref: KM	1,000
8.28	704	Quarter Rupee	1221	49	Ref: KM	1,000

Dehli – Shah 'Alam II – Rupee – Floral Border

My thanks to R. Johnston who drew my attention to the different wreath directions (Obv A & B, Rev I & II) on these coin.

8.29

sikka zad sāhib-i qirān (a)z ta'yid ilāh hāmī dīn muhammad shāh 'ālam bādshāh [AH] (= Struck coin like the second Lord of conjunctions by the help of God, Defender of the faith of Muhammad, the Emperor Shah 'Alam [AH]). Inside a wreath of roses, thistles and shamrocks

zarb dār al-khilāfa shāhjahānābād [RY] julūs maimanat mānūs (= Struck at the seat of the Caliphate, Shahjahanabad, in the [RY] year of his reign of tranquil prosperity). Surrounded by a wreath of roses, thistles and shamrocks

Actual Weight (g)	11.15-11.16
Actual Diameter (mm)	23.6-28.6
Metal	Silver
Edge	Plain

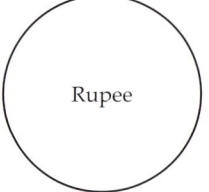

Rupee

Catalogue

Cat No.	KM	Denomination	AH	RY	Obv	Rev	Comment	Value ($)
8.29	714	Rupee	1219	47	A	I	Baldwin (2001), sale 25 (Wiggins), lot 503, 504	250
8.30		"	1219	47	B	I		250
8.30c		"	1220	47	A	II	Ref: Lingen	250
8.31		"	1220	47	B	I	See Baldwin (2007), sale 53, lot 2078	250
8.32		"	1220	48	A	I		250
8.33		"	1220	48	A	II		250
8.33c		"	1220	48	B	I	Ref: Kawale	250
8.34		"	1220	48	B	II		250
8.35		"	1221	48	A	II	Baldwin (2001), sale 25 (Wiggins), lot 504	250
8.36		Half Rupee	1219	47	A	I	Baldwin (2007), sale 50, lot 1061	500

Dehli – Shah 'Alam II – Rupee – Floral Border (cont)

Obverse Varieties

Direction of Wreath	The wreath may go clockwise or anti-clockwise

	A	B
Direction of Wreath	anti-clockwise	clockwise

A – Wreath anti-clockwise   *B – Wreath clockwise*

Reverse Varieties

Direction of Wreath	The wreath may go clockwise or anti-clockwise

	I	II
Direction of Wreath	anti-clockwise	clockwise

I – Wreath anti-clockwise   *II – Wreath clockwise*

Dehli – Shah 'Alam II – Nazarana Pice

fulus shah alam shahi (= *fulus* of Shah Alam the king) with a sun face in the *seen* of *fulus*

zarb shahjahanabad (= struck at Shahjahanabad)

Actual Weight (g)	11.64
Actual Diameter (mm)	~22?
Metal	Copper
Edge	Plain

Nazarana Pice

Catalogue

Cat No.	KM	Denomination	AH	RY	Comment	Value ($)
8.36c	-	Nazarana Pice	1221	48	Ref: Album	500

Dehli – Shah 'Alam II –Pice

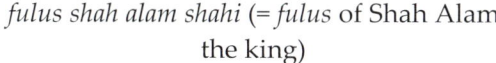

fulus shah alam shahi (= *fulus* of Shah Alam the king)

zarb shahjahanabad (= struck at Shahjahanabad)

Actual Weight (g)	12.43
Actual Diameter (mm)	19.3-20.9
Metal	Copper
Edge	Plain

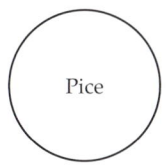

Pice

Catalogue

Cat No.	KM	Denomination	AH	RY	Comment	Value ($)
8.36e	700	Pice	1219	47	Ref: Johnston	150
8.36g		"	1220	48	Ref: Baldwin (2013), sale 84 (Fore, lot 1089)	150
8.36i		"	1221	49	Ref: Baldwin (2013), sale 84 (Fore, lot 1089)	150

Dehli – Muhammad Akbar II – Gold Nazarana Mohur

8.37

muhammad akbar shāh bādshāh ghāzī sāhib-i qirān thani sikka mubārak [AH] (= Auspicious coin of Emperor Muhammad Akbar the warrior, the second Lord of conjunctions [AH])	zarb dār al-khilāfa shāhjahānābād [RY] julūs maimanat mānūs (= Struck at the seat of the Caliphate, Shahjahanabad, in the [RY] year of his reign of tranquil prosperity)

Actual Weight (g)	?
Actual Diameter (mm)	~28
Metal	Gold
Edge	Plain

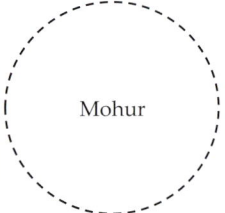

Mohur

Catalogue

Cat No.	KM	Denomination	AH	RY	Comment	Value ($)
8.37	783	Nazarana Mohur	1221	1		20,000
8.38		"	1234	12		20,000
8.39		"	1237	17		20,000

Dehli – Muhammad Akbar II – Gold Mohur

8.40

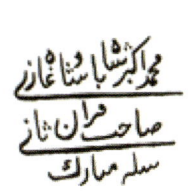

*muhammad akbar shāh bādshāh ghāzī
sāhib-i qirān thani sikka mubārak [AH] (=
Auspicious coin of Emperor
Muhammad Akbar the warrior, the
second Lord of conjunctions [AH])*

*zarb dār al-khilāfa shāhjahānābād [RY]
julūs maimanat mānūs (= Struck at the
seat of the Caliphate, Shahjahanabad,
in the [RY] year of his reign of
tranquil prosperity)*

Actual Weight (g)	10.71-10.73
Actual Diameter (mm)	19.6-20.8
Metal	Gold
Edge	Plain

Mohur

Catalogue

Cat No.	KM	Denomination	AH	RY	Comment	Value ($)
8.40	781	Mohur	122x	2		3,000
8.41	-	"	1223	3		3,000
8.42	-	"	1227	7		3,000

Gold mohur dated AH 1223, RY 3

Dehli – Muhammad Akbar II – Silver Nazarana Rupee

 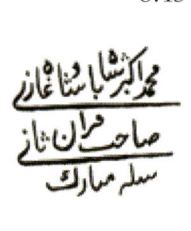 8.43

muhammad akbar shāh bādshāh ghāzī sāhib-i qirān thani sikka mubārak [AH] (= Auspicious coin of Emperor Muhammad Akbar the warrior, the second Lord of conjunctions [AH])

zarb dār al-khilāfa shāhjahānābād [RY] julūs maimanat mānūs (= Struck at the seat of the Caliphate, Shahjahanabad, in the [RY] year of his reign of tranquil prosperity)

Actual Weight (g)	11.22-11.44
Actual Diameter (mm)	28.5-28.7
Metal	Silver
Edge	Plain

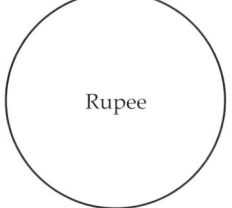

Rupee

Catalogue

Cat No.	KM	Denomination	AH	RY	Comment	Value ($)
8.43	779.1	Nazarana Rupee	1223	3		1,000
8.44		"	1224	3		1,000
8.45		"	1225	4		1,000
8.46		"	1226	5		1,000
8.47		"	1227	6		1,000
8.48		"	1227	7		1,000
8.48d			1231	11	Berlin museum. Ex Guthrie	NV
8.48f			1232	12	Ref: Baldwin	NV
8.49		"	1235	15		1,000
8.50		"	1236	16		1,000
8.51		"	1237	17		1,000
8.52		"	1239	19		1,000
8.53		"	1240	20		1,000
8.54		"	1241	21		1,000
8.55		"	1242	22		1,000

Listing continued on next page

Dehli – Muhammad Akbar II – Silver Nazarana Rupee (cont)

Catalogue

Cat No.	KM	Denomination	AH	RY	Comment	Value ($)
8.55c	779.1	Nazarana Rupee	1245	25	Berlin museum. Ex Guthrie	NV
8.55e			1246	26	Berlin museum. Ex Guthrie	NV
8.55g			1247	27	Berlin museum. Ex Guthrie	NV
8.56		"	1248	28		1,000
8.57		"	1249	29		1,000
8.58		"	125x	30		1,000
8.59	779.2	"	1251	31	Not sure why KM gives these last two a different catalogue number. See photo below	1,000
8.60		"	1252	32		1,000

8.51

Rupee dated AH 1251, RY 31

Dehli – Muhammad Akbar II – Silver Rupee *et infra*

8.68

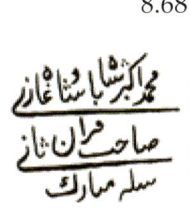

muhammad akbar shāh bādshāh ghāzī sāhib-i qirān thani sikka mubārak [AH] (= Auspicious coin of Emperor Muhammad Akbar the warrior, the second Lord of conjunctions [AH])

zarb dār al-khilāfa shāhjahānābād [RY] julūs maimanat mānūs (= Struck at the seat of the Caliphate, Shahjahanabad, in the [RY] year of his reign of tranquil prosperity)

Dehli – Muhammad Akbar II – Silver Rupee *et infra* (cont)

	Rupee	Half Rupee	Quarter Rupee
Actual Weight (g)	11.03-11.16	?	?
Actual Diameter (mm)	21.7-24.4	~19	~17
Metal	Silver		
Edge	Plain		

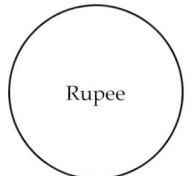 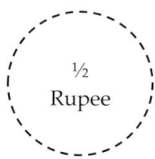 

Catalogue

Cat No.	KM	Denomination	AH	RY	Comment	Value ($)
8.61	777	Rupee	1221	1		250
8.62		"	1222	1	Some of the rupees of the early years are struck on broad flans without being nazaranas	250
8.63		"	1222	2		250
8.64		"	1223	2		250
8.65		"	1223	3		250
8.66		"	1224	3		250
8.67		"	1225	4		250
8.68		"	1226	5		250
8.69		"	1227	6		250
8.70		"	1227	7		250
8.71		"	1228	7		250
8.72		"	1228	8		250
8.73		"	1229	9		250
8.74		"	12xx	11		250
8.75		Half Rupee	1221	1		500
8.76		"	1225	4		500
8.77		Quarter Rupee	xxxx	1		500
8.78		"	122x	7		500

Dehli – Muhammad Akbar II – Copper Pice with S

The only half pice examined is struck on a very broad thin flan.

The meaning of the S is not certainly known, though it may stand for Shahjahanabad, the name of the mint.

8.86

falus shāh akbar shāh (= Copper coin of Shah Akbar Shah)

zarb shāhjahānābād (= struck at Shahjahanabad)
S by RY

	Pice	Half Pice
Actual Weight (g)	11.00-11.55	5.15
Actual Diam (mm)	18.4-22.0	27.0-27.4
Metal	Copper	
Edge	Plain	

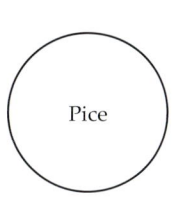 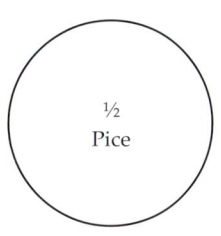

Pice   ½ Pice

Catalogue

Cat No.	KM	Denomination	AH	RY	Comment	Value ($)
8.78c	770	Pice	1222	1	No S by RY	150
8.78e		"	1222	2	No S by RY	150
8.79	771	"	1225	4		150
8.80		"	1225	5		150
8.81		"	1226	5		150
8.82		"	1226	6		150
8.83		"	1230	9		150
8.84		"	1231	10		150
8.84c		"	1232	11	Ref: Johnston	150
8.85		"	1232	12		150
8.86		"	1233	12		150
8.87	-	Half Pice?	1225	5	Broad thin flan	500

Dehli – Muhammad Akbar II – Copper Pice with S (cont)

8.87

Half pice RY 5. Very thin, large diameter

8.79

Pice RY 4. Thicker and smaller diameter than half pice

Dehli – Bahadur Shah II – Nazarana Rupee

8.88

abu al-muzaffar siraj-al dīn muhammad
bahadur shāh bādshāh ghāzī (= Father of the
victorious, of the religion, Emperor
Muhammad Bahadur Shah, the warrior

zarb dār al-khilāfa shāhjahānābād [RY]
julūs maimanat mānūs (= Struck at the seat
of the Caliphate, Shahjahanabad, in the
[RY] year of his reign of tranquil
prosperity)

Actual Weight (g)	11.02-11.44
Actual Diameter (mm)	27.0
Metal	Silver
Edge	Plain

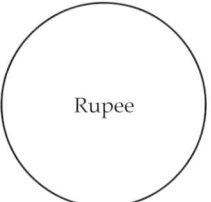

Rupee

Catalogue

Cat No.	KM	Denomination	AH	RY	Comment	Value ($)
8.88	-	Nazarana Rupee	1253	1		2,000
8.89	-	"	1254	2		2,000
8.90	-	"	1255	3		2,000
8.91	-	"	1256	4		2,000
8.92	-	"	1257	5		2,000
8.93	-	"	1258	6		2,000

Farrukhabad – Silver Rupee – Shah 'Alam II – 1802 to 1806

Local style continued after the British took over. In the style of the Bangash Nawabs of Farrukhabad. RYs appear to be fixed at 39. The Hijri years are progressive.

8.97

sikka zad bar haft kishwar sāya fazl ilāh hāmī dīn muhammad shāh 'ālam bādshāh [AH] (= Defender of the religion of Muhammad, Shah Alam Emperor, Shadow of the divine favour, put his stamp on the seven climes, [AH])

zarb ahmadnagar farruckābād sanah [RY] julūs maimanat mānūs (= Struck at Ahmadnagar Farrukhabad in the [RY] year of his reign of tranquil prosperity.)

Actual Weight (g)	10.75-11.14
Actual Diameter (mm)	23.5-26.3
Metal	Silver
Edge	Plain

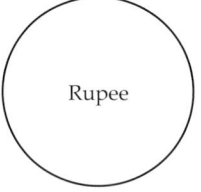

Rupee

Farrukhabad – Silver Rupee – Shah 'Alam II – 1802 to 1806 (cont)

Catalogue

Cat No.	Pr. No.	AH	RY	Comments	Value ($)
8.94	-	1217	39	Handover occurred in this year	100
8.95	-	1218	39	**Nazarana.** Not seen by author. May just be a broad-flan currency striking	NV
8.96	-	1218	39		100
8.97	-	1219	39		100
8.98	-	1220	39		100
8.99	-	1224	39	Dates not seen by author but reported in KM. Assume RY 39 but all dates after 1220 seem peculiar. See Stevens, Bengal pp. 450-451	NV
8.100	-	1225	39		NV
8.101	-	1227	39		NV
8.102	-	1228	39		100

Farrukhabad – Rupee *et infra* – Shah 'Alam – 1806 to 1819

Also struck at Calcutta and Benares.

8.103

| *sikka zad bar haft kishwar sāya faz ilāh hamī dīn muhammad shāh 'ālam bādshāh* (= Defender of the religion of Muhammad, Shah Alam Emperor, Shadow of the divine favour, put his stamp on the seven climes) | *zarb farruckābād sanah 45 julūs maimanat mānūs* (= Struck at Farrukhabad in the 45 year of his reign of tranquil prosperity.) |

Secret Marks for Farrukhabad

| *Rupee and half rupee: extra dot on obverse No dot on reverse* | *Quarter rupee: dot in centre of circle on reverse. No inverted V on obverse* |

Farrukhabad – Rupee *et infra* – Shah 'Alam II – 1806 to 1819 (cont)

	Rupee	Half Rupee	Quarter Rupee
Official Weight (g)	11.21	5.60	2.80
Actual Weight (g)	11.20-11.24	?	2.78
Actual Diameter (mm)	26.4-27.5	~20	17.4-17.8
Metal	Silver		
Edge	Grained Right		

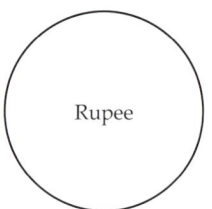
Rupee

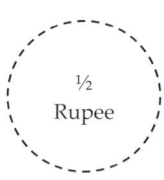
½ Rupee

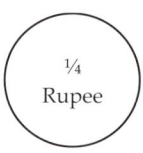
¼ Rupee

Catalogue

Cat No.	Pr. No.	Denom	Status	Comments	Value ($)
8.103	340	Rupee	Pattern	No dot mark. Edge GL. May have been struck at Calcutta before being sent to Farrukhabad	2,000
8.104	341	"	Pattern	Smaller flan. Edge GR	2,000
8.105	314	"	Currency	Forgeries occur, often in copper or brass	100
8.106	315	Half Rupee	Currency		150
8.107	316	Quarter Rupee	Currency		150

Weight for Farrukhabad Rupee – 1806 to 1819. Type 1

8.108

Minimum legal weight of oblique – milled old Fur. Rupee 171.198 grs

Legend and weight in a hexagon formed with double lines

Blank

Weight for Farrukhabad Rupee – 1806 to 1819. Type 1 (cont)

Official Weight (g)	11.09 (171.198 grains)
Actual Weight (g)	11.05
Actual Diameter (mm)	30.2
Metal	Copper
Edge	Plain

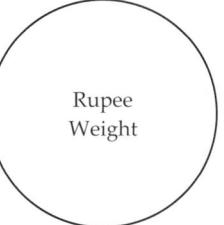

Rupee Weight

Catalogue

Cat No.	Pr. No.	Comments	Value ($)
8.108	-	Note star on obverse	150

Weight for Farrukhabad Rupee – 1806 to 1819. Type 2

8.109

Minimum legal weight of oblique – – milled old Fur. Rupee

Legend within a square formed with double lines. Above is the weight, below the units:

172.35

grs

Legend in Persian within a square formed with double lines.

Official Weight (g)	11.16 (172.35 grains)
Actual Weight (g)	11.11
Actual Diameter (mm)	26.4
Metal	Copper
Edge	Plain

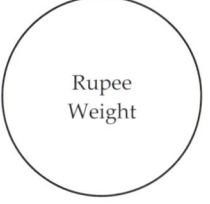

Rupee Weight

Catalogue

Cat No.	Pr. No.	Comments	Value ($)
8.109	-		150
8.110	-	star below the square on the reverse	150

Star on reverse

Farrukhabad – Single & Quarter Rupee – Shah 'Alam II, 1820 - 1824

See p. 42 for privy marks. Also struck at Calcutta and Benares. See Stevens, Bengal pp. 295-297 & 395-396

8.111

sikka zad bar haft kishwar sāya fazl ilāh hāmī dīn muhammad shāh 'ālam bādshāh
(= Defender of the religion of Muhammad, Shah Alam Emperor, Shadow of the divine favour, put his stamp on the seven climes)

zarb farruckābād sanah 45 julūs maimanat mānūs (= Struck at Farrukhabad in the 45 year of his reign of tranquil prosperity.)

	Rupee	Quarter Rupee
Official Weight (g)	11.68	2.92
Actual Weight (g)	11.26-11.61	?
Actual Diameter (mm)	25.5-26.0	~16
Metal	Silver	
Edge	Straight Grained	

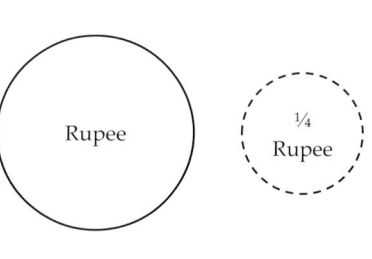

Catalogue

Cat No.	Pr. No.	Denom	Comments	Value ($)
8.111	318	Rupee	Silver plated forgeries exist	150
8.112	319	Quarter Rupee		100

Weight for Farrukhabad Rupee – 1820 to 1824

8.113

**Min. wt.
of new Stand.
Furukh^d. Rupee
[straight-milled,
and plain edged]
178.12 grs.**

The legend and weight within a plain raised rim

Blank

Official Weight (g)	11.54 (178.12 grains)
Actual Weight (g)	11.44-11.53
Actual Diameter (mm)	26.5
Metal	Copper
Edge	Plain

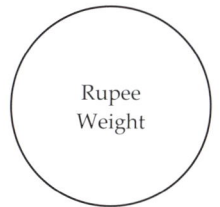

Rupee
Weight

Catalogue

Cat No.	Pr. No.	Rev	Comments	Value ($)
8.113	-	I		150
8.114	-	II	Countermarked with MC * (Mint Calcutta?)	150

Reverse Varieties

Rev I – no mark

Rev II – MC countermark

Farrukhabad – Falus (Pice) 1802 to 1806

The records contain no specific mention of copper coins being struck immediately after the Farrukhabad mint was acquired by the EIC but rare examples of falus (or pice) exist with dates that correspond to the early years of Britsh occupation.

8.116

sikka zad bar haft kishwar sāya fazl ilāh hāmī dīn muhammad shāh 'ālam bādshāh [AH] (= Defender of the religion of Muhammad, Shah Alam Emperor, Shadow of the divine favour, put his stamp on the seven climes, [AH])	*zarb ahmadnagar farruckābād sanah [RY] julūs maimanat mānūs* (= Struck at Ahmadnagar Farrukhabad in the [RY] year of his reign of tranquil prosperity.)

Actual Weight (g)	7.41
Actual Diameter (mm)	23.6-24.2
Metal	Copper
Edge	Plain

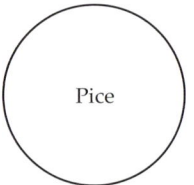

Pice

Catalogue

Cat No.	KM	Denom	AH	RY	Comments	Value ($)
8.115	C71.5	Falus	1219	39	Ref: KM South Asia	1,000
8.116		"	1220	39	Ref: Stevens collection	1,000

KM South Asia also reports a half anna in the name of Muhammad Akbar II, but this has not been confirmed

154

Farrukhabad – Pattern Pice 1806

 8.117

The value in three languages: Bengali: *ek pai sikka*. Persian: *Yek pai sikka*. Hindi: *ek pai sikka*. (Translation of all languages = One pai sikka).	*zarb farruckābād sanah 45 julūs maimanat mānūs* (= Struck at Farrukhabad in the 45 year of his reign of tranquil prosperity.)

Actual Weight (g)	6.22-6.73
Actual Diameter (mm)	26.2-26.5
Metal	Copper
Edge	Plain

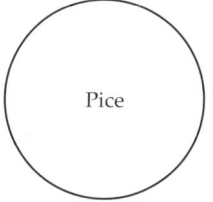

Pice

Catalogue

Cat No.	Pr. No.	Comments	Value ($)
8.117	342		1,000

Farrukhabad – Currency Pice 1806

Not certain that this coin was ever struck. A possible example is illustrated below. See Stevens. Bengal pp. 448-450

 8.118

sikka zad bar haft kishwar sāya fazl ilāh hāmī dīn muhammad shāh 'ālam bādshāh [AH] (= Defender of the religion of Muhammad, Shah Alam Emperor, Shadow of the divine favour, put his stamp on the seven climes, [AH])	*zarb farruckābād sanah 45 julūs maimanat mānūs* (= Struck at Farrukhabad in the 45 year of his reign of tranquil prosperity.)

Farrukhabad – Currency Pice 1806 (cont)

Official Weight (g)	18.43 (284½ grains) or 18.8 (290 grains)
Actual Weight (g)	?
Actual Diameter (mm)	~26.5?
Metal	Copper
Edge	Plain or grained right?

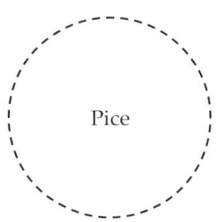

Pice

Catalogue

Cat No.	Pr. No.	Comments	Value ($)
8.118	-		NV

Farrukhabad – Double & Single Pice 1816

8.119

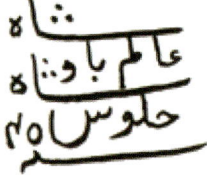

sanah julūs 45 shāh 'ālam bādshāh (= In the 45th year of the Emperor Shah 'Alam)

Value in three languages: Bengali, Persian, Hindi: *ek pai sikka* (= one pai sikka) OR *do pai sikka* (= two pai sikka)

	Double Pice	Pice
Actual Weight (g)	12.66	6.84
Actual Diam (mm)	28.1-28.5	22.5-22.7
Metal	Copper	
Edge	Plain	

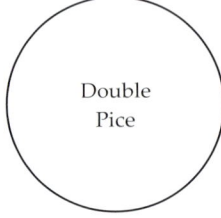

Double Pice

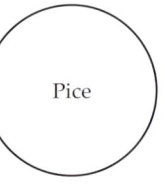

Pice

Farrukhabad – Double & Single Pice 1816

Catalogue

Cat No.	Pr. No.	Denomination	Comments	Value ($)
8.119	335	Double Pice		500
8.120	335A	Pice		300

Farrukhabad – Pice 1820 to 1824

Numerous different sizes and shapes of trident – also contemporary forgeries (Weir)

8.121

sanah julūs 45 shāh 'ālam bādshāh
(= in the 45th year of the Emperor Shah 'Alam)

Value in Persian and Hindi: *ek pai sikka*
(= One pai sikka)

Actual Weight (g)	5.80-6.47
Actual Diameter (mm)	22.0-24.0
Metal	Copper
Edge	Plain

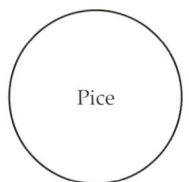

Pice

Catalogue

Cat No.	Pr. No.	Axis	Comments	Value ($)
8.121	336	↑↑		50
8.122	336	↑↓		50
8.122a	336	↑→		70

Gwalior Fort Mint

These coins were discussed by Barry Tabor in 2008[21]. According to this account, the British advanced against Gwalior in 1802, whereupon the Maratha governor, Ambaji Inglia, handed over the fort and surrounding territory without a fight. Tabor gives a quote from Malleson[22] which states:

…ceded districts were made over to Kirith Singh, successor to Lakinder Singh, by a treaty dated 17th January 1804 with the exception of the fortress and city of Gwalior, which the English retained…

Thus, the British held Gwalior fort between 1802 and 1804, and one type of rupee with a straight sword has been attributed to this period.

Gwalior Fort Mint – Silver Rupee 1802 to1806

8.123

  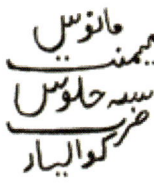

sikka zad bar haft kishwar sāya fazl ilāh hāmī dīn muhammad shāh 'ālam bādshāh [AH] (= Defender of the religion of Muhammad, Shah Alam Emperor, Shadow of the divine favour, put his stamp on the seven climes, [AH])	*zarb gwīlīār sanah 46 julūs maimanat mānūs* (= struck at Gwalior in the 46th year of tranquil prosperity)

Actual Weight (g)	10.92	
Actual Diameter (mm)	20.2-20.7	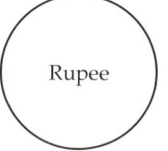 Rupee
Metal	Silver	

Catalogue

Cat No.	Pr. No.	AH	RY	Comments	Value ($)
8.123	-	1218	46	The straight sword is said to represent a British officer's sword	250

---

[21] Tabor B, (2008), The Ranas of Gohad and their occupations of Gwalior Fort – a numismatic perspective, JONS 196, pp. 27-34.

[22] Malleson Col. GB, An historical sketch of the Native States of India. Facsimile reprint, Gurgaon 1984.

Hathras Mint

Rupees appear to have been issued from a mint at Hathras in the name of Shah 'Alam II from RY 25 (1783/84) to RY 30 (1788/89). Copper coins may also have been issued.

There is some indication in the records that this mint may have continued for a short time after the British acquired control at the end of 1801 but no coins are known (see Stevens, Bengal, p. 471)

Najibabad Mint

Although some authors have believed that coins were struck at Najibabad by the British, the evidence is very flimsy and it seems more likely that the mint was closed before the British acquired the town (see Stevens, Bengal, pp. 472-474)

Saharanpur – Silver Rupee – 1803 to 1806

8.127

sikka zad bar haft kishwar sāya fazl ilāh hāmī dīn muhammad shāh 'ālam bādshāh [AH] (= Defender of the religion of Muhammad, Shah Alam Emperor, Shadow of the divine favour, put his stamp on the seven climes, [AH])

zarb dār al-sarūr sahāranpūr sanah [RY] julūs maimanat mānūs (= Struck at Dar al Sarur Saharanpur in the [RY] year of his reign of tranquil prosperity)

Actual Weight (g)	10.94-11.10	
Actual Diameter (mm)	21.8-27.0	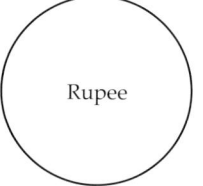
Metal	Silver	Rupee
Edge	Plain	

Catalogue

Cat No.	MW	KM	AH	RY	Rev	Comments	Value ($)
8.124	T1w	-	1218	45	I	NB different marks in *julus*	100
8.125	T1x	-	1218	45	II		100
8.126		692	1218	45	III	St Stephen's cross on reverse	200
8.127	T1y	693	1218	45	IV		100
8.128		693	1219	46	Like IV	See Baldwin (2001), sale 25 (Wiggins), lot 345	100
8.129	-	694	1220	47	2 dots in *julus*	KM reports a coin of RY 49. This could be a mistake for RY 47	100

MW = Maheshwari & Wiggins , Maratha Mints and Coinage, 1989, IIRNS

Reverse Varieties for AH1218, RY45

Symbol next to RY	The symbol to the left of the RY varies			
	I	II	III	IV
Symbol next to RY	✚♦	↓	✳	⟱

Saharanpur – Silver Rupee – 1803 to 1806 (cont)

Rev I

Rev II

Rev III

Rev IV

Saharanpur – Copper Double Pice, INO Shah 'Alam II – 1803

8.131

falūs 'alām shāhī 1218 (= Copper coin of Shah 'Alam 1218).

†in centre line

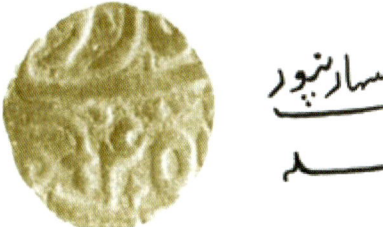

zarb sahāranpūr sanah 45 (= Struck at Saharanpur in the 45th year).

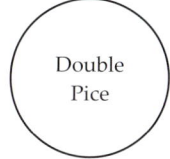 in centre line

Actual Weight (g)	See below
Actual Diameter (mm)	21
Metal	Copper
Edge	Plain

Double Pice

Catalogue

Cat No.	MW	KM	AH	RY	Weight (g)	Comment	Value ($)
8.131	T3p	-	1218	45	16.65		50
8.132	-	690	1218	45	12.9-13.8	KM calls this a pice. Their coin has a St Stephen's cross to left of RY	50

Saharanpur – Copper Pice, INO Shah 'Alam II – 1803

8.133

falūs 'alām shāhī 1218 (= Copper coin of Shah 'Alam 1218).

❖ **Ⅱ** in centre line

zarb sahāranpūr sanah 45 (= Struck at Saharanpur in the 45th year).

 in centre line

Actual Weight (g)	7.7
Actual Diameter (mm)	18
Metal	Copper
Edge	Plain

Pice

Catalogue

Cat No.	MW	AH	RY	Comment	Value ($)
8.133	T3t	1218	45		50

162

Saugor – Hammered Silver Rupee *et infra*– 1818 to 1819 – Type 1

The year 55 coins were copied at Gurrah Kotah. These copies might be distinguished by their crude nature although this is stated to be difficult to do (see Stevens, Bengal, p. 483). The year 55 coins struck by the Marathas at Saugor cannot be distinguished from those struck by the British.

8.134

  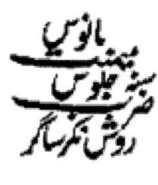

sikka zad bar haft kishwar sāya fazl ilāh hāmī dīn muhammad shāh 'ālam bādshāh [AH] (= Defender of the religion of Muhammad, Shah Alam Emperor, Shadow of the divine favour, put his stamp on the seven climes, [AH])

zarb ravishnagar sāgar sanah 55 julūs maimanat mānūs (= Struck at Ravishnagar Saugor in the 55 year of his reign of tranquil prosperity).

	Rupee	Quarter Rupee
Actual Weight (g)	11-11.08	~2.7
Actual Diameter (mm)	19-21	~12
Metal	Silver	
Edge	Plain	

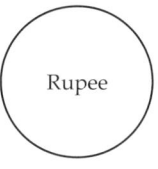 

Catalogue

Cat No.	MW. No.	Denomination	AH	RY	Comment	Value ($)
8.134	T3	Rupee	?	55	Slight differences in reverse ornaments between these two, particularly the presence of a cross on 8.135	75
8.135	T3a	Rupee	?	55		75
8.136	T3	Quarter Rupee	?	55		100

Saugor – Hammered – Silver Rupee – 1819 – Type 2

Issued to try to prevent the copying of the Saugor rupee at Gurrah Kotah. The coins have Saugor on the obverse and 1819 on the reverse. First reported by P. Kulkarni[23].

8.137

sikka zad bar haft kishwar sāya fazl ilāh hāmī dīn muhammad shāh 'ālam bādshāh Saugor (= Defender of the religion of Muhammad, Shah Alam Emperor, Shadow of the divine favour, put his stamp on the seven climes, "Saugor" in crude English letters)	*zarb ravishnagar sāgar sanah 55 julūs maimanat mānūs* (= Struck at Ravishnagar Saugor in the 55 year of his reign of tranquil prosperity). "1819" in English, above the word *julūs*

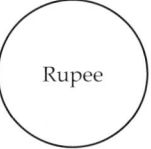

Actual Weight (g)	10.9
Actual Diameter (mm)	19-20
Metal	Silver
Edge	Plain

Rupee

Catalogue

Cat No.	MW. No.	AH	RY	AD	Comment	Value ($)
8.137	T4	?	55	1819	Ref: HK/Singapore (1997), Sale 25, Lot 676	2,000

---

[23] Kulkarni P, draft of paper in my files from RD Shah. Subsequently published: Kulkarni P, (1988/89), Numismatic Digest vol 12/13, pp. 119-122.

Saugor – Hammered – Copper Pice – 1818 to 1819 – Type 1

If copper coins were issued from the old Saugor mint during the time that the British kept it operating, then they would have been dated RY 55. However the exact style is not known. They could be identified by their Hijri dates (1234 or later). Of the two coins shown below, the Hijri date on the top coin is not clear and that on the bottom coin appears to be 1230 (and therefore not EIC).

8.139

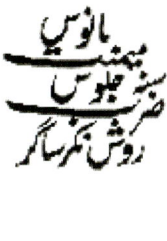

8.138

sikka zad bar haft kishwar sāya fazl ilāh hāmī dīn muhammad shāh 'ālam bādshāh [AH] (= Defender of the religion of Muhammad, Shah 'Alam Emperor, Shadow of the divine favour, put his stamp on the seven climes).

zarb ravishnagar sāgar sanah 55 julūs maimanat mānūs (= Struck at Ravishnagar Saugor in the 55 year of his reign of tranquil prosperity).

Actual Weight (g)	~15
Actual Diameter (mm)	~20
Metal	Copper
Edge	Plain

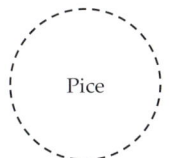
Pice

Catalogue

Cat No.	MW. No.	Denom	AH	RY	Obv	Comment	Value ($)
8.138	T5d	Takka	?	55	A		50
8.139	T5e	"	?	55	B		50
8.140	T5f	"	?	55	C		50
8.141	T5j	Pice	?	55		Wt ~12g	50

Saugor – Hammered – Copper Pice – 1818 to 1819 – Type 1 (cont)

Obverse Varieties for Takkas

Symbols on Obverse	The symbols in the three lines of the obverse vary, particularly those in the middle line

	A	B	C
Symbols on Obverse			

Saugor – Hammered – Copper Pice 1826 – Type 2

P. Kulkarni first reported this coin, which is distinguished particularly by the reverse legend[24]

8.142

sanah julūs 45 shāh 'ālam bādshāh (= in the 45th year of the Emperor Shah 'Alam)

ek pai sa (or sata) masa (= This coin weighs seven mashes).

Official Weight (g)	6.80?
Actual Weight (g)	6.34-6.52
Actual Diameter (mm)	19.9-21.2
Metal	Copper
Edge	Plain

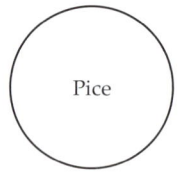

Pice

Catalogue

Cat No.	Pr. No.	Comments	Value ($)
8.142	-		300

---

24 Kulkarni P, SNC March 1985, p. 40.

Saugor – Milled – Silver Rupee – 1820 to 1831

For comments about secret marks, see p. 42.

8.143

sikka zad bar haft kishwar sāya fazl ilāh hāmī dīn muhammad shāh ʿālam bādshāh [AH] (= Defender of the religion of Muhammad, Shah Alam Emperor, Shadow of the divine favour, put his stamp on the seven climes, [AH])	*ẓarb farruckābād sanah 45 julūs maimanat mānūs* (= Struck at Farrukhabad in his 45th year of tranquil prosperity)

	Rupee	Half Rupee	Quarter Rupee
Official Weight (g)	11.66	5.83	2.91
Actual Weight (g)	11.67	?	?
Actual Diameter (mm)	24.7	~23	~17
Metal	Silver		
Edge	Straight Grained		

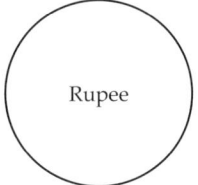 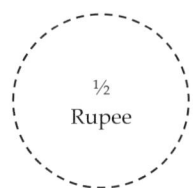 

Rupee · ½ Rupee · ¼ Rupee

Catalogue

Cat No.	Pr. No.	Denomination	Comment	Value ($)
8.143	325	Rupee	Distinguished from the Rupees struck at other mints by the absence of any privy mark – See p. 42	150
8.144	-	Half Rupee	None found but referred to in IOR. See Stevens, Bengal p. 491	NV
8.145	-	Quarter Rupee	None found but referred to in IOR. See Stevens, Bengal p. 491	NV

Saugor – Milled – Copper Pice 1826 to 1835

8.148

 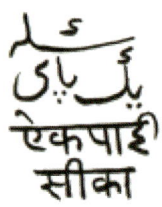

sanah julūs 45 shāh 'ālam bādshāh (= In the 45th year of the Emperor Shah 'Alam)	The value in two languages: Bengali: *ek pai sikka.* Persian: *yek pai sikka.* (Translates as one pai sikka). N.B. trisul in Persian inscription.

Official Weight (g)	6.48
Actual Weight (g)	6.11-6.50
Actual Diameter (mm)	21.5-24.1
Metal	Copper
Edge	Plain

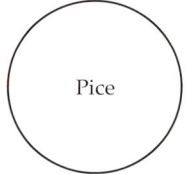

Pice

Catalogue

Cat No.	Pr. No.	Obv	Comment	Value ($)
8.146	337	A	Trident in *sīn* of *julūs*	50
8.147	338	B	Flower in *sīn* of *julūs*. Comes with thick and thin letters (R. Weir)	50
8.148	339	C	Spiky rosette or star in *sīn* of *julūs*	50

Obverse Varieties

Shape of ornament in *seen* of *julus*	The ornament in the *sīn* of *julūs* may be a trident, a flower, or an ornamental star

	A	**B**	**C**
Shape of ornament in *seen* of *julus*	Trident	Flower	Star

Trident	*Flower*	*Star*

Sohagpur Rupee

8.149

sikka mubārak bādshāh ghāzī shāh 'ālam (= The auspicious coin of the victorious Emperor Shah Alam)	*...sanah [RY] julūs maimanat mānūs* (= [zarb Sohagpur?] in the [RY] year of tranquil prosperity)

Actual Weight (g)	?
Actual Diameter (mm)	~25
Metal	Silver
Edge	Plain

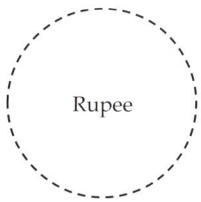

Rupee

Catalogue

Cat No.	Pr. No.	Comment	Value ($)
8.149	-	Two specimens in the British Museum	NV

Prinsep's ticket labelling the coin as issuing from Sohagpur

Bengal Presicency Calcutta Mint Introduction of Steam

Summary

By 1818 it had become clear that the Calcutta mint could not keep up with the work that was expected of it. The Calcutta mint master, Saunders, and the assay master, Wilson, were asked to prepare a report on the necessary steps to improve the situation, and in 1819 they recommended that a steam-driven mint should be obtained from England. A Lieutenant Forbes was selected to go to England and work with the supplier to ensure that local Bengal requirements would be met, and he duly arrived in England in 1820. The new mint was supplied by Boulton & Watt and was built and sent to Calcutta in pieces, arriving in October 1823. A number of experienced workmen were sent to Calcutta with the mint, and they were largely responsible for reconstructing it locally. It was completed in 1829 or 1830 and began production of copper pice in the summer of 1830. Silver rupees of the 19 sun sicca style and gold mohurs of the same style, as well as Farrukhabad rupees were produced; also Arcot rupees for use at Madras and in Bengal. In 1831 a new style of copper anna and pie was produced, but the debate about the style of the coins, and the introduction of one uniform coinage for the whole of India had by then reached a point at which it could become reality, and no further changes were made to the Bengal coins. In 1835, the new Calcutta mint led the way in producing this new uniform coinage.

Gold Pattern Mohur – Shah 'Alam II – c1830

A pattern prepared for the opening of the new mint

9.1

sikka zad bar haft kishwar sāya fazl ilāh hāmī dīn muhammad shāh 'ālam bādshāh 1202
(= Defender of the religion of Muhammad, Shah 'Alam Emperor, Shadow of the divine favour, put his stamp on the seven climes, 1202)

zarb murshīdābād sanah 19 julūs maimanat mānūs (= Struck at Murshidabad in the 19th year of his reign of tranquil prosperity.)

Official Weight (g)	13.28
Actual Weight (g)	13.27
Actual Diameter (mm)	29.2-29.3
Metal	Gold
Edge	Varies. See table below

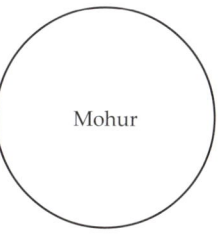

Mohur

Catalogue

Cat No.	Pr. No.	Edge	Comments	Value ($)
9.1	85	SG		5,000
9.2	86	GL	Later striking	2,000

Gold Mohur – Shah 'Alam II – 1831 to 1835

Tiny crescent at top left of reverse

9.4

sikka zad bar haft kishwar sāya fazl ilāh hāmī dīn muhammad shāh 'ālam bādshāh 1202 (= Defender of the religion of Muhammad, Shah 'Alam Emperor, Shadow of the divine favour, put his stamp on the seven climes, 1202)	*zarb murshīdābād sanah 19 julūs maimanat mānūs* (= Struck at Murshidabad in the 19th year of his reign of tranquil prosperity.)

Official Weight (g)	12.36
Actual Weight (g)	12.37
Actual Diameter (mm)	26.6-26.8
Metal	Gold
Edge	Grained Left

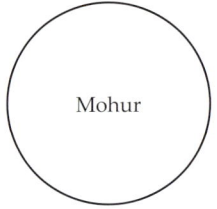

Mohur

Catalogue

Cat No.	Pr. No.	Obv	Date Issued	Comments	Value ($)
9.3	84	A	1830		1,200
9.4	-	B	1830	Ref: Baldwin/Taisei (2000), Sale 30, lot 559. Also Thompson also Chopra	1,500

Obverse Varieties

Dot Privy Mark	On some coins there is a tiny dot above the two dots in the upper left area of the design

	A	B
Dot Privy Mark	Dot	No Dot

Gold Mohur – Shah 'Alam II – 1831 to 1835 (cont)

Dot Present

No Dot Present

Silver Murshidabad Rupee *et infra* – 1831 to 1835

9.8

sikka zad bar haft kishwar sāya fazl ilāh hāmī dīn muhammad shāh 'ālam bādshāh
(= Defender of the religion of Muhammad, Shah 'Alam Emperor, Shadow of the divine favour, put his stamp on the seven climes)

zarb murshīdābād sanah 19 julūs maimanat mānūs (= Struck at Murshidabad in the 19th year of his reign of tranquil prosperity.)

	Rupee	Half Rupee	Quarter Rupee
Official Weight (g)	12.43	6.21	3.10
Actual Weight (g)	12.36-12.42	5.78-6.21	3.10-3.11
Actual Diameter (mm)	26.3-26.5	23.0-23.5	16.3-17.0
Edge	Varies. See table below		

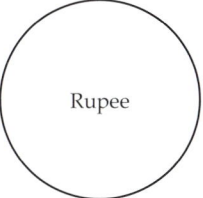

Rupee

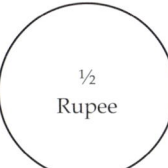

½
Rupee

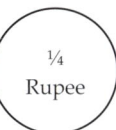

¼
Rupee

Silver Murshidabad Rupee *et infra* – 1831 to 1835 (cont)

Catalogue

Cat No.	Pr. No.	Denom	Obv	Rev	Status	Edge	Comments	Value ($)
9.5	177	Rupee	A	I	Currency	P		100
9.6	178	"	A	II	Proof	P		1,000
9.7	-	"	A	II	Pewter Die-trial		Wt = 9.60	2,000
9.8	179	"	B	II	Proof	SG	No star on obv. No crescent on rev	1,000
9.9	180	Half Rupee	-	-	Currency	P		80
9.10	181	"	-	-	Proof	P		800
9.11	182	"	-	-	Proof	SG		800
9.12	183	Quarter Rupee	-	-	Currency	P		70
9.13	184	"	-	-	Proof	P		600
9.14	185	"	-	-	Proof	SG		600

9.7

Pewter die-trial

Obverse Varieties for Rupee

Star	A star may or may not appear in the design.

	A	B
Star	Present	Absent

Silver Murshidabad Rupee *et infra* – 1831 to 1835 (cont)

Star present

Star absent

Reverse Varieties for Rupee

Crescent	There may or may not be a tiny crescent.

	I	II
Crescent	Present	Absent

Crescent present

Crescent absent

Silver Farrukhabad Rupee *et infra* – 1831 to 1833

Tiny crescent mark at top left of reverse

9.15

sikka zad bar haft kishwar sāya fazl ilāh hāmī dīn muhammad shāh 'ālam bādshāh
(= Defender of the religion of Muhammad, Shah 'Alam Emperor, Shadow of the divine favour, put his stamp on the seven climes)

zarb farruckābād sanah 45 julūs maimanat mānūs (= Struck at Farrukhabad in the 45th year of his reign of tranquil prosperity).

	Rupee	Half Rupee	Quarter Rupee
Official Weight (g)	11.68	5.84	2.92
Actual Weight (g)	11.65-11.66	5.81	2.89-2.93
Actual Diameter (mm)	26.5-26.5	22.9	16.4
Metal	Silver		
Edge	Varies. See table below		

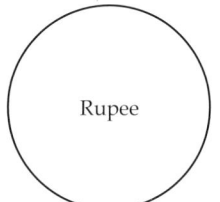 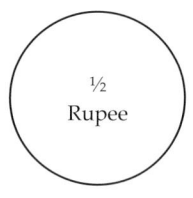 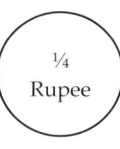

Catalogue

Cat No.	Pr. No.	Denom	Status	Edge	Comments	Value ($)
9.15	326	Rupee	Currency	P		100
9.16	327	"	Proof	P	Diam = 27.2-27.3	1,000
9.17	328	"	Proof	SG	Diam = 27.6	1,000
9.18	329	Half Rupee	Currency	P		80
9.19	330	"	Proof	P	Diam = 23.1-23.2	800
9.20	331	Quarter Rupee	Currency	P		70
9.21	332	"	Proof	P	Diam = 17.0	600

Silver Farrukhabad Rupee *et infra* – 1833 to 1835

No tiny crescent mark at top left of reverse

9.22

sikka zad bar haft kishwar sāya fazl ilāh hāmī dīn muhammad shāh 'ālam bādshāh
(= Defender of the religion of Muhammad, Shah 'Alam Emperor, Shadow of the divine favour, put his stamp on the seven climes)

zarb farruckabad sanah 45 julūs maimanat mānūs (= Struck at Farrukhabad in the 45th year of his reign of tranquil prosperity).

Official Weight (g)	11.66
Actual Weight (g)	11.65
Actual Diameter (mm)	26.5
Metal	Silver
Edge	Plain

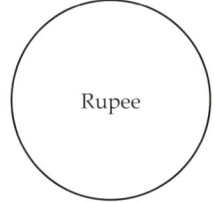

Rupee

Catalogue

Cat No.	Pr. No.	Status	Comments	Value ($)
9.22	333	Currency	Copper forgeries exist	100
9.24	334	Proof		800
9.25	334	Proof	Milled edge. Ref: R. Weir	1,000

Copper forgery (wt = 11.03g)

Copper Pice 1831

The first coins issued from the new mint

9.26

sanah julūs 37 shāh ʿālam bādshāh (= in the 37th year of the Emperor Shah ʿAlam)

The value in three languages: Bengali: *ek pai sikka*. Persian: *yek pai sikka*. Hindi: *ek pai sikka*. (Translation of all languages = One pai sikka). Within a plain, raised rim.

Official Weight (g)	6.47
Actual Weight (g)	5.87-6.58
Actual Diameter (mm)	22.8-23.0
Metal	Copper
Edge	Plain

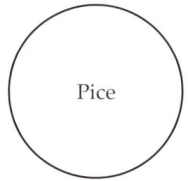

Pice

Catalogue

Cat No.	Pr. No.	Date Issued	Status	Comments	Value ($)
9.26	209	1831	Currency		50
9.27	210		Proof		500

Copper Half Anna & Pie 1831 to 1835

9.28

The value in English:
HALF ANNA
and Bengali:

(Bengali = a*dha āna* = Half Anna).
Within a raised, toothed rim.

The value in two languages:
Persian: *nīm ana.*

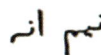

Nagari: *ādhā ānā.*

आधा आना

(= Half anna). Within a raised, toothed rim.

9.31

The value in English
ONE PIE
and Bengali:

এক পাই

(Bengali = *ek pai* = One Pie).
Within a raised, toothed rim.

The value in two languages:
Persian: *ek pai.*

ايك پاي

Nagari: *ek pai.*

एक पाई

(= One pie).

	Half Anna	Pie
Official Weight (g)	12.95	2.16
Actual Weight (g)	12.95-13.01	2.06-2.24
Actual Diameter (mm)	27.5-28.2	16.4-16.6
Metal	Copper	
Edge	Plain	

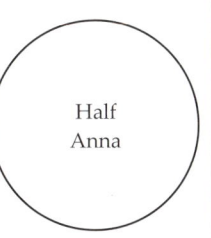

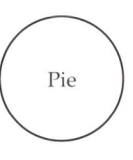

Copper Half Anna & Pie 1831 to 1835 (cont)

Catalogue

Cat No.	Pr. No.	Denom	Status	Axis	Comments	Value ($)
9.28	213	Half Anna	Currency	↑↑	Ref: Weir	70
9.29	213	"	Currency	↑↓	Ref: Weir	70
9.30	214	"	Proof			500
9.31	215	Pie	Currency			50
9.32	216	"	Proof			250

Varieties of half anna exist with 1 or 2 dots on reverse (R. Weir)

Crescent privy mark on the reverse of the half anna

Crescent privy mark on the reverse of the pie

Bengal Presidency
Soho Mint

Summary

From time to time, the Board of Directors in London contacted various people in England, particularly Boulton and Watt, with a view to their producing coins for use in India or even complete mints. Many tons of coins were produced for the Madras and Bombay Presidencies at Boulton and Watt's Soho factory in Birmingham. As far as the Bengal Presidency was concerned, only proofs and patterns were produced and these were never turned into a full circulating currency

The minting hall at Soho (from sohomint.info)

Copper Hexagonal Patterns – 1792

This was Boulton's attempt to produce a coin that could be used in very low-value transactions and replace the cowrie.

10.1

Balemark with date, 1792, below. Surrounded by three hexagonal lines, the centre line twisted.

Scales with Persian inscription between the pans (= 'adil = justice).

All surrounded by three hexagonal lines, the centre one twisted.

	Large Size	Small Size
Official Weight (g)	1.45	0.36
Actual Weight (g)	1.40-1.42	?
Actual Diameter (mm)	15.1-17.7	9.5
Metal	Copper	
Edge	Plain	

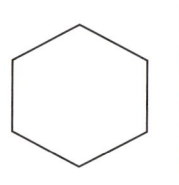

Catalogue

Cat No.	Pr. No.	Denom	Comments	Value ($)
10.1	365	Large Size		1,000
10.2	366	"	Obverse only. Reverse blank	NV
10.3	367	"	Reverse only. Obverse blank	NV
10.4	368	Small Size		2,000

Copper Pattern Pice 1795

10.5

sanah julūs 37 shāh 'ālam bādshāh
(= in the 37th year of the Emperor
Shah 'Alam)

The value in three languages:
  Bengali: *ek pai sikka.*
  Persian: *yek pai sikka.*
  Hindi: *ek pai sikka.*
  (= One pai sikka)

Actual Weight (g)	Varies. See table below
Actual Diameter (mm)	30.2
Metal	Copper
Edge	Varies. See table below

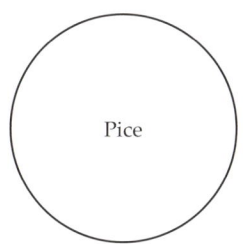

Pice

Catalogue

Cat No.	Pr. No.	Metal	Edge	Actual wt (g)	Comments	Value ($)
10.5	380	Copper	P	14.32		750
10.6	381	Copper	SG	?		NV
10.7	382	Copper Gilt	P	?		1,000
10.8	383	Pewter	P	13.20		NV

Copper Pattern Pie 1809

10.9

The arms of the Company with the date:
1809
below
The motto on the ribbon reads:
AUSP:REGIS & SENAT:ANGLIAE
Surrounded by a raised rim of pellets

The Persian inscription: *yek pai sikka:*

يك پاى سكه

Surrounded by the value in Bengali and Hindi *(ek pai sikka)*:
Bengali:

এক পাই সিক্ষ1

Hindi:

ऐक पई सिक्का

(Translation of all languages = One pai sikka) Within a toothed, raised rim.

Actual Weight (g)	7.85-7.92
Actual Diameter (mm)	27.4-27.5
Metal	Copper
Edge	Plain

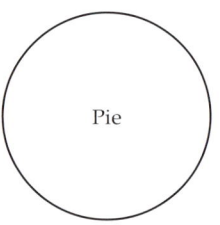

Pie

Catalogue

Cat No.	Pr. No.	Comment	Value ($)
10.9	384		750

Copper Pattern Pie 1809 – Blank Reverse

10.10

The arms of the Company with the
date:
1809
below
The motto on the ribbon reads:
AUSP:REGIS & SENAT:ANGLIAE
Surrounded by a raised, toothed rim.

Blank

Actual Weight (g)	7.59
Actual Diameter (mm)	27.4
Metal	Copper
Edge	Plain

Catalogue

Cat No.	Pr. No.	Comment	Value ($)
10.10	385		750

Copper Pattern Pie 1809 – Value on Obverse

10.14

The arms of the Company with the
date:
1809
below and the value:
ONE PIE
above.
The motto on the ribbon reads:
AUSP:REGIS & SENAT:ANGLIAE
Surrounded by a raised, toothed rim.

The Persian inscription: *yek pai sikka:*

يك پای سكه

Surrounded by the value in Bengali
and Hindi *(ek pai sikka)*:
Bengali:

এক পাই সিক্কা।

Hindi:

ऐक पाई सिक्का

(Translation of all languages = One pai
sikka) Within a toothed, raised rim.

Actual Weight (g)	Varies. See table below
Actual Diameter (mm)	27.4-27.5
Metal	Varies. See below
Edge	Plain

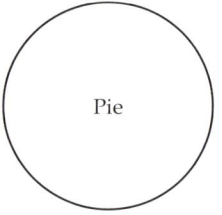

Pie

Catalogue

Cat No.	Pr. No.	Metal	Actual wt (g)	Comment	Value ($)
10.11	386	Gold	?	Value presumably indicated on obv, but not seen	NV
10.12	387	Silver	?	Value presumably indicated on obv, but not seen	NV
10.13	388	Copper Gilt	7.02-7.53		1,000
10.14	389	Copper or Bronze	See comments	Die axis may be ↑→, ↑↑ & ↑↓. Also weights of 10.88g, 8.29g, 7.75g, 7.53g, 7.49g & 6.32g.	750
10.15	390	Pewter	?	Assume that value is shown on obv, but not seen	NV

Pewter Pattern Pie 1809

10.16

The arms of the Company with the date:
1809
below and the value:
ONE PIE
above. Surrounded by a raised, toothed
rim.
Die the size of a half pie on flan the size of
a pie.

Blank

Actual Weight (g)	1.91
Actual Diameter (mm)	27.6
Metal	Pewter
Edge	Plain

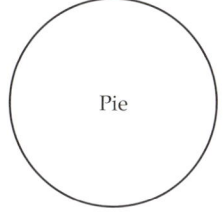

Pie

Catalogue

Cat No.	Pr. No.	Comment	Value ($)
10.16	-	Ref: SNC April 1980. Also Pr. Sale lot 694	750

Copper Mule Pie 1809

10.17

The arms of the Company with the date:

1809

below and the value:

ONE PIE

above. The motto on the ribbon reads:

AUSP:REGIS & SENAT:ANGLIAE

Surrounded by a raised, toothed rim.

The three legs of the Isle of Man triskeles surrounded by the legend:

QVOCVNQUE IECERIS STABIT

on a broad, raised rim.

Actual Weight (g)	10.96
Actual Diameter (mm)	27.5
Metal	Copper
Edge	Plain

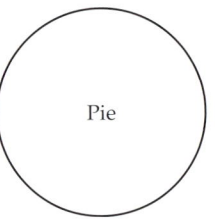

Pie

Catalogue

Cat No.	Pr. No.	Comments	Value ($)
10.17	391	Only one known at present	3,000

Copper Pattern Half Pie 1809

10.21

The arms of the Company with the date, 1809, below and the value above:
HALF PIE
Surrounded by a raised, toothed rim.

The Persian inscription (*nīm pai sikka*):

نيم پاي سكد

surrounded by the value in Bengali and Hindi:

Bengali (*ad pai sikka*):

আমা পাই সিক্কা

Hindi (*adha pai sikka*):

आधा पाई सिक्का

(Translation of all languages = Half pai sikka). Within a toothed, raised rim.

Actual Weight (g)	Varies. See table below
Actual Diameter (mm)	21.6
Metal	Varies. See table below
Edge	Plain

Half Pie

Catalogue

Cat No.	Pr. No.	Metal	Actual wt (g)	Comment	Value ($)
10.18	392	Gold	?		NV
10.19	393	Silver	?		NV
10.20	394	Copper Gilt	4.27		1,000
10.21	395	Copper or Bronze	4.00-4.31		750
10.22	-	White metal	4.07	Ref: Pr. Sale lot 696	1,000

Copper Pattern Half Pie 1809 – Blank Reverse

10.23

A lion standing to left and holding a crown.
The date: 1809
below and the value: HALF PIE
above. Surrounded by a raised, toothed rim.
(The standing lion is the crest of the
Company)

Blank

Actual Weight (g)	4.78
Actual Diameter (mm)	21.5
Metal	Varies. See below
Edge	CGL

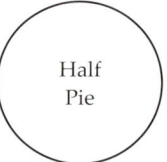

Half Pie

Catalogue

Cat No.	Pr. No.	Metal	Comment	Value ($)
10.23	396	Copper	Ref: Pr. sale, lot 697	1,000
10.24	-	Pewter	Ref: SNC June 1984, p. 161, lot 3847	1,000

Bombay Presidency Bombay Mint, Early Coinages 1672 to c1717

Summary

The coinage of Bombay, at the time of transfer from King Charles II to the EIC, was Portuguese and consisted of silver xerafins, copper pice, and tin bazaruccos, all of which were manufactured outside of Bombay itself. Sixteen bazarucco's went to one pice and 23¼ pice to one xerafin. In the books of the EIC the accounts continued to be kept in the old Portuguese way in xerafins (valued in the Company's books at 20 pence sterling), divided into 3 larins with each larin being reckoned at 80 reis and this continued for many years. However, most trade was carried out with the mainland and the coins in use there were gold mohurs and silver rupees, although other coins were also in use. Pridmore cites the use of a coin called a *Mahmudi* (with a sterling value of about one shilling), apparently issued by the Rajah of Malher in Baglan, a place about 70 miles from Surat[1].

By 1672 The EIC had determined to issue coins from a mint in Bombay. Their plan was to issue gold, silver, copper and tin coins but no gold coins were produced at this time. The copper and tin coins proved successful and continued to be issued, pretty much unchanged, throughout the period under review. However, the silver coins proved unsatisfactory because they were not widely accepted outside of Bombay Island, apparently because of their foreign appearance. In 1674 a suggestion to produce silver rupees in the name of Charles II was made, but in the Moghul style (i.e. with Persian writing) and patterns were produced but the coin was not put into full scale production. None of these coins is known to have survived. During the reign of James II, a few Moghul style rupees seem to have been produced because a few of these survive and during the reign of William and Mary, in the 1690s, more Moghul style rupees were minted but the Emperor, Aurangzeb, forced the EIC to stop production. Thus the major coins produced during this period were copper and tin (though very few tin coins survive) and most silver coins are very rare.

---

[1] Foster (1911). The English Factories in India 1634-1636. Clarendon Press, Oxford, p. 224.

Pattern Anglina – 1672

1.1

Shield of arms of the Company. No legend.

167[2]
G A

Anglina

Actual Weight (g)	2.89
Actual Diameter (mm)	21.9
Metal	Silver

Catalogue

Cat No.	Pr. No.	Comments	Value ($)
1.1	331	British Museum has the only know specimen	NV

Anglina & Half Anglina – 1672

MON:
BOMBAY
ANGLIC
REGIMS
Aº.7º.

1.2

The shield of arms of the Company within a beaded circle and surrounded by the legend
HON:SOC:ANG:IND:ORI
All within a beaded rim

A legend within a beaded circle. This, in turn, surrounded by another legend.
A:DEO:PAX:&:INCREMENTUM
All within a beaded rim.

Anglina & Half Anglina – 1672 (cont)

	Anglina	½ anglina
Actual Weight (g)	11.48-11.56	5.75
Actual Diameter (mm)	24.8-25.4	20.7
Metal	Silver	

Anglina

Half Anglina

Catalogue

Cat No.	Pr. No.	Denomination	Comments	Value ($)
1.2	12	Anglina		25,000
1.3	13	Half Anglina	Diam and Wt recorded from Pridmore. Authenticity suspect	NV

Half anglina

Anglina – Interlinking Cs – 1674

1.4

The shield of arms of the Company within a beaded circle and surrounded by the legend. All within a beaded rim.

Two interlinked Cs, crowned and surmounted by a cross, within a beaded circle. Surrounded by the legend.

Actual Weight (g)	11.62
Actual Diameter (mm)	23.2
Metal	Silver

Anglina

Anglina – Interlinking Cs – 1674 (cont)

Catalogue

Cat No.	Pr. No.	Comments	Value ($)
1.4	14		25,000

Anglina – Arms and Persian Inscription – 1674

No Picture Available

The shield of arms of the Company within a beaded circle and surrounded by the legend. All within a beaded rim.	A Persian inscription.

Metal	Silver

Catalogue

Cat No.	Pr. No.	Comments	Value ($)
1.5	-	None traced. See Pr. p. 105 who refers to Martin Folkes (1763), Tables of English Silver and Gold Coins, p. 113 .	NV

Anglina – Charles II – 1674

In 1674, the Bombay council ordered the production of patterns with Persian writing on both sides. These were sent to Surat for approval but were rejected[2].

No Picture Available

A Persian inscription: Charles II King of England etc	A Persian inscription: Money of Bombay.

Metal	Silver

Catalogue

Cat No.	Pr. No.	Comments	Value ($)
1.6	-	None traced but patterns prepared and sent to Surat	NV

---

[2] Bombay Factory Records, IOR G/3/1. 1674 p. 64. Meeting of Council 17th July 1674

Pattern Anglina – PAX DEO with Balemark – 1676

No Picture Available

Balemark of the Company	PAX DEO type
Metal	Silver

Catalogue

Cat No.	Pr. No.	Comments	Value ($)
1.7	-	None traced. See Pr. p. 105	NV

Anglina – PAX DEO – 1676 to 1692

PAX DEO

1.8

The shield of arms of the Company within a plain circle. All within a beaded rim.	A legend within a beaded circle and surrounded by another legend. MONETA BOMBAIENSIS All within a plain circle and surrounded by a beaded rim.

	Anglina	½ Anglina
Official Weight (g)	11.75	5.83
Actual Weight (g)	11.28-11.75	5.84
Actual Diameter (mm)	23.8-24.1	18.3-19.1
Metal	Silver	

Anglina | Half Anglina

Catalogue

Cat No.	Pr. No.	Denomination	Rev	Comments	Value ($)
1.8	16	Anglina	I		20,000
1.9	17	"	II	Ref: Ashmolean Museum	20,000
1.10	17	"	III		20,000
1.11	18	Half Anglina	-		20,000

Anglina – PAX DEO – 1676 to 1692 (cont)

Reverse Varieties

Letters in Legend	The letters in the legend may be correct or malformed e.g. inverted Ns		

	I	II	III
Letters in Legend	Correct	Both Ns inverted. E of MONETA is B	N in BOMBAIENSIS inverted. E of MONETA is B

Letters correct   *Both Ns inverted. E replaced by B*   *One N inverted. E replaced by B*

There are also minor variations in the obverse design. Note the floral ornament to the left of the shield

Rupee Patterns – 1677/78 – English Striking

THE RUPEE OF BOMBAIM

1.13

A legend with two roses below. Surrounded by another legend.
[date] BY AVTHORITY OF CHARLES THE SECOND
All within a plain raised rim

The royal shield of arms, crowned, and surrounded by the legend. All within a plain raised rim.

Rupee Patterns – 1677/78 – English Striking

Actual Weight (g)	Varies. See table below
Actual Diameter (mm)	"
Metal	"
Edge	"

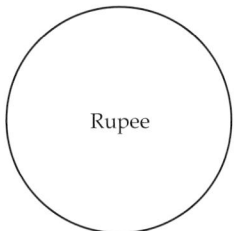

Rupee

Catalogue

Cat No.	Pr. No.	Date	Status	Obv	Edge	Actual wt (g)	Actual Diam (mm)	Comments	Value ($)
1.12	19	1677	Pattern	A	P	10.86	27	Ref: BM	NV
1.13	20	1678	Pattern	B	SG	11.45	30		50,000
1.14	23	"	Lead Die trial	B	SG	9.66	"	Authenticity suspect	NV
1.15	-	"	Pattern	C	SG	?	?	Ref: Puddester. Not sure if this is a London or Bombay striking	NV
1.16	24	"	Copper Trial	C	P	5.67	24.7	Overstruck on farthing of Charles II dated 1674. Ref: BM	NV
1.17	21	"	Pattern	-	P	13.06	30	Differing style. Authenticity suspect	NV

Obverse Varieties

Symbol in Legend	The legend may start with a cross or a star
Stop in RUPEE OF	There may or may not be a stop between RUPEE and OF

	A	**B**	**C**
Symbol in Legend	Cross	Star	Star
Stop in RUPEE OF	Yes	No	Yes

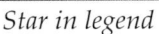

Star in legend   *No stop in RUPEE OF*

Rupee – 1677/78 – Bombay Striking

These are crudely struck versions of the previous coins. See Sainsbury E.B., (1938).
A Calendar of the Court Minutes etc of the East India Company 1677-1679, p. xii.

THE
RUPEE OF
BOMBAIM

1.18

A legend with two roses below. Surrounded by another legend.
1678 BY AVTHORITY OF CHARLES THE SECOND
All within a plain raised rim

The royal shield of arms, crowned, and surrounded by the legend. All within a plain raised rim.

Actual Weight (g)	11.53
Actual Diameter (mm)	29.0-29.4
Metal	Silver
Edge	Straight Grained

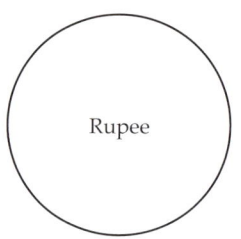

Rupee

Catalogue

Cat No.	Pr. No.	Comments	Value ($)
1.18	25		10,000
1.19	22	Pewter die trial. Wt = 7.98g	5,000

Pattern Rupee – PAX DEO – 1687

Possibly struck to commemorate the move of the seat of the Presidency from Surat to Bombay.

PAX DEO

1.20

The shield of arms of the Company with three roses added to the lower half. All within a plain raised circle.

An inscription interworked with ornamentation within a beaded circle and surrounded by the legend:
BOMBAIENSIS MONETA 1687
All within a plain circle, surrounded by a beaded rim.

Actual Weight (g)	11.56
Actual Diameter (mm)	25.0
Metal	Silver

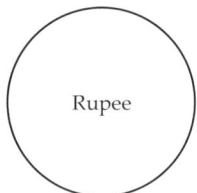

Rupee

Catalogue

Cat No.	Pr. No.	Comments	Value ($)
1.20	26	British Museum has only known specimen	NV

Rupee – James II

1.22

سكه [زد دورا]ن جانشين
كينگ جمس دي سبكن *sikka*

[zad daura] n-i-janishin-i-king jems di sekun
(=coin [of the term] of the governor-
general of king James the second)

ضرب مي سنه جلوس ۴
انگريز شادي

zarb mi [=munbai?] sanah julus [RY]
angrez [shadi?] (= struck at Bombay in the
[RY] year of English wedding [or rule?])

Reading of legend, transliteration and translation all taken from Deyell

	Rupee	Half Rupee	Quarter Rupee
Actual Weight (g)	11.45	?	2.84
Actual Diameter (mm)	22.8-23.9	~19	~16
Metal	Silver		

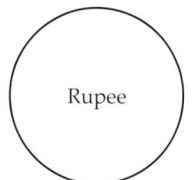

Rupee

½ Rupee

¼ Rupee

Catalogue

Cat No.	Pr. No.	Denomination	RY	Comments	Value ($)
1.21	-	Rupee	3	Deyell J., Journal of Indian Numismatics and Sigillography (JAINS), Vol III 1980 pp. 57-60. plate 5 No 10.	NV
1.22	-	"	4	Three known. There may be a few more (3?) in India.	10,000
1.23	-	Half Rupee	?	Ref: Bhandare. One known	NV
1.24	-	Quarter Rupee	4	Ref: Bhandare. One known	NV

Quarter rupee

Rupee – William & Mary

1.28

سکه زد دوران king william and queen mary (= Coin struck during the reign of King William and Queen Mary)

sanah julus [RY] angrez shaheen zarb munbai (= Struck at Bombay in the auspicious year [RY] of the English rulers)

	Rupee	**Half Rupee**
Official Weight (g)	11.50	5.77
Actual Weight (g)	11.10-11.54	?
Actual Diameter (mm)	22.4-25.7	~19
Metal	Silver	

Rupee

Half Rupee

Catalogue

Cat No.	Pr. No.	Denom	RY	Differentiating Mark	Comments	Value ($)
1.25	-	Rupee	4			3,000
1.26	27	"	5			2,000
1.27	28	"	6	Mark 1		1,000
1.28	28	"	6	Mark 2		1,000
1.29	28	"	6	Mark 3	Ref: Todywalla	1,000
1.30	28	"	6	Mark 4	Ref: Johnston	1,000
1.31	29	Half Rupee	5			NV

Mark 1

Mark 2

Rupee – William & Mary (cont)

Mark 3

Mark 4

Dots & circle

Star shape with dots

Other differentiating marks in top Part of legend (often not visible)

The numeral 4 takes different forms. The one on the left looks like a 4 lying on its back. There has been speculation that this may be an earlier form of numeral 5 but this form had not been used for 200 years. The one on the right has a more upright 4.

Countermarked Foreign Silver Coins – 1705

No Photo Available

Metal	Silver

Catalogue

Cat No.	Pr. No.	Comments	Value ($)
1.32	-	None found. See Bombay Public Consultations, 24th April 1705. IOR P/341/2, p. 174. Also Stevens (2004), SNC Vol CXII April, pp. 90-91	NV

Single and Half Copperoons – 1672 to 1678

MON(ET):
BOMBAY
ANGLIC
REGIMS
[date]

1.36-1.43

The shield of arms of the Company within a beaded circle and surrounded by the legend:
HON:SOC:ANG:IND:ORI
(= The Honourable English Company of the East Indies). All within a beaded rim.

An inscription within a beaded circle surrounded by the legend:
A:DEO:PAX:X:INCREMENTVM: (date?)
(= peace and growth from God). All within a beaded rim.
NB This one has the date 74

	Copperoon	½ Copperoon
Actual Weight (g)	11.75-14.83	6.73-7.28
Actual Diameter (mm)	17.6-24.6	15.0-18.0
Metal	Copper	

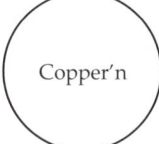

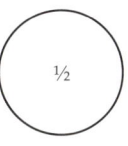

Catalogue

Cat No.	Pr. No.	Denomination	Date	Obv	Rev	Comments	Value ($)
1.33	78	Copperoon	Aº7º	A	I	Dot after Aº and 7º	1,500
1.34	79	"	Aº7º	A	II	No O in BOMBAY	1,500
1.35	80	"	Aº7º	A	III	Dot after MON. Colon after 7	1,500
1.36	81	"	Aº9º	A	IV	Dot after Aº and 9º	80
1.37	82	"	Aº9º	A	V	No dots in date	120
1.38	-	"	A9º	A	VI	Ref: Puddester. No º after A in date	150
1.39	83	"	Aº9º	A	VII	8 instead of Y in BOMBAY	120
1.40	84	"	A9º	A	VIII	No B at start of BOMBAY. May be a contemporary forgery.	150
1.41	85	"	Aº8º	A	IX	Dot after Aº and 8º	150
1.42	86	"	AºDº	A	X	Large S in BOMBAYS	100
1.43	86	"	AºDº	A	XI	Small s in BOMBAYs	100
1.44	88	"	AnDº	B	XII	BOMBAYES. Upside down G	150

Listing continued on next page

Single and Half Copperoons – 1672 to 1678 (cont)

Catalogue

Cat No.	Pr. No.	Denomination	Date	Obv	Rev	Comments	Value ($)
1.44c	-	"	AnDo	C	XII	BOMBAYES. Upside down G. Lions backwards	150
1.45	87	"	AnDo	D	XII	BOMBAYES. Normal GCE	120
1.46	-	Copperoon	AnDo	D	XIII	BONBAYES on reverse. Ref: Johnston	150
1.47	-	"	AnoDo	D	XIV	BOMBAYs on reverse	150
1.48	-	"	"	D	XV	BOMBAYES. Unbarred I in ANGLICI. Ref: Puddester	150
1.49	89	"	"	D	XVI	BOMBAYES. Barred I in ANGLICI	150
1.50	-	½ Copperoon		A	VII	ANS 1917.216.4598	750
1.51	-	"		A	X	Ref: Wiggins, SNC, Nov 1984, p. 288.	750

The earliest coins show most of the legend but are extremely rare

Obverse Varieties

Letters around Shield	The letters around the shield should be arranged GCE, or may be GGE with the second G upside-down. Alternatively there may only be scrolls around the shield and no letters.
Arms	The appointments in the Royal arms may show lions in the 1st and 4th quarter, or in the 2nd and 3rd quarters.

	A	B	C	D
Letters around Shield	Scrolls	G G(upside down) E	G G(upside down) E	G C E
Arms	Lions in 2nd & 3rd Quarters	Lions in 2nd & 3rd Quarters	Lions in 2nd & 3rd Quarters. Lions face backwards	Lions in 1st & 4th Quarters

Single and Half Copperoons – 1672 to 1678 (cont)

Moghul Sholapur pice overstruck on Bombay copperoon

Scrolls around shield

GCE around shield

Lions in 1st & 4th quarters

Lions in 2nd & 3rd quarters

Reverse Varieties

Central Legend	The legend in the centre of the reverse varies
Outer Legend	The legend around the inner circle varies

Because of the poor quality of the specimens available, the listed outer legends for each variety are the author's best guess and are subject to future revision.

	I	II	III
Central Legend	MON : BOMBAYr ANGLIC REGIMS A°.7°.	MON : B MBAYr ANGLIC REGIMS A°.7°.	MON. BOMBAY ANGLIC REGIMS A°.7:
Outer Legend	A: DEO: PAX: X: INCREMENTVM:	A: DEO: PAX: X: INCREMENTVM:	A: DEO: PAX: X: INCREMENTVM:

Single and Half Copperoons – 1672 to 1678 (cont)

	IV	V	VI
Central Legend	MON BOMBAY ANGLIC REGIMs Aᵒ.9ᵒ.	MON BOMBAY ANGLIC REGIMs Aᵒ9ᵒ	MON BOMBAY ANGLIC REGIMs A9ᵒ
Outer Legend	A DEO PAX & INCREMENTVM 74	A DEO PAX & INCREMENTVM 74	A DEO PAX & INCREMENTVM 74

	VII	VIII	IX
Central Legend	MON BOMBA8 ANGIIC REGMs Aᵒ9ᵒ	MON OMBAV ANGLIC ??GIMs A9ᵒ	MON BOMBAY ANGLIC REGIMs Aᵒ.8ᵒ.
Outer Legend	A DEO PAX & INCREMENTVM 74	A DEO PAX & INCREMENTVM 74 (retrograde)	A DEO PAX & INCREMENTVM 74

Single and Half Copperoons – 1672 to 1678 (cont)

	X	XI	XII
Central Legend	MON BOMBAYS ANGLICI REGIMs AoDo	As X but small s in BOMBAYs	MONETA BOMBAYES ANGLICI REGIMs AnDo
Outer Legend	A DEO PAX ET INCREMENTVM (date?)	As X	A DEO PAX ET INCREMENTVM 78

	XIII	XIV	XV	XVI
Central Legend	MONETA BONBAYES ANGLICI REGIMs AnDo	MONETA BOMBAYs ANGLICI REGIMs AnoDo	MONETA BOMBAYES ANGLICI REGIMs AnoDo	As XII but Barred I in ANGLICI
Outer Legend	A DEO PAX ET INCREMENTVM 78	A DEO PAX ET INCREMENTVM 78	A DEO PAX ET INCREMENTVM 78	As XV

Unlisted variety, obverse A, reverse legend incomplete. No B in Bombay, normal outer legend

Copperoons – 1692 to 1703

It is very hard to piece together the inscriptions and varieties on these very poorly made coins. My thanks to Bob Johnston for help with this. However, I feel that there is still a lot to be added to our work.

1.53

MONETA
BOMBAY
ANGLICI
REGIMS
[date]

The shield of arms of the Company with lions in the first and fourth quarters and scrolls around it within a beaded circle and surrounded by the legend:
A:DEO (date?) PAX:ET:INCREMENTVM (= peace and growth from God). All within a beaded rim.
NB the outer legend is similar to the previous issue reverse outer legend

An inscription within a beaded circle and surrounded by the legend:
HON:SOC:ANG:IND:ORIEN (= The Honourable English Company of the East Indies). All within a beaded rim.
NB the outer legend is similar to the previous issue obverse outer legend

Actual Weight (g)	12.00-13.98
Actual Diameter (mm)	18.4-24.0
Metal	Copper

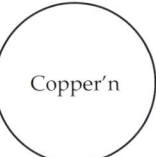

Copper'n

Catalogue

Cat No.	Pr. No.	Date	Rev	Comments	Value ($)
1.53	90	AºD9r	I		200
1.54	91	AºD9r	II	Retrograde N in MONET. This reverse has not been confirmed	NV
1.55	91	AºD9r	III	Normal N in MONET	200
1.56	92	AºD9r	IV	Retrograde N in MONET	150
1.57	93	AºD9r	V		150
1.58	-	AºD9r	VI	TEGIMS	150
1.59	-	1703	VII	Normal 3	150
1.60	94-95	1703	VIII	3 on its back	150
1.61	-	1703	IX	Backward 3. Unbarred I in ANGLIIC	150

Copperoons – 1692 to 1703 (cont)

Reverse Varieties

Central Legend	The legend in the centre of the reverse varies
Outer Legend	Reading of the outer legend is incomplete due to the small flan size. It may be HON: SOC: ANG: IND: ORIEN.

	I	II	III
Central Legend	MOET BOMBAY ANGIIC hEGIMs A⁰D9r	MONET (N retrograde) BOMBAY ANGIIC hEGIMs A⁰D9r	MONET BOMBAY ANGIIC hEGIMs A⁰D9r
		As Pr 91 but not confirmed	
	MOET BOMBAY ANG IIC hEGIMs A⁰D9r	MONET BOMBAY ANG IIC hEGIMs A⁰D9r	MONET BOMBAY ANG IIC hEGIMs A⁰D9r

	IV	V
Central Legend	MONET (N retrograde) BONBAY ANGIIC hEGIMs A⁰D9r	MONET BONBAY ANGIIC hGEIM A⁰D9r
		Photo from Pr
	MONET BONBAY ANG IIC hEGIMs A⁰D9r	MONET BONBAY ANG IIC hGEIM A⁰D9r

Copperoons – 1692 to 1703 (cont)			
	VI	**VII**	**VIII**
Central Legend	MONET BONBAV ANGIIG TEGIM A°D9r	MONET BONBAV ANGIIG TEGIM 1703	MONET BONBAV ANGIIG TEGIM 1703 (3 on its back)

	IX
Central Legend	MONET BONBAV ANGIIG TEGIM 1703 (3 reversed)

Obverse outer legend showing
…97 PAX…
(from 10 0'clock)
The date on the reverse is not visible
Photo from Craig Fernandez

Pice *et infra* – Stars Type – 1705 to 1716

AUSPICIO
REGIS ET
SENATUS
ANGLICI

1.63

A large crown. A star either side of the orb and cross, and another below. No inscription on specimens seen by Pr. or current author. The top arches are decorated with loops or circles, not beads.

The legend in four lines with ornamentation above and below. (Translates as 'Under the patronage of the King and Parliament of England'). NB Many misspellings occur.

	Pice	Half Pice	Quarter Pice
Official Weight (g)	13.75	6.87	3.44
Actual Weight (g)	12.00-13.65	6.73-6.75	?
Actual Diameter (mm)	19.3-22.7	15.0-18.0	?
Metal	Copper		

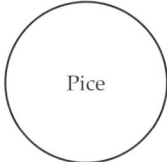

Pice

Half Pice

¼ Pice

Catalogue

Cat No.	Pr. No.	Denomination	Rev	Comments	Value ($)
1.63	97	Pice	I		200
1.64	97	"	II	letters muddled	150
1.65	98	Half Pice			150
1.66	-	Quarter Pice		None found. Mentioned in records, see Bombay Public Consultations, 24th April 1705. IOR P/341/2, p. 174.	NV

Pice *et infra* – Stars Type – 1705 to 1716 (cont)

Reverse Varieties

Arrangement of Letters	The letters may be arranged normally or may be muddled

		I	II
Arrangement of Letters		Normal	Muddled

Normal letters | *Muddled letters* | *Stars on each side of orb and cross*

Tinny or Bujerook – 1672

1.68

Balemark of the G[overnor and] C[ompany of merchants of London trading into the] E[ast Indies]. No border.

The numerals 1 (or 4) over 72, indicating value and year of issue, [16]72. No border.

	4 Tinnys	Tinny		
Actual Weight (g)	5.68	1.56		
Actual Diameter (mm)	~20?	13.0	4 Tinnys	Tinny
Metal	Tin			

Catalogue

Cat No.	Pr. No.	Denomination	Comments	Value ($)
1.67	-	4 Tinnys	Ref: Hemanth Chopra. Date not certain	NV
1.68	227	Tinny		NV

Tinny or Bujerook – 1672 (cont)

4 tinnys 1672? Date only faintly visible

Double Tinny or Bujerook – 1675

1.69

| Shield of arms of the Company, garnished. No legend. No border. | The numerals 2 over 75 indicating 2 tinnys and 1675. A plain raised border. |

Actual Weight (g)	2.69-3.05
Actual Diameter (mm)	16.8-17.0
Metal	Tin

Tinny

Catalogue

Cat No.	Pr. No.	Comments	Value ($)
1.69	228		2,000

Tinny or Bujerook – 1677 to 1694

Balemark with GCE

The date within a plain circle

Actual Weight (g)	1.40-2.68
Actual Diameter (mm)	15.1-17.0
Metal	Tin

Tinny

Catalogue

Cat No.	Pr. No.	Date	Comments	Value ($)
1.70	-	[16]77	New York sale (2016), sale XXXVII, lot 1110. Also BM. Also Peter Thompson	3,000
1.71	-	[16]94	Ref: Bob Johnston	3,000
1.71c	-	[1]701	Ref: Bob Johnston	3,000

Tinny or Bujerook – 1716 to 1720

1.72

Balemark of the V[nited] E[ast] I[ndia] C[ompany]. No border. No legend.

The date, 1716 or 1720 within a plain circle.

Actual Weight (g)	1.65-2.0
Actual Diameter (mm)	14.8
Metal	Tin
Edge	Plain

Tinny

Catalogue

Cat No.	Pr. No.	Date	Comments	Value ($)
1.72	229	1716		NV
1.73	-	1720	Mitchiner 1690The EIC had issued tin pice in 1717 so the issue of these tinnys in 1720 seems strange. Perhaps they were meant to be a smaller denomination.	NV

Tin Pice – 1717

AUSPICIO
REGIS ET
SENATUS
ANGLIAE

1.76

A large crown with GR above. The GR is divided by the orb and cross of the crown. Below the crown is the legend: BOMB All within a border of half loops.

The motto of the Company in four lines (By the authority of the King and Parliament of England) with or without the date below. Scrolled ornaments above and below. All within a border of half loops.

	Double Pice	Pice	
Actual Weight (g)	32?	16.23	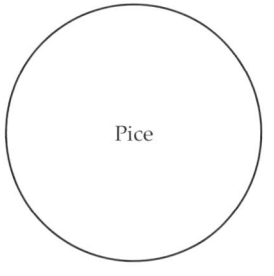
Actual Diameter (mm)	?	33.5-34.7	Pice
Metal	Tin		

Catalogue

Cat No.	Pr. No.	Denomination	Date	Comments	Value ($)
1.74	230	Double Pice	1717	Not seen by Pridmore. Recorded from Atkins. May not exist	NV
1.75	231	"	1718	Recorded from Pridmore. Probably tin	NV
1.76	241	Pice	1717	XRF analysis shows tin	1,000
1.77	-	"	1717	Retrograde Ss in SENATUS	1,000

Pice with retrograde Ss in SENATUS

Bombay Presidency c1890

Bombay Presidency Bombay Mint, Hammered Coins 1717 to 1799

Summary

In 1717 the Bombay council succeeded in getting permission to strike Moghul style rupees, and these 'munbai rupees' were struck throughout the eighteenth century. However, it was only one of many types of rupee issued by different authorities in the region (e.g. Ahmadabad, Broach and Surat rupees). In particular the Surat rupee competed with that of Bombay, and the Nawab of Surat found it convenient to debase his rupee by a few percent from time to time. This caused many problems for the Bombay authorities and these problems were not resolved until Bombay adopted the Surat standard in 1800 (see next section).

Gold coins were issued from time to time, usually struck in the style of the silver rupees, although some European style gold coins were tried in the 1760s and 1770s. The mintages of these gold coins, where known, are very small and these coins are all extremely rare.

Copper coins were also issued from time to time during the century but for most of the time, lower value coins were produced in tutenague (zinc) although by the 1770s forgery was such a problem that these coins were called in and replaced by copper coins.

Rupee *et infra* – Farrukh Siyar – 1713 to 1719

2.3

sikka zad az fazl hagg bar sim wa zar badshah bahar wa bar farrukhsiyar [AH] (= Struck money of gold and silver by the grace of God Emperor of sea and land. Farrukh-Siyar [AH])

zarb munbai sanah [RY] julūs maimanat mānūs (= Struck at Bombay in the [RY] year of tranquil prosperity)

	Rupee	Half Rupee
Actual Weight (g)	11.51-11.54	5.32-5.71
Actual Diameter (mm)	24.5-26.8	23.0-24.2
Metal	Silver	

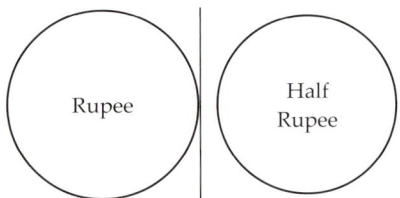

Catalogue

Cat No.	Pr. No.	Denomination	AH	RY	Mark	Comments	Value ($)
2.1	30	Rupee	112x	6	1	Ref: Bob Johnston	400
2.2		"	1129	6	2	Ref: Bob Johnston	200
2.3		"	112x	6	3		300
2.4	31	"	1130	7	3	AH 1130 – ref: Baldwin (2003), sale 35, lot 1711	200
2.5	31	"	1130	7	4		300
2.6	-	Half Rupee	112x	6	?	Ref: Todywalla. Mark not clear	800
2.7	-	"	xxxx	7	4	Crown mark. Ref: Shatrughan Jain, personal communication.	800

N.B. A Farrukh Siyar rupee apparently without a RY has been offered for sale (Album list 197 No. 363). It has a weight of 10.89g and diameter of 22.5-23.3. It also has a different arrangement of the obverse legend and a different differentiating mark. It therefore does not fit into this series and is either from a different mint or a counterfeit.

Rupee *et infra* – Farrukh Siyar – 1713 to 1719 (cnt)

Reverse Varieties

Differentiating Mark	The mark, in the *sīn* of *julus*, varies

Mark 1, 'Flower'   *Mark 2 'Open Carrot'*   *Mark 3, 'Carrot'*   *Mark 4, Crown*

Half rupee

Rupee with last digits of AH (30) just visible on left of centre row on obverse

219

Mohur – Shah Jahan II – 1719

No photo available. See photo of rupee

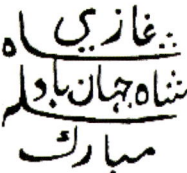 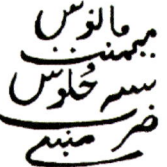

sikka mubarak. badshah ghazi shah jahan (= the auspicious coin of the victorious Emperor Shah Jahan)	*zarb munbai sanah ahd julūs maimanat mānūs* (= Struck at Bombay in the 1st year of his reign of tranquil prosperity).

Actual Weight (g)	?
Actual Diameter (mm)	~25
Metal	Gold

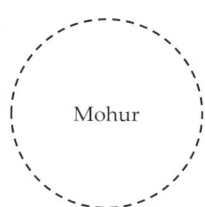

Mohur

Catalogue

Cat No.	Pr. No.	Comments	Value ($)
2.8	1	No specimens traced	NV

Rupee – Shah Jahan II – 1719

2.9

sikka mubarak badshah ghazi shah jahan 1131 (= The auspicious coin of the victorious Emperor Shah Jahan 1131)	*zarb munbai sanah ahd julūs maimanat mānūs* (= Struck at Bombay in the 1st year of tranquil prosperity)

Rupee – Shah Jahan II – 1719 (cont)

	Rupee	Half Rupee
Actual Weight (g)	11.53-11.54	5.75
Actual Diameter (mm)	24.4-25.6	19.8-20.6
Metal	Silver	

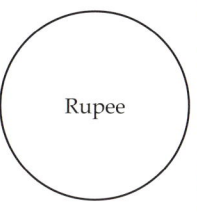

Rupee

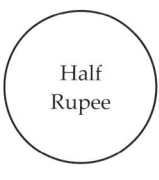

Half Rupee

Catalogue

Cat No.	Pr. No.	Denomination	AH	RY	Comments	Value ($)
2.9	32	Rupee	[11]31	Ahd (1)		200
2.10	33	Half Rupee	[11]31	Ahd (1)		800

On the Surat coins the King's name is usually in the top line but there is a specimen with the King's name in the middle line, like the Bombay coins (noted by Bob Johnston), so this is not a way of identifying coins without the mint name.

Mohur – Muhammad Shah – 1719 to 1748

2.12

sikka mubarak. badshah ghazi muhammad shah[AH] (= the auspicious coin of the victorious Emperor Muhammad Shah [AH])

zarb munbai sanah [RY] julūs maimanat mānūs (= Struck at Bombay in the [RY] year of his reign of tranquil prosperity).

Actual Weight (g)	10.94-10.95
Actual Diameter (mm)	21.6-22.7
Metal	Gold

Mohur

Mohur – Muhammad Shah – 1719 to 1748 (cont)

Catalogue

Cat No.	Pr. No.	AH	RY	Comments	Value ($)
2.11	-	113x	8	Ref:: Todywalla sale 97, lot 994	14,000
2.12	-	114x	11	Ref: ONSNL (1998), 157, p. 15.	10,000
2.13	2	1145	15	Caldecott lot 58	NV
2.14	3	11[xx]	29	Caldecott lot 59	NV

Oswal auction 48 had a similar coin apparently without a regnal year but it looks like a weakly struck RY 11.

Rupee *et infra* – Muhammad Shah – 1719 to 1748

2.23

sikka mubarak badshah ghazi Muhammad Shah [AH] (= the auspicious coin of the victorious Emperor Muhammad Shah [AH])

zarb munbai sanah [RY] *julūs maimanat mānūs* (= Struck at Bombay in the [RY] year of tranquil prosperity)

	Rupee	Half Rupee	Quarter Rupee	Eighth Rupee
Official Weight (g)	11.55	5.76	2.89	1.44
Actual Weight (g)	11.18-11.57	5.57-5.81	?	?
Actual Diameter (mm)	20.3-27.3	18.0-21.6	~18	~16
Metal	Silver			

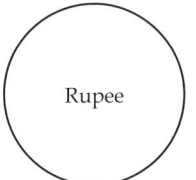

Rupee

Half Rupee

¼

⅛

Rupee *et infra* – Muhammad Shah – 1719 to 1748 (cont)

Catalogue

Cat No.	Pr. No.	Denom	AH	RY	Differ. Mark	Comments	Value ($)
2.14c	35	Rupee	1131	1	1	Ref: Craig Fernandez	400
2.15	35	"	1132	2	?	Recorded from Pr. Mark not known maybe 1?	150
2.16		"	xxxx	2	1	Ref: Johnston	200
2.17		"	113x	3	1	Ref: Johnston	200
2.18		"	113x	3	2	Ref: Todywalla, sale 35 lot 249	200
2.19	-	"	113x	3	3	Ref: Johnston	200
2.20	36	"	113x	4	3?		200
2.21	37	"	1135	5	3	Ref: Johnston	100
2.22	-	"	1136	5	4	Ref: Johnston	200
2.23	38	"	1136	6	4	Ref: Todywalla, sale 5 lot 271	200
2.24	-	"	113x	6	5	Ref: Rajgor sale 33, lot 189	150
2.25	39	"	1136	7	?	Taken from Pr. But AH & RY do not correspond. May be a mistake?	100
2.26	40	"	1137	7	5		100
2.27	41	"	1138	8	5		100
2.28	42	"	1139	9	5		100
2.29	-	"	1140	10	5	Numeral 0 written as small circle (not dot).	100
2.30	-	"	xxxx	10/9	5	Last numeral has 0 over 9. May be a light weight counterfeit (10.12g)?	100
2.31	-	"	xxxx	11	6	Ref: Johnston. Straight 1s in RY	100
2.32	43	"	114x	11	7	Curved 1s in RY	100
2.33	44	"	114x	12	7		100
2.34	-	"	114x	13	7	Ref: Mitchiner M1694. Also Puddester	100
2.35	45	"	114x	14	7		100
2.36	46	"	1145	15	8	Numeral 5 written as kidney shape	100
2.37	47	"	114x	16	8		100
2.38	48	"	1147	17	8		100
2.39	49	"	1148	18	8		100
2.40	50	"	1149	19	8		100
2.41	51	"	1150	19	8		200
2.42	-	"	1150	20	8	Ref: Johnston. Numeral 0 written as small circle (not dot).	100

Listing continued on next page

Rupee *et infra* – Muhammad Shah – 1719 to 1748 (cont)

Catalogue

Cat No.	Pr. No.	Denom	AH	RY	Differ. Mark	Comments	Value ($)
2.43	52	Rupee	115x	21	8		100
2.44	-	"	115x	22	8	Ref: Puddester. Also Todywalla sale 6, lot 211	100
2.45	-	"	1153	23	8		100
2.46	-	"	1154	23	8	Ref: Puddester. Baldwin (2006), sale 47 (Stiller), lot 851	100
2.47	-	"	11xx	24	8	Ref: Puddester	150
2.48	53	"	1155	25	8	Numeral 5 kidney shaped	100
2.49	54	"	1156	26	8	Ref: Puddester	100
2.50	55	"	1157	27	8	Ref: Puddester	100
2.51	-	"	115x	28	8	Ref: Noble (1995), sale 48 lot 2059. Also Puddester	100
2.52	-	"	1159	29	8		100
2.53	-	"	116x	30	8	Numeral 0 written as dot or small circle	100
2.54	56	"	1161	31	8		100
2.55	57	Half Rupee	xxxx	4	-		350
2.56	-	"	11xx	5	3	Ref: Johnston	350
2.57	-	"	xxxx	6	4		350
2.58	-	"	xxxx	7	5		350
2.59	-	"	11xx	9	5	Ref: Johnston	350
2.60	58	"	1147	17	8		350
2.61	-		xxxx	19	-	Ref: Puddester	350
2.62	59	"	11xx	21	-		350
2.63	-	"	115x	25	-	Ref: Chopra	350
2.64	-	"	1xxx	29	-	Ref: ClassNG, sale 9, lot 932	350
2.65	-	"		31	-	Ref: Wiggins.	350
2.66	-	¼ Rupee	?	2x	-	Ref: Bhandare.	500
2.67	-	⅛ Rupee	11xx	?	-	Michiner M1697	NV

See also fifth & twelfth rupees for use on the Malabar Coast.

My thanks to Bob Johnston who has done an enormous amount of work on these coins and kindly provided me with the results of his studies.

Rupee *et infra* – Muhammad Shah – 1719 to 1748 (cont)

The numeral 0 appears to be written as a small circle whilst 5 is larger and kidney shaped.
The photos show 10 on the left and 15 on the right

Differentiating Marks (see catalogue above)

| Mark 1 | Mark 2 | Mark 3 | Mark 4 |

| Mark 5 | Mark 6 | Mark 7 | Mark 8 |

Dam – Muhammad Shah

2.68

sikka mubarak badshah ghazi Muhammad Shah [AH] (= the auspicious coin of the victorious Emperor Muhammad Shah [AH])

zarb munbai sanah [RY] julūs maimanat mānūs (= Struck at Bombay in the [RY] year of tranquil prosperity)

Actual Weight (g)	20.11-20.96
Actual Diameter (mm)	23.3-24.6
Metal	Copper

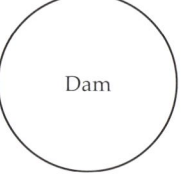

Dam

Catalogue

Cat No.	Pr. No.	AH	RY	Comments	Value ($)
2.68	-	1140?	10?	At least five known	700

Rupee *et infra* – Ahmad Shah – 1748 to 1754

2.73

sikka mubarak badshah ghazi ahmad shah bahadur [AH] (= The auspicious coin of the Victorious Emperor Ahmad Shah the valiant. [AH])

zarb munbai sanah [RY] julūs maimanat mānūs (= Struck at Bombay in the [RY] year of tranquil prosperity)

Rupee et infra – Ahmad Shah – 1748 to 1754 (cont)

	Rupee	Half Rupee
Official Weight (g)	11.60	5.80
Actual Weight (g)	11.40-11.56	5.63-5.73
Actual Diameter (mm)	20.0-23.2	17.3-18.1
Metal	Silver	

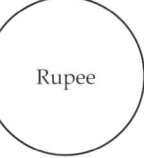 Rupee  Half Rupee

Catalogue

Cat. No.	Pr. No.	Denomination	AH	RY	Comments	Value ($)
2.69	-	Rupee	xxxx	2	Not certain. Could be RY 3	200
2.70	-	"	xxxx	3	Ref: Puddester	200
2.71	65	"	xxxx	4		200
2.72	66	"	xxxx	5		200
2.73	67	"	1167	6		200
2.74	-	Half Rupee	xxxx	4	RY 2 or 3 might also exist but not clear	500
2.75	-	"	xxxx	6	Ref: Withers, Mahapatra.	500

Mohur et infra – Alamgir II – 1774

2.76

sikka mubarak. badshah ghazi alamgir (= the auspicious coin of the victorious Emperor Alamgir)

zarb munbai sanah [RY] julūs maimanat mānūs (= Struck at Bombay in the [RY] year of tranquil prosperity)

	Mohur	Eighth Mohur	Fifteenth Mohur
Official Weight (g)	11.55	1.44	0.76
Actual Weight (g)	11.50-11.52	1.40-1.42	?
Actual Diameter (mm)	17.5-19.4	11.8-12.3	9.5 (from Pr)
Metal	Gold		

Mohur *et infra* – Alamgir II – 1774 (cont)

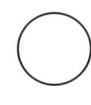

Mohur

Eighth Mohur

Catalogue

Cat No.	Pr. No.	Denomination	AH	RY	Comments	Value ($)
2.76	8	Mohur	1188	9	4 known	5,000
2.77	-	Eighth Mohur	11xx	9	The records contain no mention of an eighth and the three published coins seen have no mint name but are of the same style as the mohur and panchia	3,500
2.78	11	Fifteenth Mohur	xxxx	9		1,000

See also third mohur (panchia) for use on the Malabar Coast (p. 310). Pridmore lists a half mohur but none have been found and the quarter he lists is the weight of a third mohur.

Rupee *et infra* – Alamgir II – 1754 to 1759 – RY 1

2.79

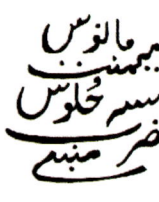

sikka mubarak badshah ghazi Alamgir [AH] (= the auspicious coin of the victorious Emperor Alamgir [AH])

zarb munbai sanah [RY] julūs maimanat mānūs (= Struck at Bombay in the [RY] year of tranquil prosperity)

	Rupee	Half Rupee	Eighth Rupee
Actual Weight (g)	11.46-11.52	5.71	?
Actual Diameter (mm)	20.2-23.0	17.2-18.0	~9
Metal	Silver		

Rupee *et infra* – Alamgir II – 1754 to 1759 – RY 1 (cont)

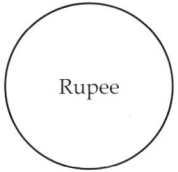
Rupee

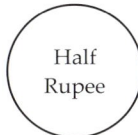
Half Rupee

⅛

Catalogue

Cat No.	Pr. No.	Denomination	Obv	AH	RY	Comments	Value ($)
2.79	-	Rupee	A	1167	Ahd (Ry1)	Dot above *julus*	500
2.80	-	"	B	1168	Ahd (Ry1)	No dot above *julus*	500
2.81	-	Half Rupee	-	(1168)	Ahd (Ry1)	Ref: Chopra. No dot above *julus*	700
2.82	-	Eighth Rupee	-	xxxx	xx	Ref: Paris museum. Attributed by design	NV

Obverse Varieties

Date Position	The AH date may be in different positions in the legend.
Vowel mark	The vowel mark at the bottom right varies with the date

	A	B
Date Position	Top part of legend	Bottom part of legend
Vowel mark	Open	Closed

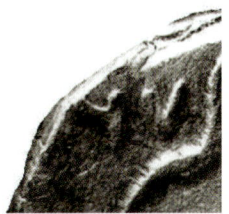

A – Date in top part of legend.
Vowel mark - Open

B – Date in bottom part of legend
Vowel mark - Closed

Half rupee

Rupee – Alamgir II – 1754 to 1759 – RY 2 to 9

2.85

sikka mubarak badshah ghazi alamgir [AH] (= The auspicious coin of the Victorious Emperor Alamgir [AH])

zarb munbai sanah [RY] julūs maimanat mānūs (= Struck at Bombay in the [RY] year of tranquil prosperity)

	Rupee	Half Rupee	Quarter Rupee	Eighth Rupee
Actual Weight (g)	11.46-11.57	5.72-5.78	2.77	?
Actual Diameter (mm)	19.1-22.5	17.2-18.1	15.3-15.8	~12
Metal	Silver			

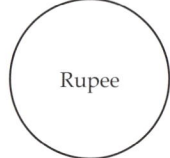

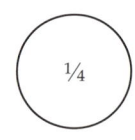

Catalogue

Cat No.	Pr. No.	Denomination	AH	RY	Comments	Value ($)
2.83	68	Rupee	1169	2		100
2.84	69	"	1170	2		100
2.85	-	"	xxxx	3	Ref: Puddester, Album list 202, No 628	100
2.86	-	"	xxxx	4	Ref: Puddester	100
2.87	70	"	1173	5	Ref: Puddester	100
2.88	71	Half Rupee	11xx	2		500
2.89	-	"	xxxx	4	Ref: Puddester	500
2.90	72	"	xxxx	5		500
2.91	-	Quarter Rupee	xxxx	x	Ruler not visible but mark similar to that on other denominations. Could be a coin of Ahmad Shah?	500
2.92	-	Eighth Rupee	xxxx	2	Ref: Noble (1995), sale 48, lot 2069. Mint off flan so might be Surat	500

See also rupees for use on the Malabar Coast (pp. 313-316)

Mohur *et infra* – 1765

2.93

The shield of arms of the Company within a plain circle and surrounded by the legend. All within a beaded circle.

An inscription with floral ornaments above and below. All within a beaded boarder.

	Mohur	Half Mohur	Quarter Mohur
Official Weight (g)	10.95	5.48	2.74
Actual Weight (g)	10.94	?	2.72
Actual Diameter (mm)	23.6-24.2	20 (from Pr)	17.0-17.7
Metal	Gold		

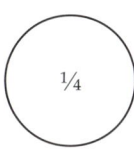

Catalogue

Cat No.	Pr. No.	Denomination	Comments	Value ($)
2.93	4	Mohur		150,000
2.94	5	Half Mohur		120,000
2.95	6	Quarter Mohur		100,000

Mohur – 1770

BOMBAY
1770

---

15 RUPEES

2.96

An inscription surrounded by ornaments. All within a plain circle. Surrounded by a raised toothed rim.

sikka mubarak sanah 9 alamgir badshah ghazi sanah 1184 (= Auspicious coin of the 9th year of Alamgir, The victorious Emperor. Year 1184.) Within a plain circle all surrounded by a raised toothed rim.

Official Weight (g)	10.95
Actual Weight (g)	10.87
Actual Diameter (mm)	22.8-23.7
Metal	Gold

Mohur

Catalogue

Cat No.	Pr. No.	AH	RY	Comments	Value ($)
2.96	7	1184(=AD 1770/71)	9 (=AD 1767/68)	Forgeries exist	120,000

Double Pice *et infra* – GR Type – 1728 to 1749

2.98

A large crown. G R separated by the orb and cross of the crown. BOMB below the crown. All within a beaded rim.
The top arches of the crown are decorated with beads not loops or circles

AUSPICIO
REGIS ET
SENATUS
ANGLIAE
(date)

The legend (= under the patronage of the King and parliament of England) and date. Within a beaded rim.

Double Pice *et infra* – GR Type – 1728 to 1749 (cont)

	Double Pice	Pice	Half Pice
Actual Weight (g)	15.06-19.05	8.01-10.13	3.23-4.57
Actual Diameter (mm)	21.5-26.3	17.6-21.6	15.0-17.5
Metal	Copper		

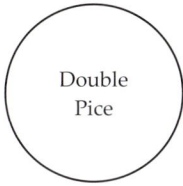 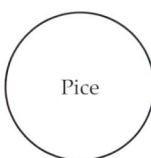 

Catalogue

Cat No.	Pr. No.	Denomination	Date	Comments	Value ($)
2.97	99	Double Pice	1728		200
2.98	100	"	1730		300
2.99	101	"	1733		300
2.100	-	"	1733	BOMB mis-spelt BMOB	500
2.101	-	"	1733	Overstruck on falus of Iranian mint of Qazvin. Ref: Goron, S, (1997), ONSNL 154, p. 22	500
2.102	102	"	1735		300
2.103	103	"	1737		300
2.104	(104)	Pice	1728	With complete date visible	150
2.105	(104)	"	173x		200
2.106	-	"	xxxx	BOMB mis-spelt BMOB. Ref: Noble (1995), Sale 48, lot 2080	250
2.107	106	"	1749	Weight 5.90-6.13g	200
2.108	105	Half Pice	xxxx	Loops on arch of crown	100
2.109	105	"	xxxx	Beads on arch of crown	100

Half pice with loops (left photo) and beads (right photo)

Double Pice *et infra* – GR Type – 1728 to 1749 (cont)

Double pice 1735

Double pice over-struck on Persian falus

Pice with complete 1728 date

Double Pice – Balemark Type – 1773 to 1784

2.110

The balemark of the Company

Crown with G R above separated by the orb and cross. The legend and date below the crown.

Actual Weight (g)	10.25-10.28
Actual Diameter (mm)	19.2-22.5
Metal	Copper

Double Pice

Catalogue

Cat No.	Pr. No.	Denomination	Date	Comments	Value ($)
2.110	107	Double Pice	1773		100
2.111		"	"	Transposed balemark. Ref: Puddester.	150
2.112	108	"	1775		200
2.113		"	1777	Ref: Puddester	200
2.114	109	"	1783		200
2.115	-	"	1784		200

Correct balemark

Transposed balemark

Pice – Balemark Type – 1773 to 1784

| The balemark of the Company | The legend PICE BOMB and date below (not visible on this specimen but see photo below). |

Actual Weight (g)	4.79-4.87
Actual Diameter (mm)	17.1-19.0
Metal	Copper

Pice

Catalogue

Cat No.	Pr. No.	Denomination	Date	Comments	Value ($)
2.116	110	Pice	1773		80
2.117		"	1777	Ref: Puddester	100
2.118	111	"	1783		100
2.119	112	"	1784		100
2.120	113	"	1788		100

Pice 1783

Half & Quarter Pice – Balemark Type – 1773 to 1784

2.121

The balemark of the Company

The numeral ½ or ¼

	Half Pice	Quarter Pice
Actual Weight (g)	2.56-2.63	1.15-1.22
Actual Diameter (mm)	14.2-15.0	11.0-12.0
Metal	Copper	

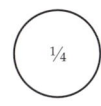

Quarter pice

Catalogue

Cat No.	Pr. No.	Denomination	Comments	Value ($)
2.121	114	Half Pice		500
2.122	115	Quarter Pice		700

Pice – Countermarked – 1788

2.123

Old native copper coin countermarked
with an oblong stamp containing
BOMB
1788
within a beaded border.

Blank

Actual Weight (g)	5.20-19.84
Actual Diameter (mm)	19.3-23.7
Metal	Copper

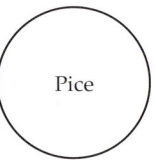

Pice

Catalogue

Cat No.	Pr. No.	Comments	Value ($)
2.123	116/117		700

There are a number of different varieties of these coins. Pridmore records large and small dates and a few other specimens have appeared on the market since then. The tremendous variation in weights suggest that there may have been more than one denomination but their rarity makes it difficult to come to any conclusion. More research is needed.

Zinc Double Pice *et infra* – Balemark Type 1717 to 1771

2.134

AUSPICIO
REGIS ET
SENATUS
ANGLIAE

A large crown with GR above. The GR is divided by the orb and cross of the crown. Below the crown is the word: BOMB. All within a border of half loops.

The motto of the Company in four lines (By the authority of the King and Parliament of England) with or without the date below. Scrolled ornaments above and below. All within a border of half loops.

	Double Pice	Pice	Half Pice
Official Weight (g)	27.2	13.6	6.8
Actual Weight (g)	27.72-33.35	13.14-17.72	?
Actual Diameter (mm)	37.1-41.0	32.0-35.5	27
Metal	Zinc (by XRF analysis)		

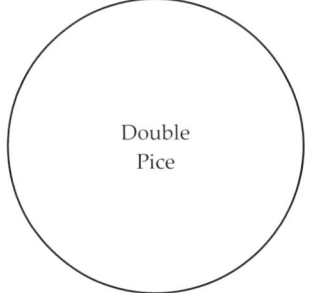
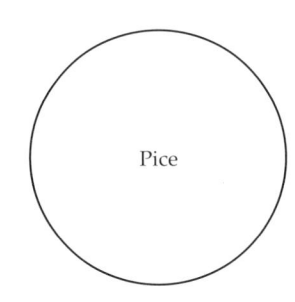
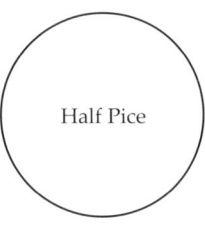

Double Pice

Pice

Half Pice

Zinc Double Pice *et infra* – Balemark Type 1717 to 1771 (cont)

Catalogue

Cat No.	Pr. No.	Denomination	Date	Comments	Value ($)
2.124	232	Double Pice	1732	Not seen by Pridmore. Recorded from Atkins	NV
2.125	233	"	1741		1,000
2.126	234	"	1742	Not seen by Pridmore. Recorded from Atkins	NV
2.127	235	"	1743		1,000
2.128	-	"	1747	Ref: Stevens Collection	1,000
2.129	236	"	1748	Stevens collection	1,000
2.130	237	"	1761	Not seen by Pridmore. Recorded from Atkins	NV
2.131	238	"	1771	Obv legend reads BOMB	800
2.132	238	"	1771	Obv legend reads BONB	1,000
2.133	239	"	1771	Rev legend reads SENATUT	1,000
2.134	240	"	No Date		800
2.135	-	"	No Date	Struck in lead. Wt=41g. Ref: Chopra. Not sure about authenticity	NV
2.136	242	Pice	1741		800
2.137	243	"	1743	Not seen by Pridmore. Recorded from Atkins	NV
2.138	-	"	1744	Ref: Todywalla, sale 31, lot 230 but date not certain from photo	1,000
2.139	244	"	1747		800
2.140	245	"	1771		700
2.141	246	"	No Date		500
2.142	247	Half Pice	No Date	Only one known	2,000

1748 on double pice

Zinc Half and Quarter Pice – Value Type – No Date

2.143

Balemark of the Company

The value in English within a plain raised border

	½ Pice	¼ Pice
Actual Weight (g)	5.31-6.15	?
Actual Diameter (mm)	22.8-23.5	~18
Metal	Zinc	

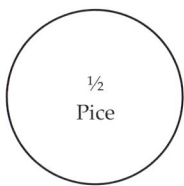

Catalogue

Cat No.	Pr. No.	Denomination	Comments	Value ($)
2.143	248	½ Pice		2500
2.144	249	¼ Pice	Recorded from Pridmore	NV

Original miniature paintings by Cherryl Stevens

Bombay Presidency

Bombay Mint, Hammered Coins, 1800 to c1830

Summary

During the period under consideration several important numismatic events occurred. Firstly, because the Malabar Coast was transferred from the Bombay to the Madras Presidency, the focus of Bombay shifted to the north. Surat was acquired by the Company and the Bombay mint began to strike Surat standard rupees in place of the Munbai rupees that had been struck during most of the previous century. Secondly, the acquisition of more territories after 1818 meant that the Bombay mint was unable to meet all the coin requirements for the Presidency. The mint had not been mechanised like those at Calcutta and Madras and the quality and quantity of the coins was not good. In addition, a recurring theme throughout the period was the poor state of the mint buildings. Neither the mint machinery nor the buildings were properly replaced until new machinery was brought from England but attempts to introduce machinery were made between about 1818 and 1820 and these will be discussed later. Thus, although the mint began striking coins of a different standard, the operational aspects of the mint did not change very much until about 1830. The coinage consisted of gold mohurs and silver rupees both with the mint name Surat. Various fractions were struck. In addition copper coins of different denominations were produced.

Mohur *et infra* – Shah Alam – 46 Sun

3.4

| *sikka mubarak. badshah ghazi shah alam* (= The auspicious coin of the victorious Emperor Shah Alam). | *zarb surat sanah 46 julūs maimanat mānūs* (= Struck at Surat in the 46th year of tranquil prosperity) |

	Mohur	Panchia (⅓)	Rupee (¹⁄₁₅)
Official Weight (g)	11.59/11.66	3.86/3.88	0.77
Actual Weight (g)	11.52-11.66	3.83-3.88	0.76-0.77
Actual Diameter (mm)	17.0-19.0	12.7-15.0	7.5-9.7
Metal	Gold		

The official weight of the mohur was 11.59g from 1800-1824 and 11.66g from 1825-1831

 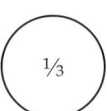

Mohur ⅓ ¹⁄₁₅

Catalogue

Cat No.	Pr. No.	Denomination	Privy Marks	Date Issued	Comments	Value ($)
3.1	257	Mohur	2 crescent	1801-02		1,000
3.2	-	"	3 1802 upside-down on panel + Leopard's head on rev	"	Ref: Todywalla	10,000
3.3	261	"	4 Crown	1803-24		1,000
3.4	262	"	4a Inverted crown	"		1,000
3.5	266	"	5 Star + crown	1825-31	Official wt = 11.66g	1,000

Listing continued on next page

Mohur *et infra* – Shah Alam – 46 San (cont)

Catalogue

Cat No.	Pr. No.	Denom	Privy Marks	Date Issued	Comments	Value ($)
3.6	258	Panchia	2 crescent	1801-02		800
3.7	260	"	3 1802 on panel + Leopard's head on rev	"		5,000
3.8	263	"	4 Crown	1803-24		800
3.9	264	"	4a Inverted crown	"		800
3.10	267	"	5 Star + crown	1825-31	Official wt = 3.88g	800
3.11	-	"	8 Star + crown at top	1825-31?	Ref: Album (2012), sale 13, lot 1413. Looks like a local imitation	800
3.12	268	"	5a Star + inverted crown at bottom	"		800
3.13	259	Rupee	2 crescent	1801-02		750
3.14	265	"	4b Star to right	1803-24		700
3.15	269	"	5b Start to left	1825-31		700

See also Surat Mint (pp. 305-306).

Privy Marks

A number of different privy marks occur on the gold and silver Surat style coins issued from the Surat and Bombay mints. Pridmore has undertaken a study of these marks and arrived at a proposed assignment of date for them. He was only able to confirm one of these (for the 1802 gold coinage) from literature sources and the rest remain a matter of his deduction, which he considered required further research.

Mohur, with leopard's head MM on obverse and 1802 upside down on panel on reverse
(reverse as privy mark 3)

Privy Marks on 46 san Gold and Silver

Gold

Privy mark 1 (for Surat mint (see pp. 307-309)

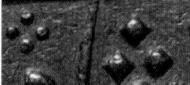

Privy mark 2

Privy mark 3 (1802 upside-down on panel)

Privy mark 4 (crown to right)

Privy mark 4a (inverted crown to right)

Privy mark 4b (star to right)

Privy mark 5 (star + crown)

Privy mark 5A (from Pridmore)

Privy mark 5B

Silver

Privy Mark 6 (star to left)

Privy Mark 7 (star below + crown)

Privy Mark 8 (star above + crown)

Privy Mark 9 (crown below)

Silver Rupee *et infra* – Shah Alam – 46 Sun

The AH date is almost never visible but one or two specimens show AH 1215 at the top of the obverse.

3.16

sikka mubarak badshah ghazi Shah Alam (= the auspicious coin of the victorious Emperor Shah Alam.)	*zarb surat sanah 46 julūs maimanat mānūs* (= Struck at Surat in the 46th year of tranquil prosperity)

The official weight of the mohur was 11.59g from 1800-1824 and 11.66g from 1825-1831

	Rupee	Half Rupee	Quarter Rupee	Eighth Rupee
Official Weight (g)	11.59/11.66	5.76/5.83	2.88/2.91	1.44/1.46
Actual Weight (g)	11.55-11.66	5.73-5.86	2.89-2.94	1.44-1.49
Actual Diameter (mm)	17.8-20.8	14.6-17.8	11.8-13.4	10.0-11.0
Metal	Silver			

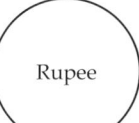
Rupee

Half Rupee

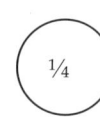
¼

⅛

Silver Rupee *et infra* – Shah Alam – 46 San (cont)

Catalogue

Cat No.	Pr. No.	Denom	Privy Mark	Issued AD	Comments	Value ($)
3.16	270	Rupee	6	1800-1824		60
3.17	274	"	7	1825	Silver-plated forgeries exist	60
3.18	276	"	8	1825-31	Official wt = 11.66g. Base metal forgeries exist	60
3.19	280	"	9	"		250
3.20	271	Half Rupee	6	1800-24		100
3.21	275	"	7	1825		100
3.22	277	"	8	1825-31	Official wt = 5.83g	100
3.23	281	"	9	"		100
3.24	272	Quarter Rupee	6	1800-24		125
3.25	278	"	8	1825-31		125
3.26	-	"	7	1825		125
3.27	282	"	9	"	Not traced by Pridmore or current author. Official wt = 2.91g	NV
3.28	273	Eighth Rupee	6	1800-24		150
3.29	279	"	8	1825-31	Official wt = 1.46g	150
3.30	283	"	9	"		150

See also Surat Mint (pp.307-309)

Rupee showing 1825 on panel

Rupee – Shah Alam – 1823 to 1824

3.31

sikka mubarak badshah ghazi Shah Alam (= The auspicious coin of the victorious Emperor Shah Alam)	*zarb Surat sanah [RY] julus maimanat manus* (= Struck at Surat in the [RY] year of tranquil prosperity)

Official Weight (g)	11.66	
Actual Weight (g)	11.54-11.67	
Actual Diameter (mm)	26.7-27.6	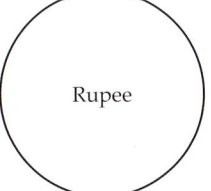
Metal	Silver	Rupee
Edge	Straight Grained	

Catalogue

Cat No.	Pr. No.	Denomination	Status	AH	RY	Comments	Value ($)
3.31	284	Rupee	Currency	1215	46		100
3.32	285	"	Proof	"	"		1,000

Four Pice *et infra*– 1802 to 1829

3.51

Balemark with date below. Within a toothed border. The border is not usually visible.

Balanced scales with *adil* (= justice) written in Arabic between the pans. There may be a numeral to indicate value. All within a toothed border that is not usually visible.

	4 Pice	Two Pice	Pice	½ Pice	¼ Pice
Official Weight (g)	42.51	21.25	10.62	5.31	2.65
Actual Weight (g)	41.07-42.88	19.22-21.31	8.64-10.69	4.77-5.56	2.46-2.73
Actual Diameter (mm)	26.3-30.0	20.0-25.0	17.7-22.8	14.5-18.6	12.0-14.8
Metal	Copper				

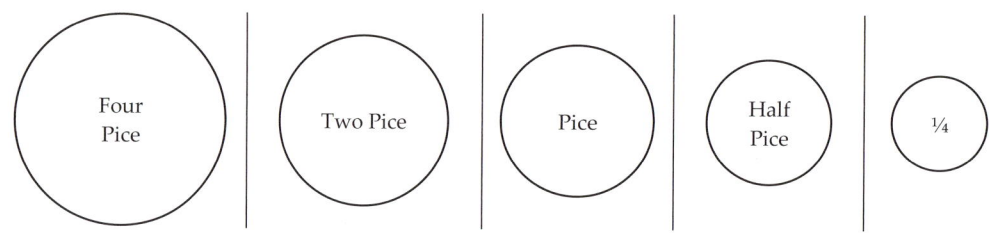

Catalogue

Cat No.	Pr. No.	Denomination	Date	Comments	Value ($)
3.33	141	Four Pice	1802		100
3.34	142	"	1803		100
3.35	143	"	1804		100

Listing continued on next page

| | | Four Pice *et infra*– 1802 to 1829 (cont) | | | | |

Catalogue

Cat No.	Pr. No.	Denomination	Rev	Date	Comments	Value ($)
3.36	144	Two Pice	I	1802		90
3.37	145	"	I	1803		70
3.38	146	"	I	1804		70
3.39	147	"	I?	1808		90
3.40	148	"	I	1809	Ref: ANS, also Johnston	70
3.41	149	"	I	1810		70
3.42	150	"	II	1812		90
3.43	146A	"	I	1813		70
3.44	151	"	II	1813		90
3.45	-	"	II	1815?	Noble (1995), Sale 48, lot 2092. May be 1816?	90
3.46	152	"	II	1816		70
3.47	153	"	II	δ181	Local imitation?	70
3.48	154	"	II	1818		90
3.49	155	"	II	8118	Local imitation?	70
3.50	156	"	II	1819		70
3.51	157	"	II	1825		70
3.52	158	"	II	1826		70
3.53	159	"	II	1827		90
3.54	159A	"	II	1828		90
3.55	160	"	II	1829		70

Listing continued on next page

Reverse I. Numeral 2 present

Reverse II. No numeral 2 present

Four Pice *et infra*– 1802 to 1829 (cont)

Catalogue

Cat No.	Pr. No.	Denomination	Date	Comments	Value ($)
3.56	161	Pice	1802		50
3.57	162	"	1803		50
3.58	163	"	1804		70
3.59	164	"	1808		50
3.60	165	"	1809		70
3.61	166	"	1810		50
3.62	-	"	1811?	Ref: Noble (1995), sale 48, lot 2093	70
3.63	167	"	1813		50
3.64	168	"	1815		50
3.65	169	"	1816		50
3.66	170	"	1818		70
3.67	171	"	1819		50
3.68	172	"	1825		50
3.69	173	"	1826		50
3.70	174	"	1827		50
3.71	175	"	1828		70
3.72	176	"	1829		50
3.73	177	Half Pice	1802		80
3.74	178	"	1803		60
3.75	179	"	1808		80
3.76	180	"	1810		60
3.77	181	"	1813		60
3.78	182	"	1815		80
3.79	183	"	1816		60
3.80	184	"	18ठ1	Local imitation	60
3.81	-	"	ठ881	Local imitation	60
3.82	185	"	1818		60

Listing continued on next page

Four Pice *et infra*– 1802 to 1829 (cont)

Catalogue

Cat No.	Pr. No.	Denomination	Date	Comments	Value ($)
3.83	186	Half Pice	1819		80
3.84	187	"	1825		50
3.85	188	"	1826		60
3.86	189	"	1827		60
3.87	190	"	1829		80
3.88	191	Quarter Pice	1816		100
3.89	192	"	1821	Date may be 1825 with only the top of the last digit visible. No other coins of this series were issued between 1819 and 1825	100
3.90	193	"	1825		100
3.91	-	"	1826	Last numeral of date not completely clear, but most likely 6. Ref: Baldwin (2001), sale 25 (Wiggins), lot 729	100
3.92	-	"	xxx9	First three numerals of date not visible, could be 1819 or 1829 but 1829 most likely	100

Obverse Notes

On the pice, 1803 and 1808 are often difficult to differentiate

Example of contemporary forgery. Note the date.

The EIC records seem to indicate that these coins were struck by other local rulers such as Angria. It is possible that the coins described here as local imitations fall into this category and are a type of Katchcha pice[3].

---

[3] Bombay Consultations. P/411/51. No. 171 (11th July 1832). Letter from the principal collector in the Concan to government, dated 29th June 1832.

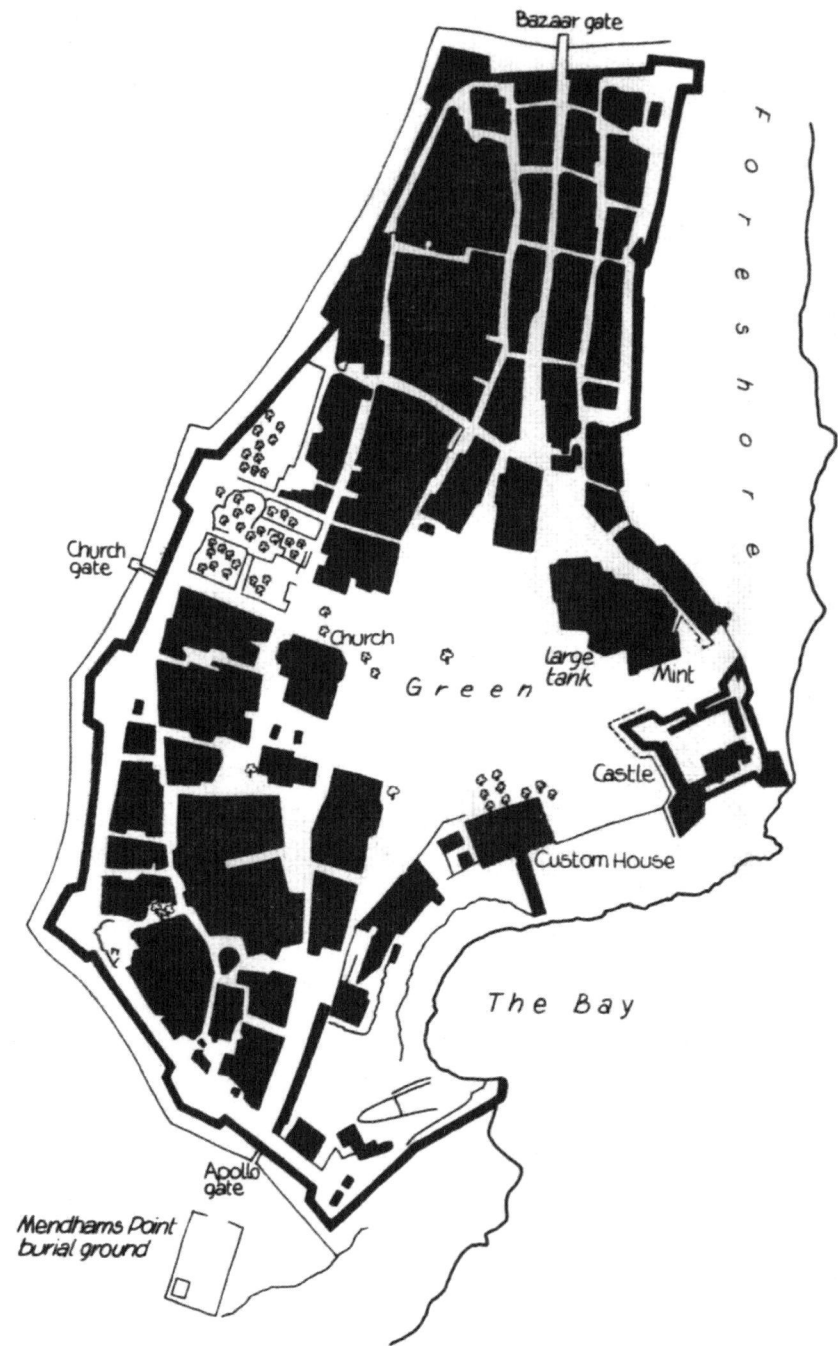

THE FORT CIRCA 1750 – after Grose

Position of the mint c1750 (middle right)

Bombay Presidency Bombay Mint, Dr. Stewart's Copper Coins Dated 1820 & 1821

Summary

The EIC mints at Calcutta and Madras had both been mechanised in the early 1790s or early 1800s respectively. However, Bombay continued with the old hammered method of coin production for many more years. In 1817 or 1818 the Bombay mint master, Dr. Stewart, had begun to investigate the possibility of building machines that could be used to strike the coinage for that Presidency. However, probably due to illness, Stewart had to leave India and the project passed to the new mint master, Henderson, who spent several more years trying to perfect the machinery. Because the directors of the EIC decided to ship a new mint from Europe, the local production of machinery was limited to a few machines for striking copper coins and was eventually halted altogether and it never went into full production[4]. A number of pattern coins for a proposed new copper coinage were produced and are discussed in this chapter.

---

[4] Stevens PJE, ONSNL (2008), vol 195, pp. 31-35

Pattern Quarter Anna – 1820

No value on reverse

4.1

The arms of the Company surrounded by the legend:
EAST INDIA COMPANY 1820
On the ribbon is the motto:
AUSPICIO REGIS & SENATUS ANGLIAE
All within a raised toothed rim

Balanced scales with Persian legend between the pans (translation = 'adil = justice).

عدل

AH date in Arabic figures below (=1235).
All within a raised toothed rim.

Actual Weight (g)	6.22-6.65
Actual Diameter (mm)	26.1-26.3
Metal	Copper
Edge	Plain

Quarter Anna

Catalogue

Cat No.	Pr. No.	Date	Comments	Value ($)
4.1	-	1820	Ref: Bonhams (1997), sale 27299, lot 415e	2,000

Pattern Pie – 1820

No value on reverse

4.2

The arms of the Company surrounded by the legend: EAST INDIA COMPANY 1820 On the ribbon is the motto: AUSPICIO REGIS & SENATUS ANGLIAE All within a raised toothed rim

Balanced scales with Persian legend between the pans (translation = 'adil = justice).

عدل

AH date in Arabic figures below (=1235). All within a raised toothed rim.

Actual Weight (g)	?
Actual Diameter (mm)	~19
Metal	Copper
Edge	Plain

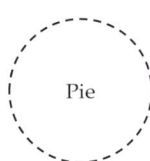

Pie

Catalogue

Cat No.	Pr. No.	Date	Comments	Value ($)
4.2	-	1820	Ref: Bonhams (1997), sale 27299, lot 416	1,600

Pattern Anna – 1821

4.3

The arms of the Company surrounded by the legend: EAST INDIA COMPANY 1821 On the ribbon is the motto: AUSPICIO REGIS & SENATUS ANGLIAE All within a raised toothed rim	Balanced scales with Persian legend between the pans (translation = 'adil = justice). AH date in Arabic figures below (=1231). عدل The value above: ANNA All within a raised toothed rim.

Actual Weight (g)	25.9-26.3
Actual Diameter (mm)	35
Metal	Copper
Edge	Plain

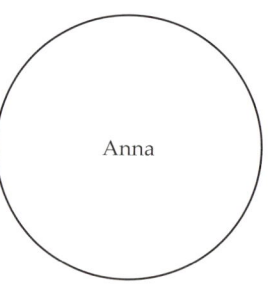

Anna

Catalogue

Cat No.	Pr. No.	Date	Comments	Value ($)
4.3	-	1821	Ref: Bonhams (1997), sale 27299, lot 413	4,000

Pattern Half Anna – 1821 – Type 1

Value HALF ANNA

4.4

The arms of the Company surrounded by the legend: EAST INDIA COMPANY 1821 On the ribbon is the motto: AUSPICIO REGIS & SENATUS ANGLIAE All within a raised toothed rim	Balanced scales with Persian legend between the pans (translation = 'a*dil* = justice). 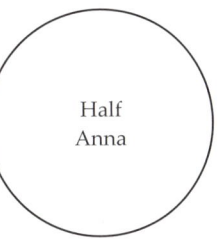 AH date in Arabic figures below (=1231). The value above: HALF ANNA All within a raised toothed rim.

Actual Weight (g)	12.77
Actual Diameter (mm)	30.0-30.1
Metal	Copper
Edge	Plain

Half Anna

Catalogue

Cat No.	Pr. No.	Date	Comments	Value ($)
4.4	334	1821		2,000

259

Pattern Half Anna – 1821 – Type 2

Value ONE HALF ANNA

4.5

The arms of the Company surrounded by the legend:
EAST INDIA COMPANY 1821
On the ribbon is the motto:
AUSPICIO REGIS & SENATUS ANGLIAE
All within a raised toothed rim

Balanced scales with Persian legend between the pans (translation = 'a*dil* = justice).

عدل

AH date in Arabic figures below (=1231). The value above:
ONE HALF ANNA
All within a raised toothed rim.

Actual Weight (g)	12.77
Actual Diameter (mm)	30.0-30.1
Metal	Copper
Edge	Plain

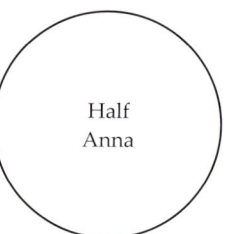

Half Anna

Catalogue

Cat No.	Pr. No.	Date	Comments	Value ($)
4.5	-	1821	Ref: Pridmore sale, lot 560	3,000

Pattern Quarter Anna – 1821

Value on reverse: ONE QR ANNA

4.6

The arms of the Company surrounded by the legend:
EAST INDIA COMPANY 1821
On the ribbon is the motto:
AUSPICIO REGIS & SENATUS ANGLIAE
All within a raised toothed rim

Balanced scales with Persian legend between the pans (translation = 'adil = justice).

عدل

The value above:
ONE Qr ANNA
AH date in Arabic figures below (=1231).
All within a raised toothed rim.

Actual Weight (g)	6.22
Actual Diameter (mm)	26.1-26.3
Metal	Copper
Edge	Plain

Quarter Anna

Catalogue

Cat No.	Pr. No.	Date	Comments	Value ($)
4.6	335	1821		3,000

Pattern Pie – 1821

Value on reverse: PIE

4.7

The arms of the Company surrounded by the legend:
EAST INDIA COMPANY 1821
On the ribbon is the motto:
AUSPICIO REGIS & SENATUS ANGLIAE
All within a raised toothed rim

Balanced scales with Persian legend between the pans (translation = 'adil = justice).

عدل

AH date in Arabic figures below (=1231).
All within a raised toothed rim.

Actual Weight (g)	2.1-2.2
Actual Diameter (mm)	19
Metal	Copper
Edge	Plain

Pie

Catalogue

Cat No.	Pr. No.	Date	Comments	Value ($)
4.7	-	1821	Ref: Bonhams (1997), sale 27299, lot 418	1,600
4.8	-	1821	Silvered flan. Ref: Bonhams (1997), sale 27299, lot 417. May have been caused by storage in a particular way e.g. an oak cabinet?	1,600

Bombay Presidency Bombay Mint, Introduction of Steam, 1831 to 1844

Summary

After much deliberation the Court of Directors finally decided that the new Bombay mint would be equipped with the machinery that was then installed at the Soho mint in Birmingham. The mint was disassembled, shipped to Bombay, arriving there in 1825. This and the building of the new mint and reassembly of the machinery were overseen by Captain Hawkins, although the work did not go particularly smoothly. The new mint was ready for operations at the end of 1830 but Hawkins fell ill and died early in 1831 before it went into full production. The first coins to be produced were copper quarter annas but enormous difficulties were encountered in getting these copper coins into circulation. Even by 1836 not all of the territories under the Bombay Presidency were using the new copper coins. The major problem was the token nature of the copper coins. They were much lighter than the old coins and deliberately did not contain their intrinsic value of metal[5]. The silver coins proved easier because they were the same weight and style as those already in circulation.

In 1835 the new Uniform Coinage for all of India was introduced and replaced the Bombay silver coinage, although the copper currency of Bombay continued to be minted until the middle of the 1840s

---

[5] Stevens PJE (2114), JONS 221, pp. 37-41

Silver Pattern Mohur – Shah Alam – 46 San. Issued 1833

 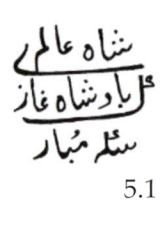

5.1

sikka mubarak badshah ghazi shah alam 1215 (= the auspicious coin of the victorious Emperor Shah Alam. AH 1215)	*zarb surat sanah 46 julus maimanat manus* (= Struck at Surat in the 46th year of tranquil prosperity).

Official Weight (g)	11.66?	
Actual Weight (g)	11.71	
Actual Diameter (mm)	27.7	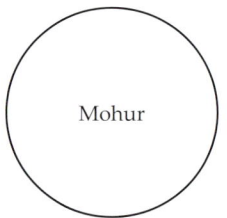
Metal	Silver	Mohur
Edge	SG	

Catalogue

Cat No.	Pr. No.	Axis	Comments	Value ($)
5.1	333	↑↓		2,000

Copper Pattern Mohur 1828

A lion facing left with a
palm tree above.
Obverse B or Reverse II

A star and garter with the
legend and date
Obverse A

*zarb surat sanah [RY] julus
maimanat manus* (= Struck
at Surat in the [RY] year
of tranquil prosperity).
Reverse I

Actual Weight (g)	6.54-9.51
Actual Diameter (mm)	27.1-27.3
Metal	Copper
Edge	Plain

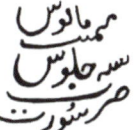

Pattern
Mohur

Catalogue

Cat No.	Pr. No.	Obv	Rev	Comments	Value ($)
5.2	336	A	II	Lion & garter. Thick flan. Wt = 8.93-9.51. Brand sale part 9, lot 182 & 183 (8.96g, 8.99g). Spink Taisei, sale 9, lot 627 & 628 (8.98g, 9.01g).	800
5.3	-	A	II	Lion & garter. Thin flan. Wt = 6.54-6.78. Pr. sale, lot 561 (6.54). Bob Johnston (6.78g).	1,000
5.4	337	A	I		1,000
5.5	338	B	I		1,000

Pattern Mohur 1828 (cont)

Obverse Varieties

Obverse A

Obverse B

Reverse Varieties

Reverse I

Reverse II

Pattern Rupee *et infra* 1832

5.6

sikka mubarak badshah ghazi shah alam 1215 (= The auspicious coin of the victorious Emperor Shah Alam, AH 1215)

zarb surat sanah 46 julus maimanat manus (= Struck at Surat in the 46th year of tranquil prosperity).

Pattern Rupee *et infra* 1832

	Rupee	Half Rupee
Official Weight (g)	11.66	5.83
Actual Weight (g)	11.66	?
Actual Diameter (mm)	~27	~23
Metal	Silver	
Edge	Plain	

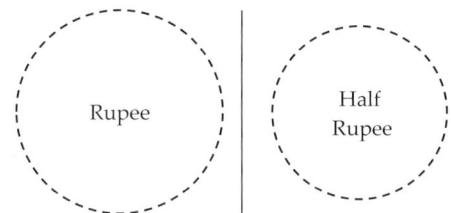

Catalogue

Cat No.	Pr. No.	Status	Comments	Value ($)
5.6	332	Pattern Rupee	Minor differences in ornamentation compared to currency issues	1,500
5.7	-	Pattern Half Rupee	Ref: Pridmore sale lot 559.	1,200

Rupee *et infra* – Shah Alam – 1832 to 1835

5.8

sikka mubarak badshah ghazi shah alam 1215 (= The auspicious coin of the victorious Emperor Shah Alam, AH 1215)

zarb surat sanah 46 julus maimanat manus (= Struck at Surat in the 46th year of tranquil prosperity).

Rupee & half have slightly different dot patterns

Rupee *et infra* – Shah Alam – 1832 to 1835 (cont)

	Rupee	Half Rupee	Quarter Rupee
Official Weight (g)	11.66	5.83	2.91
Actual Weight (g)	11.60-11.62	5.81-5.82	2.89-2.93
Actual Diameter (mm)	27.7-27.8	22.7	17.5-17.6
Metal	Silver		
Edge	Plain		
Axis	↑↓		

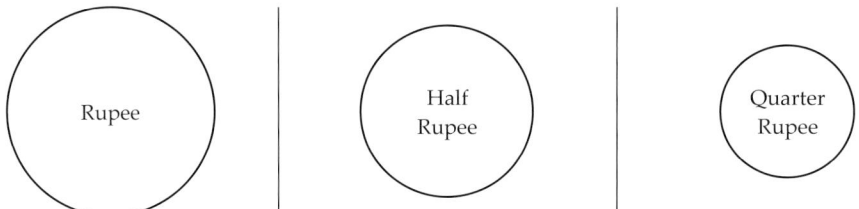

Catalogue

Cat No.	Pr. No.	Denomination	Status	Comments	Value ($)
5.8	286	Rupee	Currency		100
5.9	286	"	Currency	Axis ↑↑. Ref: Rajesh Jagtiani.	100
5.10	287	"	Proof		1,000
5.11	288	Half Rupee	Currency		90
5.12	289	"	Proof		800
5.13	290	Quarter Rupee	Currency		80
5.14	291	"	Proof		600

Half Anna *et infra* – 1830 to 1833

5.15

The arms of the Company surrounded by the legend: EAST INDIA COMPANY (date) On the ribbon is the motto: AUSP:REGIS & SENAT:ANGLIAE All within a plain raised rim.

Balanced scales with Persian legend between the pans (translation = *Adil* = justice).

عدل

The value above. AH date (1246) in Arabic figures below. All within a raised toothed rim.

	Half Anna	Quarter Anna	Twelfth Anna
Official Weight (g)	12.95	6.97	2.16
Actual Weight (g)	12.72	6.27-6.58	2.09-2.16
Actual Diameter (mm)	30.4-30.5	25.0-25.6	17.6-17.7
Metal	Copper		
Edge	Plain		

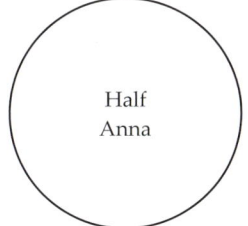

Half Anna

Quarter Anna

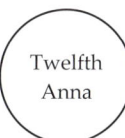

Twelfth Anna

Half Anna *et infra* – 1830 to 1833 (cont)

Catalogue

Cat No.	Pr. No.	Denomination	AD	AH	Status	Axis	Comments	Value ($)
5.15	204	Half Anna	1832	1246	Proof	↑↓	Pr states proof only but Weir claims that some circulated pieces exist (see Baldwin (2013), sale 82 (Fore), lot 932)	1,000
5.16	205	Quarter Anna	1830	1246	Currency	Varies. Mostly ↑↓	There are various varieties of the quarter anna: Different size letters in *Adil*, plain and beaded lines to ropes holding pans, pivot of the scales may be plain or have horizontal lines (R. Weir)	60
5.17	206	"	1830	1246	Proof	↑↓		500
5.18	-	"			Pattern?		Smaller scales. Ref: Puddester. Not seen by author.	1,000
5.19	207	"	1832	1246	Currency	Varies. Mostly ↑↓		60
5.20	208	"	1832	1247	Currency	↑↓		60
5.21	209	"	-	1246	Mule		Double reverse	500
5.22	210	Twelfth Anna	1830	1246	Proof	↑↓	Ref: Johnston	250
5.23	211	"	1831	1246	Currency	↑↓		50
5.24	212	"	1831	1246	Proof			250

Quarter anna double reverse mule

Half Anna – 1833 to 1844

5.26

The arms of the Company surrounded by the legend:
EAST INDIA COMPANY 1834
On the ribbon is the motto:
AUSP:REG & SEN:ANG:
All within a plain raised rim.

Balanced scales with the Persian legend between the pans (translation = *Adil* = justice).

عدل

The value above:
HALF ANNA
AH date (1249) in Arabic figures below.
All within a plain raised rim.

Official Weight (g)	12.95
Actual Weight (g)	12.82-13.10
Actual Diameter (mm)	29.5-29.6
Metal	Copper
Edge	Plain

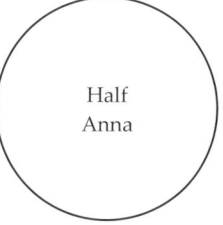

Half Anna

Catalogue

Cat No.	Pr. No.	AD	AH	Status	Rev	Axis	Comments	Value ($)
5.25	213	1834	1249	Currency	I	↑↓		60
5.26	214	"	"	Proof	I	↑↑	The Calcutta proofs are larger (30.9mm) with broad rims	500
5.27	214	"	"	Proof	I	↑↓	The Bombay proofs are 29.6mm with narrow rims	500
5.28	-	"	"	Gilt Proof	I	↑↓	Ref: Johnston but some doubt about authenticity	800
5.29	215	"	"	Silver Proof	I			1,000
5.30	216	"	"	Currency	II	↑↓		60
5.31	217	"	"	Currency	III	↑↓		60

Half Anna – 1833 to 1844

Reverse Varieties

Size of letters	The letters may be different heights. One way of identifying these differences is the position of the letters relative to the scales. Rev I the H & A are inside the top of the scales; Rev II the H & A are outside the top of the scales. Rev III H & A are well above the top of the scales..

	I	II	III
Size of letters	1.8mm	2.2mm	1.2mm

| *I – Letters 1.8mm* | *II - Letters 2.2mm* | *III – Letters 1.2mm* |

Quarter Anna – 1833 to 1844

5.34

The arms of the Company.
On the ribbon is the motto:
AUSP:REG & SEN:ANG:
All within a plain raised rim.

Balanced scales with Persian legend between
the pans (translation = *Adil* = justice).

The value above:
QUARTER ANNA
AH date in Arabic figures below (=1249). All
within a raised toothed rim.

Quarter Anna – 1833 to 1844 (cont)

Official Weight (g)	6.47
Actual Weight (g)	6.36-6.62
Actual Diameter (mm)	24.9-25.5
Metal	Copper
Edge	Plain

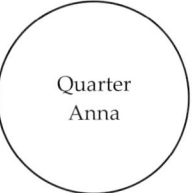

Quarter Anna

Catalogue

Cat No.	Pr. No.	AD	AH	Status	Obv	Rev	Axis	Comments	Value ($)
5.32	217A	1833	1247	Currency Mule	B	I		Pr. states this is a pattern with a small shield but The Pr lot 502 & Fore lot 1908 appear to be straight-forwards currency mules..	500
5.33	218	"	1249	Currency	A	II	↑↓		50
5.34	219	"	"	Proof	A	II	↑↑	26.0mm. Broad rims	500
5.35	-	"	"	Gilt Proof	A	II	↑↓	Ref: Johnston. Some doubt about authenticity	800
5.36	219	"	"	Proof	A	III	↑↓	25.1mm. Narrow rims	500
5.37	220	"	"	Currency	B	IV	↑↓		50
5.38	221	1832	"	Currency	C	IV			400

Different size letters in *adil*, and differences in the pivot of the scales have also been observed but are not recorded.

Obverse Varieties

Base of Lion	The base under the lion above the shield may be plain or beaded
Design	May be as 1830-1833 issue

	A	B	C
Base of Lion	Beaded	Plain	-
Design	Normal	Normal	As previous issue

Quarter Anna – 1833 to 1844 (cont)

Lion with plain base

Lion with beaded base

Normal design

Design from previous issue

Reverse Varieties

Size of letters	The letters may be different heights described herein as medium or large.
Length of Ropes	The length of the ropes, from which the pans of the scales hang, may be long (6.7mm) or short (6.0mm)
Design	May be as 1830-1832 issue

	I	II	III	IV
Size of letters	-	Large 1.6mm	Medium 1.3mm	Medium 1.3mm
Length of Ropes	-	Long 6.7mm	Short 6.0mm	Long 6.7mm
Design	As previous issue	Normal	Normal	Normal

Quarter Anna – 1833 to 1844 (cont)

Rev I – Design from previous issue

Rev II. Large letters, long ropes

N.B. Different AH date on the designs

Rev III. Medium letters, short ropes

Rev IV. Medium letters, long ropes

Twelfth Anna – 1833 to 1844

5.39

The arms of the Company. On the ribbon is the legend:
AUSP:REG & SEN:ANG:
All within a plain raised rim.

Balanced scales with Persian legend between the pans (translation = *Adil* = justice).

The value above:
PIE
AH date (1248) in Arabic figures below. All within a plain raised rim.

Official Weight (g)	2.16
Actual Weight (g)	1.91-2.17
Actual Diameter (mm)	17.8-18.0
Metal	Copper
Edge	Plain

Twelfth Anna

Catalogue

Cat No.	Pr. No.	AD	AH	Status	Obv	Rev	Axis	Comments	Value ($)
5.39	222	1833	1248	Currency	A	I	↑↓	Large PIE	40
5.40	223	"	"	Proof	A	I		18.7mm. Broad rim. Pr sale lot 498. Large PIE	250
5.41	224	"	"	Currency	A	II		Small PIE	40
5.42	-	"	"	Proof	A	II	↑↓	Small PIE	250
5.43	225	"	1246	Mule	A	III	↑↓	Small PIE	300
5.44	226	1831	1248	Mule	C	II	↑↓	Small PIE	300

Twelfth Anna – 1833 to 1844 (cont)

Obverse Varieties

Design	The design may be of this coinage or the previous coinage

	A	B
Design	This coinage	Previous coinage

This coinage	*Previous coinage*

Reverse Varieties

Design	The design may be of this coinage or the previous coinage
Size of Letters	The letters spelling the value may be large (1.3mm) or small (1.0mm).

	I	II	III
Design	This coinage	This coinage	Previous coinage
Size of Letters	1.3	1.0	-

Letters 1.3mm	*Letters 1.0mm*

This coinage	*Previous coinage*

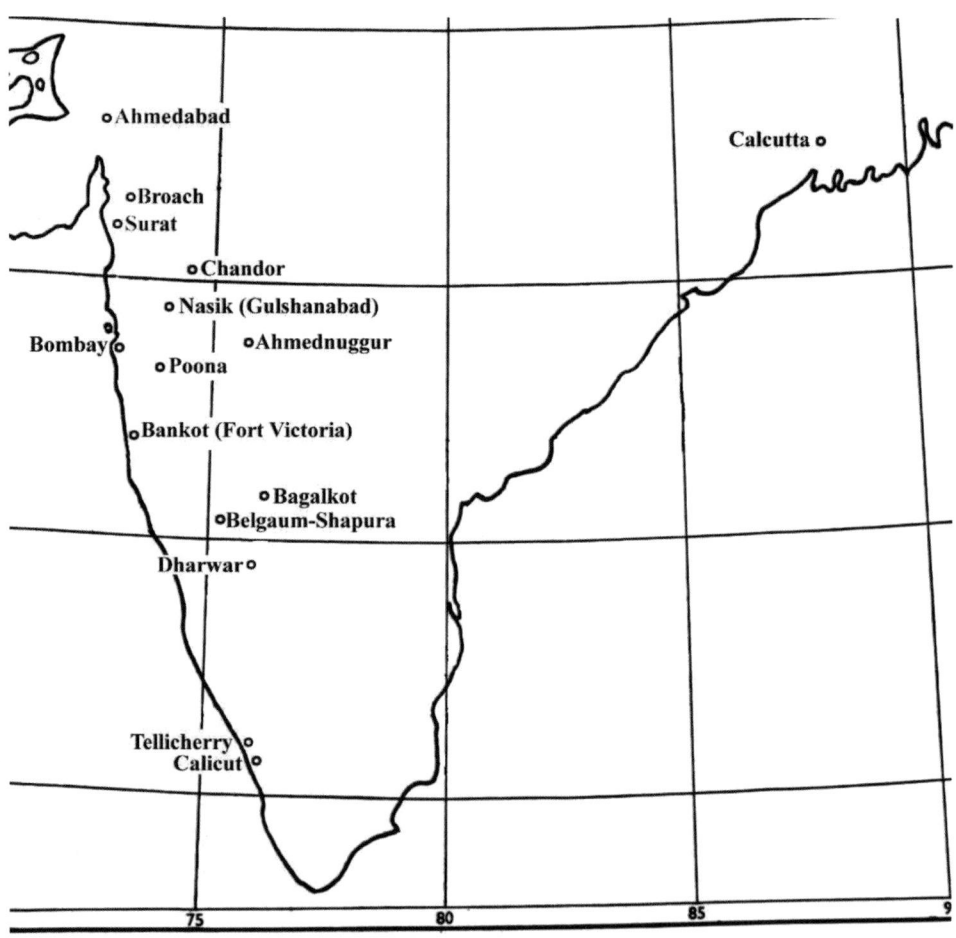

Bombay Presidency Transitional & Local Mints

Summary

As the British extended their control of India during the late eighteenth and early nineteenth centuries, a number of areas that had active mints fell under their management. Some of these mints were kept in operation for a number of years after they were taken over by the British.

Inland from Bombay was the area known as the Deccan, with the mints of Poona, Nasik/Chandore and Ahmadnuggur, which were all acquired in 1817/1818. To the north lay the mints of Surat, Ahmadabad and Broach and to the south were the mints of the "Southern Maratha Country", Bagalkot and Belgaum-Shahpur. Bankot, though not strictly a 'transitional' mint, is included here because it behaved as a local mint.

The records are not completely clear about the operations of these mints, but what archival evidence does exist can be combined with knowledge of the coins themselves to produce a much clearer picture than has hitherto been seen[6].

---

[6] Stevens P.J.E., JONS No. 179, pp. 28-32.
Stevens P.J.E., JONS No. 180 p. 27-31.
Stevens P.J.E., JONS No. 181 p. 24-30.
Stevens P.J.E., JONS No. 182 pp. 25-32.
Stevens P.J.E., JONS No. 183 pp. 20-22.

Ahmadabad Mint – Gold Fractional (Third?) Mohur

These gold coins came onto the market in the early 2000s and appear to be cut from a necklace.

 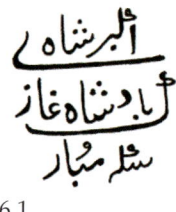  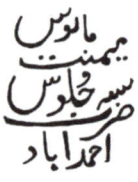

6.1

sikka mubārak bādshāh ghāzī akbar shāh [AH date] (= The auspicious coin of the victorious Emperor Muhammad Akbar Shah [AH date])

zarb ahmadabad sanah [RY] julūs maimanat mānūs (= Struck at Ahmadabad in his [RY] year of tranquil prosperity)

⅓ Mohur

Actual Weight (g)	3.00-3.07
Actual Diameter (mm)	14.2-15.5
Metal	Gold

Catalogue

Cat No.	AH	RY	Comments	Value ($)
6.1	[1]249	?	Ref: HK/Singapore (2002), sale 35, lot 732. Also Baldwin (2003), sale 33, lot 1025, also others	1,000

Ahmadabad Mint – Silver Rupee *et infra*

Ma. Refers to Masters (1914), Numismatic Supplement No. XXII, pp. 153-173

  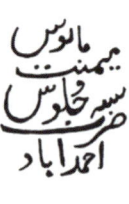

6.9

sikka mubārak bādshāh ghāzī akbar shāh [AH date] (= the auspicious coin of the victorious Emperor Muhammad Akbar Shah [AH date])

zarb ahmadabad sanah [RY] julūs maimanat mānūs (= Struck at Ahmadabad in his [RY] year of tranquil prosperity)

Ahmadabad Mint – Silver Rupee *et infra* (cont)					
	Double Rupee	**Rupee**	**Half Rupee**	**¼ Rupee**	**⅛ Rupee**
Actual Weight (g)	~22	11.38-11.78	5.69-5.87	2.83-2.87	1.44-1.46
Actual Diameter (mm)	~28	20.6-24.8	17.0-19.7	14.4-15.7	12.5-13.9
Metal	Silver				

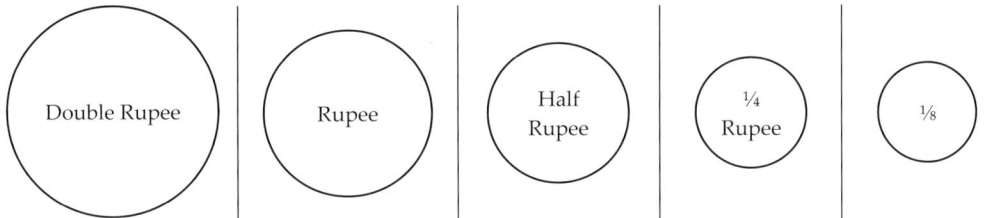

Catalogue

Cat No.	Ma. No.	Denom	Obv	AH	RY	Comments	Value ($)
6.2	-	Double Rupee	A	1231?	?	Ref: Bhandare. Has been mounted. Extremely rare	NV
6.3	-	Rupee	A	1231	15	Full Flan strike on copper. Flattened on obverse. 16.16g, 30.0-31.3mm	800
6.4	51	"	A	123[3]	11		70
6.5	53	"	A	1233	12	Baldwin (2001), sale 25 (Wiggins), lot 742	70
6.6	-	"	A	1234	12	Ref: Johnston	70
6.7	54		A	1236	13	Ref: Johnston	70
6.8	56	"	A	1239	15	Baldwin (2001), sale 25 (Wiggins), lot 742. BM	70
6.9	57	"	A	1241	16	Ref: BM	70
6.10	59	"	B	1242	22	Ref: BM	70
6.11	61	"	B	1243	2x		70
6.12	63	"	B	1244	24	Ref: Johnston	70
6.13	65	"	B	1248	28		70
6.14	67	"	B	1249	xx		70
6.15	-	"	B	1249	xx	Retrograde 9 in AH date.	70
6.16	-	"	B	1249/p	29	Last digit 9 over retrograde 9 in AH date. ANS1988.81.56	70

Variety A coins with full AH date and variety B coins with full RY are rare

Listing continued on next page

	Ahmadabad Mint – Silver Rupee *et infra* (cont)

Catalogue

Cat No.	Ma. No.	Denomination	Obv	AH	RY	Comments	Value ($)
6.17	52	Half Rupee	A	xxxx	11		90
6.18	-	"	A	123x	12		90
6.19	55	"	A?	12xx	13	Ref: BM	90
6.20	-	"	A	xxxx	15	Ref: Baldwin (2013), sale 84 (Fore), lot 1962	90
6.21	58	"	A?	12xx	16		90
6.22	60	"	B	1242	xx		90
6.23	62	"	B	1243	xx	Baldwin (2001), sale 25 (Wiggins), lot 742	90
6.24	64	"	B	1244	xx		90
6.25	66	"	B	1248	xx	Mitchiner 1764	90
6.26	68	"	B	1249	xx	Ref: BM	90
6.27	-	Quarter Rupee	A	xxxx	11	Ref: Todywalla (2009), sale 36, lot 232. Wt not given and there is some doubt about whether this is a half or a quarter.	150
6.28	-	"	A	xxxx	12		150
6.29	-	"	B	1243		Ref: Wiggins	150
6.30	-	"	B	1249		Ref: Johnston	150
6.31	-	Eighth Rupee	B	1244	xx	Baldwin (2001), sale 25 (Wiggins), lot 745	200
6.32	-	"	B	1248	xx	Ref: Stevens	200

Obverse Varieties

Date	The date may occur above or below the top line on the obverse

	A	B
Date	Above & right	Below & left

A – date above & right   *B – date below & left*   *Full flan strike on copper*

Ahmadabad Mint – Copper Single and Half Pice

Pice dated 1232 were issued by the Maratha authorities. These coins have a trisul mark in the *seen* of *julus* instead of the flower mark on the EIC coins.

6.34

Akbar Shah fulus [AH] (= falus of Akbar Shah [AH])

Ahmadabad [RY] julus (= [struck at] Ahmadabad in the [RY] year)

	Pice	Half Pice
Actual Weight (g)	7.33-7.84	3.72-3.79
Actual Diameter (mm)	18.8-22.9	15.2-16.6
Metal	Copper	

Pice Half Pice

Catalogue

Cat No.	Ma. No.	Denom	AH	RY	Comments	Value ($)
6.33	-	Pice	1233	12	Ref: Baldwin (2001), sale 25 (Wiggins), lot 742	50
6.34	53b	"	1234	12	Ref: Baldwin (2001), sale 25 (Wiggins), lot 742	50
6.35	53c	"	1234	13	Ref: Noble (1995), sale 48, lot 2170	50
6.36	53d	"	1235	1[4]	Ref: Noble (1995), sale 48, lot 2170	50
6.37	53e	"	1236	14	Ref: Noble (1995), sale 48, lot 2170	50
6.38	53a	Half Pice	1233	12	Ref: BM. Also called pai (pie) by Masters	70
6.39	-	"	1234	xx	Ref: ANS 1921.54.1388	70
6.40		"	1235	14	Ref: Piyush Khaitan	70
6.41		"	1236	14	Ref: GP Taylor JBBRAS Vol XX. Also sold on eBay in July 2005	70

Ahmadnagar Mint – Pattern for Rupee

Only the rupee is known to exist.. See Gupta P.L. An Unknown Rupee Pattern of East India Company. Numismatic Digest Vol.1, part II, 1977.

1820
सरकार
कपनी अगरेज
बाहादुर सन
१२२०

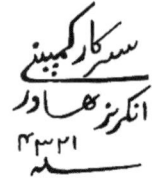

The date, 1820, above a Nagari inscription surrounded by the legend THE HONBLE EAST INDIA COMPANY. *Sarkar/Kampany Angrez/Bahadur San/1220* [or, more probably, 1221] (= The Honourable English Company)

A Persian inscription surrounded by the legend BRITISH INDIA DECCAN ONE RUPEE. *Sarkar Kampany/Angrez Bahadur/4321 Sanah* (= The Honourable English Company)

Actual Weight (g)	?
Actual Diameter (mm)	~27
Metal	Copper

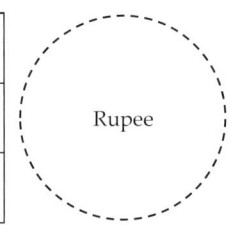

Rupee

Catalogue

Cat No.	Denomination	AH	AD	Comments	Value ($)
6.42	Rupee	1234	1820 or 1821	Only known specimen in Prince of Wales Museum, Bombay.	NV

Ahmadnagar – Pattern for Pice

No Photo available

Catalogue

Cat No.	Denomination	AH	Comments	Value ($)
5.43	Pice	?	No known existing specimen but mentioned in the EIC records[7]	NV

---

[7] Stevens PJE, (2004), ONSNL vol 181, pp. 24-30

Bagalkot Mint – Single & Half Rupee

6.44

The date 1819 with a Persian Inscription: *sikka mubarak taban mihr-o-mah azizuddin shah alam ghazi badshah* (= Struck the auspicious coin shining like sun and moon. Aziz-ud-din Shah Alam, the Warrior and Emperor)

zarb dār al-khilāfa shāhjahānābād bagadkut sanah julūs [RY] maimanat mānūs (= Struck at Bagalkot in the [RY] reign of tranquil prosperity)

	Rupee	Half Rupee
Actual Weight (g)	11.05-11.10	5.48
Actual Diameter (mm)	20.1-21.5	16.8-17.6
Metal	Silver	

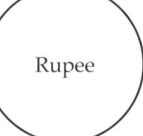

Rupee

Half Rupee

Catalogue

Cat No.	Pr. No.	Denomination	AD	Comments	Value ($)
6.44	-	Rupee	1819		150
6.45	-	Half Rupee	1819	Baldwin (2001), sale 25 (Wiggins), lot 743	750

Half Rupee

Bankot Mint – Half Anna, Pice and Half Pice – 1820 to 1821

पैसा

6.49

Balemark with date below. All within a toothed border.	Balanced scales with Hindi inscription (= *Paisa* = Pice, or other values) between the pans. The date below in Devanagiri script. All within a toothed border.

	Half Anna	Pice	Half Pice
Official Weight (g)	15.06	7.53	3.76
Actual Weight (g)	14.0-15.33	7.2-8.85	3.65-3.93
Actual Diameter (mm)	21.2-23.5	18.9-22.0	15.3-17.7
Metal	Copper		

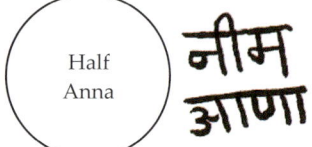 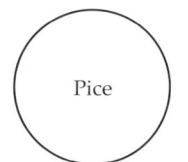 

Half Anna   नीम आणा   Pice   Half Pice   अर्धा पैसा

Catalogue

Cat No.	Pr. No.	Denomination	Date	Comments	Value ($)
6.46	322	Half Anna	1820		1000
6.47	323	"	1821		200
6.48	-	"	1821	Transposed E in balemark	300
6.49	324	Pice	1820		1500
6.50	325	"	1821		150
6.51	326	Half Pice	1820		1000
6.52	327	"	1821		100
6.53	-	"	"	Mule 1820 obv/1821 rev. Ref: Noble (1995), sale 48, lot 2121	NV

Transposed letter E

Belgaum-Shahpur Mint – Rupee – 1821

MW = Maheshwari & Wiggins (1989), Maratha Mints and Coinage, IIRNS, Nasik

6.54

The date, 1821, with a Persian inscription: *sikka zad dar jahan balutf-I-ilah badshah zaman muhammad shah* (= Struck coin in the world by favour of God, Muhammad Shah, Emperor of the Age)

zarb azamnagar bagadkut sanah julūs maimanat mānūs (= Struck at Azamnagar in the [RY] reign of tranquil prosperity)

	Rupee	Half Rupee	Quarter Rupee
Actual Weight (g)	11.21	5.45	2.77
Actual Diameter (mm)	20.3-20.9	~15	~14
Metal	Silver		

Rupee

Half Rupee

¼ Rupee

Half rupee   *Quarter rupee*

Catalogue

Cat No.	MW	Denomination	AD	Comments	Value ($)
6.54	T3	Rupee	1821	Baldwin (2001), sale 25 (Wiggins), lot 743.	120
6.55	T3	Half Rupee	1821	Recorded from Maheshwari & Wiggins	NV
6.56	-	Quarter Rupee		Ref: Album (2009), auction 7, lot 628	750

Bhakkar Mint – Silver Rupee – Lion & Hare Type

Bhakkar came into the possession of the EIC in 1842 (AH 1258)

6.57

mahmud shah (Durrani) surrounded by a Persian inscription. Hare above	*zarb bhakkar sanah [RY] julus maimanat manus* (= struck at Bhakkar in the [RY] year of tranquil prosperity) A lion in the *seen* of *julus*

Actual Weight (g)	9.59-9.97	
Actual Diameter (mm)	19.5-21.8	Rupee
Metal	Silver	

Catalogue

Cat No.	KM	AH	Comments	Value ($)
6.57	C11	1259		70
6.58	"	1260	Ref: SACG. Photo posted by Jim Farr	100
6.59	"	1261		70

Rupee dated AH 1261

Bhakkar Mint – Rupee – Floral Type

6.66

mahmud shah (Durrani) surrounded by a Persian inscription

zarb bhakkar sanah [RY] julus maimanat manus (= struck at Bhakkar in the [RY] year of tranquil prosperity) various floral designs in the legend

Actual Weight (g)	9.73-9.92
Actual Diameter (mm)	18.7-21.8
Metal	Silver

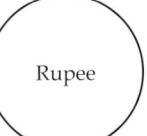

Rupee

Catalogue

Cat No.	KM	AH	Comments	Value ($)
6.60	C12	1262		60
6.61	"	1264		60
6.62	"	1265		60
6.63	"	1266		60
6.64	"	1267		60
6.65	"	1268		60
6.66	"	1269		60

Rupee dated AH 1264

Bhakkar Mint – Rupee – Hare and Peacock Type

6.67

 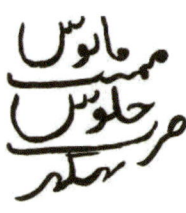

mahmud shah (Durrani) surrounded by a Persian inscription	*zarb bhakkar sanah [RY] julus maimanat manus* (= struck at Bhakkar in the [RY] year of tranquil prosperity)
The head of a hare at top right	Peacock facing right in *seen* of *julus*. Looks like a snake in front of the peacock

Actual Weight (g)	9.87	
Actual Diameter (mm)	19.5-20.5	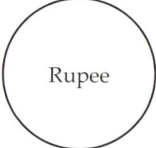 Rupee
Metal	Silver	

Catalogue

Cat No.	KM	AH	Comments	Value ($)
6.67	C13	1259		100

Broach Mint – Silver Single & Half Rupee

See Baldwin (2001), sale 25 (Wiggins), lot 110. Some of those are described as EIC coins. Identified by the cross but distinguishing between EIC coins and those produced by other authorities is very difficult, if not impossible.

  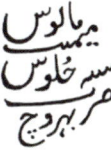

6.68

sikka mubarak bdshah ghazi shah alam (= The auspicious coin of the victorious Emperor Shah Alam)

zarb broach sanah [RY] julus maimanat manus (= Struck at Broach in his [RY] year of tranquil prosperity)

	Rupee	Half Rupee
Actual Weight (g)	11.36-11.52	5.62-5.72
Actual Diameter (mm)	19.5-20.6	15.8-17.0
Metal	Silver	

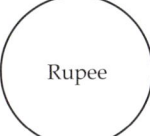 

Catalogue

Cat No.	Pr. No.	Denom	AH	RY	Comments	Value ($)
6.68	-	Rupee	xxxx	22	ONS Newsletter No. 132, Feb-Apr 1992, which refers to a list issued by Stephen Album in which this coin appears	150
6.69	-	Half Rupee	xxxx	xx	Ref: KM A36.	100

Broach Mint – Early? Copper Pice

See Baldwin (2001), sale 25 (Wiggins), lot 110. Some of those are described as EIC coins. Identified by cross.

6.70
Undetermined Legend

Undetermined legend with the cross of St Thomas prominently displayed

Actual Weight (g)	6.94
Actual Diameter (mm)	16.4-17.4
Metal	Copper

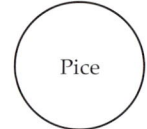

Pice

Catalogue

Cat No.	Pr. No.	Comments	Value ($)
6.70	-	Issued 1803 to 1806	50

Broach Mint – Later Copper Pice

6.71

Balemark of the EIC

Balemark of the EIC

Actual Weight (g)	10.23-10.50
Actual Diameter (mm)	18.6-19.8
Metal	Copper

Pice

Catalogue

Cat No.	Pr. No.	Comments	Value ($)
6.71	300	Issued first quarter of 19th century There is a possibility that a half pice denomination of this coin was issued. Todywalla sale 26, lot 244 appears to show a pice with a smaller coin with the same design. No weight or diameter is given so this must remain speculation for the moment. My thanks to Bob Johnston.	250
6.72	–	Overstruck on copper coins of Baroda	250

Over-struck on coins of Baroda. (Photos from Jan Lingen)

Chandore Mint – Silver Rupee

The type of rupee issued from the Chandore mint by the British is not known. The coin illustrated below is a possible candidate (from Jan Lingen)

 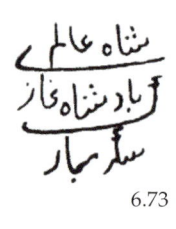  

6.73

sicca mubarak shah alam badshah ghazi (= The auspicious coin of the victorious Emperor Shah Alam)

zarb Ja'afarabad urf chandor. sanah [RY] julus maimanat manus (= struck at Chandor In the [RY] year of tranquil prosperity)

Actual Weight (g)	?	
Actual Diameter (mm)	~21	
Metal	Silver	

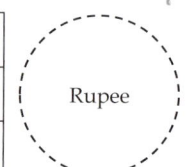

Rupee

Catalogue

Cat No.	AH	RY	Comments	Value ($)
6.73	XXXX	XX		NV

294

Dharwar Mint – Pagoda?

Coins appear to have been struck at Dharwar under the authority of the British, but they have not yet been identified. They may well have been gold pagodas[8].

Catalogue

Cat No.	Date	Comments	Value ($)
6.74	-	Not sure what coins were issued from Dharwar under British control	NV

---

[8] Stevens PJE, (2005), ONSNL 183, pp. 20-22

Bandar Dholara Mint – Copper Pice

 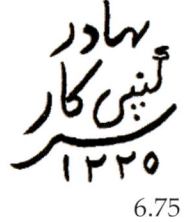  

6.75

sarkar kampani bahadur [AD] (= Honourable Company. [AD]). Coins dated 1226 have a slightly different arrangement with the date at the top of the legend

zarb bandar dholarah (= struck at Bandar Dholarah)

Actual Weight (g)	7.68-9.51
Actual Diameter (mm)	19.7-21.8
Metal	Copper

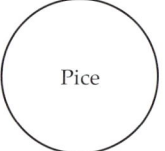

Pice

Catalogue

Cat No.	Pr. No.	AH	AD	Comments	Value ($)
6.75	-	1225	1810/11		150
6.76	-	1226	1811/12		150

Pice 1226

Jambusir Mint – Silver Rupee *et infra*

 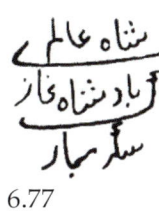

6.77

sicca mubarak shah alam badshah ghazi (=
The auspicious coin of the victorious
Emperor Shah Alam)

*zarb jambusir sanah [RY] julus maimanat
manus* (= Struck at Jambusir in his [RY]
year of tranquil prosperity)
NB mace symbol in *seen* of *julus*

	Rupee	Half Rupee
Actual Weight (g)	11.60	5.82
Actual Diameter (mm)	20.6-21.3	~18
Metal	Silver	

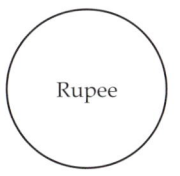

Rupee

Half Rupee

Catalogue

Cat No.	Pr. No.	Denomination	AH	RY	Comments	Value ($)
6.77	-	Rupee	xxxx	22		150
6.78		Half Rupee	xxxx	22		400

Half Rupee

Nasik (Gulshanabad) Mint – Silver Rupee *et infra*

The coins have a distinctive mark of a pennant on the reverse

6.79

sikka mubarak badshah ghazi shah alam (= the auspicious coin of the victorious Emperor Shah Alam).

(zarb gulshanabad) sanah [RY] julus maimanat manus (= struck at Gulshanabad in the [RY] year of tranquil prosperity)

	Rupee	Half Rupee	¼ Rupee	⅛ Rupee
Actual Weight (g)	11.09-11.21	5.7	2.7	1.3
Actual Diameter (mm)	19.8-20.8	~18	~14	~11
Metal	Silver			

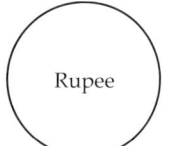   

Rupee   Half Rupee   ¼ Rupee   ⅛

Catalogue

Cat No.	MW	Denomination	Fasli	Comments	Value ($)
6.79	T6a	Rupee	1234		150
6.80	"	"	1235		150
6.81	"	"	1236	See Baldwin (2004), sale 39, lot 2928.	150
6.82	"	"	1237		150
6.83	"	"	1244		150
6.84	"	"	1247		150
6.85	"	"	1248		150
6.86	"	"	1249		150
6.87	"	"	1251	Listed from KM	150
6.88	T6a	Half Rupee	1235		250
6.89	"	"	1236		250
6.90	-	"	1241	Ref: ClassNG (2012), sale 9, lot 931.	250
6.91	T6a	Quarter Rupee	1236		200
6.92	T6a	Eighth Rupee	1236		150

Dates are usually called Hijri but are more likely Fasli

Poona Mint – Silver Rupee – *Ankusi* Type

6.95

sikka mubarak shah ali gauhar badshah ghazi (= The auspicious coin of Shah Ali Gauhar the Emperor and Warrior)

zarb muhiabad pune sanah [RY] julus maimanat manus (= Struck at Poona in his [RY] year of tranquil prosperity)

	Rupee	Half Rupee	Quarter Rupee	Eighth Rupee
Actual Weight (g)	10.99-11.21	5.57-5.64	2.64-2.87	?
Actual Diameter (mm)	19.4-22.0	16.4-17.5	13.5-14.7	13.5
Metal	Silver			

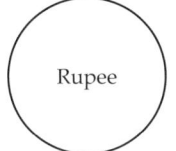 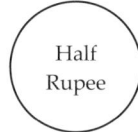 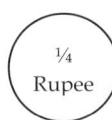 

Rupee   Half Rupee   ¼ Rupee   ⅛

Catalogue

Cat No.	MW	Denomination	Fasli	Comments	Value ($)
6.93	T4b	Rupee	1230		100
6.94	"	"	1231		100
6.95	"	"	1232		100
6.96	"	"	1233		100
6.97	"	"	1234		100
6.98	"	"	1235		100
6.99	"	"	1236		100
6.100	"	"	1237/38	Last numeral 7 over 8	100
6.101	"	"	1238		100
6.102	"	"	1239		100

Listing continued on next page

Poona Mint – Silver Rupee – *Ankusi* Type (cont)

Catalogue

Cat No.	MW	Denomination	Fasli	Comments	Value ($)
6.103	″	Rupee	1240		100
6.104	″	″	1241		100
6.105	″	″	1242		100
6.106	″	″	1243		100
6.107	″	″	1244		100
6.108	T4b	Half Rupee	1232		200
6.109	-	″	1233		200
6.110	-	″	1236		200
6.111	-	″	1240		200
6.112	-	″	1242		200
6.113	-	Quarter Rupee	1233		300
6.114	-	″	1234		300
6.115	T4b	″	1237		300
6.116	″	″	1238		300
6.117	″	″	1241		300
6.119	″	″	1242		300
6.120	″	″	1243		300
6.121	T4b	Eighth Rupee	1233		300

Poona Mint – Silver Rupee *et infra* – *Hali sicca* Type

6.123

sikka mubarak shah ali gauhar badshah ghazi
(= the auspicious coin of Shah Ali
Gauhar the Emperor and Warrior)

*zarb muhiabad pune sanah [RY] julus
maimanat manus* (= Struck at Poona in
his [RY] year of tranquil prosperity)

	Rupee	Half Rupee	Quarter Rupee
Actual Weight (g)	11.07-11.32	5.64	?
Actual Diameter (mm)	21.9-25.1	18.8-19.4	~14
Metal	Silver		

Poona Mint – Silver Rupee *et infra* – *Hali sicca* Type (cont)

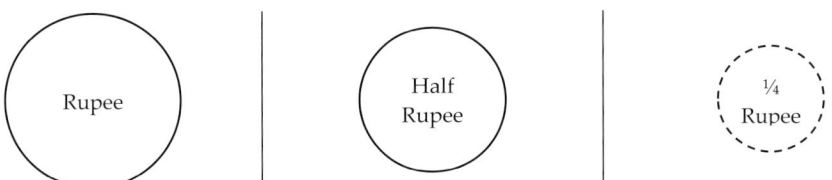

Catalogue

Cat No.	MW	Denomination	Fasli	Comments	Value ($)
6.122	T3a	Rupee	1230		150
6.123	"	"	1231		150
6.124	"	"	1232		150
6.125	"	"	1233		150
6.126	"	"	1234		150
6.127	"	"	1235		150
6.128	"	"	1236		150
6.129	"	"	1237		150
6.130	"	"	1238		150
6.131	"	"	1239		150
6.132	"	"	1240		150
6.133	"	"	1241		150
6.134	"	"	1242		150
6.135	"	"	1243		150
6.136	"	"	1244		150
6.137	T3a	Half Rupee	1233		200
6.138	"	"	1236		200
6.139	T3a	Quarter Rupee	1230		300
6.140	"	"	1238		300

Poona Mint – Copper Pice

Copper pice from the mints of Poona and Satara are indistinguishable[9]

6.145

Shri Raja Siva (= the illustrious king Shiva)

Chhatra Pati (= Lord of the [royal] umbrella)

Actual Weight (g)	9.78-10.01
Actual Diameter (mm)	18.5-20.0
Metal	Copper

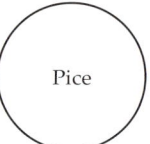

Pice

Catalogue

Cat No.	Fasli	Comments	Value ($)
6.141	1230	Ref: BM	100
6.142	1231	Ref: BM	100
6.143	1232	Ref: BM	100
6.144	1233	Ref: BM	100
6.145	1234	Ref: BM	100
6.146	1235	Ref: BM	100
6.147	1237	Ref: KM old South Asia catalogue No. 192, p. 98	100
6.148	1238	Ref: KM old South Asia catalogue No. 192, p. 98	100
6.149	1239	Ref: BM	100
6.150	1240	Ref: BM	100

---

[9] Bombay Consultations. P/411/50. No. 281 (27th July 1831). Letter from the Junior Principal Collector, Poona, to government, dated 11th July 1831.

Rahimatpur Mint
Half Anna & Pice (Imitations of Bankot Coins) – 1828 to 1829

6.151

Balemark with date below (8281=1828). All within a toothed border.

Balanced scales with the date below.

	Half Anna	Pice
Actual Weight (g)	13.61-14.26	6.78-7.23
Actual Diameter (mm)	21.4-23.3	18.0-22.5
Metal	Copper	

Half Anna

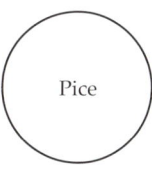

Pice

Catalogue

Cat No.	Pr. No.	Denomination	Date	Comments	Value ($)
6.151	328	Half Anna	1828	Retrograde date on obverse	150
6.152	329	"	1829	No date on obverse	150
6.153	-	Pice	1828	Retrograde date on obverse. Noble (1995), sale 48, lot 2122 also Steve Album sale 18, lot 1820. The photo of the SA coin shows single lines in shield.	300
6.154	-	"	"	Noble (1995), sale 48, lot 2122. The description implies that the date is not retrograde. No photo shown so existence not certain	NV
6.155	330	"	1829	No date on obverse	100

Round pice

Square pice

Pice come in different shapes: round and square

Surat Mint – Gold Mohur *et infra* – Shah Alam – 46 Sun

 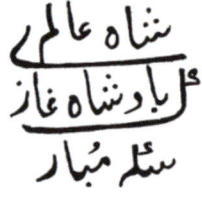  

6.156

sikka mubarak badshah ghazi shah alam (=
the auspicious coin of the victorious
Emperor Shah Alam).

zarb surat sanah 46 julus maimanat manus
(= Struck at Surat in the 46th year of
tranquil prosperity).

	Mohur	Panchia (Third Mohur)	Eighth Mohur	Rupee ($\frac{1}{15}$ Mohur)
Official Weight (g)	11.59	3.86	1.4	0.77
Actual Weight (g)	11.50-11.58	3.85-3.86	1.33 (but has been mounted)	0.60-0.76
Actual Diameter (mm)	17.6-19.1	13.0-14.0	12.3-13.2	7.0-8.0
Metal	Gold			

  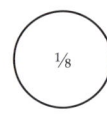

Mohur ⅓ Mohur ⅛ ¹⁄₁₅

Catalogue

Cat No.	Pr. No.	Denomination	Date Issued	Comments	Value ($)
6.156	250	Mohur	1800-1815		800
6.157	251	Panchia	"		900
6.158	-	Eighth mohur	"	Ref: Johnston. The coin looks a bit crude and may be a local imitation	NV
6.159	252	Gold Rupee	"		600

See also Bombay Mint (pp. 244-246)

Privy mark for Surat mint
Four dots to left and 3 diamonds to right

Surat Mint – Silver Rupee *et infra* – Shah Alam – 46 Sun

 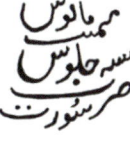

6.163

sikka mubarak badshah ghazi shah alam (= The auspicious coin of the victorious Emperor Shah Alam)

zarb surat sanah 46 julus maimanat manus (= Struck at Surat in the 46th year of tranquil prosperity)

	Rupee	Half Rupee	Quarter Rupee	Eighth Rupee
Official Weight (g)	11.59	5.78	2.89	1.45
Actual Weight (g)	11.53-11.58	5.74-5.79	2.85	1.47
Actual Diameter (mm)	18.4-21.3	16.3-17.7	~15	13.4-14.3
Metal	Silver			

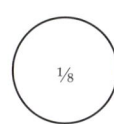

Silver Rupee *et infra* – Shah Alam – 46 Sun (cont)

Only RY 46 can definitely be attributed to the EIC. Surat-type Rupees in the name of Shah 'Alam II with other dates (43, 44, 45, 47, 49, 50, 51, 53) have been known for some time and have proved enigmatic. There have been various suggestions as to who may have issued them ranging from the local Nawab, the French, to the Marathas, while it has been assumed that they were not struck by the East India Company. There has not been any documentary evidence to support any of these possible attributions.

Catalogue

Cat No.	Pr. No.	Denomination	RY	Comments	Value ($)
6.160	-	Rupee	43	No example found but predicted to exist	NV
6.161	-	"	44	Ref: Lingen	150
6.162	-	"	45		150
6.163	253	"	46		80
6.164	-	"	49		80
6.165	-	"	50		80
6.166	-	"	51		80
6.167	-	"	52		80
6.168	-	Half Rupee	44	Ref: Oswal auction (2012), sale 33, lot 305. Mint not visible but probably Surat or Bombay. See comments above	200
6.169	-	"	45	Ref: Johnston. See comments above	200
6.170	254	"	46		70
6.171	-	"	47	Ref: Lingen. See comments above	100
6.172	255	Quarter Rupee	46		80
6.173	256	Eighth Rupee	46		100

See also Bombay Mint (pp. 249-250). A sixteenth of this series may exist

Half rupee

Surat Mint – Copper Pice

Photo from a coin in Ashmolean. Not sure that this is actually the type struck under the EIC.

6.174

fulus badshah shah alam (= fulus of the Emperor Shah Alam)

(zarb) surat sanah [RY] julus (= struck at surat in [RY])

Actual Weight (g)	10.47
Actual Diameter (mm)	25.3
Metal	Copper

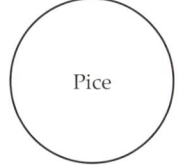

Pice

Catalogue

Cat No.	Pr. No.	Comments	Value ($)
6.174	-		NV

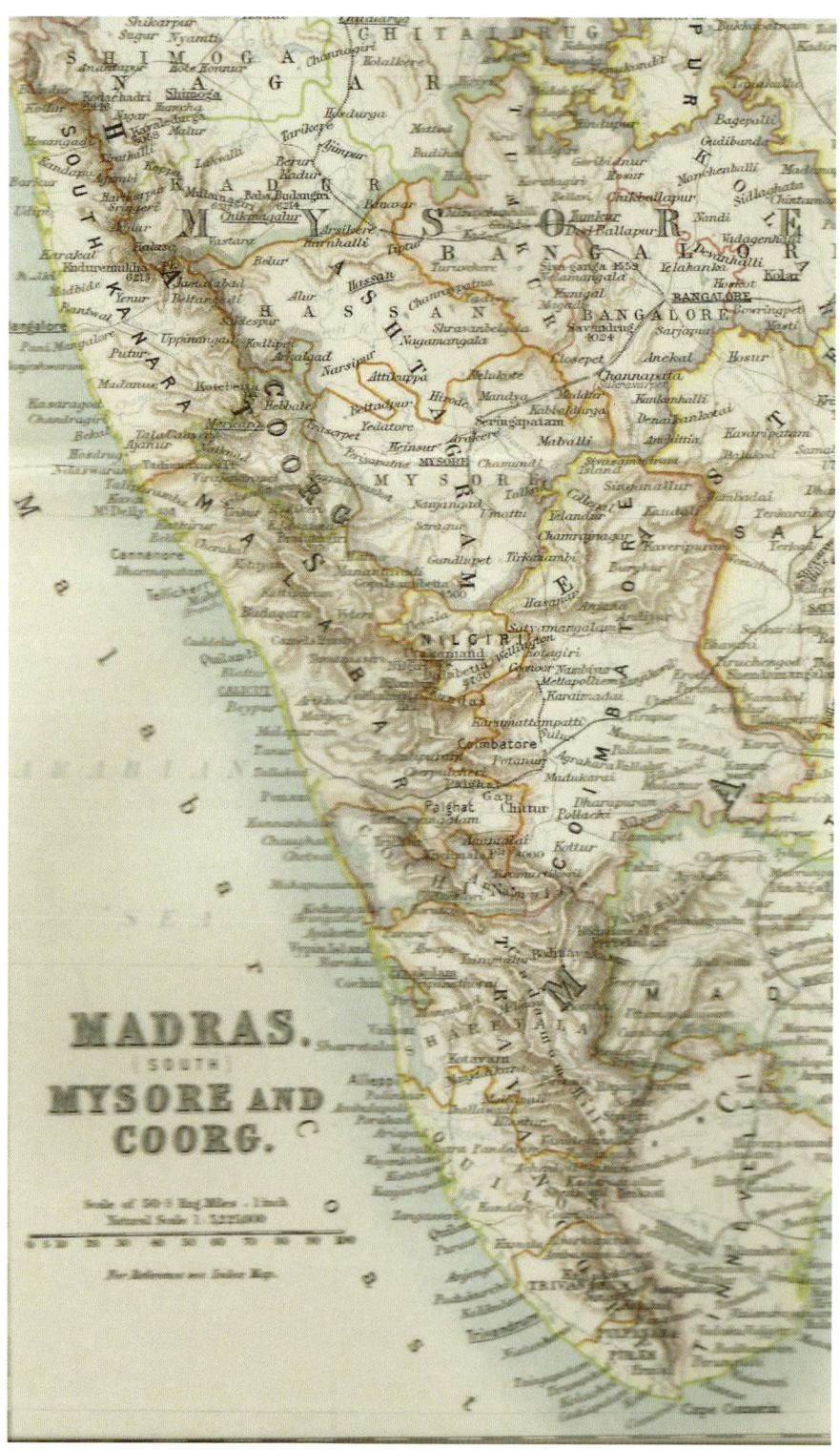

Bombay Presidency Malabar Coast

Summary

To the British tradesmen the term 'Malabar' meant the entire coast of Kerala from Mount Dilla (South of Mangalore) to Cape Comorin (Kanniyakumari). Traditionally, however only the northern part of the Keralan coast bears the geopolitical designation "Malabar". The history of the region centres on the coastal towns of Tellicherry, Mahé, Calicut and Cannanore.

The British established a factory at Tellicherry (now called Thalasserry) in 1683 but did not introduce their silver 'Velli Fanams' until sometime after 1719-20. In British correspondence the coins are referred to by the sobriquet 'Billy' Fanams or 'Bombay Billys'[10].

Copper and gold coins for use in Malabar by the EIC are also known although the site of production of all the coins, including silver, is not certainly known. Some were struck in Bombay but others appear to have been struck locally, mainly at Tellicherry. I have attempted to assign coins to various mints on the basis of style but this must remain conjecture at present.

---

[10] Bhandare & Stevens, ONSNL 172 Supplement, pp. 1-22. My thanks to Dr Bhandare for his considerable help on this section

Bombay Mint – Third Mohur or Pagoda – Alamgir II (1774)

  7.1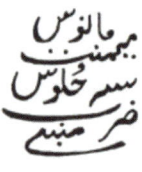

sikka mubarak. badshah ghazi alamgir (= the auspicious coin of the victorious Emperor Alamgir) | *zarb munbai sanah [RY] julus maimanat manus (= Struck at Bombay in the [RY] year of his reign of tranquil prosperity)*

⅓ Mohur

Official Weight (g)	3.84
Actual Weight (g)	3.79-3.85
Actual Diameter (mm)	14.7-16.0
Metal	Gold

Catalogue

Cat No.	Pr. No.	AH	RY	Comments	Value ($)
7.1	10	118x	9	See HK/Singapore (2002), sale 35, lot 734. Also Baldwin *et al*, New York Sale 2008, lot 394. Pr. records this as a quarter but the weight corresponds to a third.	2500

Tellicherry Mint – Pagoda – 1809

 T.99
نشین
سكه
1809   7.2

جلوس
ضرب
تالچري

sikka nishini 1809 T.99. (= Government coin. 1809. T[ellicherry 17] 99. Within a beaded rim) | *zarb tellicherri julus (= Struck at Tellicherry in[RY])*

Pagoda

Actual Weight (g)	?
Actual Diameter (mm)	~13
Metal	Gold

Catalogue

Cat No.	Pr. No.	Comments	Value ($)
7.2	292	No sales known in last 40 years. Recorded from Pridmore.	NV

Calicut Mint *Vir Raya* Fanam – 1790 to 1809?

7.3

Kali Figure

Dots and other symbols

Official Weight (g)	0.38
Actual Weight (g)	0.37
Actual Diameter (mm)	7.7-8.1
Metal	Gold

Catalogue

Cat No.	Pr. No.	Comments	Value ($)
7.3	293	Not possible to distinguish mint and date of manufacture for an individual specimen	50

Bombay Mint – Rupee *et infra* – Alamgir II

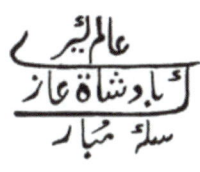

7.6

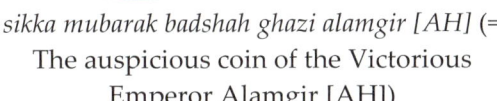

sikka mubarak badshah ghazi alamgir [AH] (= The auspicious coin of the Victorious Emperor Alamgir [AH])

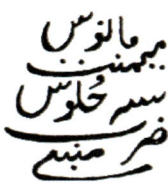

zarb munbai sanah [RY] julus maimanat manus (= Struck at Bombay in the [RY] year of tranquil prosperity)

	Rupee	Half Rupee	Quarter Rupee
Actual Weight (g)	11.47-11.55	5.76	2.77
Actual Diameter (mm)	19.0-22.7	16.4-17.1	14
Metal	Silver		

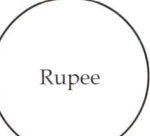

Rupee

½ Rupee

¼ Rupeee

Bombay Mint – Rupee *et infra* – Alamgir II (cont)

Catalogue

Cat No.	Pr. No.	Denomination	Obv	AH	RY	Possible Mint	Comments	Value ($)
7.4		Rupee	B	117x	5	Tellicherry		150
7.5		"	D	xxxx	6	Tellicherry	Ref: Johnston. See below for rupees struck at Calcutta with inverted crescent.	150
7.6	75	"	A	118x	9	Bombay		150
7.7	75	"	B	1188	9	Tellicherry		150
7.8	75	"	C	118x	9	Tellicherry		150
7.9	-	"	E	118x	9	Tellicherry		150
7.10	-	"	F	11xx	9	Tellicherry		150
7.11	73/76	Half Rupee	A	1xxx	9	Bombay	Ref: Johnston	300
7.12	73/76	"	B	xxxx	x	Tellicherry	This seems to be the most common type of half rupee	150
7.13	73/76	"	C	118x	x	Tellicherry		150
7.14	73/76	"	E?	xxxx	9	Tellicherry	No coin seen. Recorded from the Wiggins sale but no clear photo available	NV
7.15	77	Quarter Rupee	A	xxxx	9	Bombay		200
7.16	-	Sixteenth Rupee	?	xxxx	x		Pridmore Sale Lot 459. Has a crescent.	500

See also rupees for use in Bombay (pp. 230-231)

Rupee RY 5

Bombay Mint – Rupee *et infra* – Alamgir II (cont)

Obverse Varieties

Differentiating Mark & Design	A number of different marks occur on the obverse. The designs may be neat, fairly crude or very crude					

Differentiating Mark & Design	A	B	C	D	E	F
	Neat, Crescent	Fairly Crude, Crescent	Crude, Crescent	Inverted Crescent	Rosette	Circle

A- Neat with crescent   B - Fairly crude with crescent   C - Crude with crescent

D - Inverted crescent   E - Dots forming a rosette   F - Circle

Calcutta Mint – Rupees for Use on the Malabar Coast – 1810 to 1813

These are derived from the earlier crescent marked rupees struck at Bombay or Tellicherry. Distinguishing features are the upside-down crescent, the simplified legend and the neat appearance of the coins. The full legend never appears and the coins appears to have been deliberately struck in this way.

7.17

Part of: *sikka mubarak badshah ghazi Alamgir [AH]* (= The auspicious coin of the Victorious Emperor Alamgir [AH])

Part of: *zarb munbai sanah [RY] julus maimanat manus* (= Struck at Bombay in the [RY] year of tranquil prosperity)

	Double Rupee	Rupee
Official Weight (g)	23.18 (estimated)	11.59
Actual Weight (g)	?	11.53-11.56
Actual Diameter (mm)	~28	25.1-25.8
Metal	Silver	

Catalogue

Cat No.	Pr. No.	Denomination	Comments	Value ($)
7.17	-	Double Rupee	Ref: Baldwin (2000), Sale 22 (Wheeler), lot 123	2,000
7.18	294	Rupee		250

Fifth Rupee – Bombay Mint?
Types 1 & 2. Normal 5, Top Word *ghazi*

   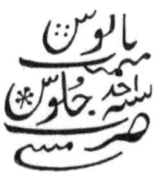

7.19

sikka mubarak [Bad]shah ghazi Sha[h Jaha]n 5 [AH] (= the auspicious coin of the victorious [Emperor] Sha[h Jaha]n [AH]. 1/5th)

zarb munbai sanat [RY] julus maimanat manus (= Struck at Bombay in the [RY] year of tranquil prosperity)

Actual Weight (g)	2.16-2.33
Actual Diameter (mm)	11.9-15.5
Metal	Silver

1/5 Rupee

Catalogue

Cat No.	Pr. No.	Emperor	Type	Obv	Rev	AH	RY	Comments	Value ($)
7.19	34	Muham'd Shah	1	A	I	1131	*Ahd*	Probably issued post c1725. Certainly from the Bombay Mint	100
7.20	-	"	1c	A1	Ia	113x	*Ahd*	Ref: Johnston	100
7.21	34	"	1a	A1	IIa	-	*Ahd*		100
7.22	-	"	1b	A1	IIb	xxxx	11	Ref: Mitchiner M1738	100
7.23	-	"	1b	A1	IIb	xxxx	12	.	100
7.24	63	"	?	A1	?	1143	13	Ref: Herrli. Baldwin (2006), sale 47, lot 852	100
7.25	-	"	1a	A1	IIa	xxxx	22	Ref: Puddester	100
7.26	-	"	1b	A1	IIb	xxxx	25	Ref: Puddester	100
7.27	-	"		A1	II?	xx62	30	Not sure exactly which reverse. Must have been struck posthumously.	100
7.28	-	Alamgir II	2	B	II	xxxx	2		100
7.29	60	"	2	B	II	1133?	3		100
7.30	61	"	2	B	II	113x?	5		100
7.31	-	"	2	B	II	xxxx	6	This may be mistake for RY 2?	100
7.32	-	"	?	?	?	xxxx	8	Ref: Mitchiner M1737	100
7.33	62/ 74	"	2	B	II	1188	9	AH date usually not visible and could be different on posthumous coins	100

Fifth Rupee – Bombay Mint?
Types 1 & 2. Normal 5, Top Word *ghazi* (cont)

Obverse Varieties

Obv A. This is derived from the designs of the 'munbai' rupees of Shah Jahan II and bears a neatly executed figure 5 in the centre. In addition, it bears vestiges of an AH date in the bottom left field which, being faithful to the prototype design, is usually 1131. However, there exists a specimen in the BM collection that has a date 1143, corresponding to 1730 AD. The word in the top line in this case is *Ghazi*.

This design further degrades into what may be termed obverse A1, where it retains most details of obverse A. A distinct change, which is carried forward in all subsequent types as a stylised vestige, is the vowel sign of 'u' appearing over 'm' in the word *Mubarak* (last line). In most cases the chronological detail is seen to degenerate into vestigial numerals. However in the case of a solitary coin it has been observed to read AH 1154.

Obv B. This shows a noteworthy degradation in the execution of the legend as compared to the previous obverse. It retains the word *Ghazi* in the top line. However, in the last line, the chronological details after the word *mubarak* no longer exist and also the vowel and other signs in the word such as the sign of 'u' over 'm' and the 'S'-shaped sign to identify the 'k' as the last letter of the word – have all been jumbled up.

The second significant observation that can be made regarding this obverse is the execution of the figure '5'. There are three distinct varieties depending on the length of the oblique stroke that joins the curve and the top horizontal line of the numeral – with short, medium and long stroke. Depending on the way the stroke has been executed, the numeral assumes a progressively lanky appearance. For the entire design, two styles of execution are seen in general – one where the letters are fine and the other, where they are bolder.

Fifth Rupee – Bombay Mint?
Types 1 & 2. Normal 5, Top Word *ghazi* (cont)

Obv A.
Very neat, AH often visible

Obv A1.
Some degradation. AH sometimes visible

Obv B.
Much cruder

Obv A

Obv B

Long

Medium

Short

Different length shanks to numeral 5

Reverse Varieties

Reverse I: Reverse I matches with obverse A inasmuch as it too is a direct derivation of the design of the Shah Jahan II munbai issue. The chronological detail is RY *ahd* or 1; the mint name is munbai and even the small differentiating mark of a flower is faithfully reproduced in the *aeen* of *julus*. This flower then becomes a group of dots in **reverse Ia**

317

Fifth Rupee – Bombay Mint?
Types 1 & 2. Normal 5, Top Word *ghazi* (cont)

Reverse II: The most noteworthy feature of this design is the word *julus* and the way in which the flow of execution between the *jim*, *laam* and *waav* characters has been affected. In fact this remains a point worthy of note for all the succeeding reverse types. In this particular case the 'knot' of *laam* and *waav* has the shape of an almost isosceles triangle. The differentiating mark in the *seen* of *julus* is a cluster of five or six dots. The regnal years observed for this design are 12, 21, 24?, 25, 2, 3, 5 and 9. There are some coins that show figures other than these, but in most cases they turn out to be jumbled die engravings – like 6 occurring as a result of an incorrectly engraved 2. On a couple of coins '01' was seen, which is probably an error for 9, with the '0' emerging as the misconstrued *nuqta* of *noon* in *sanah*, above which the RY is usually placed. Extant specimens indicate RYs 12 and 21 may also be a case of wrongly engraved dies.

Depending on minor variations, reverse 2 may be further classified into:–

Reverse IIa: Like rev I but no (or dot?) differentiating mark. Only seen with RY 1 and RY 22. The vowel sign for 'u' points towards the bottom of the upstroke of the *laam*

Reverse IIb: Like rev II but with flower differentiating mark (flower differs from rev III, see below.)

Rev I   Rev. II

Rev I   Rev Ia   Rev II

Bombay Mint – Fifth Rupee
Type 3. Normal 5, Top Word *alamgir* c1730 to c1798

7.34

| *sikka mubarak badshah ghazi alamgir* (= The auspicious coin of the Victorious Emperor Alamgir) | *zarb munbai sanah julus maimanat manus* (= Struck at Bombay in the year of tranquil prosperity) |

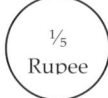

¹/₅ Rupee

Actual Weight (g)	2.25-2.27
Actual Diameter (mm)	11.9-15.5
Metal	Silver

Catalogue

Cat No.	Pr. No.	Obv	Rev	AH	RY	Comments	Value ($)
7.34	-	C	III	xxxx	9	Very distinct style	100

Obverse Varieties

Obverse C: The top line in this case clearly spells out *alamgir*, so here there is no ambiguity about whose designs have been used as a prototype. The execution of legends in this case seems to be quite accurate, and the extant specimens show it to be of superior workmanship. The figure '5' survives in the centre. Although there is no explicit chronological detail seen, a group of small vertical strokes just below the *ain'* of *alamgir* indicates a vestige of the Hijri date as it appeared on the prototype.

Reverse Varieties

Reverse III: This is similar to reverse II, but differs in depicting a flower with a stalk as the differentiating mark, rather than a cluster of dots. Only one RY is noted for this reverse type, and that is 9.

Tellicherry Mint? – Fifth Rupee
Types 4 & 5. Distorted 5, Top Word *manoos* c1762/63

7.36

Distorted legend:
sikka mubarak badshah ghazi alamgir
(= The auspicious coin of the Victorious
Emperor Alamgir)

zarb munbai sanat julus maimanat manus
(= Struck at Bombay in the year of
tranquil prosperity)

Actual Weight (g)	2.22-2.25
Actual Diameter (mm)	11.9-15.5
Metal	Silver

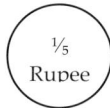

⅕ Rupee

Catalogue

Cat No.	Pr. No.	Obv	Rev	AH	RY	Comments	Value ($)
7.35	297	D1	II		9		100
7.36	297	D1	IV		-		100

Obverse Varieties

Obv D1. On this variety the word in the top line seems to be *manoos*, which one would expect as the top line on the reverse given the usual legend arrangement. This obverse type is also noteworthy for a most peculiarly engraved '5'. The shank of the numeral is at its longest here and that gives the numeral a very lanky appearance. The partial letters seen on the last line are remnants of *mubarak*, which makes this design stylistically closer to obverse 2. Also noteworthy is the shape of the 'knot' in the top line and the way it curves in a sigmoid fashion towards the end of the stroke. There is no chronological detail, not even in a vestigial form.

Obv D1   *Obv D1*

Tellicherry Mint? – Fifth Rupee
Types 4 & 5. Distorted 5, Top Word *manoos* c1762/63 (cont)

Reverse Varieties

Rev IV. This reverse forms a link between the previous reverses and the subsequent ones in being the first where the RY 9 seems to have become a 'fossilised' detail. This reverse has many other interesting characteristics in terms of its execution and differentiating mark. Firstly, the execution is crude as compared to any of the reverses listed so far, but it has a distinct style. Its manifestations can be judged on the same parameters as the previous reverses – the execution of the word *julus* and its constituent characters. The *jim* has a distinct 'upward' bent at its beak, the vowel sign of the 'u' above it often seems attached to the vertical stroke of *laam*, and the knot of *waav* is not isosceles but projects higher vertically, on some coins being hollow. It also extends outwards from the vertical stroke much closer to its top end. The differentiating mark is a flower with a stalk, but the stalk has additional curves besides it and the flower itself has a 'blob'-like execution. A set of vertical lines appears below the RY, indicating corruption of the curves of *seen* in the word *sanah*.

Rev IV

Rev II (NB RY 9 visible)

Tellicherry Mint – Fifth Rupee
Types 6. 7 & 8. Inverted 5, Top Word *manoos* – c1762/3 to c1780

7.37

Distorted legend:
sikka mubarak badshah ghazi alamgir
(= The auspicious coin of the Victorious
Emperor Alamgir)

zarb munbai sanah julus maimanat manus
(= Struck at Bombay in the year of
tranquil prosperity)

Actual Weight (g)	2.15-2.27
Actual Diameter (mm)	11.9-15.5
Metal	Silver

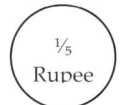

Catalogue

Cat No.	Pr. No.	Type	Obv	Rev	AH	RY	Comments	Value ($)
7.37		6	D2	IV	-	9		200
7.38		7	D3	IVa	-	9		100
7.39		8	E	V	-	9		100

Obverse Varieties

Obv D2. This is by far the rarest obverse type – there were only three coins represented in the group of 300 that were examined (although others with less readable legend may have been of this type). Consequently, it has not been possible to reconstruct the design to the extent that has been done with the other types. Stylistically it bears close links with obverse D1, in terms of the execution of the extant characters and the 'knot' in the top line that retains the same flow in its course. However, the most significant distinguishing feature is that the numeral '5' now appears inverted – the form that Pridmore erroneously described as the 'Malayalim'. This is a significant deviation in the type characteristics and continues in all succeeding obverse types.

Tellicherry Mint – Fifth Rupee
Types 6. 7 & 8. Inverted 5, Top Word *manoos* – c1762/3 to c1780
(cont)

Obv D3. This bears a direct link with the previous varieties insofar as the word in the top line is still *manoos*, however the execution of the characters seems to be of better workmanship. The 'knot' in the top line no longer bears the sigmoid end. The figure of 5 is seen in the inverted form and bears a close resemblance to that seen on the previous variety.

Obv E. This obverse retains the word in the top line as *manoos* and continues to bear the inverted figure '5'. But the execution of characters is noticeably better than that seen in obverses D1 and D2. It lacks chronological details and the bottom line shows vestiges of *mubarak*.

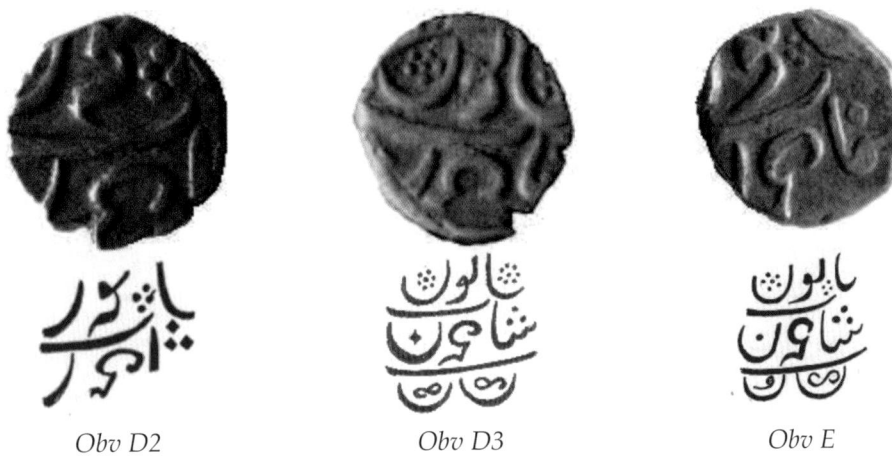

Obv D2   *Obv D3*   *Obv E*

Reverse Varieties

Rev IVa. The major difference here lies in the fact that although much of the execution of the inscription is very similar to that seen on reverse IV, here the differentiating mark of the flower is replaced with a cluster of dots. On some coins it appears to be a vestige of the 'flower' seen on reverse IV, but without the small curvy lines that flank the stalk. The reverse retains the chronological detail of frozen RY 9.

Rev V. Here again the execution is markedly superior to that seen on reverse IV. However, the most noteworthy aspect is the chronological detail, where the RY is seen now definitely 'frozen' at 9. The differentiating mark in the *seen* of *julus* is a flower, but without a stalk, and the execution of the word itself bears close similarities with reverse II rather than reverse IV, with the 'knot' being triangular in shape, but not hollow or projecting vertically.

Tellicherry Mint – Fifth Rupee
Types 6. 7 & 8. Inverted 5, Top Word *manoos* – c1762/3 to c1780
(cont)

| Rev IV | Rev IVa | Rev V |

Tellicherry or Calicut Mint – Fifth Rupee
Type 9. Inverted 5, Top word *shah alam* – c1792 to c1798

7.40

sikka mubarak badshah ghazi shah 5 (= the auspicious coin of the victorious Emperor 1/5th)

zarb munbai sanah julus maimanat manus (= Struck at Bombay in the year of tranquil prosperity)

Actual Weight (g)	2.21-2.33
Actual Diameter (mm)	11.9-15.5
Metal	Silver

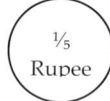

1/5 Rupee

Catalogue

Cat No.	Pr. No.	Type	Obv	Rev	RY	Comments	Value ($)
7.40	295	9	F	VI	9	Neat variety. RY 9.	100

Tellicherry or Calicut Mint – Fifth Rupee
Type 9. Inverted 5, Top word *shah alam* – c1792 to c1798 (cont)

Obverse Varieties

Obverse F: Executionally, this is the most singular of all the obverse types and shows no similarity with any of those listed above. The only sequential link it offers in the design is the inverted figure '5' in the centre. Almost all characters are vestigial, but one can certainly discern the top line as derived from *shah alam*, while the central and bottom lines are *badshah* and *sikka mubarak*. The central line has some noticeable peculiarities – to the right of the numeral and beyond 'Sha', the vestige of the *alif* in what remains of 'Ba' has assumed a sharply backward slash-like form and there is a circle to its right. To the left, there is a cluster of four dots within a curve and one of those always bears a small prong coming out of it. No chronological details are visible.

Obv F

Reverse Varieties

Reverse VI: Like obverse F, this is by far the most distinct reverse type and there are many noteworthy aspects to it. Firstly, the execution of the word *julus* is very different from what has been listed so far. The chronological detail is clearly 9, the frozen regnal year that becomes a feature from reverse IV onwards. The mint name is preceded by what looks like a remnant of 'Fi', but is most likely a version of *zarb*, even though a downward sloping stroke appears to its right.

Rev VI

325

Tellicherry Mint – Fifth Rupee – 1799

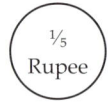

T.99
نشين

سكه
١٢١٤ 7.41

جلوس
ضرب
تالچري

T.99 sikka nishini ah1214 (=T[ellicherry 17]99. Government coin. AH 1214). Within a beaded rim.

zarb tellicherri julus (= Struck at Tellicherry [under] royal [orders])Within a beaded rim.

Official Weight (g)	2.32
Actual Weight (g)	2.26-2.27
Actual Diameter (mm)	11.9-12.9
Metal	Silver

⅕ Rupee

Catalogue

Cat No.	Pr. No.	Comments	Value ($)
7.41	298	See Herrli H., (2007), JONS 193, p. 31	100

Tellicherry Mint – Fifth Rupees – 1805

Since Malabar had been moved from the Bombay Presidency in 1800, this really belongs to the Madras Presidency but has been placed here for completeness of the series.

7.42

ضرب منبي
شاه عالم
جلوس

Scales with T (=Tellicherry) between the pans and 1805 below.

zarb munbai shah alam julus (= Struck at Bombay in the reign of Shah Alam)

Actual Weight (g)	2.20-2.24
Actual Diameter (mm)	12.0-13.1
Metal	Silver

⅕ Rupee

Catalogue

Cat No.	Pr. No.	Comments	Value ($)
7.42	299	Issued under the authority of the Madras Presidency	100

Tellicherry Mint? – Eighth Rupee?

This coin is a bit of an enigma. It occurs in round and square shapes and usually weighs the same as the 1/5th rupees. It has the same fineness (as measured by XRF) so the meaning of the 8 is not clear. The light-weight square coin may possibly be a cut down round coin.

   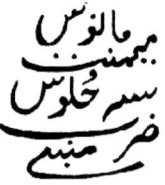

7.43

sikka mubarak badshah ghazi shah 8 (= the auspicious coin of the victorious Emperor 1/8th)

zarb munbai sanah julus maimanat manus (= Struck at Bombay in the year of tranquil prosperity)

Actual Weight (g)	1.42-2.26
Actual Diameter (mm)	12.6-13.2
Metal	Silver

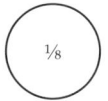

⅛

Catalogue

Cat No.	Pr. No.	Comments	Value ($)
7.43	-	Ref: Ashmolean Museum, Wilford, Herrli.	500

   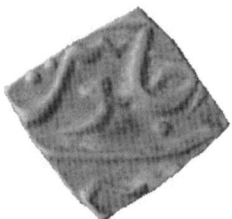

These coins can be round or square

Bombay Mint – Twelfth Rupee – For use at Anjengo

 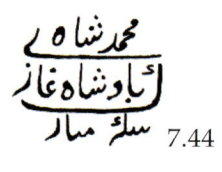

7.44

 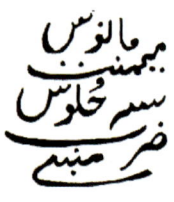

sikka mubarak badshah ghazi muhammad Shah (= the auspicious coin of the victorious Emperor Muhammad Shah) | *zarb munbai sanah 8 julus maimanat manus* (= Struck at Bombay in the 8th year of tranquil prosperity)

Actual Weight (g)	0.97
Actual Diameter (mm)	11 (from Pr)
Metal	Silver

$\frac{1}{12}$

Catalogue

Cat No.	Pr. No.	AH	RY	Comments	Value ($)
7.44	64	xxxx	8	Only known example is in the Ashmolean Museum[11]	NV

Madras Mint? – Pattern Possibly for the Malabar Coast 1798

7.45

Balemark | *Date within a plain circle*

Actual Weight (g)	6.14
Actual Diameter (mm)	19.8
Metal	Copper

Pice

Catalogue

Cat No.	Pr. No.	Date	Comments	Value ($)
7.45	341	1798	Pattern? Ref: ANS	600

[11] Bhandare S, (1995), ONSNL 182, p. 32

Tellicherry Mint – Double Pice *et infra* – c1705 to c1791

7.46

Balemark within a plain circle

Date within a plain circle

	Double Pice	Pice	Half Pice
Actual Weight (g)	5.42-6.38	2.43-3.22	1.20-1.98
Actual Diameter (mm)	17.2-19.7	14.2-19.6	7.7-12.8
Metal	Copper		

Double Pice

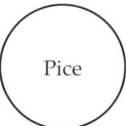

Pice

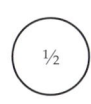

½

Catalogue

Cat No.	Pr. No.	Denomination	Date	Comments	Value ($)
7.46	302	Double Pice	1729	Ref:: Johnston, Stevens, Pridmore	200
7.47	304	"	1732	Ref: Johnston, Pridmore	200
7.48	305	"	1734	Intermediate weight 3.92g & 4.33g. Stevens, Pridmore	200
7.49	306	"	1739	Ref: Johnston, Pridmore	200
7.50	307	"	1742	Ref: Johnston, Pridmore	200
7.51	308	"	1743	Ref KM. Wt. unknown	200
7.52	309	"	1747	None traced. Parsons sale[12]. Wt. unknown	200
7.53	310	"	1752	None traced. Recorded from Atkins. Wt. unknown	200
7.54	311	"	1773	None traced. Parsons sale[12]. Wt. unknown	200
7.55	-	"	1774	Baldwin (2000), sale 22 (Wheeler), lot 126. Slightly different design.	200
7.56	312	"	1779	None traced. Parsons sale[12]. Wt. unknown	200

Entries with Wt unknown may be pice

[12] Parsons sale, 1954, lot 892

Tellicherry Mint – Double Pice *et infra* – c1705 to c1791 (cont)

Catalogue

Cat No.	Pr. No.	Denomination	Date	Comments	Value ($)
7.57	301	Pice	1705	Ref: Pridmore	200
7.58	303	"	1731	Ref: Pridmore	200
7.59	-	"	1732	Ref: Johnston	200
7.60	-	"	1791	Ref: Johnston	200
7.61	313	Half Pice	1710	Ref: Wiggins. Also Jackson, Coin Collecting in the Deccan. See Pr. sale	150
7.62	-	"	1712	Ref: KM	150
7.63	314	"	1726		150
7.64	315	"	1741	None traced. Recorded from Pridmore	NV
7.65	316	"	1753	None traced. Recorded from Pridmore	NV
7.66	317	"	1759	None traced. Recorded from Pridmore	NV
7.67	-	"	1780	Wt. = 1.23g. No balemark. Ref: Ashmolean Museum.	NV
7.68	318	"	1785		150
7.69	-	"	1786	Ref: Steve Album (2012), sale 14, lot 1324.	150

Half pice 1780, no balemark

Half Pice 1786

Bombay Presidency Soho Mint

Summary

Up until very late in the eighteenth century, the copper coins of the Bombay Presidency were poorly manufactured and very crude although they do appear to have circulated quite widely in India. Plans to send copper coins manufactured in England, to India, started as early as 1786[13]:

In 1790, the Bombay authorities were informed that the existing circulating copper coins were to be replaced by a new coinage sent out from England. They considered that replacing all of the copper coin in one go would be too expensive and so they determined to do it gradually[14]:

However, by 1791 a decision was taken to replace all circulating copper coins in one go with 100 tons of new coins. Accordingly, 35 tons of coins were sent from England to Bombay aboard the "Essex" with instructions not to open the casks until the rest of the shipment arrived[15]: A further 65 tons was duly received aboard the "Rockingham" with instructions on how to issue them[16]:

2 Pice @ 50 to a rupee; 1½ @ 66 ⅔ to a rupee; Pice @ 100 and halves @ 200 to a rupee

The weight was intended to make one rupee worth 10,000 grains avoirdupois weight of copper (e.g. 200 x 50) compared to the then existing rate of 7314 grains i.e. the coins contained less than their intrinsic value of copper. This, combined with the greatly increased quality of the design, would reduce the amount of forgery that was obviously worrying the authorities at the time.

---

[13] Dispatches to Bombay. IOR E/4/1004 (1786-1786), p. 277. Dispatch dated 31st July 1787
[14] Dispatches to Bombay. IOR E/4/1006 (1789-90), p. 393-394 Dispatch dated 21st April 1790
[15] Dispatches to Bombay. IOR E/4/1007 (1790-91), p. 549-551. Dispatch dated 3rd May 1791
[16] Dispatches to Bombay. IOR E/4/1008 (1791-93), p. 59. Dispatch dated 8th February 1792

Pridmore records that further deliveries occurred in 1792, 1793 and 1794. The delivery for 1792 was probably the second load of 1791 coins and perhaps more of these were delivered in 1793 although this has not been confirmed. However, a second coinage was undertaken in 1793 and shipped to India in 1794 (Doty[17]). The coinage consisted of double pice, pice and half pice. The coins were dated 1794[18]. Further shipments were made in 1804.

Matthew Boulton

---

[17] Doty R, (1998), The Soho Mint & the Industrialisation of Money, pp. 205-226.
     Smithsonian Institution, British Numismatic Society & Spink
[18] Dispatches to Bombay. IOR E/4/1009 (1793-94), p. 53. Dispatch dated 19th February 1794

Soho Mint – Pattern Double Pice - 1794

The Persian inscription on the reverse of this coin occurs on a number of patterns prepared for the dub coinage of the Northern Circars struck at Soho.

8.1

Balemark with date below. All within a tooth-bordered rim.

Persian inscription within a raised toothed rim. The inscription reads:

سكه كمپني عيسوي ۱۷۹۳

= *Sikka Kampani 'Isavi 1793* (= Money of the Company. Christian year 1793)

Actual Weight (g)	14.02
Actual Diameter (mm)	30.8
Metal	Copper
Edge	ENGLISH . UNITED . EAST . INDIA . COMPANY &.. (incuse)

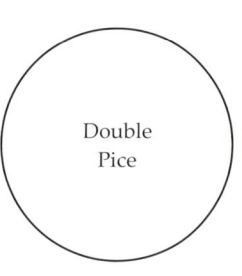

Double Pice

Catalogue

Cat No.	Pr. No.	Axis	Comments	Value ($)
8.1	Bengal 372	↑←	Ref: BM. Also Baldwin (2013), sale 82 (Fore), lot 882	2,000

Soho Mint – Double Pice – 1791 to 1794

8.2

Balemark with date below. All within a tooth-bordered rim.

Balanced scales with Persian inscription between the pans. All within a raised, toothed border. The inscription reads:

عدل

Adil (= Justice)

Official Weight (g)	12.95
Actual Weight (g)	12.13-13.57
Actual Diameter (mm)	29.5-31.6
Metal	Copper
Edge	Grained Right

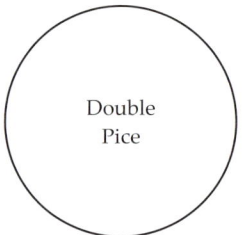

Double Pice

Catalogue

Cat No.	Pr. No.	Date	Status	Obv	Rev	Axis	Comments	Mintage (Doty)	Value ($)
8.2	118	1791	Currency	A	II	↑↓			150
8.3	119	"	Proof	A	II	"			400
8.4	119	"	Proof	A	I	"		1,174,630	400
8.5	120	"	Gilt Proof	A	I	"			600
8.6	118	"	Currency	B	III	"			150
8.7	121	1794	Currency	B	I	↑↓			150
8.8	122	"	Proof	B	I	"			500
8.9	-	"	Currency	B	III	↑↑	N.B. Die axis. Edge Plain. This coin is heavier than average (13.20g) and slightly mis-struck.	1,569,330	250
8.10	122	"	Proof	B	III	↑↓			500
8.11	122	"	Proof	B	II	"	Ref: Seen at Baldwin's		500
8.12	123	"	Gilt Proof	B	I	"			600

334

Soho Mint – Double Pice – 1791 to 1794 (cont)

Obverse Varieties

Privy Mark	There may or may not be a tiny dot below the letter V in the shield.

	A	B
Privy Mark	Dot present	No Dot

Dot below V

No dot below V

Reverse Varieties

Pivot	The length and style of the pivot varies.

	I	II	III
Pivot	Medium length and fairly sharp point	Longer and blunter point	Short and sharp point

Medium length and fairly sharp

Longer and blunter

Short and sharp

Soho Mint – One & a Half Pice Pattern

Smaller scales than on the currency type

8.13

Balemark with date below. All within a tooth-bordered rim.

Balanced scales with Persian inscription between the pans. All within a raised, toothed border. The inscription reads:

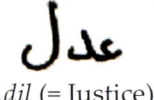

Adil (= Justice)

Actual Weight (g)	?
Actual Diameter (mm)	~28
Metal	Copper
Edge	SG

1½ Pice

Catalogue

Cat No.	Pr. No.	Date	Status	Comments	Value ($)
8.13	124	1791	Pattern	Edge straight grained. Rev has small scales	2,000

336

Soho Mint – One & a Half Pice – 1791 to 1794

8.16

Balemark with date below. All within a tooth-bordered rim.

Balanced scales with Persian inscription between the pans. All within a raised, toothed border. The inscription reads:

عدل

Adil (Justice)

Official Weight (g)	9.71
Actual Weight (g)	8.74-10.48
Actual Diameter (mm)	27.4-28.8
Metal	Copper
Edge	Grained Right

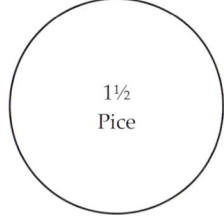

1½ Pice

Catalogue

Cat No.	Pr. No.	Date	Status	Obv	Rev	Axis	Comments	Mintage (Doty)	Value ($)
8.14	124	1791	Pattern	-	-	?	Edge straight grained. Rev has small scales		2,000
8.15	-	None	White Metal Trial	Blank	Too weakly struck to be sure	-	Wt.=9.06g. Diam=31.3-31.8mm. Edge Plain. Uniface trial striking.	2,690,351	250
8.16	125	1791	Currency	A	I	↑↓			100
8.17	126	"	Proof	A	I	"			400
8.18	126	"	Proof	A	II	"			400
8.19	126	"	Proof	B	I	"	Ref: BM		400
8.20	127	"	Gilt Proof	A	II	"			600
8.21	128	1794	Proof	A	I	"			500

Soho Mint – One & a Half Pice – 1791 to 1794 (cont)

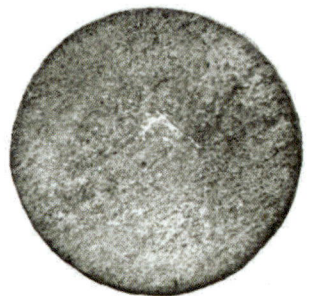 

White metal trial

Obverse Varieties

Privy Mark	There may or may not be a tiny dot below the letter V in the shield. See double pice for photos.

	A	B
Privy Mark	No Dot	Dot Present

There are other variations for instance in the outline of the balemark, but these have not been listed

Reverse Varieties

Chain Holder	The holders (looking like tassels), from which the chains are suspended, vary in size.

	I	II
Chain Holder	Narrow	Wide

Narrow holders   *Wide holders*

Single Pice – 1791 to 1794

8.28

Balemark with date below. All within a tooth-bordered rim.

Balanced scales with Persian inscription between the pans. All within a raised, toothed border. The inscription reads:

عدل

Adil (= Justice)

Official Weight (g)	6.47
Actual Weight (g)	5.95-6.85
Actual Diameter (mm)	24.8-25.9
Metal	Copper
Edge	Grained Right

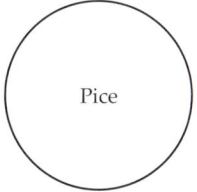

Pice

Catalogue

Cat No.	Pr. No.	Date	Status	Rev	Axis	Comments	Mintage (Doty)	Value ($)
8.22	129	1791	Currency	I	↑↓			100
8.23	129	"	Currency	IV	"			100
8.24	129	"	Currency	V	"			100
8.25	129	"	Currency	VI	"		5,472,740	100
8.26	129	"	Currency	VII	"	Ref: Morris		150
8.27	130	"	Proof	I	"			300
8.28	130	"	Proof	III	"			300
8.29	131	"	Gilt Proof	III	"			500
8.30	-	"	Silver Proof	I	"	Only one known at present	?	1,000
8.31	132	1794	Currency	II	"			100
8.32	133	"	Proof	III	"		2,371,779	300
8.33	134	"	Gilt Proof	III	"			500

Single Pice – 1791 to 1794 (cont)

Reverse Varieties

Pivot	The shape of the pivot varies. One specimen has no pivot.
Dots	There may be three dot privy marks: one immediately below the pivot, one next to the top of the last Arabic letter, and the third between the first two chains of the left pan. The one below the pivot is probably the real mark and the others die flaws.
Hanging Loop	There may be just one loop at the top of the scales, or this may be linked to another. Single loops may be round or flattened.
Pans	The depth of the pans can vary

	I	II	III	IV	V	VI	VII
Pivot	Long	Medium	Medium	Short	Short	Fat	None
Dots	Yes	None	None	None	None	None	None
Hanging Loop	One	One	One	Two	Slightly flattened	Slightly flattened	Two?
Pans	Deep	Deep	Shallow	Deep	Deep	Deep	Deep

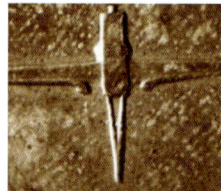
Long pivot

Medium pivot

Short pivot

Fat pivot

No pivot

Soho Mint – Single Pice – 1791 to 1794 (cont)

Dots

No dots

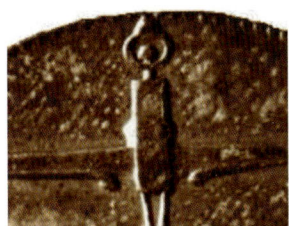

One loop

Two loops

Flattened loop

Deep pans

Shallow pans

Soho Mint – Half Pice – 1791 to 1794

8.41

Balemark with date below.
All within a tooth-bordered
rim.

Balanced scales with Persian inscription between
the pans. All within a raised, toothed border. The
inscription reads:

عدل

Adil (Justice)

Official Weight (g)	3.23
Actual Weight (g)	2.92-3.47
Actual Diameter (mm)	19.8-21.0
Metal	Copper
Edge	Grained Right

Half Pice

Catalogue

Cat No.	Pr. No.	Date	Status	Rev	Axis	Comments	Mintage	Value ($)
8.34	135	1791	Currency	IV	↑↓			90
8.35	135	"	"	V	"			90
8.36	135	"	"	VI	"			90
8.37	135	"	"	VI	↑↑		7,903,280	90
8.38	135	"	"	VII	↑↓			90
8.39	135	"	"	VIII	"			90
8.40	135	"	"	IX	"			90

Listing continued on next page

Soho Mint – Half Pice – 1791 to 1794 (cont)

Catalogue

Cat No.	Pr. No.	Date	Status	Rev	Axis	Comments	Mintage	Value ($)
8.41	136	1791	Proof	I	"			250
8.42	136	"	Proof	II	"			250
8.43	136	"	Proof	III	"			250
8.44	136	"	Proof	IV	"			250
8.45	137	"	Gilt Proof	I	"	Wt. = 3.45g		300
8.46	138	1794	Currency	X	"			90
8.47	138	"	Currency	XI	"			90
8.48	138	"	Currency	XII	"		4,711,998	90
8.49	138	"	Currency	XIII	"			90
8.50	139	"	Proof	I	"			250
8.51	136	"	Proof	III	"	Heavy weight 3.64g		300
8.52	140	"	Gilt Proof	I	"	Extremely rare		800

Reverse Varieties

Pivot	The shape of the pivot varies
Hanging loop	The hanging loop may be slightly distorted
Privy Mark	There may be a dot privy mark below the pivot.

	I	II	III	IV	V	VI	VII
Pivot	Short and delicate	Delicate & long	Delicate & long	Coarse & narrow	Coarse & narrow	Coarse & fat	Open & fairly delicate. Tapering
Hanging loop	Round	Round	Round	Elongated	Round	Round	Round
Privy Mark	None	Yes	None	None	None	None	None

Soho Mint – Half Pice – 1791 to 1794 (cont)

	VIII	IX	X	XI	XII	XIII
Pivot	Wide and pointed	Coarse & narrow	Fairly delicate. Pointed	Coarse narrow & blunt	Open & fairly delicate. Stubby.	Coarse narrow & sharp.
Hanging loop	Elongated	Round	Filled	Round	Round	Round
Privy Mark	None	None	None	None	None	None

I – Short and delicate

II – Delicate & long

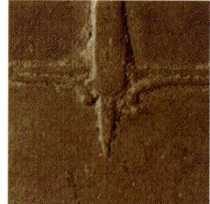

IV- Coarse & narrow

VI – Coarse & fat

VII – Open & fairly delicate. Tapering

VIII – Wide and pointed

X – Fairly delicate. Pointed

XI - Coarse narrow & blunt

XII – Open & fairly delicate. Stubby.

XIII – Coarse narrow & sharp.

Soho Mint – Half Pice – 1791 to 1794 (cont)

Round loop   *Elongated loop*   *Filled loop*

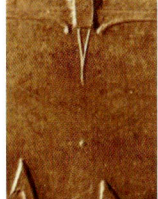 

Privy mark   *No privy mark*

Soho Mint – Double, Single and Half Pice – 1804

8.54

The arms of the Company surrounded by the legend:
EAST INDIA COMPANY 1804
The motto on the ribbon reads:
AUSPICIO REGIS & SENATUS ANGLIAE
All within a raised toothed rim.

Balanced scales with Persian legend between the pans:

عدل

(translation = *Adil* = just or fair). AH date (1219) in Arabic figures below. All within a raised toothed rim.

	Double Pice	Pice	Half Pice
Official Weight (g)	12.95	6.47	3.23
Actual Weight (g)	Varies. See below	6.3-6.53	3.14-3.33
Actual Diameter (mm)	30.6-30.7	25.6-25.7	21.0-21.2
Metal	Copper		
Edge	Plain		

345

Soho Mint – Double, Single and Half Pice – 1804 (cont)

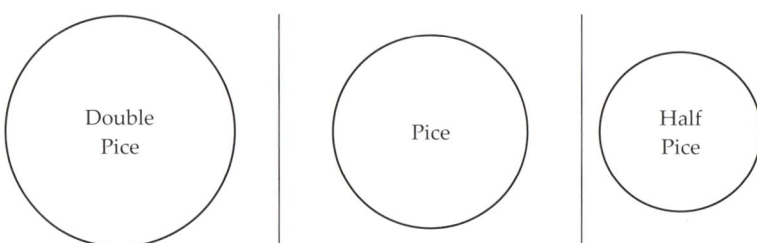

Catalogue

Cat No.	Pr. No.	Denomination	Status	Axis	Actual wt (g)	Comments	Value ($)
8.53	194	Double Pice	Currency	↑↓	12.04-12.88		80
8.54	195	"	Proof	↑↑	"		300
8.55	196	"	Gilt Proof	↑↓	"		400
8.56	197	"	Obverse Mule	"	10.62-10.93		300
8.57	198	Pice	Currency	↑↓	6.3-6.53		75
8.58	199	"	Proof	"	"		250
8.59	200	"	Gilt Proof	"	"		350
8.60	201	Half Pice	Currency	↑↓	3.14-3.33		80
8.61	202	"	Proof	"	"	May come with serifs on 4 arranged differently	200
8.62	203	"	Gilt Proof	"	"		300

Double pice mule

Madras Presidency Madras Mint Early Coinages

Summary

The building of Fort St George at Madras began in 1640 and a mint was established in 1643. The coins copied the types struck in the area at the time, small gold coins called pagodas and copper coins called cash. At various times multiple cash coins were struck (2, 3, 5 and 10 cash coins) as well as silver coins called fanams, also issued in various denominations. These coins continued to be issued at various times and with different designs, until 1806 when a new mint was built (see later).

Gold Pagoda c1643

This coin is recorded from Pridmore although the ability to assign any single design to the EIC is almost impossible.

1.1

Crude representation of a Hindu deity

Blank

Official Weight (g)	3.45
Actual Weight (g)	3.42
Actual Diameter (mm)	11.0-14.0
Metal	Gold

Pagoda

Catalogue

Cat No	Pr. No.	Comments	Value ($)
1.1	1	Ref: Pridmore; Lingen (1979), SNC 87 pp. 2-3. Very difficult to determine the type of this crude coin.	300

Another crude coin that may be of this type. (Au 85.5%, Ag 11.5%, Cu 2.3% by XRF)

Gold Pagoda c1678 to c1740

This was the standard gold coin of the EIC for many years. Easily confused with Dutch pagodas, see pictures below.

1.2

A standing deity holding a sword in his left hand and surrounded by various symbols.

Granulated

Official Weight (g)	3.45
Actual Weight (g)	3.36-3.42
Actual Diameter (mm)	11.0-11.5
Metal	Gold

Pagoda

Catalogue

Cat No	Pr. No.	Status	Comments	Value ($)
1.2	2	Currency	Single, standing figure of Vishnu.	200

Gold Pagoda c1678 to c1740 (cont)

Example of probable Dutch pagoda (Au 86%, Ag 12%, Cu 2%, by XRF)

Example of probable Negapatam pagoda (Au 62%, Ag 8%, Cu 29%, by XRF). See p. 522

Normal figure	*Squat figure*	*Fairly normal figure*

Examples of contemporary forgeries

Gold Three Swami Pagoda 1691 to 1806

Apparently issued at the same time as the coins with a single deity and others.

1.4

Three standing figures, each with a star above their head.

Granulated

	Pagoda	Half Pagoda	Quarter Pagoda
Official Weight (g)	3.43	1.71	0.85
Actual Weight (g)	3.43-3.46	1.68	0.85
Actual Diameter (mm)	11.2-13.0	10	8
Metal	Gold		

Pagoda

Catalogue

Cat No.	Pr. No.	Denomination	Obv	Date Issued	Comments	Value ($)
1.3	3A	Pagoda	A	c1691-1740	Full figures	200
1.4	3B	Pagoda	B	1740-1806	Half figures	150
1.5	4	Half Pagoda	A	c1691-1740	BM. Possibly jeweler's copy	NV
1.6	5	Quarter Pagoda	A	"	BM. Possibly jeweler's copy	NV

Obverse Varieties

Size of Figures	The complete figures may be visible or only half

	A	**B**
Size of Figures	Full	Half

Full figures

Half figures

351

Gold Alamgir Pagoda 1692 to 1707

1.9

Nisar Badshah Alamgir (= The gift of the Emperor Alamgir)

zarb chinapatan (= Struck at Chinapatan (Madras))

Pagoda

Official Weight (g)	2.98
Actual Weight (g)	2.99
Actual Diameter (mm)	10.8-11.3
Metal	Gold

Catalogue

Cat No.	Pr. No.	AH	RY	=AD	Comments	Value ($)
1.7	6	1103	35	1691/92		1,000
1.8	-	1111	?	1699/1700	Ref: BM	NV
1.9	7	1113	47	1703	AH may be 1114	1,000

Gold MM Pagoda 1730 to 1735

1.10

A single standing deity with the letter M on each side. Indicative Picture – No specimen available

Granulated. Indicative Picture – No specimen available

Pagoda

Actual Weight (g)	?
Actual Diameter (mm)	~11.5?
Metal	Gold

Catalogue

Cat No.	Pr. No.	Comments	Value ($)
1.10	8	Not traced	NV

Gold Star Pagoda 1740 to 1806

This became the standard bullion coin of the EIC in the second half of the eighteenth century

1.11

Half a standing figure with dots on each side. | A star surrounded by dotted circles

Actual Weight (g)	3.32-3.40
Actual Diameter (mm)	10.0-12.7
Metal	Gold

Pagoda

Catalogue

Cat No.	Pr. No.	Obv	Rev	Comments	Value ($)
1.11	9	A	I		150
1.12	-	A	II	Ref: Wiggins	150
1.13	-	B	I	Ref: Hemanth Chopra Full figure on obverse. Star and dots on reverse look very different from usual. Perhaps a local copy?	NV

Obverse Varieties

Design	The design may vary. Normally there is only part of the figure of Vishnu visible. Rarely there is the whole figure visible. Forgeries have all sorts of crude figures

	A	B
Design	Normal	Full figure

Normal design | *Crude design on typical contemporary forgery* | *Full standing figure as 1.13*

Gold Star Pagoda 1740 to 1806 (cont)

Reverse Varieties

Star within	The star is normally held within a circle of dots. Sometimes the dots are arranged in the shape of a pentagon rather than a circle

	I	II
Star within	Circle	Pentagon

Star within Circle   *Star within Pentagon*

Gold Fanam c1643 to 1693

1.14

A single standing deity (Vishnu) within a beaded border

Not deciphered.

Actual Weight (g)	0.27
Actual Diameter (mm)	7
Metal	Gold

Catalogue

Cat No.	Pr. No.	Comments	Value ($)
1.14	11	None traced. Many South Indian gold fanams exist that resemble this design.	NV

Silver Double Fanam *et infra* – 1689

1.16

| Full standing figure of Vishnu within a beaded border | Two interlinked Cs the ends of one separated by the figure 1. Within a beaded border. |

	Double Fanam	**Fanam**	**Half Fanam**
Official Weight (g)	2.46	1.23	0.62
Actual Weight (g)	?	0.95-1.03	?
Actual Diameter (mm)	~12	8.7-10.3	~8
Metal	Silver		

2

1

½

Catalogue

Cat No.	Pr. No.	Denomination	Comments	Value ($)
1.15	12	Double fanam	Two strokes between the ends of the C. Private collection. One known	NV
1.16	13	Single fanam		1300
1.17	14	Half fanam	None traced	NV

Silver Double Fanam *et infra* 1690 to 1763

See Stevens (August 1992) ONS Occasional Paper No. 22, for examination and discussion of these coins.

1.18

Full standing figure of Vishnu, within a beaded border.	Two interlinked Cs, with one, two or three dots. Surrounded by a beaded border.

	Double Fanam	Fanam	Half Fanam
Official Weight (g)	2.07	1.03	0.51
Actual Weight (g)	2.00-2.08	1.00-1.05	0.482
Actual Diameter (mm)	9.1-11.3	7.8-9.4	7.1-7.9
Metal	Silver		

Catalogue

Cat No	Pr. No.	Denom	Obv	Rev	Comments	Value ($)
1.18	15	Double fanam	A	I	Three dots on reverse	100
1.19	-	"	A	II	Two dots on Reverse. Usually only one visible.	80
1.20	-	"	B	II	Same weight but cruder design (as later issue). Only one dot visible on specimens examined, but could be two on specimens showing full die impression.	100
1.21	16	Single fanam	A	III	One dot on reverse.	80
1.22		"	A	IV	Two dots on reverse. One in centre and one between ends of C. Wiggins	80
1.23	17	Half fanam	A	?	The only one seen by the author is very crude and looks like a contemporary forgery. However, the ANS apparently has one Ref: 1973.56.1232	NV

Silver Double Fanam *et infra* 1690 to 1763

Obverse Varieties

Shape of Figure	The shape of the figure varies. Normally a full figure is visible. On some coins a cruder figure is shown and is only partially visible.

	A	B
Shape of Figure	Normal	Cruder

A – Normal figure   *B – Cruder figure*   *Forgery?*

Reverse Varieties

Dots	There may be three, two or one dot visible

	I	II	III	IV
Dots	Three	Two. Between ends of each C	One	Two. One in centre & one between ends of C

I – Three Dots (Double Fanam)   *II – Two Dots (Double Fanam)*   *III – One Dot (Single Fanam)*

Silver Double & Single Fanams – 1764 to 1806

1.24

| Partial standing figure of Vishnu (crude compared with 1st & 2nd issues). Within a beaded border. | Two interlinked Cs, one end separated by a dot, which is often not visible. Surrounded by a beaded border. |

	Double Fanam	Single Fanam
Official Weight (g)	1.83	0.91
Actual Weight (g)	1.65-1.88	0.80-0.96
Actual Diameter (mm)	7.4-11.1	7.0-7.9
Metal	Silver	

Catalogue

Cat No.	Pr. No.	Denomination	Comments	Value ($)
1.24	18	Double fanam		50
1.25	19	Single fanam		50

NB the ANS has two crude copper coins which look like the silver fanams Ref: 1988.84.47 (1.184g) & 1988.84.46 (1.686g). These are probably contemporary forgeries. Thanks to Bob Johnston for spotting these.

Silver Double & Single Fanams – 1764 to 1806

Double fanam
Example showing bead on reverse

fanam
Example showing beaded border on obverse

fanam
Example showing beaded border on reverse

Copper Ten Cash (Dudu) – 1691 to 1745

Balemark with GCE within a decorative stroke border

1.33

Date between wavy lines within a beaded circle

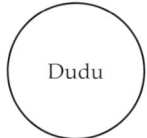
Dudu

Official Weight (g)	8.85
Actual Weight (g)	7.66-8.79
Actual Diameter (mm)	13.7-22.0
Metal	Copper

Catalogue

Cat No.	Pr. No.	Date	Comments	Value ($)
1.26	20	1691	Manchester Museum	150
1.27	21	1693		50
1.28	22	1695		50
1.29	24	1702		50
1.30	25	1703		50
1.31	28	1704	4 shaped like y. Could be 9. Example in BM.	50
1.32	26	1705	Noble sale 48, lot 1986 (1995). Not examined	80
1.33	27	1706		50
1.34	29	1716		80
1.35	30	1720	Ashmolean museum	NV
1.36	31	1721	Manchester Museum. ANS also Johnston	50
1.37	32	1722		50
1.38	33	1725	Not examined.	NV
1.39	34	1726		50
1.40	35	1728	Ref: Jan Lingen	80
1.41	36	1731	None traced. Recorded from Pridmore	NV
1.42	37	1739		50
1.43	38	1741		50
1.44	39	1744		50
1.45	40	1745	Not examined	NV

See also Fort St David mint for dudus struck 1748-1752, p. 503

Copper Ten Cash (Dudu) – 1755 to 1806

1.65

Balemark containing GCE within a wavy line circle.

Date between wavy lines and within a circle.

Official Weight (g)	6.30
Actual Weight (g)	5.06-6.36
Actual Diameter (mm)	11.9-19.0
Metal	Copper

Dudu

Catalogue

Cat No	Pr. No.	Date	Comments	Value ($)
1.46	45	1755		50
1.47	46	1756		50
1.48	-	1758	Ref: Baldwin sale 84, lot 2021	80
1.49	47	1761		50
1.50	48	1765	Ref: Wiggins.	80
1.51	49	1768		50
1.52	50	1769		50
1.53	51	1774		50
1.54	-	1776	Ref: Puddester	80
1.55	52	1777	Ref: Wiggins, Puddester	50
1.56	-	1778	Ref: Puddester	80
1.57	53	1780	Ref: Snartt (1980). SCMB pp. 279-280.	80
1.58	54	1784		50
1.59	55	1786		50
1.60	56	1787	None traced. Recorded from Pridmore	NV
1.61	57	1788	None traced. Recorded from Pridmore	NV
1.62	58	1789	Ref: Puddester, Wiggins	50
1.63	59	1790	None traced. 1791 might also exist (Johnston)	NV
1.64	60	1795		50
1.65	61	1796	Ref: Snartt (1980). SCMB pp. 279-280.	50
1.66	62	1798	None traced. Recorded from Pridmore	NV
1.67	63	1800		50
1.68	64	1801		50
1.69	65	1806	None traced. Recorded from Pridmore	NV

Copper Five Cash (Half Dudu) – 1691 to 1742

1.74

Balemark with GCE within a beaded border. | Date in one or two lines within a plain raised circle.

Official Weight (g)	4.43
Actual Weight (g)	3.73-4.22
Actual Diameter (mm)	12.1-15.5
Metal	Copper

Half Dudu

Catalogue

Cat No.	Pr. No.	Date	Rev	Comments	Value ($)
1.70	66	1691	I		200
1.71	67	1699	I	Not traced. Recorded from Pridmore	NV
1.72	23&68	1700	II	Date in one line	300
1.73	69	1702	I	Ref: Johnston	300
1.74	70	1705	I	NB shape of 5 shown in photo above	200
1.75	-	1706	I	Ref: Lingen	300
1.76	71	1720	I	Not traced. Recorded from Pridmore	NV
1.77	-	1722 or 1723	I	Ref: Lingen. Date not clear	200
1.78	72	1726	I		200
1.79	73	1737	I	Not traced. Recorded from Pridmore	NV
1.80	74	1739	I	Ref: Wiggins	200
1.81	75	1742	I	Not traced. Recorded from Pridmore	NV

Copper Five Cash (Half Dudu) – 1691 to 1742 (cont)

Reverse Varieties

Date	The date may be in one line, or split between two lines.

		I	II
	Date	Two lines	One Line

Date in two lines   *Date in one line*

Copper Five Cash (Half Dudu) 1755 to 1804

1.82

Balemark with GCE within a beaded   Date in two lines
border.

Official Weight (g)	3.15
Actual Weight (g)	2.65-3.14
Actual Diameter (mm)	10.5-13.6
Metal	Copper

½ Dudu

Copper Five Cash (Half Dudu) 1755 to 1804 (cont)

Catalogue

Cat No.	Pr. No.	Date	Comments	Value ($)
1.82	76	1755		200
1.83	-	1757	Ref: Thompson	300
1.84	77	1758	Not traced. Recorded from Pridmore	NV
1.85	78	1761	Ref: Wiggins	200
1.86	79	1768	Ref: Wiggins	200
1.87	-	1776	Manchester Museum	NV
1.88	80	1777		200
1.89	-	1778	Manchester Museum	NV
1.90	-	1781	Ref: Wiggins	300
1.91	81	1784		200
1.92	82	1785	Ref: Wiggins	200
1.93	83	1786		200
1.94	84	1790	Not traced. Recorded from Pridmore	NV
1.95	85	1791	Ref: Puddester	200
1.96	86	1802	Not traced. Recorded from Pridmore	NV
1.97	87	1804	Not traced. Recorded from Pridmore	NV

Copper Cash – 1660 to 1678

1.99

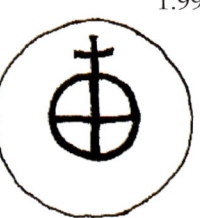

Outline of the balemark of the Company.

Telugu inscription. Translation *Sri Ranga*. Possibly a royal title.

Official Weight (g)	0.53
Actual Weight (g)	0.36-0.70
Actual Diameter (mm)	5.7-7.4
Metal	Copper

	Copper Cash – 1660 to 1678 (cont)	

Catalogue

Cat No	Pr. No.	Rev	Comments	Value ($)
1.98	89	I	Reverse often difficult to distinguish	500
1.99	90	II		500

Varieties exist without the lower vertical bar in the balemark. See ANS website

Reverse Varieties

Telugu Inscription	May be Normal or a Variety with the letters of the legend in the wrong order.

	I	II
Telugu Inscription	Normal	Variety

I – Normal inscription   *II – Variety*

	Copper Cash – 1678 to 1680	

A new style of cash coin was issued in 1678 with a weight of 9.11 troy grains. There appear to be three denominations.

1.102

Balemark with GCE   *Sri Ranga* title in 2 lines. Surrounded by a beaded circle.

	Treble Cash	Double Cash	Cash
Official Weight (g)	1.77	?	0.59
Actual Weight (g)	1.46-1.68	1.18	0.61-0.62
Actual Diameter (mm)	8.5-9.7	9.5-10.8	7.6-10.6
Metal	Copper		

Copper Cash – 1678 to 1680 (cont)

Catalogue

Cat No	Pr. No.	Denomination	Comments	Value ($)
1.100	88	Three (Great) Cash	Very rare. See also ANS 1919.999.133	1500
1.101	-	Two Cash	Ref: Johnston	800
1.102	91	Cash		500

Three Cash | *Two Cash*

Copper Cash – 1678 to 1722

1.104

Balemark with date. Surrounded by a beaded circle. | Telugu inscription. Translation: *Sri Ranga* Possibly a royal title.

	2 Cash	Cash
Official Weight (g)	?	0.88
Actual Weight (g)	1.57-1.66	0.64-0.82
Actual Diameter (mm)	9.5-10.8	7.1-9.0
Metal	Copper	

Copper Cash – 1678 to 1722 (cont)

Catalogue

Cat No	Pr. No.	Denom	Date	Obv	Rev	Comments	Value ($)
1.103	-	2 Cash	[16]78	A	I	Ref: Johnston	500
1.104	-	"	[16]78	A	II	Ref: Johnston, Chopra	500
1.105	92	Cash	[16]78	A	II		100
1.106	-	"	6187	A	?	(1678) Fitzwilliam Museum	NV
1.107	-	"	1691	?	?	Fitzwilliam Museum	NV
1.108	-	"	1697	C?	?	Ref: Johnston.	100
1.109	94	"	1698	B	II		100
1.110	93	"	1698	B	III		100
1.111	-	"	1698	C	II	Ref: Chopra.	200
1.112	-	"	1700	C	?	Ref: Chopra.	200
1.113	95	"	1702	C	III		100
1.114	-	"	1703			Ref: Wiggins	100
1.115	-	"	1704	C	III	Ref: Johnston	100
1.116	96	"	1705	C	III	Figure 5 same shape as on half dudu	100
1.117	-	"	1708	?	?	Fitzwilliam Museum	NV
1.118	-	"	1722	C	III	ANS 1919.60.226	NV

Obverse Varieties

Design	The design may consist of a balemark with the date in the lower half and the top half empty, the date in two lines in a plain circle, or a balemark with the date divided between the top and bottom.

	A	B	C
Design	Date in lower half	No balemark	Full date in balemark

A – Date in lower half   *B – Date with no balemark*   *C – Full date in balemark*

Copper Cash – 1678 to 1722 (cont)

Reverse Varieties

Title	The bottom part of the title may be spelt correctly or the letters may be reversed. The oval in the centre may be missing

I	No Oval	II	Mis-spelt	III	Correct

Reverse I

Copper Cash – 1725 to 1740

1.123

A heart shaped shield with a 4 on top. Triply divided. In each third is a letter E I C. A wavy line above. All within a beaded border?

Date within a dotted circle.

Official Weight (g)	1.20
Actual Weight (g)	1.07-1.65
Actual Diameter (mm)	7.4-11.0
Metal	Copper

Copper Cash – 1725 to 1740 (cont)

Catalogue

Cat No	Pr. No.	Date	Obv	Comments	Value ($)
1.119	-	1725	A	Ref: Lingen	80
1.120	97	1731	A	Specimens exist with a bar across the 7	30
1.121	98	1733	A		30
1.122	99	1734	A		30
1.123	100	1736	A		30
1.124	101	1737	A	Ref: Johnston	30
1.125	101	1737	B		30
1.126	102	1739	A		30
1.127	-	1740	A	Ref: Johnston	100

See also Fort St David mint for cash struck 1748-1752, p. 506

Obverse Varieties

Letters in balemark	The letters in the balemark may be arranged clockwise or anticlockwise.

	A	B
Letters in balemark	Clockwise	Anticlockwise

Letters Clockwise   *Letters Anticlockwise*

1725 cash. (Photo from Jan Lingen). 1.6g

Copper Single and Half Pice – 1803 to 1808

1.128

Balemark within a plain circle

Date within a plain circle

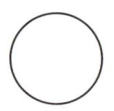

	Pice	Half Pice
Actual Weight (g)	2.11-2.85	0.88-1.20
Actual Diameter (mm)	10.6-13.2	7.5-10.6
Metal	Copper	

Catalogue

Cat No	Pr. No.	Denomination	Date	Comments	Value ($)
1.128	319	Pice	1803		80
1.129	-	"	1804?	Date not certain	120
1.130	320	"	1807		80
1.131	321	Half Pice	1803		70
1.132	-	"	1808	Ref: Puddester	NV

Possibly 1804 Pice? 2.20g. 10.6-11.3mm

Half pice reverse showing complete date

Madras Presidency
Madras Mint
Early Coinages
Moghul Style

Summary

Once the state of Golconda had been conquered by the Moghul Emperor, Aurangzeb, in 1687, Moghul style coins began to be used in the area. These were based on the rupee. The authorities at Madras obtained permission to strike Moghul style coins in 1692 and this included both gold mohurs and silver rupees although very few gold coins were struck. Initially the coins bore the mint name: Chinapatan, the local name for Madras, but later, this was changed to Arkot, the name of a neighbouring town whose rupees were widely used, especially in Bengal. The EIC had extensive trading interests in Bengal but did not acquire the right to mint coins there until 1757 (see Bengal section) so bullion was often shipped to Madras for coinage into Arkot rupees before onward passage to Bengal.

Gold Mohur – Aurangzeb Alamgir 1658-1707 – Chinapatan

2.1

 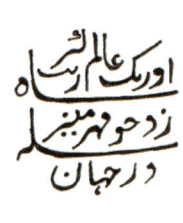    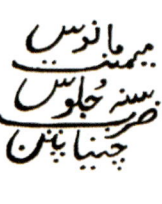

sikka zad dar jahan chau muhr munir Shah Aurangzeb Alamgir (= Struck money through the world like the shining sun. Shah Aurangzeb Alamgir)	*zarb chinapatan sanat [RY] julus maimanat manus* (= Struck at Chinapatan in the [RY] year of tranquil prosperity)

Official Weight (g)	11.01
Actual Weight (g)	11.01
Actual Diameter (mm)	19.8-20.7
Metal	Gold

Mohur

Catalogue

Cat No.	Pr. No.	AH	RY	Comments	Value ($)
2.1	109	1114	47	One sold privately in 2004. Another in 2007	10,000

Silver Rupee – Aurangzeb Alamgir 1658 to 1707 – Chinapatan

2.6

     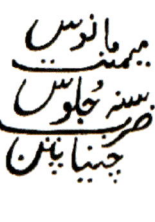

sikka zad dar jahan chau badr munir shah aurangzeb 'Alamgir (= Struck money through the world like the shining moon Shah Aurangzeb 'Alamgir)	*zarb chinapatan sanat [RY] julus maimanat manus* (= Struck at Chinapatan in the [RY] year of tranquil prosperity)

Silver Rupee – Aurangzeb Alamgir 1658 to 1707 – Chinapatan (cont)	
Official Weight (g)	11.59
Actual Weight (g)	11.03-11.62
Actual Diameter (mm)	21.0-24.0
Metal	Silver

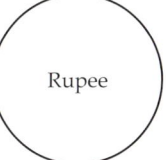

Rupee

Catalogue

Cat No.	Pr. No.	AH	RY	Comments	Mintage (from Banerji[1])	Value ($)
2.2	-	1103	38	Two styles exist. One with AH and one without		200
2.3	-		39	Neither the author nor the contributors have seen a RY 35 coin. Pridmore illustration is unclear and may be RY 39. Specimen in BM may be 35 or 39.		200
2.4	113		40			200
2.5	114		41			200
2.6	115		42	Also KM		200
2.7	-		43	Ref: Lingen		200
2.8	116		45			200
2.9	-		46			200
2.10	-		47	Reported, not confirmed. KM		NV
2.11	-		48	Ref: Johnston		200
2.12	117		49			200
2.13	-		50	Ref: Puddester	156,915	200
2.14	118		51		541,380	200

Although AH dates have been reported, no trace of an AH date has been seen on any specimens examined, except for the AH 1103, RY 38, shown below (Lingen).

Rupee dated 1103/38. The AH date is in the loop at top centre on the obverse. The style of the mint name differs from later coins.

---

[1] Banerji R.N. (1974). Economic Progress of the East India Company on the Coromandel Coast, 1702-1746. Nagpur, 1974.

Silver Rupee – Shah Alam I Bahadur 1707 to 1712 – Chinapatan

2.19

Shah 'Alam Badshah ghazi sanah [AH]
(= Shah 'Alam. Victorious Emperor.
[AH] Year)

zarb chinapatan sanah [RY] julus
(= Struck at Chinapatan in the [RY] year
of his reign)

Official Weight (g)	11.57
Actual Weight (g)	10.93-11.61
Actual Diameter (mm)	21.3-23.6
Metal	Silver

Rupee

Catalogue

Cat No.	Pr. No.	AH	RY	Comments	Mintage (from Banerji[2])	Value ($)
2.15	119	1119	Ahd(=1)			150
2.16	120	1120	2			150
2.17	121	1121	3		1,579,220.	150
2.18	122	1122	4	AH1122 confirmed		150
2.19	123	1123	5			150
2.20	124	1124	6			150

Rupee 1120/ 2

---

[2] Banerji R.N. (1974). *Economic Progress of the East India Company on the Coromandel Coast, 1702-1746.* Nagpur, 1974.

Silver Rupee – Jahandar Shah 1712 to 1713 – Chinapatan

2.21

sikka bezad bar mah chau sahib qiran jahandar shah. badshah jahan (= Struck money like the shining moon. The Great Emperor Jahandar Shah. King of the World)

zarb chinapatan sanah [RY] julus maimanat manus (= Struck at Chinapatan in the [RY] year of tranquil prosperity)

Official Weight (g)	11.57
Actual Weight (g)	11.50-11.58
Actual Diameter (mm)	23.0-24.1
Metal	Silver

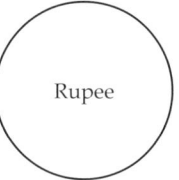

Rupee

Catalogue

Cat No.	Pr. No.	RY	Comments	Value ($)
2.21	125	Ahd (=1)		1500

Silver Rupee – Farrukh-Siyar 1713 to 1719 – Chinapatan

2.22

   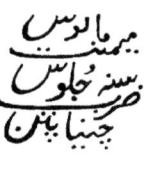

sikka zad az fazl hagg bar sim wa zar badshah bahar wa bar farrukh-siyar (= Struck money of gold and silver by the grace of God Emperor of sea and land. Farrukh-Siyar)

zarb chinapatan sanat [RY] julus maimanat manus (= Struck at Chinapatan in the [RY] year of tranquil prosperity)

Silver Rupee – Farrukh-Siyar 1713 to 1719 – Chinapatan (cont)

	Rupee	Half Rupee	Quarter Rupee
Official Weight (g)	11.57	5.78	2.89
Actual Weight (g)	10.69-11.78	5.89	2.91
Actual Diameter (mm)	23.7-24.7	18.1	~15
Metal	Silver		

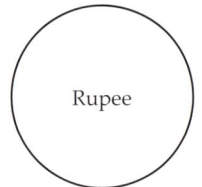

Rupee

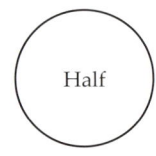

Half

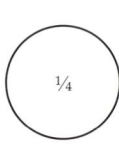

¼

Catalogue

Cat No.	Pr. No.	Denomination	AH	RY	Comments	Mintage (from Banerji[3])	Value ($)
2.22	126	Rupee	1125	2			150
2.23	127	"	[11]26	3			150
2.24	128	"	1128	5			150
2.25	-	"	[112]9	6	Ref: Puddester	359,250	200
2.26	129	"	1130	7		1,652,575	150
2.27	-	Half Rupee	1129	6	Ashmolean Museum.		NV
2.28	-	Quarter Rupee	1128	5	HK/Singapore (2003), sale 37, lot 527		1250

Gold Mohur – Muhammad Shah 1719 to 1748 – Chinapatan

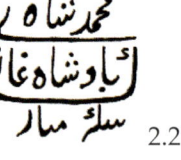

2.29

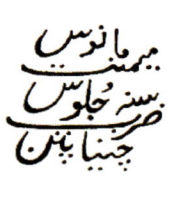

sikka mubarak badshah ghazi Muhammad Shah (= the auspicious coin of the Victorious Emperor Muhammad Shah)	*zarb chinapatan sanat [RY] julus maimanat manus* (= Struck at Chinapatan in the [RY] year of tranquil prosperity)

---

[3] Banerji R.N. (1974). Economic Progress of the East India Company on the Coromandel Coast, 1702-1746. Nagpur, 1974.

Gold Mohur – Muhammad Shah 1719 to 1748 – Chinapatan (cont)

	Mohur	Quarter Mohur
Official Weight (g)	10.88	2.72
Actual Weight (g)	10.89	2.70
Actual Diameter (mm)	18.7-19.5	11
Metal	Gold	

 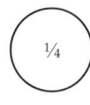

Catalogue

Cat No.	Pr. No.	Denomination	RY	Comments	Value ($)
2.29	110	Mohur	26?		12,000
2.30	-	Quarter Mohur		Nick Rhodes from a private collection in Calcutta	NV

Silver Rupee – Muhammad Shah 1719 to 1748 – Chinapatan

2.39

 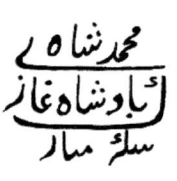  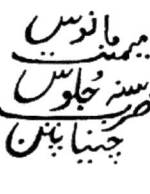

sikka mubarak badshah ghazi muhammad shah (= the auspicious coin of the Victorious Emperor Muhammad Shah)

zarb chinapatan sanat [RY] julus maimanat manus (= Struck at Chinapatan in the (RY) year of tranquil prosperity)

	Rupee	Quarter Rupee
Official Weight (g)	11.57	2.89
Actual Weight (g)	10.82-11.57	2.80-2.84
Actual Diameter (mm)	19.0-22.5	15-16
Metal	Silver	

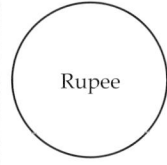 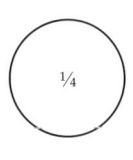

Silver Rupee – Muhammad Shah 1719 to 1748 – Chinapatan (cont)

Catalogue

Cat No.	Pr. No.	Denomination	AH	RY	Comments	Mintage (from Banerji[4])	Value ($)
2.31	-	Rupee	xxxx	2	Ref: HK/Singapore (2003), sale 37, lot 523. However, the smaller diameters seen suggest this is probably RY 2x, e.g. 23		150
2.32	-	"	11xx	3	Ref: Puddester	241,720	150
2.33	-	"	xxxx	4	Ref: HK/Singapore (2003), sale 37, lot 523		150
2.34	-	"	"	5	Ref: Puddester, Wiggins	63,770	150
2.35	-	"	"	6	None traced. The coin in the Noble sale (lot 1991) is of Ahmad Shah.	24,050	150
2.36	130	"	11xx	7		47,820	150
2.37	131	"	xxxx	8		105,935	150
2.38	132	"	"	9			150
2.39	133	"	"	11			150
2.40	-	"	1142?	13	Ref: Johnston		150
2.41	-	"	xxxx	14	S. Album Feb 1985		150
2.42	-	"	"	18	RC Senior List 5, issued 1984. Cat No. 591. Also SNC Nov 1984		150
2.43	-	"	"	23	Ref: Chopra, Johnston		200
2.44	-	Quarter Rupee	xxxx	3	Ref: HK/Singapore (1999), Sale 28, lot 1014. Also Ashmolean. Specially prepared small dies.		1000

Quarter rupee from small dies

---

[4] Banerji R.N. (1974). Economic Progress of the East India Company on the Coromandel Coast, 1702-1746. Nagpur, 1974.

Silver Rupee – Ahmad Shah 1748 to 1754 – Chinapatan

2.45

 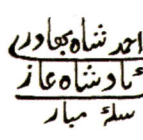    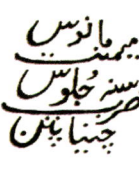

sikka mubarak badshah ghazi ahmad shah bahadur (= the auspicious coin of the victorious emperor Ahmad Shah the valiant)	*zarb chinapatan sanat [RY] julus maimanat manus* (= Struck at Chinapatan in the [RY] year of tranquil prosperity)

Official Weight (g)	11.59
Actual Weight (g)	11.24
Actual Diameter (mm)	20.9-21.4
Metal	Silver

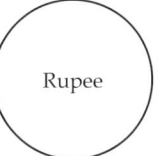

Rupee

Catalogue

Cat No.	Pr. No.	Denomination	AH	RY	Comments	Value ($)
2.45	-	Rupee	xxxx	6	Ref: Johnston	1,000

Another example showing the date but less of the mint and ruler.
The mint is identified by the star on the reverse

379

Gold Mohur – Muhammad Shah 1719 to 1748 – Arkot

Permission to strike coins with the Arkot mint name was obtained on 4th November 1742. Both gold and silver coins were initially issued from a new mint at Chintadripetta just outside Madras[5]. No gold coins are currently known.

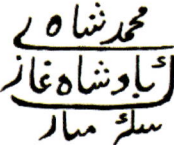

sikka mubarak badshah ghazi muhammad shah (= the auspicious coin of the Victorious Emperor Muhammad Shah)

zarb arket sanat [RY] julus maimanat manus (= Struck at Arkat in the [RY] year of tranquil prosperity)

Official Weight (g)	10.88
Actual Weight (g)	?
Actual Diameter (mm)	?
Metal	Gold

Catalogue

Cat No.	Pr. No.	Comments	Value ($)
2.46	111	None known to exist. Recorded from Pridmore	NV

Silver Rupee – Muhammad Shah 1719 to 1748 – Arkot

2.47

sikka mubarak badshah ghazi muhammad shah (= the auspicious coin of the Victorious Emperor Muhammad Shah)

zarb arket sanat [RY] julus maimanat manus (= Struck at Arkat in the [RY] year of tranquil prosperity).
Note the lotus to the right of julus. This is the mark of the EIC at Arkot

---

5 Pridmore

Silver Rupee – Muhammad Shah 1719 to 1748 – Arkot		

Official Weight (g)	11.43
Actual Weight (g)	11.67
Actual Diameter (mm)	20.0
Metal	Silver

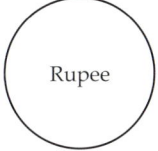

Rupee

Catalogue

Cat No.	Pr. No.	AH	RY	Comments	Value ($)
2.47	-	11xx	x	Fitzwilliam Museum. Also Hemanth Chopra. Very rare	500

Another example

Silver Rupee – Ahmad Shah 1748 to 1754 – Arkot

The French occupied Madras from 1746 until 1749 and the mint was not rebuilt there until 1754. Thus, most of these coins must have been struck at Fort St. David (Cuddalore).

2.54

sikka mubarak badshah ghazi ahmad shah bahadur (= the auspicious coin of the Victorious Emperor Ahmad Shah the Valiant)

zarb arkat sanat [RY] julus maimanat manus (= Struck at Arkat in the [RY] year of tranquil prosperity)

Silver Rupee – Ahmad Shah 1748 to 1754 – Arkot (cont)

	Rupee	Half Rupee
Official Weight (g)	11.43	5.72
Actual Weight (g)	10.83-11.78	5.72
Actual Diameter (mm)	19.9-21.2	17.0
Metal	Silver	

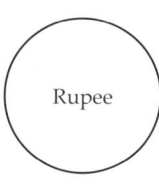 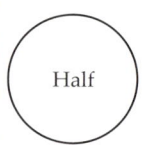

Rupee   Half

Catalogue

Cat No.	Pr. No.	Denomination	AH	RY	Comments	Value ($)
2.48	135	Rupee	[11]62	Ahd(=1)		100
2.49	136	"	1163	2		100
2.50	-	"	1164	3	Ref: Lingen	100
2.51	137	"	xxxx	4	Ref: Format 3/95.	100
2.52	-	"	[116]6	5	Ref: Puddester	100
2.53	-	"	[xx]66	6	Ref: Craig Fernandez, Johnston	100
2.54	-	"	1167	7	Ref: Wiggins, Puddester	100
2.55	141	Half Rupee	xxxx	Ahd(=1)		250

Gold Mohur – Alamgir II 1754 to 1759 – Arkot

2.56

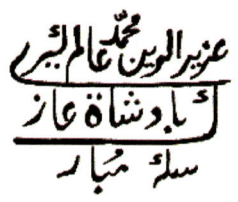  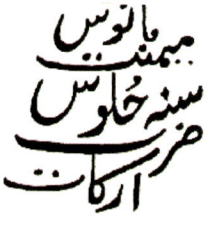

sikka mubarak badshah ghazi aziz-al-din muhammad alamgir (= the auspicious coin of the Victorious Emperor 'Alamgir. Chosen of the faith of Muhammad)

zarb arkat sanat [RY] julus maimanat manus (= Struck at Arkat in the [RY] year of tranquil prosperity)

Actual Weight (g)	10.77
Actual Diameter (mm)	18.2
Metal	Gold

Mohur

Gold Mohur – Alamgir II 1754 to 1759 – Arkot (cont)

Catalogue

Cat No.	Pr. No.	AH	RY	Comments	Value ($)
2.56	-	xxxx	3		5,000
2.57	-	xxxx	6	Ref: Puddester	5,000

Silver Rupee – Alamgir II (1754 to 1759) – Arkot

2.58

  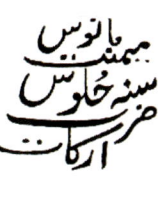

sikka mubarak badshah ghazi Aziz-ul-din Muhammad. Alamgir (= the auspicious coin of the Victorious Emperor 'Alamgir. Chosen of the faith of Muhammad)

zarb Arkat sanat [RY] julus maimanat manus (= Struck at Arkat in the [RY] year of tranquil prosperity)

	Rupee	Half Rupee	Quarter Rupee	Eighth Rupee	Sixteenth Rupee
Official Weight (g)	11.43	5.72	2.86	1.42	0.71
Actual Weight (g)	10.64-11.57	5.38-5.74	2.76-2.82	1.35-1.42	0.58
Actual Diameter (mm)	20.0-25.0	16.5-18.5	13.5-15.1	10.0-11.0	8.0
Metal	Silver				

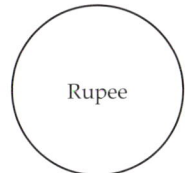 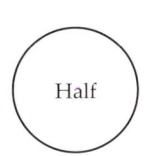 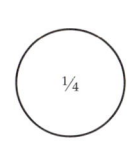 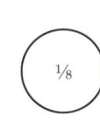 

Rupee · Half · ¼ · ⅛

Silver Rupee – Alamgir II (1754 to 1759) – Arkot

Catalogue

Cat No.	Pr. No.	Denomination	AH	RY	Comments	Value ($)
2.58	-	Rupee	1167	Ahd (=1)	Ref: Chopra, Lingen	100
2.59	138	"	xxxx	2		100
2.60	-	"	1169	3	AH not certain but likely. Ref: Johnston	100
2.61	139	"	1170	4	Ref: Johnston	100
2.62	139A	"	1171	5		100
2.63	140	"	1172	6	Fixed regnal year. Also recorded under Bengal as 2.196. A coin dated 1182 has been seen but this may be a mistake for 1172?	60
2.64	142	Half Rupee	"	6		250
2.65	143	Quarter Rupee	"	6		150
2.66	144	Eighth Rupee	"	6		150
2.67	145	Sixteenth Rupee	"	6		200

NB. Examples of coins with AH dates are very rare.

Sometimes it is difficult to determine which emperor a coin belongs to. There are some dot groupings that might help with this. The groups below julus on the reverse seem to vary as follows: Md Shah usually has a diamond and 4 dots right, Ahmed Shah has a diamond and 3 dots right and Alamgir has 3 dots and a diamond right. Pridmore recorded this but my thanks go to Bob Johnston for pointing this out.

Muhammad Shah   Ahmad Shah   Alamgir II

Madras Presidency Madras Mint Reformation 1807 to 1818

Summary[6]

In 1806 a decision was taken to introduce machinery into the Madras mint and Benjamin Roebuck was appointed mint master. Machinery was imported from Calcutta and a new series of coin designs was adopted with minting beginning in 1807. Some of the coins were slightly redesigned in 1808 but coinage was stopped in 1812 by orders from London, although striking of gold coins continued until about 1818. One of the most notable features of the coins, particularly the silver coins, is the huge number of different varieties found. This indicates the use of a large number of different dies. The larger silver coins such as the half and quarter pagodas and the double rupee, were struck directly onto imported Spanish dollars which contained a higher proportion of alloy than the silver coins struck at Calcutta, making the metal harder and causing the dies to break, sometimes after as few as 15 strikes. The smaller silver coins were struck from silver from the same source. An attempt has been made to catalogue as many of these varieties as possible but there is no doubt that many others remain to be found. It is possible that some of the varieties may be contemporary forgeries. Many coins have been examined by XRF and almost all contained the correct quantity of silver, so most varieties appear to be genuine.

---

[6] See Stevens (2004), BNJ vol 74 pp. 121-144 for a fuller account of this period

Gold Two Pagodas 1808 to 1817

3.2

Seven tiered Gopuram of a temple, standing on stony ground. Between seven and nine stars on each side. All this surrounded by a buckled garter. On the garter is the value in English:
TWO PAGODAS
and Persian. (Persian = *do hun* = Two hun):

دو هون

Figure of Vishnu holding a sword in his left hand and rising from a lotus flower. Dotted and other symbols on each side.
All surrounded by three circles of beads. All this within a ribbon, the ends separated by a star. On the ribbon is the value in Tamil and Telugu:

உவராகண

౩ వరహూవి

All within a beaded border. (Tamil = *2 vara kun*, Telugu = *2 vara hun* = 2 hun)

Official Weight (g)	5.94
Actual Weight (g)	5.89-5.92
Actual Diameter (mm)	20.1-21.6
Edge	Grained Right
Metal	Gold
Axis	↑↑
Mintage	1,063,912

Two Pagodas

386

Gold Two Pagodas 1808 to 1817 (cont)

Catalogue

Cat No.	Obv	Rev	Obverse				Reverse		Comments	Value ($)
			Stars	Stops	Buckle	Gopuram	3 Circles	Stop		
3.1	A	I	9/9	End	Oval	OD	Yes	No	Ref: Johnston. Gopuram may point to D	1,000
3.2	A	II	9/9	End	Oval	OD	Yes	No		1,000
3.3	A	IV	9/9	End	Oval	OD	No	No	Ref: BM	1,000
3.4	B	I	9/9	End	Oval	O	Yes	Yes		1,000
3.5	B	II	9/9	End	Oval	O	Yes	No	Ref: BM	1,000
3.6	B	IV	9/9	End	Oval	O	No	No		1,000
3.7	C	II	9/9	End	Oval	G	Yes	No		1,000
3.8	C	III	9/9	End	Oval	G	No	Yes		1,000
3.9	D	I	9/9	End	Oval	GO	Yes	Yes	Ref: Baldwin (2007), sale 53, lot 2079	1,000
3.10	D	III	9/9	End	Oval	GO	No	Yes		1,000
3.11	D	IV	9/9	End	Oval	GO	No	No		1,000
3.12	E	II	9/9	End	Oval	D	Yes	No		1,000
3.13	F	II	9/9	End	Square	GO	Yes	No	Ref: BM	1,000
3.14	F	IV	9/9	End	Square	GO	No	No	Ref: BM	1,000
3.15	G	IV	9/9	End	Square	G	No	No		1,000
3.16	H	III	9/9	End	Square	O	No	Yes		1,000
3.17	H	IV	9/9	End	Square	O	No	No		1,000
3.18	I	I	9/9	C+E	Oval	GO	Yes	Yes	Ref: Puddester	1,000
3.19	I	IV	9/9	C+E	Oval	GO	No	No		1,000
3.20	J	II	9/9	C+E	Oval	OD	Yes	No		1,000
3.21	K	II	9/9	C+E	Oval	O	Yes	No		1,000
3.22	K	IV	9/9	C+E	Oval	O	No	No		1,000
3.23	L	IV	9/9	None	Oval	O	No	No		1,000
3.24	M	IV	7/7	None	Square	G	No	No	Ref: BM	1,000
3.25	N	IV	7/7	None	Oval	G	No	No		1,000
3.26	O	IV	7/7	End	Square	GO	No	No		2,000

Gold Two Pagodas 1808 to 1817 (cont)

Obverse Varieties

Number of stars	The number of stars on each side of the gopuram can vary.
Stops in Legend	There may be no stops, an end stop alone, or a centre stop plus an end stop in the English legend
Shape of Buckle	The buckle may be oval or square
Gopuram	The gopuram may point between the letters G and O, between the letters O and D, or directly at the letter G, O or D.

	A	B	C	D	E	F	G
Number of stars	9/9	9/9	9/9	9/9	9/9	9/9	9/9
Stops in Legend	E	E	E	E	E	E	E
Shape of Buckle	Oval	Oval	Oval	Oval	Oval	Square	Square
Gopuram	OD	O	G	GO	D	GO	G

	H	I	J	K	L	M	N	O
Number of stars	9/9	9/9	9/9	9/9	9/9	7/7	7/7	7/7
Stops in Legend	E	C+E	C+E	C+E	None	None	None	E
Shape of Buckle	Square	Oval	Oval	Oval	Oval	Square	Oval	Square
Gopuram	O	GO	OD	O	O	G	O	GO

No stops

End stop

Centre & end stops

Oval buckle

Square buckle

Gold Two Pagodas 1808 to 1817 (cont)

9 Stars

7 Stars

Gopuram points between G & O

Gopuram points between O & D

Gopuram points to G

Gopuram points to O

Gopuram points to D

Reverse Varieties

3 circles of beads	All three circles of beads are complete, or the stalk of the lotus flower or other symbols interrupt one or more of the circles.
Bead in Telugu legend	There may or may not be a bead in the Telugu legend.

	I	II	III	IV
3 circles of beads	Yes	Yes	No	No
Bead in Telugu legend	Yes	No	Yes	No

3 complete circles of beads

Circle of beads interrupted

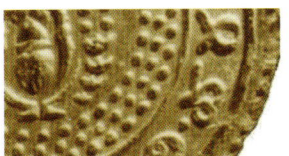

Bead in Telugu legend

No bead in Telugu legend

Gold Pagoda 1808 to 1817

3.28

Seven tiered Gopuram of a temple, standing on stony ground. Five stars on each side. All this surrounded by a buckled garter. On the garter is the value in English:
PAGODA
and Persian:

لی هن

All within a beaded border. (Persian = *hun* = hun)

Figure of Vishnu holding a sword in his left hand and rising from a lotus flower. Dotted and other symbols on each side. All surrounded by one circle of beads. All this within a ribbon, the ends separated by a star. On the ribbon is the value in Tamil and Telugu:
வராகண
వరహాని
Separated by a bead. All within a beaded border. (Tamil = *vara kun* Telugu = *vara hun* = hun)

Official Weight (g)	2.97
Actual Weight (g)	2.93-3.05
Actual Diameter (mm)	16.8-17.4
Edge	Grained Right
Axis	↑↑
Mintage	1,381,809

Pagoda

Gold Pagoda 1808 to 1817

Catalogue

Cat No.	Obv	Rev	Obverse		Reverse		Comments	Value ($)
			Buckle	Gopuram	Stop	Beads in Cross		
3.27	A	I	Oval	O	Yes	11/9		800
3.28	A	II	Oval	O	Yes	13/11		800
3.29	B	I	Oval	OD	Yes	11/9	Ref: Puddester	800
3.30	B	III	Oval	OD	Yes	11/11	Ref: Thompson	800
3.31	C	I	Oval	D	Yes	11/9	Ref: Todywalla	800
3.32	C	III	Oval	D	Yes	11/11		800
3.33	D	I	Square	OD	Yes	11/9		800
3.34	D	IV	Square	OD	No	11/9	Authenticity suspect.	800
3.45	E	I	Square	D	Yes	11/9		800
3.36	F	I	Square	O	Yes	11/9		800
3.37	F	IV	Square	O	No	11/9	Ref: BM	800

Jeweller's copy

Probably a modern forgery (as 3.34). NB the way the dots are joined by a line. This represents the 'no stop' variety'

Gold Pagoda 1808 to 1817 (cont)

Obverse Varieties

Buckle Shape	The buckle may be oval or square.
Gopuram	The gopuram may point between the letters O and D, directly at the letter O, or directly at the letter D.

	A	B	C	D	E	F
Buckle Shape	Oval	Oval	Oval	Square	Square	Square
Gopuram	O	OD	D	OD	D	O

Oval buckle

Square buckle

Gopuram points to O

Gopuram between O & D

Gopuram points to D

Reverse Varieties

Stop in Legend	There is usually a stop between the Tamil and Telugu legends. On some coins this stop is not present.
Top Left Cross	To the left of Vishnu is an arrangement of dots topped by a cross shape, representing one of his wives. The number of dots that form this figure varies.
Top Right Cross	To the right of Vishnu is an arrangement of dots topped by a cross shape, representing one of his wives. The number of dots that form this figure varies.

	I	II	III	IV
Stop in Legend	Present	Present	Present	Absent
Top Left Cross	11	13	11	11
Top Right Cross	9	11	11	9

Gold Pagoda 1808 to 1817 (cont)

Stop in legend

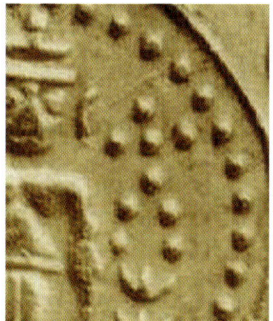

Top right cross – 9

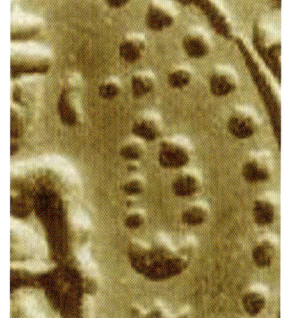

Top right cross – 11 (ignore tiny dots)

Top left cross – 11

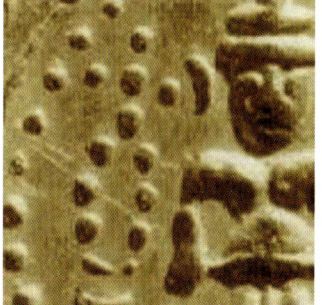

Top left cross – 13

Silver Half Pagoda 1807 to 1808

3.50

Nine tiered Gopuram of a temple, standing on stony ground. Between eight and eighteen stars on each side. All this surrounded by a ribbon, the ends of which are separated by a star. On the ribbon is the value in English:
HALF PAGODA
and Persian:

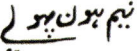

(Persian = *Nim hun phuli* = half a flower, or star, pagoda)

Figure of Vishnu holding a sword in his left hand and rising from a lotus flower. Dotted and other symbols on each side. All surrounded by three, four or five circles of beads. Around this is the value in Tamil and Telugu:

அரை பூவராகண

అరవూవరహుఎ

All within a beaded or toothed border.
(Tamil = *Arai pu vara kun*, Telugu = *Ara pu vara hun* = half a flower, or star, pagoda)

Official Weight (g)	21.17
Actual Weight (g)	20.69-21.27
Actual Diameter (mm)	35.1-37.4
Metal	Silver
Edge	Grained Right
Axis	↑↑
Mintage	500,800

Half Pagoda

Silver Half Pagoda 1807 to 1808 (cont)

Catalogue

Cat No.	Obv	Rev	Obverse		Reverse				Comments	Value ($)
			Stars	Persian	Circles	Crosses	Tamil	Telugu		
3.38	A	I	18	Inward	5	?/14	Left Inward	Right Outward		1,000
3.39	A	VIII	18	Inward	5	13/14	Left Outward	Right Outward	Ref: BM. Bead count not verified	1,000
3.40	B	IX	17+1+17	Outward	4	16/11	Left Inward	Right Outward		1,000
3.41	C	VIII	16+17	Inward	5	13/14	Left Outward	Right Outward		1,000
3.42	D	III	16	Inward	5	17/16	Left Inward	Right Inward	ANS 1917.216.4753	1,000
3.43	E	V	15	Inward	5	16/13	Left Inward	Right Inward		1,000
3.44	E	VI	15	Inward	5	15/13	Left Inward	Right Inward	Baldwin sale 54, lot 185	1,000
3.45	F	VII	14	Inward	5	15/14	Right Inward	Left Inward		1,000
3.46	G	II	14	Outward	5	15/13	Left Inward	Right Outward		1,000
3.47	G	IX	14	Outward	4	16/11	Left Inward	Right Outward		1,000
3.48	G	X	14	Outward	4	14/16	Left Inward	Right Outward	Ref: Baldwin sale 54, lot 184	1,000
3.49	H	IX	13	Outward	4	16/11	Left Inward	Right Outward	Ref: ANS 1919.148.1	1,000
3.50	I	IV	12	Inward	5	16/14	Left Inward	Right Inward		1,000
3.51	J	XI	8	Outward	3	16/13	Left Inward	Right Outward	Ref: Pr. sale part 2, Oct 1982, lot 370. Then Baldwin (2000), Sale 22 (Wheeler), lot 20. Axis: ↑↑	3,000

Silver Half Pagoda 1807 to 1808 (cont)

Obverse Varieties

There is usually a centre and end stop in the English legend. However, on one variety (C) there is only a centre stop. Since this only occurs on this one obverse variety, and the number of stars is a more obvious distinguishing feature, the stops in the legend are not included as part of the variety identifiers.

Number of stars	The number of stars on each side of the gopuram can vary.
Persian Legend	The top of the Persian legend may face inward or outward

	A	B	C	D	E
Number of stars	18	17+1+17	16+17	16	15
Persian Legend	Inward	Outward	Inward	Inward	Inward

	F	G	H	I	J
Number of stars	14	14	13	12	8
Persian Legend	Inward	Outward	Outward	Inward	Outward

18 stars   *17+1+17 stars*   *16+17 stars*

Silver Half Pagoda 1807 to 1808 (cont)

15 stars

14 stars

13 stars

12 stars

8 stars

Persian legend faces outward

Persian legend faces inward

Silver Half Pagoda 1807 to 1808 (cont)

Reverse Varieties

Circles of Beads	There may be 3, 4 or 5 circles of beads.
Top Left Cross	To the left of Vishnu is an arrangement of dots topped by a cross shape, representing one of his wives. The number of dots that form this figure varies.
Top Right Cross	To the right of Vishnu is an arrangement of dots topped by a cross shape, representing one of his wives. The number of dots that form this figure varies.
Tamil Legend	The Tamil legend may be to the left or right of Vishnu, and the top of the letters may face inward or outward
Telugu Legend	The Telugu legend may be to the left or right of Vishnu, and the top of the letters may face inward or outward.

	I	II	III	IV	V	VI
Circles of Beads	5	5	5	5	5	5
Top Left Cross	?	15	17	16	16	15
Top Right Cross	14	13	16	14	13	13
Tamil Legend	Left Inward	Left Inward	Left Inward	Left Inward	Left Inward	Left Inward
Telugu Legend	Right Outward	Right Outward	Right Inward	Right Inward	Right Inward	Right Inward

	VII	VIII	IX	X	XI
Circles of Beads	5	5	4	4	3
Top Left Cross	15	13	16	14	16
Top Right Cross	14	14	11	16	13
Tamil Legend	Right Inward	Left Outward	Left Inward	Left Inward	Left Inward
Telugu Legend	Left Inward	Right Outward	Right Outward	Right Outward	Right Outward

5 circles of beads	*4 circles of beads*	*3 circles of beads*

Silver Half Pagoda 1807 to 1808 (cont)

Top Left Cross – 13

Top Left Cross – 14

Top Left Cross – 15

Top Left Cross – 16

Top Right Cross – 11

Top Right Cross – 13

Top Right Cross – 14

Top Right Cross – 16

Tamil legend – Left, Inward

Tamil legend – Left, Outward

Tamil legend – Right, Inward

Telugu legend – Right, Outward

Telugu legend – Right, Inward

Telugu legend – Left, Inward

Silver Quarter Pagoda 1807 to 1808

3.53

Seven tiered Gopuram of a temple, standing on stony ground. 9, 11 or 13 stars on each side. All this surrounded by a ribbon, the ends of which are separated by a star. On the ribbon is the value in English:

QUARTER PAGODA

and Persian:

پاو هن پهلی

All within a beaded or toothed border. (Persian = *Pau hun Phuli* = Quarter of a flower, or star, pagoda)

Figure of Vishnu holding a sword in his left hand and rising from a lotus flower. Dotted and other symbols on each side. All surrounded by three or four circles of beads. Around this is the value in Tamil and Telugu:

காலவராகண

కాలవరహూని

All within a beaded border. (Tamil = *Kal vara kun*, Telugu = *Kai vara hun* = quarter pagoda)

Official Weight (g)	10.58
Actual Weight (g)	10.41-10.74
Actual Diameter (mm)	25.8-27.2
Metal	Silver
Edge	Grained Right
Axis	↑↑
Mintage	1,772,896

Quarter Pagoda

Silver Quarter Pagoda 1807 to 1808

Catalogue

Cat No.	Obv	Rev	Obverse			Reverse				Comments	Value ($)
			Stars	Persian	Letters	Circles	Stops	Beads	Tamil		
3.52	A	I	13+1+13	Outward	AGO	4	Quintets	16	8		800
3.53	B	II	11+1+11	Outward	AGO	4	Single	16	8	Ref: SNC Sept 1976 p. 319. SNC April 1980 p. 147	800
3.54	B	III	11+1+11	Outward	AGO	3	Single	14	8		800
3.55	C	IV	9+9	Inward	AGO	3	Quintets	15	8		500
3.56	C	VI	9+9	Inward	AGO	3	4+5	15	8	Ref: Puddester and photo in Pridmore	500
3.57	D	IV	9+9	Inward	GOD	3	Quintets	15	8		500
3.58	D	V	9+9	Inward	GOD	3	Quintets	15	9	Ref: Kaslove	500
3.59	E	IV	9+9	Inward	AGOD	3	Quintets	15	8		500
3.60	E	V	9+9	Inward	AGOD	3	Quintets	15	9	Ref: Wiggins	500

Obverse Varieties

Number of stars	The number of stars on each side of the gopuram can vary.
Persian Legend	The top of the Persian legend may face inwards or outwards
Letters under Gopuram	The base of the gopuram may be above the letters AGO, AGOD or GOD of PAGODA. An easy way to distinguish these varieties is that the central line of the gopuram points straight to G in the AGO variety, straight to O on the GOD variety and between G & O (or at least to one side of the O) in the AGOD variety.

	A	B	C	D	E
Number of stars	9+9	9+9	9+9	11+1+11	13+1+13
Persian Legend	Inward	Inward	Inward	Outward	Inward
Letters under Gopuram	AGO	GOD	AGOD	AGO	AGOD

9+9 Stars

11+1+11 Stars

13+1+13 Stars

Silver Quarter Pagoda 1807 to 1808 (cont)

Persian Legend Inward

Persian Legend Outward

Letters under Pagoda - AGO

Letters under Pagoda - GOD

Letters under Pagoda - AGOD

Reverse Varieties

Circles of Beads	There may be three or four circles of beads surrounding Vishnu.
Stops in legend	The Tamil and Telugu legends may be separated by two quintets of dots arranged roughly in the shape of a diamond, a quartet of dots above Vishnu plus a quintet below, or by two single dots.
Beads in Cross to Left of Vishnu	The number of beads to the left of Vishnu can vary
Letters in Tamil Legend	There can be different numbers of letters in the Tamil legend.

	I	II	III	IV	V	VI
Circles of Beads	4	4	3	3	3	3
Stops in legend	Quintets	Single	Single	Quintets	Quintets	Quartet + quintet
Beads in Cross to left of Vishnu	16	16	14	15	15	15
Letters in Tamil Legend	8	8	8	8	9	8

Silver Quarter Pagoda 1807 to 1808 (cont)

4 Circles of beads   *3 Circles of beads*

Quintets of stops   *Single stops*

16 Beads   *15 Beads*   *14 Beads*

8 letters in Tamil legend   *9 letters in Tamil legend*

Silver Five Fanams 1807 to 1808

3.61

The value in Persian:

within a plain circle and surrounded by the value in English: FIVE FANAMS

All within a plain border. (Persian = *Panj falam* = Five fanams)

The value in Telugu:

ఆయిదు రూకలు

in two lines within a plain circle. Around this is the value in Tamil:

அ ரு சு பணம

All within a plain border. (Tamil = *Anacu panam*, Telugu = *Aedu rukalu* = Five fanams)

Official Weight (g)	4.65
Actual Weight (g)	4.42-4.70
Actual Diameter (mm)	16.3-17.8
Metal	Silver
Edge	Grained Right
Axis	Not Fixed
Mintage	988,423

Five Fanams

Silver Five Fanams 1807 to 1808 (cont)

Catalogue

Cat No.	Obv	Rev	Obverse				Reverse		Comments	Value ($)
			F & A	V & F	S	Stops	Tamil Letter	Stop		
3.61	A	I				4+1		Yes		300
3.62	B	I				1+4		Yes		300
3.63	B	II				1+4		No	Ref: Hemanth Chopra	300
3.64	B	III				1+4	Open	No		300
3.65	B	IV				1+4	Retrograde	Yes?	Ref: Kaslove; also Hemanth Chopra	300
3.66	C	II				4+4		No		300
3.67	D	I			Retrograde	1+4		Yes	S of FANAMS, retrograde	300
3.68	E	I		Wrong		1+4		Yes	Ref: Thompson	300
3.69	F	I	Wrong			1+4		Yes		300

Obverse Varieties

F & A in FANAMS	The first two letters of FANAMS may be mal-formed
V in FIVE & F in FANAMS	V in FIVE represented by an upside-down A. F in FANAMS represented by an E.
S in FANAMS	The S in the word FANAMS may be retrograde.
Stops in Legend	The stops in the English legend may be composed of single dots (1), or a quartet of dots (4) arranged roughly in the shape of a diamond. These can be mixed on a single coin (e.g. 4+1 means quartet after FIVE and single after FANAMS, 1+4 means single after FIVE and quartet after FANAMS)

	A	B	C	D	E	F
F & A in FANAMS	OK	OK	OK	OK	OK	Mal-formed
V in FIVE & F in FANAMS	OK	OK	OK	OK	Incorrect	OK
S in FANAMS	OK	OK	OK	Retrograde	OK	OK
Stops in Legend	Q+1	1+Q	Q+Q	1+Q	1+Q	1+Q

Silver Five Fanams 1807 to 1808 (cont)

F & A – OK

F & A – mal-formed

S – OK

S – retrograde

Stops in legend – 4+1

Stops in legend – 1+4

Stops in legend – 4+4

Reverse Varieties

Last Tamil Letter	The last letter in the Tamil legend may be the normal closed type, or open. This is a die or striking error rather than a variety. On one variety the letter is retrograde.
Stop in Tamil legend	There may or may not be stops in the Tamil legend.

	I	II	III	IV
Last Tamil Letter	Closed	Closed	Open	Retrograde
Stop in Tamil legend	Yes	No	No	Yes

Silver Five Fanams 1807 to 1808 (cont)

Last Tamil letter closed   *Last Tamil letter open*   *Last Tamil letter retrograde*

Stops in Tamil legend – Yes   *Stops in Tamil legend – No*

Silver Two Fanams 1807 to 1808

3.71

The value in Persian:

دو فلم

With or without a plain circle around. This is surrounded by the value in English:
DOUBLE FANAM
All within a plain border. (Persian = *Do falam* = Double fanam)

The value in Telugu:

రెండు రూకలు

in two lines with or without a plain circle around. Around this is the value in Tamil:

இரண்டு பணம

All within a plain border. (Tamil = *Irantu panam*, Telugu = *Renddu rukalu* = Two fanams)

Official Weight (g)	1.85
Actual Weight (g)	1.70-1.87
Actual Diameter (mm)	12.1-13.2
Metal	Silver
Edge	Plain
Axis	Not fixed
Mintage	1,511,087

2
Fans

Silver Two Fanams 1807 to 1808 (cont)

Catalogue

Cat No.	Obv	Rev	Obverse			Reverse			Comments	Value ($)
			Circle	Stops	Spelling	Circle	Legend U/S down	Stops		
3.70	A	III	Yes	1+1		Yes	No	0	Ref: Puddester	150
3.71	B	I	Yes	1+4		Yes	Yes	4+4		150
3.72	B	II	Yes	1+4		Yes	No	4+4	Ref: Withers & Hemanth Chopra	150
3.73	B	III	Yes	1+4		Yes	No	0	Ref: Withers	150
3.74	B	IV	Yes	1+4		Yes	No	1+1		150
3.75	B	V	Yes	1+4		No	No	1+4	ANS 1988.84.184	150
3.76	B	VIII	Yes	1+4		No	No	4+1	Ref: Todywalla	150
3.77	C	III	Yes	1+4	гΛNΛN	Yes	No	0		150
3.78	D	III	Yes	1+4	гANAM	Yes	No	0		150
3.79	E	VI	Yes	0		Yes	No	1+1	Ref: Puddester	150
3.80	F	?	No	0+1		-	-	-	Recorded from Pridmore. Probably Rev I, II or III.	150
3.81	G	II	No	1+1		Yes	No	4+4		150
3.82	H	II	No	1+4		Yes	No	4+4	Ref: SNC Sept 1976, pp319	150
3.83	H	V	No	1+4		No	No	1+4		150
3.84	H	VII	No	1+4		No	muddled	0	Ref: Todywalla	150
3.85	H	VI	No	1+4		No	No	1+1	Ref: Withers	150
3.86	I	V	No	B.L		No	No	1+4	Ref: Kaslove. DOUB.LE	150

Obverse Varieties

Centre Circle	There may or may not be a plain circle surrounding the Persian legend.
Stops in Legend	The stops in the English legend may be composed of single dots (1), or a quartet of dots (4) arranged roughly in the shape of a diamond. (E.g. 1+4 means single after DOUBLE and quartet after FANAM). Alternatively there may be no stops at all (0) or a stop between the B & L of DOUBLE.
F & A's of FANAM	The second bar of F of FANAM is missing. A's of FANAM are upside-down V's.
Second bar of F	The second bar of the F is missing

Silver Two Fanams 1807 to 1808 (cont)

	A	B	C	D	E	F	G	H	I
Centre Circle	Yes	Yes	Yes	Yes	Yes	No	No	No	No
Stops in Legend	1+1	1+4	1+4	1+4	0+0	0+1	1+1	1+4	B.L
F & A's of FANAM	OK	OK	Incorrect		OK	OK	OK	OK	OK
Second bar of F	OK	OK		Missing	OK	OK	OK	OK	OK

Centre circle – Yes

Centre circle – No

Stops in legend – 1+1

Stops in legend – 1+4

Stops in legend – 0+0

F & A – incorrect

Second bar of F – missing

Silver Two Fanams 1807 to 1808 (cont)

Reverse Varieties

Centre Circle	The Telugu legend may or may not be surrounded by a plain circle.
Legend U/S Down	The Telugu legend may or may not be upside-down relative to the Tamil legend. On one variety the Tamil legend is muddled at top left.
Stops in Legend	The stops in the Tamil legend may be composed of single dots (1), or a quartet of dots (4) arranged roughly in the shape of a diamond. Alternatively there may be no stops at all (0).

	I	II	III	IV	V	VI	VII	VIII
Centre Circle	Yes	Yes	Yes	Yes	No	No	No	No
Legend U/S Down	Yes	No	No	No	No	No	muddled	No
Stops in Legend	4+4	4+4	0+0	1+1	1+4	1+1	0+0	4+1

Centre circle – Yes

Centre circle – No

Legend upside-down – No

Legend upside-down – Yes

Legend muddled top left

Silver Two Fanams 1807 to 1808 (cont)

Stops in legend – 4+4

Stops in legend – 0+0

Stops in legend – 1+1

Stops in legend – 1+4

Stops in legend – 4+1

Silver Fanam 1807 to 1808

3.89

A five pointed star with or without a plain circle around. Crossed branches below. The value in English above.
FANAM
All within a plain border. (Persian = *falam* = fanam).

A five pointed star within a plain circle. This is surrounded by the value in Tamil and Telugu:

రూక

பணம

All within a plain rim. (Tamil = *panam*, Telugu = *ruka* = fanam)

Official Weight (g)	0.92
Actual Weight (g)	0.74-0.95
Actual Diameter (mm)	9.5-10.6
Metal	Silver
Edge	Plain
Axis	Not Fixed
Mintage	386,352

Fanam

411

Silver Fanam 1807 to 1808

Catalogue

Cat No.	Obv	Rev	Obverse				Reverse			Comments	Value ($)
			Circle	Spelling	Branches	Star	Stops	Device	Circle		
3.87	A	?	Yes	BANAM	Yes	Yes	-	-	Yes	Recorded from Pridmore	NV
3.88	B	III	Yes		No	Square ends	4+4	Star	Yes	Ref: BM	100
3.89	C	I	No		Yes	Yes	1+1	Star	Yes		100
3.90	C	II	No		Yes	Yes	1+1	Flower	Yes	The flowers on the reverse come in different shapes.	100
3.91	C	V	No		Yes	Yes	4+1	Star	Yes		100
3.92	C	VI	No		Yes	Yes	4+1	Star	No	Ref: Johnston	100
3.93	D	III	No		No	Yes	4+4	Star	Yes		100
3.94	D	IV	No		No	Yes	4+4	Flower	Yes	Very crude reverse	100
3.95	E	I	No	bANAM	Yes	Yes	1+1	Star	Yes		100
3.96	F	IV	No		Yes	No	4+4	Flower	Yes	Ref: Wiggins	100
3.97	G	I	No	EANAW	Yes	Yes	1+1	Star	Yes		100

Obverse Varieties

Centre Circle	There may or may not be a plain circle surrounding the star.
Spelling of FANAM	FANAM may be mis-spelt
Branches	There may or may not be crossed branches below the star.
Star	The central star may be present or absent

	A	B	C	D	E	F	G
Centre Circle	Yes	Yes	No	No	No	No	No
Spelling of FANAM	BANAM	FANAM	OK	OK	bANAM	OK	EANAW
Branches	Yes	No	Yes	No	Yes	Yes	Yes
Star	Present	Present but with square ends	Present	Present	Present	Absent	Present

Silver Fanam 1807 to 1808 (cont)

Centre circle – No

Centre circle – Yes

Spelling of Fanam – OK

Spelling of FANAM – bANAM

EANAW

Branches – Yes

Branches – No

Star – present

Star – present but with square ends

No star

Silver Fanam 1807 to 1808 (cont)

Reverse Varieties

Stops in Legend	The stops in the legend may be composed of single dots (1), or a quartet of dots (4) arranged roughly in the shape of a diamond.
Central Device	There is usually a star in the centre of the reverse design. A flower can sometimes replace this.
Centre Circle	There may or may not be a circle around the star

	I	II	III	IV	V	VI
Stops in Legend	1+1	1+1	4+4	4+4	4+1	4+1
Central Device	Star	Flower	Star	Flower	Star	Star
Centre Circle	Yes	Yes	Yes	Yes	Yes	No

Stops in legend – 1+1

Stops in legend – 4+4

Central device – Star

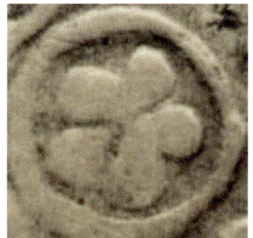
Central device – Flower

414

Silver Half Pagoda 1808 to 1812

Two coins have been observed, one with obverse P and another with obverse F, struck with an identical reverse die. This obviously provides a die link between obverses P & F (information from H. Kaslove).

3.124

Nine tiered Gopuram of a temple, standing on stony ground. Nine stars on each side. All this surrounded by a buckled garter. On the garter is the value in English:
HALF PAGODA
and Persian:

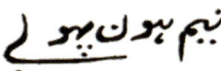

All within a beaded border. (Persian = *nim hun phuli* = half a flower, or star, pagoda)

Figure of Vishnu holding a sword in his left hand and rising from a lotus flower. Dotted and other symbols on each side. All surrounded by three circles of beads. All this within a ribbon, the ends of which are separated by a star. On the ribbon is the value in Tamil and Telugu:

அரை பூவராகன
అరవూదరహూవి

All within a beaded border. (Tamil = *Arai pu vara kun*. Telugu = *Ara pu vara hun* = half a flower, or star, pagoda)

Official Weight (g)	21.17
Actual Weight (g)	20.73-21.41
Actual Diameter (mm)	34.9-37.1
Metal	Silver
Edge	Grained Right
Axis	↑↑
Mintage	1,999,601

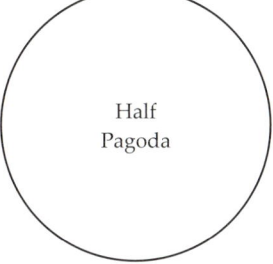

Half Pagoda

415

Silver Half Pagoda 1808 to 1812 (cont)

Catalogue

Cat No.	Obv	Rev	Obverse						Reverse						Comments	Value ($)
			Stars	Stops	Gopuram	Shading	Letters	Spelling	Circles	Crosses	Stop	Beads Below	Telugu Letter	Tails		
3.98	A	VIII	9+9	End	O/D	No	Large		3	16/14	Yes	2				800
3.99	A	IX	9+9	End	O/D	No	Large		3	16/14	Yes	2		4		1200
3.100	A	XIII	9+9	End	O/D	No	Large		3	14/16	Yes	2				800
3.101	B	XII	9+9	End	O/D	No	Small		3		No	2				800
3.102	C	II	9+9	End	G/O	No	Large		3	14/12	Yes	0			Ref: Kaslove	800
3.103	C	VI	9+9	End	G/O	No	Large		3	16/14	Yes	2 above			Ref: Puddester	800
3.104	C	VII	9+9	End	G/O	No	Large		3	16/14	Yes	0			Ref: Kaslove	800
3.105	C	VIII	9+9	End	G/O	No	Large		3	16/14	Yes	2			Ref: BM. Also Baldwin (2009), June Argentum, lot 58	800
3.106	D	VII	9+9	End	G/O	Yes	Small		3	16/14	Yes	0				800
3.107	E	VII	9+9	End	O	No	Large		3	16/14	Yes	0			Ref: Wiggins	800
3.108	E	VIII	9+9	End	O	No	Large		3	16/14	Yes	2				800
3.109	E	VIII	9+9	End	O	No	Large		3	16/14	Yes	2			O over D. Ref: Johnston	1500
3.110	E	IX	9+9	End	O	No	Large		3	16/14	Yes	2		4	Ref: Johnston	1200
3.111	E	XII	9+9	End	O	No	Large		3	16/14	No	2				800

Listing continued on next page

Silver Half Pagoda 1808 to 1812 (cont)

Catalogue

Cat No.	Obv	Rev	Obverse						Circles	Reverse					Comments	Value ($)
			Stars	Stops	Gopuram	Shading	Letters	Spelling		Crosses	Stop	Beads Below	Telugu Letter	Tails		
3.112	F	VIII	9+9	End	O	No	Small		3	16/14	Yes	2			Ref: ANS 1917.216.4756	800
3.113	F	XI or XII	9+9	End	O	No	Small		3	16/14	No	1 or 2			Ref: Puddester. Not sure about reverse. Also Noble sale 48, lot 2003. Also Sotheby (1985), Brand, lot 142	800
3.114	F	X	9+9	End	O	No	Small		3	16/14	No	0	Upside-down		Ref: Puddester.	1200
3.115	G	II	9+9	End	O	Yes	Large		3	14/12	Yes	0				800
3.116	G	IV	9+9	End	O	Yes	Large		3	11/13	Yes	0				800
3.117	G	VII	9+9	End	O	Yes	Large		3	16/14	Yes	0			Ref: Johnston	800
3.118	H	III	9+9	End	G	No	Large		3	14/14	Yes	0			Ref: Johnston. As normal obv H but with large letters	800
3.119	H	XI	9+9	End	G	No	Small		3	16/14	No	1			Ref: May be a centre stop on obverse but probably die faults	800
3.120	I	VIII	9+9	End	D	No	Large		3	16/14	Yes	2			Ref: BM	800
3.121	I	XI	9+9	End	D	No	Large		3	16/14	No	1			Ref: Baldwin (2007), sale 50, lot 742	800
3.122	J	II	9+9	C+E	G/O	No	Large		3	14/12	Yes	0			Ref: Todywalla	800
3.123	J	VI	9+9	C+E	G/O	No	Large		3	16/14	Yes	2 above			Ref: Kaslove	800
3.124	J	VIII	9+9	C+E	G/O	No	Large		3	16/14	Yes	2			Ref: Wiggins & BM	800

Listing continued on next page

Silver Half Pagoda 1808 to 1812 (cont)

Catalogue

Cat No.	Obv	Rev	Obverse						Reverse						Comments	Value ($)
			Stars	Stops	Gopuram	Shading	Letters	Spelling	Circles	Crosses	Stop	Beads Below	Telugu Letter	Tails		
3.125	J	XII	9+9	C+E	G/O	No	Large		3	16/14	No	2			Ref: Withers	800
3.126	K	?	9+9	C+E	G/O	Yes	Large		-	-	-	-	-	-	Ref: BM?	800
3.127	L	II	9+9	C+E	G	No	Large		3	14/12	Yes	0				800
3.128	L	V	9+9	C+E	G	No	Large		3	15/12	Yes	0			Ref: Baldwin (2009), June Argentum, lot 59	800
3.129	L	VII	9+9	C+E	G	No	Large		3	16/14	Yes	0				800
3.130	L	VIII	9+9	C+E	G	No	Large		3	16/14	Yes	2			Kaslove has one without a centre stop (on rev?)	800
3.131	L	XI	9+9	C+E	G	No	Large		3	16/14	No	1				800
3.132	M	II	9+9	C+E	O	No	Large		3	14/12	Yes	0			Baldwin (2006), sale 47, lot 1111	800
3.133	M	IV	9+9	C+E	O	No	Large		3	11/13	Yes	0			Reverse certainly has 11/13 beads but not certain it is IV. Ref: Kaslove	800
3.134	M	VII	9+9	C+E	O	No	Large		3	16/14	Yes	0				800
3.135	M	VIII	9+9	C+E	O	No	Large		3	16/14	Yes	2				800
3.136	M	XII	9+9	C+E	O	No	Large		3	16/14	No					800
3.136c	M	XIIc	9+9	C+E	O	No	Large		3	16/15	Yes	1			Ref: Johnstone	800

Listing continued on next page

418

Silver Half Pagoda 1808 to 1812 (cont)

Catalogue

Cat No.	Obv	Rev	Obverse						Reverse						Comments	Value ($)
			Stars	Stops	Gopuram	Shading	Letters	Spelling	Circles	Crosses	Stop	Beads Below	Telugu Letter	Tails		
3.137	N	II	9+9	L&F+E	O	No	Large		3	14/12	Yes	0			Singapore/HK (1997), sale 121, lot 1018	800
3.138	O	IV	9+9	None	O	No	Large		3	11/13	Yes	0			Ref: Johnston	800
3.139	O	VI	9+9	None	O	No	Large		3	16/14	Yes	2 above				800
3.140	O	XI	9+9	None	O	No	Large		3	16/14	No	1			Ref: Johnston	800
3.141	P	VI	9+9	None	G	No	Large		3	16/14	Yes	2 above			Ref: Kaslove	800
3.142	P	VII	9+9	None	G	No	Large		3	16/14	Yes	0				800
3.143	P	VIII	9+9	None	G	No	Large		3	16/14	Yes	2			Ref: Kaslove	800
3.144c	Q	XI	9+9	None	G/O	No	Large		3	16/14	No	1			Ref: Johnston. Like obv. Q but with large letters	800
3.144	Q	X	9+9	None	G/O	No	Small		3	16/14	No	0	Upside-down		Ref: Kaslove	1,500
3.145	R	VIII	9+9	None	D	No	Large	PGODA	3	16/14	Yes	2				2,500
3.146	S	I	22+24	C+E	O/D	No	Small		5	14/11	Yes	1			SNC, Sep. 1976. Also BM	5,000

Silver Half Pagoda 1808 to 1812 (cont)

Second type over-struck on first (from H. Kaslove)

Obverse Varieties

Number of stars	There are usually 9 stars on each side of the gopuram. On rare varieties there are other numbers.
Stops in Legend	The English legend may contain no stops, an end stop alone, or a centre stop between the two words plus an end stop (C+E). In one example the centre stop is between the L & F of HALF (L&F+E).
Gopuram	The gopuram may point directly at the letter G, O or D, between the letters G and O, or between the letters O and D. This can best be ascertained by holding a ruler up the central spine of the gopuram. If the ruler touches a letter, then the gopuram is considered to point to that letter.
Shading in buckle	The shading may or may not extend into the buckle.
Size of Letters	The letters in the English legend may be large (about 2.5-3mm) or small (about 2mm). This is often difficult to determine and could perhaps be ignored.
Spelling of PAGODA	PAGODA spelt PGODA

Silver Half Pagoda 1808 to 1812 (cont)

	A	B	C	D	E	F	G	H	I
Number of stars	9+9	9+9	9+9	9+9	9+9	9+9	9+9	9+9	9+9
Stops in Legend	End	End	End	End	End	End	End	End	End
Gopuram	O/D	O/D	G/O	G/O	O	O	O	G	D
Shading in buckle	No	No	No	Yes	No	No	Yes	No	No
Size of Letters	Large	Small	Large	Small	Large	Small	Large	Small	Large
Spelling of PAGODA	OK	OK	OK	OK	OK	OK	OK	OK	OK

	J	K	L	M
Number of stars	9+9	9+9	9+9	9+9
Stops in Legend	C+E	C+E	C+E	C+E
Gopuram	G/O	G/O	G	O
Shading in buckle	No	Yes	No	No
Size of Letters	Large	Large	Large	Large
Spelling of PAGODA	OK	OK	OK	OK

	N	O	P	Q	R	S
Number of stars	9+9	9+9	9+9	9+9	9+9	22+24
Stops in Legend	L&F+E	None	None	None	None	C+E
Gopuram	O	O	G	G/O	D	O/D
Shading in buckle	No	No	No	No	No	No
Size of Letters	Large	Large	Large	Small	Large	Small
Spelling of PAGODA	OK	OK	OK	OK	PGODA	OK

Number of Stars – 9+9

Number of Stars – 22+24

Silver Half Pagoda 1808 to 1812 (cont)

Stops in Legend – End

Stops in Legend – C+E

Stops in Legend – L&F+E (showing stop between L & F)

Stops in Legend – None

Gopuram – G

Gopuram – O

Gopuram – D

Gopuram – O/D

Gopuram – G/O

Shading in buckle – No

Shading in buckle – Yes

Size of Letters – Large

Size of Letters – Small

Spelling of pagoda – correct

Spelling of Pagoda – PGODA

Silver Half Pagoda 1808 to 1812 (cont)

Reverse Varieties

Circles of Beads	There are usually three circles of beads. On a rare variety there may be 5 circles.
Top Left Cross	To the left of Vishnu is an arrangement of dots topped by a cross shape, representing one of his wives. The number of dots that form this figure varies.
Top Right Cross	To the right of Vishnu is an arrangement of dots topped by a cross shape, representing one of his wives. The number of dots that form this figure varies.
Stop in Legend	There may or may not be a stop between the Tamil and Telugu legends.
Beads below Vishnu	There are varying numbers of beads below Vishnu. These beads are usually within the stalk, but sometimes they may be above the stalk. Beads from the inner circle often extend into the stalk. Only those beads that are *definitely* not part of the circles of beads count as beads below Vishnu.
Rotation of first letter of Telugu Legend	The first letter of the Telugu legend may be upside-down.
Tails to Top Right Cross	The top right cross arrangement may have four 'tails' as opposed to the usual two. In this circumstance the top left cross has additional tiny dots.

	I	II	III	IV	V	VI	VII
Circles of Beads	5	3	3	3	3	3	3
Top Left Cross	14	14	14	11	15	16	16
Top Right Cross	11	12	14	13	12	14	14
Stop in Legend	Yes	Yes	Yes	Yes	Yes	Yes	Yes
Beads below Vishnu	1	0	0	0	0	2 above stalk	0
Rotation of first letter of Telugu Legend	OK	OK	OK	OK	OK	OK	OK
Tails to Top Right cross	Two	Two	Two	Two	Two	Two	Two

Silver Half Pagoda 1808 to 1812 (cont)							
	VIII	IX	X	XI	XII	XIIc	XIII
Circles of Beads	3	3	3	3	3	3	3
Top Left Cross	16	16	16	16	16	16	14
Top Right Cross	14	14	14	14	14	15	16
Stop in Legend	Yes	Yes	No	No	No	Yes	Yes
Beads below Vishnu	2	2	0	1	2	1	2
Rotation of first letter of Telugu Legend	OK	OK	Upside down	OK	OK	OK	OK
Tails to Top Right cross	Two	Four	Two	Two	Two	Two	Two

Circles of beads – 5

Circles of beads – 3

Top left cross – 11

Top left cross – 14

Top left cross – 15

Top left cross – 16

Top right cross – 11

Top right cross – 12

Top right cross – 13

Top right cross – 14

Silver Half Pagoda 1808 to 1812 (cont)

Stop in legend – Yes

Stop in legend – No

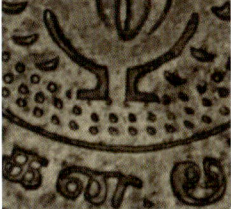

Beads below Vishnu – 0

Beads below Vishnu – 1

Beads below Vishnu – 2

Beads below Vishnu – 2 above stalk

Rotation of first letter of Telugu legend – Normal

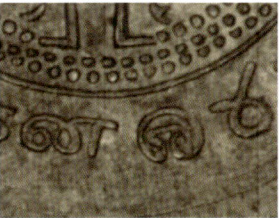

Rotation of first letter of Telugu legend – Upside-Down

Tails to top right cross – Two

Tails to top right cross – 4

Silver Quarter Pagoda 1808 to 1812

3.169

Seven tiered Gopuram of a temple, standing on stony ground. Between seven and nine stars on each side. All this surrounded by a buckled garter. On the garter is the value in English:
QUARTER PAGODA
and Persian:

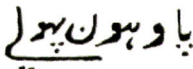

All within a beaded border. (Persian = *Pau hun phuli* = quarter of a flower, or star, pagoda)

Figure of Vishnu usually holding a sword in his left hand and rising from a lotus flower. Dotted and other symbols on each side. All surrounded by two circles of beads. All this within a ribbon, the ends separated by a star. On the ribbon is the value in Tamil and Telugu:

கால்வராகன்

కా లవరహాని

All within a beaded border. (Tamil = *Kal vara kun*, Telugu = *Kal vara hun* = quarter of a pagoda)

Official Weight (g)	10.58
Actual Weight (g)	10.26-10.71
Actual Diameter (mm)	25.6-28.3
Metal	Silver
Edge	Grained Right
Mintage	7,091,587
Axis	↑↑

Quarter Pagoda

Silver Quarter Pagoda 1808 to 1812 (cont)

Catalogue

Cat No.	Obv	Rev	Obverse							Reverse						Comments	Value ($)
			Buckle	Stars	Stops	Shading	Tongue	QUARTER	PAGODA	Bead Below	Beads in Cross	Sword	Stop	Bead Above	Tamil		
3.157	A	I (V)	Square	7+7	End	No	No			2	13/11					7 Stars. Ref: Kaslove also Baldwin (2013), sale 84, lot 2065. Kaslove believes his specimen to be reverse V but the one from the Baldwin's sale is reverse I. There may be more than one reverse for this variety	2,000
3.158	B	I	Square	8+8	None	No	Yes			2	13/11					8 Stars	2,000
3.159	C	III	Square	9+9	End	No	Yes			2	13/11		No				500
3.160	C	VI	Square	9+9	End	No	Yes			0	13/11					Ref: Kaslove	500

Listing continued on next page

Silver Quarter Pagoda 1808 to 1812 (cont)

Catalogue

Cat No.	Obv	Rev	Obverse							Reverse						Comments	Value ($)
			Buckle	Stars	Stops	Shading	Tongue	QUARTER	PAGODA	Beads in Cross	Bead Below	Sword	Stop	Bead Above	Tamil		
3.161	C	I	Square	9+9	End	No	Yes			13/11	2					Ref: Johnston	500
3.162	C	II	Square	9+9	End	No	Yes			13/11	2	None				Ref: Johnston	2000
3.163	C	VII	Square	9+9	End	No	Yes			13/11	0	None				Todywalla	2000
3.164	C	XVI	Square	9+9	End	No	Yes			11/9	0			No		Ref: seen at Baldwin's	500
3.165	D	XVI	Oval	9+8	None	No	Yes			11/9	0			No		9+8 Stars	1000
3.166	E	VI	Oval	9+9	None	Yes	Yes			13/11	0						300
3.167	E	VIII	Oval	9+9	None	Yes	Yes			13/11	0			No			300
3.168	E	XIV	Oval	9+9	None	Yes	Yes			11/9	0						300
3.169	E	XVI	Oval	9+9	None	Yes	Yes			11/9	0			No		Can occur with large As and O particularly noticeable in pAGOdA (Ref: Thompson)	300
3.170	E	XVII	Oval	9+9	None	Yes	Yes			11/9	0			No		Reverse crosses of dots incorporated into circles of beads	500

Listing continued on next page

Silver Quarter Pagoda 1808 to 1812 (cont)

Catalogue

Cat No.	Obv	Rev	Obverse									Reverse				Comments	Value ($)
			Buckle	Stars	Stops	Shading	Tongue	QUARTER	PAGODA	Beads in Cross	Bead Below	Sword	Stop	Bead Above	Tamil		
3.171	E	XIX	Oval	9+9	None	Yes	Yes			11/9	0	RH		No		Sword in right hand	1,500
3.172	F	XVI	Oval	9+9	None	Yes	No			11/9	0			No		Todywalla	300
3.173	F	XVIII	Oval	9+9	None	Yes	No			11/9	0		No	No			300
3.174	G	V	Oval	9+9	None	No	Yes			13/11	0		No			Ref: Johnston	300
3.175	G	VI	Oval	9+9	None	No	Yes			13/11	0					Ref: Johnston	300
3.176	G	VIII	Oval	9+9	None	No	Yes			13/11	0			No			300
3.177	G	IX	Oval	9+9	None	No	Yes			13/11	0		No				300
3.178	G	XVI	Oval	9+9	None	No	Yes			11/9	0			No			300
3.179	G	XVI	Oval	9+9	None	No	No			11/9	0			No		Ref: Kaslove	300
3.180	I	XVI	Oval	9+9	None	Yes	Yes	QUARTE		11/9	0			No		Ref: Puddester. QUARTE	800
3.181	J	XVI	Oval	9+9	Centre	Yes	Yes			11/9	0			No			300
3.182	K	VI	Oval	9+9	Centre	No	Yes			13/11	0						300
3.183	L	VIII	Oval	9+9	End	Yes	Yes			13/11	0			No			300
3.184	L	X	Oval	9+9	End	Yes	Yes			13/11	0		No	No			300

Listing continued on next page

Silver Quarter Pagoda 1808 to 1812 (cont)

Catalogue

Cat No.	Obv	Rev	Obverse							Reverse						Comments	Value ($)
			Buckle	Stars	Stops	Shading	Tongue	QUARTER	PAGODA	Beads in Cross	Bead Below	Sword	Stop	Bead Above	Tamil		
3.185	L	XI	Oval	9+9	End	Yes	Yes			11/11	0						300
3.186	L	XII	Oval	9+9	End	Yes	Yes			11/11	0			No		Centre stop might be present.	300
3.187	L	XIV	Oval	9+9	End	Yes	Yes			11/9	0						300
3.188	L	XV	Oval	9+9	End	Yes	Yes			11/9	0				Missing	Ref: Hemanth Chopra	800
3.189	M	VI	Oval	9+9	End	Yes	Two			13/11	0					ref: Kaslove, Album	300
3.190	N	XVI	Oval	9+9	End	Yes	No			11/9	0			No			300
3.191	O	IV	Oval	9+9	End	No	Yes			13/11	1						300
3.192	O	VI	Oval	9+9	End	No	Yes			13/11	0						300
3.193	O	VIII	Oval	9+9	End	No	Yes			13/11	0			No			300
3.194	O	XVI	Oval	9+9	End	No	Yes			11/9	0			No			300
3.195	P	VI	Oval	9+9	C+E	Yes	Yes			13/11	0						300
3.196	P	VIII	Oval	9+9	C+E	Yes	Yes			13/11	0			No			300
3.197	P	XI	Oval	9+9	C+E	Yes	Yes			11/10	0						300
3.198	P	XIII	Oval	9+9	C+E	Yes	Yes			9/11	0			No			300
3.199	P	XIV	Oval	9+9	C+E	Yes	Yes			11/9	0						300
3.200	P	XVI	Oval	9+9	C+E	Yes	Yes			11/9	0			No			300

Listing continued on next page

Silver Quarter Pagoda 1808 to 1812 (cont)

Catalogue

Cat No.	Obv	Rev	Obverse						Reverse							Comments	Value ($)
			Buckle	Stars	Stops	Shading	Tongue	QUARTER	PAGODA	Beads in Cross	Bead Below	Sword	Stop	Bead Above	Tamil		
3.201	P	XVIII	Oval	9+9	C+E	Yes	Yes			11/9	0		No	No			300
3.202	P	XX	Oval	9+9	C+E	Yes	Yes			11/9	0	None					2,000
3.203	Q	XIV	Oval	9+9	C+E	Yes	No			11/9	0					Ref: Thompson	300
3.204	Q	XVI	Oval	9+9	C+E	Yes	No			11/9	0			No			300
3.205	R	IV	Oval	9+9	C+E	No	No			13/11	1					Ref: Wiggins	300
3.206	R	XIII	Oval	9+9	C+E	No	No			11/9	0			No			300
3.207	S	I	Oval	9+9	C+E	No	Yes			13/11	2					Ref: Wiggins	300
3.208	S	VI	Oval	9+9	C+E	No	Yes			13/11	0						300
3.209	S	VI	Oval	9+9	C+E	No	Yes			13/11	0					Plain edge. Design and XRF look good	800
3.210	S	VI	Oval	9+9	C+E	No	Yes			13/11	0			No			300
3.211	S	XIV	Oval	9+9	C+E	No	Yes			11/9	0					Ref: Wiggins	300
3.212	S	XVI	Oval	9+9	C+E	No	Yes			11/9	0			No			300
3.213	S	XIX	Oval	9+9	C+E	No	Yes			11/9	0	RH		No			1,500
3.214	T	XVI	Oval	9+9	C+E	No	Yes		PAPAGODA	11/9	0			No			2,000
3.215	U	XVI	Oval	9+9	End	No	Yes		PAGOD	11/9	0			No		Ref: Kaslove, Johnston.	2,000
3.216	V	XVI	Oval	9+9	C+E	Yes	Yes	QUARTE		11/9	0			No			2,000

Silver Quarter Pagoda 1808 to 1812 (cont)

Obverse Varieties

Buckle Shape	The buckle may be square or oval.
Number of stars	The number of stars on each side of the gopuram can vary.
Stops in Legend	The English legend may contain no stops, a centre stop alone, an end stop alone, or a centre stop plus an end stop (C+E).
Shading in buckle	The shading may or may not extend into the buckle.
Cross tongue	The buckle may or may not have a cross-tongue. Sometimes there are two
Spelling of QUARTER	QUARTER may be mis-spelt QUARTE
Spelling of PAGODA	PAGODA may be mis-spelt PAPAGODA or PAGOD.

	A	B	C	D	E	F	G	H
Buckle Shape	Square	Square	Square	Oval	Oval	Oval	Oval	Oval
Number of stars	7+7	8+8	9+9	9+8	9+9	9+9	9+9	9+9
Stops in Legend	End	None	End	None	None	None	None	None
Shading in buckle	No	No	No	No	Yes	Yes	No	No
Cross tongue	No	Yes	Yes	Yes	Yes	No	Yes	No
Spelling of QUARTER	Correct	Correct	Correct	Correct	Correct	Correct	Correct	Correct
Spelling of PAGODA	Correct	Correct	Correct	Correct	Correct	Correct	Correct	Correct

	I	J	K	L	M	N	O
Buckle Shape	Oval	Oval	Oval	Oval	Oval	Oval	Oval
Number of stars	9+9	9+9	9+9	9+9	9+9	9+9	9+9
Stops in Legend	None	Centre	Centre	End	End	End	End
Shading in buckle	Yes	Yes	No	Yes	Yes	Yes	No
Cross tongue	Yes	Yes	Yes	Yes	Two	No	Yes
Spelling of QUARTER	QUARTE	Correct	Correct	Correct	Correct	Correct	Correct
Spelling of PAGODA	Correct	Correct	Correct	Correct	Correct	Correct	Correct

Silver Quarter Pagoda 1808 to 1812 (cont)

	P	Q	R	S	T	U	V
Buckle Shape	Oval	Oval	Oval	Oval	Oval	Oval	Oval
Number of stars	9+9	9+9	9+9	9+9	9+9	9+9	9+9
Stops in Legend	C+E	C+E	C+E	C+E	C+E	End	C+E
Shading in buckle	Yes	Yes	No	No	No	No	Yes
Cross tongue	Yes	No	No	Yes	Yes	Yes	Yes
Spelling of QUARTER	Correct	Correct	Correct	Correct	Correct	Correct	QUARTE
Spelling of PAGODA	Correct	Correct	Correct	Correct	PAPAGODA	PAGOD.	Correct

Buckle shape – Square

Buckle shape – Oval

Number of stars – 7+7

Number of stars – 8+8

Number of stars – 9+8

Number of stars – 9+9

Stops in legend – None

Stops in legend – End

Silver Quarter Pagoda 1808 to 1812 (cont)

Stops in legend – C+E

Stops in legend – Centre

Shading in buckle – No

Shading in buckle – Yes

Cross tongue – Yes

Cross tongue – No

Cross tongue – Two

Spelling of PAGODA – PAGOD. NB last E of QUARTER looks like R over T

Spelling of QUARTER – QUARTE

Spelling of PAGODA – PAPAGODA

Silver Quarter Pagoda 1808 to 1812 (cont)

Reverse Varieties

Top Left Cross	To the left of Vishnu is an arrangement of dots topped by a cross shape, representing one of his wives. The number of dots that form this figure varies. Very rarely, two of the beads may be incorporated into the inner circle of beads. The number of beads in the cross is then expressed as, e.g. 9/11.
Top Right Cross	To the right of Vishnu is an arrangement of dots topped by a cross shape, representing one of his wives. The number of dots that form this figure varies. Very rarely, one of the beads may be incorporated into the inner circle of beads. The number of beads in the cross is then expressed as, e.g. 8/9.
Bead below Vishnu	There may be zero, one or two beads below Vishnu's feet within the stalk of the lotus flower. These beads are separate from those that form part of the circles of beads.
Vishnu's Sword	The facing figure of Vishnu usually holds a sword in his left hand, but rare examples exist with the sword in his right hand, or no sword at all.
Stop in Legend	There may or may not be a stop between the Tamil and Telugu legends.
Bead above Vishnu	There is sometimes a single bead above Vishnu's head. This bead is sometimes incorporated into the inner ring of beads and it is then difficult to determine if there is a separate bead or not. If there is doubt, then NO bead is considered to be present.
Tamil	The third letter from the bottom of the Tamil legend may be missing

	I	II	III	IV	V	VI	VII	VIII	IX	X
Top Left Cross	13	13	13	13	13	13	13	13	13	13
Top Right Cross	11	11	11	11	11	11	11	11	11	11
Bead below Vishnu	2	2	2	1	1	0	0	0	0	0
Vishnu's Sword	Left Hand	None	Left Hand	Left Hand	Left Hand	Left Hand	None	Left Hand	Left Hand	Left Hand
Stop in Legend	Yes	Yes	No	Yes	No	Yes	Yes	Yes	No	No
Bead above Vishnu	Yes	Yes	Yes	Yes	Yes	Yes	Yes	No	Yes	No
Tamil	OK	OK	OK	OK	OK	OK	OK	OK	OK	OK

Silver Quarter Pagoda 1808 to 1812 (cont)

	XI	XII	XIII	XIV	XV	XVI	XVII	XVIII	XIX	XX
Top Left Cross	11	11	9	11	11	11	9/11	11	11	11
Top Right Cross	10	11	11	9	9	9	8/9	9	9	9
Bead below Vishnu	0	0	0	0	0	0	0	0	0	0
Vishnu's Sword	Left Hand	Left Hand	Left Hand	Left Hand	Left Hand	Left Hand	Left Hand	Left Hand	Right Hand	None
Stop in Legend	Yes	Yes	Yes	Yes	Yes	Yes	Yes	No	Yes	Yes
Bead above Vishnu	Yes	No	No	Yes	No	No	No	No	No	Yes
Tamil	OK	OK	OK	OK	Missing	OK	OK	OK	OK	OK

Top left cross – 9

Top left cross – 9/11

Top left cross – 11

Top left cross – 13

Top right cross – 8/9

Top right cross – 9

Top right cross – 11

Bead Below Vishnu – 2

Bead Below Vishnu – 1

Silver Quarter Pagoda 1808 to 1812 (cont)

Vishnu's Sword – Left Hand

Vishnu's Sword – Right Hand

Vishnu's Sword – None

Stop in Legend – Yes

Stop in Legend – No

Bead Above Vishnu – Yes

Bead above Vishnu included in Circle but distinct

Bead Above Vishnu – No

Tamil Legend – Correct

Tamil Legend – Wrong (letter missing)

Silver Five Fanams 1808 to 1812

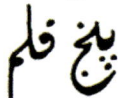

3.234

The value in Persian within a
buckled garter:

The value in Telugu in two lines:

అయిదు రూకలు

Separated by a bead and surrounded by a
ribbon, the ends of which are separated by a
star. On the ribbon is the value in Tamil:

அஞ்சு பணம

On the garter is the value in
English:
FIVE FANAMS
All within a beaded border.
(Persian = *Panj Falam* = Five
fanams)

All within a beaded border. (Tamil = *Anacu
panam*, Telugu = *Aedu rukalu* = Five fanams).

Official Weight (g)	4.65
Actual Weight (g)	3.92-4.74
Actual Diameter (mm)	20.5-22.7
Metal	Silver
Edge	Grained Right
Axis	↑↑
Mintage	3,953,694

Five
Fanams

Silver Five Fanams 1808 to 1812 (cont)

Catalogue

Cat No.	Obv	Rev	Obverse					Reverse		Comments	Value ($)
			Buckle	Stops	Shading	Tongue	FIVE	Tamil	Star		
3.217	A	I	Lrg Sq	None	No	-		Inward			200
3.218	B	II	Sh Sq	None	No	No		Outward		Ref: Chopra	200
3.219	C	I	Sh Sq	Centre	No	No		Inward		SNC. April 1980, p. 147.	200
3.220	D	I	Sh Sq	Centre	No	Yes		Inward		No stop visible in Telugu legend on some specimans but present on others	200
3.221	E	I	Long Square	Centre	No	-		Inward		Ref: Chopra	200
3.222	F	I	Long Square	None	No	-		Inward			200
3.223	F	II	Long Square	None	No	-		Outward			200
3.224	G	I	Square	None	No	No		Inward		Ref: Kaslove; also Chopra	200
3.225	H	I	Square	None	No	Yes		Inward		Ref: Kaslove; also Chopra	200
3.226	I	I	Oval	None	No	Yes		Inward			200
3.227	I	I	Oval	None	No	Yes		Inward		Axis: ↑↓	200
3.228	I	II	Oval	None	No	Yes		Outward		Ref: Chopra	200
3.229	J	I	Oval	None	Yes	Yes		Inward			200
3.230	J	I	Oval	None	Yes	Yes		Inward		Edge grained left.	200
3.231	K	I	Oval	None	Yes	No		Inward			200
3.232	L	I	Dots	None	No	Yes		Inward		Ref: Puddester	200
3.233	L	II	Dots	None	No	Yes		Outward		Ref: Puddester	200
3.234	M	I	Oval	Centre	No	Yes		Inward			200
3.235	N	I	Oval	Centre	Yes	Yes		Inward			200
3.236	O	I	Oval	Centre	Yes	No		Inward			200
3.237	P	I	Dots	Centre	No	-		Inward		Proof-like specimen in BM	NV
3.238	P	II	Dots	Centre	No	-		Outward			200
3.239	P	III	Dots	Centre	No	-		Inward	Absent	Ref: Chopra	200
3.240	Q	I	Dots	Centre	No	-	FIVB	Inward		FIVB Ref: Kaslove	200
3.241	R	I	?	C+E	?	?		Inward		Ref: Lingen.	200

Silver Five Fanams 1808 to 1812 (cont)

Obverse Varieties

Buckle Shape	The buckle may be square (large, long or short), oval, or formed with dots. Some oval buckles may appear square but can be differentiated by the rounded corners and the shape of the tongue.
Stops in legend	There may be no stops in the English legend, or there may be a centre stop.
Shading in buckle	The shading may or may not extend into the buckle.
Cross tongue	The buckle may or may not have a cross-tongue.
Spelling of FIVE	FIVE may be mis-spelt FIVB

	A	B	C	D	E	F	G	H	I
Buckle Shape	Large Square	Short Square	Short Square	Short Square	Long Square	Long Square	Square	Square	Oval
Stops in legend	None	None	Centre	Centre	Centre	None	None	None	None
Shading in buckle	No	No	No	No	No	No	No	No	No
Cross tongue	-	Yes	No	Yes	No	No	No	Yes	Yes
Spelling of FIVE	Correct	Correct	Correct	Correct	Correct	Correct	Correct	Correct	Correct

	J	K	L	M	N	O	P	Q	R
Buckle Shape	Oval	Oval	Dots	Oval	Oval	Oval	Dots	Dots	?
Stops in legend	None	None	None	Centre	Centre	Centre	Centre	Centre	C+E
Shading in buckle	Yes	Yes	No	No	Yes	Yes	No	No	?
Cross tongue	Yes	No	Yes	Yes	Yes	No	-	-	?
Spelling of FIVE	Correct	Correct	Correct	Correct	Correct	Correct	Correct	FIVB	Correct

Silver Five Fanams 1808 to 1812 (cont)

*Buckle shape –
Large Square*

*Buckle shape –
Long Square*

*Buckle shape –
Square*

*Buckle shape –
Short Square*

*Oval buckle that looks
square*

Buckle shape – Oval

Buckle shape – Dots

Stops in legend – None

Stops in legend – Centre

Shading in buckle – No

Shading in buckle – Yes

Cross tongue – No

Cross tongue – Yes

Silver Five Fanams 1808 to 1812 (cont)

Reverse Varieties

There is usually a bead in the centre of the reverse legend. However, it is often difficult to see, and using the presence or absence of this bead as a distinguishing feature for a variety is not reliable. I have not, therefore, used this feature.

Tamil Legend	The top of the Tamil legend may face inward or outward
Star	The star between the ends of the ribbon may be present or absent

	I	II	III
Tamil Legend	Inward	Outward	Inward
Star	Present	Present	Absent

Tamil legend – Inward

Tamil legend – Outward

Star present

No star

Silver Two Fanams 1808 to 1812

3.250

The value in Persian within a buckled garter:

On the garter is the value in English:
DOUBLE FANAM
All within a beaded border.
(Persian = *Do falam* = Double fanam)

The value in Telugu in two lines:

రెండు రూకలు

Surrounded by a ribbon, the ends of which are separated by a star. On the ribbon is the value in Tamil:

இரண்டுபணம

All within a beaded border. (Telugu = *Renddu rukalu*, Tamil = *Irantu panam* = Two fanams).

Official Weight (g)	1.85
Actual Weight (g)	1.70-1.92
Actual Diameter (mm)	14.1-15.9
Metal	Silver
Edge	Grained Right
Axis	↑↑
Mintage	6,044,350

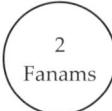
2 Fanams

Silver Two Fanams 1808 to 1812 (cont)

Catalogue

Cat No.	Obv	Rev	Obverse					Reverse	Comments	Value ($)
			Buckle	Legend	Marks	Stop	Shading	Tamil		
3.242	A	II	Short Square		U	No	No	Outward	Kaslove has one with no diacritical marks. Also occurs with the axis ↑↓.	100
3.243	B	II	Short Square		U	Yes	No	Outward	Ref: Thompson	100
3.244	C	II	Short Square		U+M	No	No	Outward		100
3.245	D	II	Short Square		?	Yes	No	Outward		100
3.246	E	II	Short Square	DOBLE	U	No	No	Outward	DOBLE	120
3.247	F	II	Square	FANM	U	No	No	Outward	FANM	120
3.248	G	II	Square	DOBBLE	U	No	No	Outward	U over first B in DOBBLE	120
3.249	H	II	Square		?	No	No	Outward	Seen at Baldwin's . Also Johnston	100
3.250	I	I	Short Oval		U+M	No	No	Inward		100
3.251	J	I	Short Oval		U+M	No	Yes	Inward	Recorded from Pridmore	100
3.252	K	I	Short Oval		M	No	No	Inward		100
3.253	L	I	Short Oval		U	No	Yes	Inward		100
3.254	M	I	Short Oval		U	No	No	Inward		100
3.255	N	I	Short Oval		None	No	No	Inward		100
3.256	O	I	Long Oval		U+M	No	No	Inward		100
3.257	P	I	Long Oval		M	No	No	Inward		100
3.258	P	II	Long Oval		M	No	No	Outward	Ref: Johnston	100

Listing continued on next page

Silver Two Fanams 1808 to 1812 (cont)

Catalogue

Cat No.	Obv	Rev	Obverse					Reverse	Comments	Value ($)
			Buckle	Legend	Marks	Stop	Shading	Tamil		
3.259	Q	I	Long Oval		U	No	No	Inward		100
3.260	R	I	Long Oval		U+M+L	No	No	Inward		100
3.261	S	I	Long Oval		M+L	Yes	No	Inward		100
3.262	T	I	Long Oval	FANAW	U	No	No	Inward	Ref: Wiggins	100
3.263	U	I	Dots		U+M	No	No	Outward	Beaded buckle, Ref: Chopra	100
3.264	U	II	Dots		U+M	No	No	Outward	Beaded buckle	100
3.265	V	II	Dots		U	No	No	Outward	Ref: Wiggins, Chopra	100
3.266	W	II	Dots	FANAMꙄ	U	No	No	Outward	Ref: BM	100
3.267	X	?	None		U	No	-	?	Ref: Kaslove	100

Double fanam A/II

Silver Two Fanams 1808 to 1812 (cont)

Obverse Varieties

Buckle Shape	The buckle may be short square, square, short oval, long oval or formed with dots or have no buckle
Spelling of Legend	The legend may be mis-spelt, e.g. DOUBLE may be spelt DOBLE, and FANAM spelt FANM or FANAW.
Diacritical marks	There should be one diacritical mark in the Persian legend. This mark is above the central legend (upper mark - U). There may be an extra dot within the letters (mid mark - M), or another mark below the letters (lower mark - L). Some coins have no marks.
Stop in Legend	There may or may not be a stop in the legend
Shading in Buckle	The shading may or may not extend into the buckle

	A	B	C	D	E	F	G	H
Buckle Shape	Short Square	Short Square	Short Square	Short Square	Short Square	Square	Square	Square
Spelling of Legend	Correct	Correct	Correct	Correct	DOBLE FANAM	DOUBLE FANM	DOBBLE FANAM	Correct
Diacritical marks	U	U	U+M	Not Clear	U	U	U	Not Clear
Stop in Legend	No	Yes	No	Yes	No	No	No	No
Shading in Buckle	No	No	No	No	No	No	No	No

	I	J	K	L	M	N
Buckle Shape	Short Oval	Short Oval	Short Oval	Short Oval	Short Oval	Short Oval
Spelling of Legend	Correct	Correct	Correct	Correct	Correct	Correct
Diacritical marks	U+M	U+M	M	U	U	None
Stop in Legend	No	No	No	No	No	No
Shading in Buckle	No	Yes	No	Yes	No	No

Silver Two Fanams 1808 to 1812 (cont)

	O	P	Q	R	S	T
Buckle Shape	Long Oval	Long Oval	Long Oval	Long Oval	Long Oval	Long Oval
Spelling of Legend	Correct	Correct	Correct	Correct	Correct	FANAW
Diacritical marks	U+M	M	U	U+M+L	M+L	U
Stop in Legend	No	No	No	No	No	Yes
Shading in Buckle	No	No	No	No	No	No

	U	V	W	X
Buckle Shape	Dots	Dots	Dots	No Buckle
Spelling of Legend	Correct	Correct	FANAMS (retrograde S)	Correct
Diacritical marks	U+M	U	U	U
Stop in Legend	No	No	No	No
Shading in Buckle	No	No	No	-

Buckle shape – Short Square

Buckle shape – Square

Buckle shape – Short Oval

Buckle shape – Long Oval

Buckle shape – Dots

Spelling of legend – DOBLE FANAM

Spelling of legend – DOUBLE FANM

Spelling of legend – DOBBLE FANAM

Silver Two Fanams 1808 to 1812 (cont)

Diacritical marks –	*Diacritical marks –*	*Diacritical marks –*	*Diacritical marks –*
U	*U+M*	*M*	*M+L*

Stop in legend – No   *Stop in legend – Yes*

Shading in buckle – No   *Shading in buckle – Yes (very faint)*

Reverse Varieties

Tamil legend	The top of the Tamil legend may face inwards or outwards

	I	II
Tamil legend	Inward	Outward

Tamil legend – Inward   *Tamil legend – Outward*

Silver Fanam 1808 to 1812

3.268

The value in Persian:

Surrounded by a buckled garter. On the garter is the value in English. All within a beaded border. (Persian = *falam* = fanam)

The value in Telugu in one line:

రూక

Surrounded by a ribbon, the ends of which are separated by a star. On the ribbon is the value in Tamil:

பணம

All within a beaded border (Telugu = *ruka*, Tamil = *panam* = fanam)

Official Weight (g)	0.88
Actual Weight (g)	0.83-0.94
Actual Diameter (mm)	10.4-12.4
Metal	Silver
Edge	Grained Right
Axis	↑↑
Mintage	1,545,412

Fanam

449

Silver Fanam 1808 to 1812 (cont)

Catalogue

Cat No.	Obv	Obverse			Comments	Value ($)
		Buckle	Marks	FANAM		
3.268	A	Oval	Yes			80
3.269	B	Oval	No			80
3.270	C	Oval	No	Retrograde N	Reported by Hemanth Chopra	100
3.271	D	Round	No			100
3.272	E	Square	Yes		Ref: SNC April 1980, p. 147. No Picture. None zeen by author	100
3.273	F	Dots	Yes		Ref: SNC September 1976, p. 319. Also SNC April 1980, p. 147. Also Kaslove. May occur with and without the diacritical mark on the obverse.	100
3.274	G	None	Yes			100

Obverse Varieties

Buckle Shape	The buckle may be oval, round, square or formed with dots
Diacritical mark	There may or may not be a diacritical mark.
Letters in FANAM	The letters in FANAM may be correct or there may be a retrograde N

	A	B	C	D	E	F	G
Buckle Shape	Oval	Oval	Oval	Round	Square	Dots	No Buckle
Diacritical mark	Yes	No	No	No	Yes	Yes	Yes
Letters in FANAM	Correct	Correct	retro N	Correct	Correct	Correct	Correct

Buckle shape – Oval   *Buckle shape – Round*

Silver Fanam 1808 to 1812 (cont)

Buckle shape – Dots

Buckle shape – No Buckle

The dot buckle may take a number of different forms

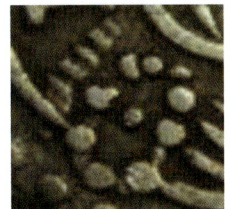

The dot buckle may take a number of different forms

Diacritical mark – Yes

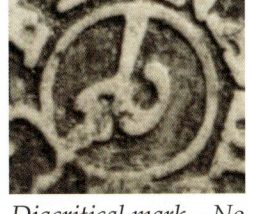

Diacritical mark – No

Letters in FANAM – correct

Letters in FANAM – retrograde N

Copper Forty Cash 1807

3.278

The value in Persian and English.

XL.CASH

(Persian = *In chahal kas ast* = This is forty cash)

Value in Tamil and Telugu.

(Telugu = *Idi nalabhai kasulu*, Tamil = *Idu naipadu kasu* = this is forty Cash)

Official Weight (g)	19.31
Actual Weight (g)	18.03-19.26
Actual Diameter (mm)	35.0-37.7
Metal	Copper
Edge	Plain
Axis	Varies. See below
Mintage (to March 1808)	514,922

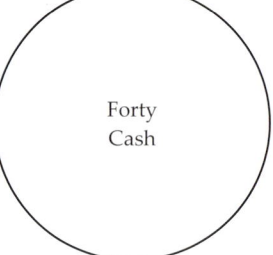

Forty Cash

Copper Forty Cash 1807 (cont)

Catalogue

Cat No.	Obv	Rev	Obverse		Reverse			Axis	Comments	Value ($)
			Separator	XL	Tamil	Separator	Letters			
3.275	A	I	Plain	XL.	Correct	Dots/Star	4	↑↑	Ref: BM	600
3.276	A	II	Plain	XL.	Correct	Dot	4	↑↑		400
3.277	A	VII	Plain	XL.	Square	None	4 small	↑↑	Ref: Puddester, BM	400
3.278	B	I	2 Plain	XL.	Correct	Dots/Star	4	↑↑	Ref: BM	450
3.279	B	I	2 Plain	XL.	Correct	Dots/Star	4	↑↓	Ref: Withers	450
3.280	B	II	2 Plain	XL.	Correct	Dot	4	↑↑		450
3.281	B	II	2 Plain	XL.	Correct	Dot	4	↑↓	Ref: BM	450
3.282	B	III	2 Plain	XL.	Modified	None	4	↑↑	Ref: Weir	300
3.283	B	IV	2 Plain	XL.	Square	None	3	↑↑	Ref: BM	350
3.284	B	VII	2 Plain	XL.	Square	None	4 small	↑↑		300
3.285	C	III	Dash/3 dots/star	XL.	Modified	None	4	↑↑		300
3.286	C	V	Dash/3 dots/star	XL.	Square	Dot	4 large	↑↑	Ref: Johnston	400
3.287	C	VII	Dash/3 dots/star	XL.	Square	None	4 small	↑↑	Ref: BM	300
3.288	D	V	Dash/4 dots/star	XL.	Square	Dot	4 large	↑↑		300
3.289	D	V	Dash/4 dots/star	XL.	Square	Dot	4 large	↑↓	Ref: Hemanth Chopra	300
3.290	E	VII	Dash/5 dots/star	XL.	Square	None	4 small	↑↑		300
3.291	F	VI	Dash/5 dots/star	X.L	Square	None	4 large			350

Obverse Varieties

Separator	The line separating the Persian from the English legends differs. It may be a single plain line, two parallel plain lines, or a number of dots and stars.
XL	The numerals XL are usually followed by a dot. On some coins the dot comes between the X and L

	A	B	C	D	E	F
Separator	Plain	2 Plain	Dash/3 dots/star	Dash/4dots/star	Dash/5 dots/star	Dash/5 dots/star
XL	XL.	XL.	XL.	XL.	XL.	X.L

Copper Forty Cash 1807 (cont)

Separator – Plain

Separator – 2 Plain

Separator – Dash/3 dots/star

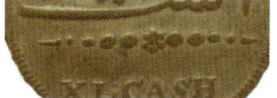

Separator – Dash/4 dots/star

Separator – Dash/5 dots/star

XL.

X.L

Reverse Varieties

First Tamil Letter	The first letter in the Tamil legend may take a number of different forms. This might be the correct form, a modified form or a square form. Other letters in the first line also vary (see photos below).
Separator	The line separating the Tamil from the Telugu legends differs. It may be a number of dots and stars, or no separator.
Letters on bottom line	Coins with the square form of the first Tamil letter come in three varieties of the bottom line. One with small letters and the usual 4 letters, one with larger (normal) letters and the usual 4 letters, and the last with larger letters and only 3 letters on the bottom line. The letter that normally appears at the start of the bottom line, appears at the end of the previous line in the last variety.

	I	II	III	IV	V	VI	VII
First Tamil Letter	Correct	Correct	Modified	Square	Square	Square	Square
Other Tamil Letters	2 square	2 square	1 rounded	1 rounded	1 rounded	1 rounded	1 rounded
Separator	Dots/Stars	Single Dot	None	None	Single Dot	None	None
Letters on bottom line	4	4	4	3	4 large	4 large	4 small

Copper Forty Cash 1807 (cont)

First Tamil letter – Correct *First Tamil letter – Modified* *First Tamil letter – Square*

Middle Tamil letters – 2 Square *Middle Tamil letters – 1 Rounded*

Separator – Dots/Star *Separator – Single Dot (often hard to see)* *Separator – None*

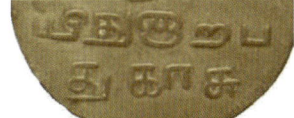 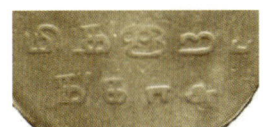 

Letters on bottom Line – 4 Large *Letters on bottom Line – 4 Small* *Letters on bottom Line – 3*

Copper Twenty Cash 1807

3.293

The value in Persian and English

كاس
اين بيست
است
XX.CASH

(Persian = *In bist kas ast* = this is twenty cash)

Value in Tamil and Telugu.

(Telugu = *Idi iravai kasulu*, Tamil = *Idu irubadu kasu* = this is twenty cash)

455

Copper Twenty Cash 1807 (cont)

Official Weight (g)	9.65
Actual Weight (g)	7.97-10.25
Actual Diameter (mm)	25.9-27.4
Metal	Copper
Edge	Plain
Axis	Varies. See below
Mintage (to March 1808)	3,016,822

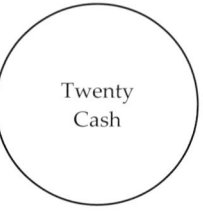

Twenty Cash

Catalogue

Cat No.	Obv	Rev	Obverse			Reverse		Axis	Comments	Value ($)
			Persian	Separator	Bead	Tamil	Letters			
3.292	A	I	3 Lines	Plain	Yes	Correct		↑↑	Pr. 342, 30mm flan	300
3.293	A	II	3 Lines	Plain	Yes	Modified		↑↑		100
3.294	A	V	3 Lines	Plain	Yes	NoU		?	Recorded from Pridmore	NV
3.295	B	I	3 Lines	Dash/3 dots/Star	Yes	Correct		↑↑	Ref: Baldwin (2009), June Argentum, lot 77	100
3.296	B	II	3 Lines	Dash/3 dots/Star	Yes	Modified		↑↑		100
3.297	B	III	3 Lines	Dash/3 dots/Star	Yes	Square		↑↓		100
3.298	C	II	3 Lines	Dash/4 dots/Star	Yes	Modified		↑↑		100
3.299	C	II	3 Lines	Dash/4 dots/Star	Yes	Modified		↑↓		150
3.300	C	III	3 Lines	Dash/4 dots/Star	Yes	Square		↑↓		100
3.301	D	II	3 Lines	Dash/4 dots/Star	No	Modified		↑↑		100
3.302	D	III	3 Lines	Dash/4 dots/Star	No	Square		↑↑		100
3.304	D	III	3 Lines	Dash/4 dots/Star	No	Square		?	Striking in lead. SNC April 1980. Not sure about authenticity	NV
3.305	D	IV	3 Lines	Dash/4 dots/Star	No	Square	Missing	↑↓		200
3.306	E	III	3 Lines	Dash/4 cups/Star	No	Square		↑↑		100

Listing continued on next page

Copper Twenty Cash 1807 (cont)

Catalogue

Cat No.	Obv	Rev	Obverse			Reverse		Axis	Comments	Value ($)
			Persian	Separator	Bead	Tamil	Letters			
3.308	F	III	2 Lines	Dash/4 dots/Star	Yes	Square		↑↑	Exists as a special strike. Ref: Johnston	200
3.309	F	III	2 Lines	Dash/4 dots/Star	Yes	Square		↑↓		200
3.310	G	III	2 Lines	Dash/4 dots/Star	No	Square		↑↑		200
3.311	G	III	2 Lines	Dash/4 dots/Star	No	Square		↑↓		200
3.312	H	III	2 Lines	Dots	Yes	Square		↑↑		200
3.313	H	III	2 Lines	Dots	Yes	Square		↑↓	Ref: Weir.	200

Obverse Varieties

Arrangement of legend	The Persian letters may be arranged in different ways. Normally in three lines but may be in two
Separator	The line separating the Persian from the English legends differs. It may be a single plain line, a number of dots and stars, a number of dots alone, or 4 'cups' and stars. Only worn specimens with no separator have been examined. The absence of the separator may therefore simply be due to wear and is not recorded as a variety.
Bead After XX	There is usually a stop after the value letters XX. Sometimes this is missing.

	A	B	C	D	E	F	G	H
Arrangement of legend	3 lines	3 lines	3 lines	3 lines	3 lines	2 lines	2 lines	2 lines
Separator	Plain	Dash/ 3 dots/Star	Dash/ 4 dots/Star	Dash/ 4 dots/Star	Dash/ 4 cups/Star	Dash/ 4 dots/Star	Dash/ 4 dots/Star	Dots
Bead After XX	Yes	Yes	Yes	No	No	Yes	No	Yes

Copper Twenty Cash 1807 (cont)

Arrangement of legend – 3 lines

Arrangement of legend – 2 lines

Separator – Plain

Separator – Dash/3dots/Star

Separator – Dash/4 Dots/Star

Separator – Dash/4 cups/star

Separator – Dots

Bead after XX

No bead after XX

Copper Twenty Cash 1807 (cont)

Reverse Varieties

There may or may not be a bead in the centre of the reverse, separating the Tamil and Telugu legends. This is often difficult to see, and has not therefore been used as a distinguishing feature. Rev I seems to have smaller letters than other varieties.

Tamil Letter	The first & third letter in the Tamil legend may take a number of different forms. This might be the correct form, a modified form, a square form, or a square form without the central upright (NoU). This last variety has been recorded from Pridmore and may be the result of the letter not being fully visible on the flan, rather than a die variety.
Missing Letters	On one variety many letters are missing from the reverse

	I	II	III	IV	V
Tamil Letter	Correct	Modified	Square	Square	NoU
Missing Letters	No	No	No	Yes	No

Tamil Letter – Correct

Tamil Letter – Modified

Tamil Letter – Square

Example of Square letter off edge of coin

Letters missing. Seems to read iruvathu kasu

Normal reverse

Copper Ten Cash 1807

The diameter of the flans can vary quite considerably. Pridmore records a separate catalogue entry for a very large flan specimen. However, investigations indicate that this is simply a coin at the extremity of the spectrum of diameters.

3.317

X CASH

| The value in Persian and English. (Persian = *In dah kas ast* = this is ten cash) | The value in Tamil and Telugu. (Telugu = *Idi padi kasulu*, Tamil = *Idu pattu kasu* = this is ten Cash) |

Official Weight (g)	4.83
Actual Weight (g)	4.24-4.95
Actual Diameter (mm)	22.7-26.5
Metal	Copper
Edge	Plain
Mintage (to March 1808)	2,127,922

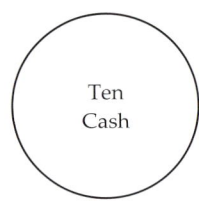

Ten Cash

Copper Ten Cash 1807 (cont)

Catalogue

Cat No.	Obv	Rev	Obverse		Reverse			Axis	Comments	Value ($)
			Separator	Stop	Separator	Tamil	Letter at Bottom			
3.314	A	I	Plain	Yes	None	Correct		?	See Baldwin (2009), June Argentum lot 83	100
3.315	A	II	Plain	Yes	None	Modified		?	See Baldwin (2009), June Argentum lot 86	80
3.316	A	IV	Plain	Yes	None	Square		↑↑		80
3.317	A	V	Plain	Yes	Line	Square		↑↑	Some have larger diameter than others (Pr 233)	80
3.318	B	II	2 Plain	No	None	Modified		↑↑		80
3.319	B	V	2 Plain	No	Line	Square		↑↑	Ref: Thompson	80
3.320	C	II	Dots/Stars	Yes	None	Modified		↑↑		80
3.321	C	III	Dots/Stars	Yes	None	Modified	Inverted	↑↓	Ref: Johnston also Wilford	100
3.322	C	IV	Dots/Stars	Yes	None	Square		↑↑		80
3.323	D	II	5 dots/dash	Yes	None	Modified		↑↑	Ref: Johnston	80
3.324	D	IV	5 dots/dash	Yes	None	Square		↑↑	Ref: Seen at Baldwin's	80
3.325	E	IV	5 dots/dash	No	None	Square		↑↑	Ref: Johnston	80
3.326	F	IV	6 dots/dash	Yes	None	Square		↑↑	Ref: Seen at Baldwin's	80
3.327	G	II	7 dots	Yes	None	Modified		↑↑	Ref: Baldwin (2009), June Argentum, lot 85	80
3.328	G	IV	7 dots	Yes	None	Square		↑↑		80
3.329	H	II	9 dots	Yes	None	Modified		↑↑		80

Copper Ten Cash 1807 (cont)

Obverse Varieties

Separator	The line separating the Persian from the English legends differs. It may be a plain line, two plain lines, a number of dots and stars, or a number of dots alone. The single plain line variety often has a second thin line immediately underneath. The double plain line variety is two clearly separated lines of about the same width
Stop After X	There is usually a stop after the X value letter. Sometimes this is missing.

	A	B	C	D	E	F	G	H
Separator	Plain	Two Plain	Dots/Stars	5 dots/dash	5 dots/dash	6 dots/dash	7 Dots	9 Dots
Stop After X	Yes	No	Yes	Yes	No	Yes	Yes	Yes

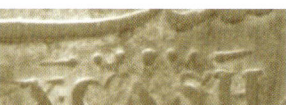

Separator – Plain   *Separator – Two Plain*   *Separator – Dots/Stars*   *Separator – 5 dots/dash*

Separator – 6 dots/dash   *Separator – 7 dots*   *Separator – 9 Dots*

Stop after X – Yes   *Stop after X – No*

Reverse Varieties

Dividing Line	There may or may not be a dividing line between the Tamil and Telugu legends. The line often has a thin second line associated with it.
First Tamil Letter	The first letter in the Tamil legend may take a number of different forms. This might be the correct form, a modified form or a square form.

	I	II	III	IV	V
Copper Ten Cash 1807 (cont)					
Separator	None	None	None	None	Plain Line
First Tamil Letter	Correct	Modified	Modified	Square	Square
Centre Letter at Bottom	Correct	Correct	Inverted	Correct	Correct

Dividing Line – None   *Dividing Line – Single Plain Line*

First Tamil Letter – Correct   *First Tamil Letter – Modified*   *First Tamil Letter – Square*

Normal letter in centre at bottom   *Inverted letter in centre at bottom*

Copper Five Cash 1807

3.332

V CASH

The value in Persian and English (Persian = *In panj kas ast* = this is five cash)

The value in Tamil and Telugu. (Telugu = *Idu anacu kasu*, Tamil = *Idi aedu kasulu* = this is five Cash)

Copper Five Cash 1807 (cont)	
Official Weight (g)	2.41
Actual Weight (g)	2.24-2.59
Actual Diameter (mm)	19.6-21.1
Metal	Copper
Edge	Plain
Axis	Varies. See below
Mintage (to March 1808)	1,216,822

Five Cash

Catalogue

Cat No.	Obv	Obverse Separator	Axis	Comments	Value ($)
3.330	A	None	↑↓		80
3.331	A	None	↑↑	Ref: BM	80
3.332	B	7 Dots	↑↑		60
3.333	B	7 Dots	↑↓		60
3.333c	B	9 Dots	↑↑		60
3.333e	B	9 Dots	↑↓		60

Obverse Varieties

Separator	The line separating the Persian from the English legends differs. It may be a number of dots alone, or no separator.

There may also be varieties with large and small English letters. Not enough examples have been examined to clarify this point.

		A	B
Separator		None	Dots

Separator – None   *Separator – 7 Dots*   *Separator – 9 Dots*

Copper Two & a Half Cash 1807

3.334

٢ ½ CASH

The value in Persian and English (Persian = *In do va-nim kas ast* = This is two and a half cash). Within a beaded circle.

The value in Tamil and Telugu. (Tamil = *Idu 2½ kasu*, Telugu = *Idi 2 1/2 kasulu* = this is 2 1/2 cash). Within a beaded circle.

Copper Two & a Half Cash 1807 (cont)

Official Weight (g)	1.21
Actual Weight (g)	Varies. See table below
Actual Diameter (mm)	"
Metal	Copper
Edge	Plain
Mintage(up to March 1808)	561,622
Axis	Varies. See below

2½
Cash

Catalogue

Cat No	Obv	Axis	Actual wt (g)	Actual Diam (mm)	Comments	Value ($)
3.334	A	↑↓	1.06-1.30	15.8-17.6		50
3.335	B	↑↑	"	"		50
3.336	B	↑↓	"	"		50
3.337	?	?	2.32	21	Same size and weight as five cash. Recorded from Pridmore. BM has an example, as has Kaslove. The letters are noticeably larger and spread out to fill the flan. This is probably a pattern or trial for a larger sized coin.	NV

Obverse Varieties

Size of 2	The numeral 2 may be large or small relative to the ½

	A	B
Size of 2	Large	Small

Size of 2 – Large

Size of 2 – Small

Silver Double Rupee *et infra* 1807

The rupee and double rupee were struck directly onto Spanish 8 reale coins after the latter had been cut to the correct weight. Examples of 8 realles exist countermarked with the impression of the rupee. These were probably die trails.

Design for Double, Single & Half Rupee

3.340

sikka mubarak badshah Ghazi Aziz-ud-din Muhammad. Alamgir. [AH] (= The auspicious coin of the Victorious Emperor. Chosen of the faith of Muhammad. Alamgir. [AH]}. All within a toothed border for double rupee and plain for single and half.

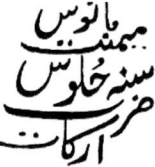

zarb arkot sanat [RY] julus maimanat manus (= Struck at Arkot in the [RY] year of his reign of tranquil prosperity). All within a toothed border for double rupee and plain for single and half.

Design for Quarter & Eighth Rupee

3.350

sikka Badshah Alamgir. 1172. (= Coin of the Emperor. Alamgir). *1172.* All within a plain border.

Zarb Arkot sanat RY (= Struck at Arkot in the RY year). All within a plain border

Silver Double Rupee *et infra* 1807 (cont)

	Double Rupee	Rupee	Half Rupee	Quarter Rupee	Eighth Rupee
Official Weight (g)	24.19	12.10	6.05	3.02	1.51
Actual Weight (g)	24.00-24.17	12.14-12.17	6.06-6.07	2.99-3.05	1.54
Actual Diameter (mm)	39.0-39.4	26.8-28.2	21.8-22.4	16.5-17.2	16.4-16.8
Mintage	165,172	2,144,806	108,180	18,216	20,046
Metal	Silver				
Edge	Grained Right				

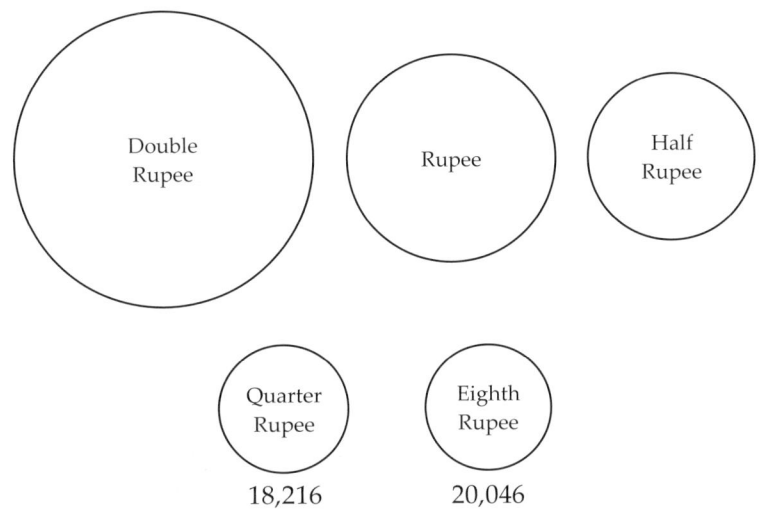

Catalogue

Cat No	Pr No.	Denomination	Obv	Rev	AH	RY	Axis	Comments	Value ($)
3.338	245	Double Rupee	A	I	1172	6	↑↑		1,500
3.339	245	"	A	I	1172	6	↑↓	Ref: BM	1,500
3.340	245	"	A	III	1172	2	↑↑	Described as mint specimen. Baldwin (2008), sale 54, lot 183	3,000
3.341	-	"	A	I	1177	6	↑↑	Ref: Puddester	2,000
3.342	-	"	A	I	No date	6		Ref: Hemanth Chopra	2,000
3.343	246	"	B	II	1172	2	↑↑		1,800

Silver Double Rupee *et infra* 1807 (cont)

Catalogue

Cat No	Pr No.	Denomination	Obv	Rev	AH	RY	Axis	Comments	Value ($)
3.344	247	Rupee	-	-	1172	6	↑↑		300
3.345	247	"	-	-	1172	6	↑↓		300
3.346	-	Copper uniface Rupee	-	-	1172	-	-	Ref: Baldwin et al (2008), New York sale, lot 401. 10.53g	NV
3.347	-	8 reales overstruck with rupee die	-	-		-	-		1,000
3.348	248	Half Rupee	-	-	1172	6	↑↑		500
3.349	-	Proof Half Rupee	-	-	1172	6	↑↑	Ref: BM	NV
3.350	249	Quarter Rupee	-	-	1172	6	↑↑		3,000
3.351	250	Eighth Rupee	-	-	1172	6	↑↑		4,000

Double rupee with no Hijri date

Silver Double Rupee *et infra* 1807 (cont)

Copper uniface rupee
(reverse blank)

Normal silver rupee

8 reales of Potsi mint overstruck with rupee dies. Probably a trial striking in the old mint[7].

Obverse Varieties for Double Rupee

Decorative Dots	There may or may not be decorative dots in the legend.

	A	B
Decorative Dots	Yes	No

Decorative dots – Yes

Decorative dots – No
Note the undertype is visible in this photo

---

[7] Boards Collections. IOR F/4/299 No 6931 referring to a public letter from Fort St George dated 24th October 1808

Silver Double Rupee *et infra* 1807 (cont)

Reverse Varieties for Double Rupee

Decorative Dots	There may or may not be decorative dots in the legend.
Extra dot group	There may or may not be an extra group of dots at the top left of the reverse legend

	I	II	III
Decorative Dots	Yes	No	Yes
Extra Dot Group	No	No	Yes

Decorative dots – Yes

Decorative dots – No
Note the undertype is visible in this photo

Extra dot group – No

Extra dot group – Yes

Silver Four Annas 1808

جهار آنه
روپيه

3.352

The value in Persian within a buckled garter. On the garter is the value in English.
FOUR ANNAS
All within a beaded border. (Persian = *Chahar ana rupiya* = Four annas of a rupee)

వెలుగు ఆఽవెలు
గనలు అణ్ణా

The value in Telugu in two lines separated by a bead surrounded by a ribbon, the ends of which are separated by a star. On the ribbon is the value in Tamil. (Tamil = *Nalu ana*, Telugu = *Nalugu analu* = Four annas).

Official Weight (g)	2.97
Actual Weight (g)	2.74-2.96
Actual Diameter (mm)	16.4-17.0
Metal	Silver
Edge	Grained Right
Mintage	165,712

Four Annas

Catalogue

Cat No	Pr No.	Obv	Axis	Comments	Value ($)
3.352	305	A	↑↑		1000
3.353	306	B	↑↑		1200

Obverse Varieties

Stops in Legend	There may be no stops in the English legend, or there may be a centre stop between the two words.

	A	B
Stops in Legend	None	Centre

Stops in Legend – None

Stops in Legend – Yes

Silver Two Annas 1808

3.357

The value in Persian within a buckled garter. On the garter is the value in English.
TWO ANNAS
All within a beaded border. (Persian = *Do ana rupiya* = Two annas of a rupee)

The value in Telugu in two lines separated by a bead surrounded by a ribbon, the ends of which are separated by a star. On the ribbon is the value in Tamil. All within a beaded border. (Tamil = *Irantu ana*, Telugu = *Renddu analu* = Two annas).

Official Weight (g)	1.48
Actual Weight (g)	1.51
Actual Diameter (mm)	16.1-16.8
Metal	Silver
Edge	Grained Right
Mintage	64,558

Two Annas

Catalogue

Cat No	Pr No.	Obv	Rev	Axis	Comments	Value ($)
3.354	309	A	I	?	Probably a pattern. Although they do come in worn condition	1000
3.355	307	B	II	↑↑		500
3.356	308	B	III	"	Taken from Pridmore	NV
3.357	-	C	II	"		400

Silver Two Annas 1808 (cont)

Obverse Varieties

Stop in Legend	There may or may not be a stop in the legend.

	A	B	C
Stop in Legend	See photo below	None	Present

Stop in Legend – None   *Stop in Legend – Present*

Reverse Varieties

Star	There may or may not be a star separating the ends of the ribbon.

	I	II	III
Star	See photo below	Yes	No

Pattern two annas. 3.357

Copper Two Dubs 1807-1808

3.358

A Persian Inscription in four lines: *do fulus Hanarabal Kampini isavi 1807* (= Two fulus of the Honourable Company. Christian year 1807).

The value in Telugu in three lines within a plain circle. Around this is the value in Tamil. All within another plain circle. (Telugu = *Kampini varuvesana renddu dabbulu*, Tamil = *Kumpini yarapotta irantu dabbu* = Honourable Company, two dubs).

Official Weight (g)	20.61
Actual Weight (g)	20.69
Actual Diameter (mm)	39.9-40.3
Metal	Copper
Edge	Plain
Axis	↑↓

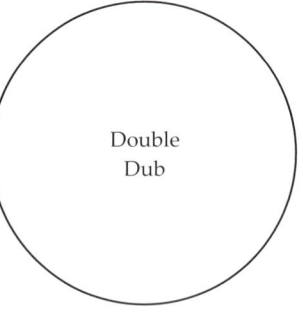

Double Dub

Catalogue

Cat No	Pr No.	Date	Comments	Value ($)
3.358	327	1807	There appear to be two obverse varieties – one with the bottom of the Persian legend reaching almost to the rim of the coin, and one with it somewhat shorter (R. Weir). Because of the rarity of these coins, insufficient specimens have been examined to catalogue these as different varieties	15,000

Copper Dub 1807 to 1808 – Type 1

3.359

A Persian Inscription in four lines: *Fulus Hanarabal Kampani isavi 1807* (= Fulus of the honourable Company. Christian year 1807). All within a toothed rim.

The value in Telugu in three lines. Within a toothed rim. (Telugu = *Kampini varuvesana dabbulu* = Honourable Company, dub). All within a toothed rim.

Official Weight (g)	10.31
Actual Weight (g)	9.88-10.49
Actual Diameter (mm)	26.4-27.9
Metal	Copper
Edge	Plain
Axis	↑↑

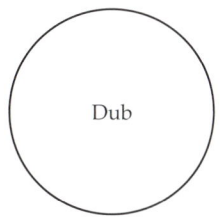

Dub

Catalogue

Cat No	Pr No.	Date	Comments	Value ($)
3.359	328	1807		300

Copper Dub 1807 to 1808 – Type 2

This coin appears to use the obverse design of the dub shown above and the reverse design of the half dub shown below. Only one specimen has been seen so far.

3.360

A Persian Inscription in four lines: *Fulus Hanarabal Kampani isavi 1807* (= Fulus of the honourable Company. Christian year 1807). All within a toothed rim.

The value in Telugu in three lines within a plain circle. Around this is the value in Tamil. All within another plain circle. (Telugu = *Kampini varuvesana dabbu*, Tamil = *Kumpini yarapotta dabbu* = Honourable Company, dub).

Official Weight (g)	10.31
Actual Weight (g)	10.57
Actual Diameter (mm)	~26
Metal	Copper
Edge	Plain
Axis	↑↑

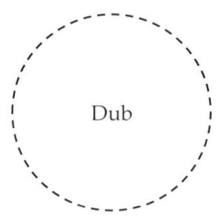

Dub

Catalogue

Cat No	Pr No.	Date	Comments	Value ($)
3.360	-	1807	Ref: Baldwins	1,000

Copper Half Dub 1807 to 1808

3.361

A Persian Inscription in four lines: *Nim fulus Hanarabal Kampani isavi 1807* (= Half fulus of the honourable Company. Christian year 1807)

The value in Telugu in three lines within a plain circle. Around this is the value in Tamil. All within another plain circle. (Telugu = *Kampini varuvesana Ara dabbu*, Tamil = *Kumpini yarapotta Arai dabbu* = Honourable Company, half dub).

Official Weight (g)	5.15
Actual Weight (g)	5.05-5.25
Actual Diameter (mm)	21.6-22.3
Metal	Copper
Edge	Plain
Axis	Varies. See below

Half Dub

Catalogue

Cat No	Pr No.	Date	Obv	Axis	Comments	Value ($)
3.361	329	"	A	↑↑	Ref: BM. Large and small date varieties (R. Weir)	100
3.362	329	1807	A	↑↓	Large and small date varieties (R. Weir)	100
3.363	330	"	B	↑↓		100

Copper Half Dub 1807 to 1808 (cont)

Obverse Varieties

Date	The date may be correct (1807) or incorrect (7107).

	A	B
Date	Correct	Incorrect

Date – Correct (1807)   *Date – Incorrect (7107)*

Copper Quarter Dub 1807 to 1808

కంపిని
వరువెశిన
కల డబ్బు

3.365

The value in Telugu. (Telugu = *Kampini varuvesana kal dabbu* = Honourable Company quarter dub).

கும்பினி
யாராபொட்ட
கால டபு4

The value in Tamil in three lines. (Tamil = *Kumpini yarapotta kal dabbu* = Honourable Company, quarter dub).

Official Weight (g)	2.57
Actual Weight (g)	2.54-2.68
Actual Diameter (mm)	16.2-16.6
Metal	Copper
Edge	Plain
Axis	Varies. See below

Quarter Dub

Catalogue

Cat No	Pr No.	Axis	Comments	Value ($)
3.364	331	↑↑	Ref: Withers	80
3.365	331	↑↓		80

Copper Regulating Dub 1807 to 1808

3.366

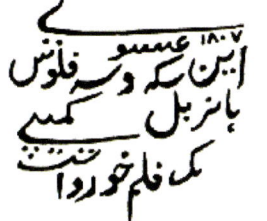

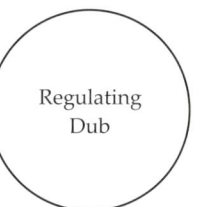

In four lines: *In sikka Hanarabal Kampani seh fulus yek falam-i-Khurd ast. Isavi 1807* (= this coin of the Honourable Company and three fulus are one small fanam. Christian year 1807)

The value in Telugu in five lines within a plain circle. Around this is the value in Tamil. All within another plain circle. (Telugu = *idi nara mudu kadta dabbulu numera cinara ruku*, Tamil = *idu ammunu pudu dabbum oru sinna panam* = this and three new dubs are one small fanam)

Official Weight (g)	7.56
Actual Weight (g)	7.40-7.61
Actual Diameter (mm)	26.4-26.8
Metal	Copper
Edge	Plain
Axis	Varies. See below

Regulating Dub

Catalogue

Cat No	Pr No.	Date	Axis	Comments	Value ($)
3.366	336	1807	↑↓	Ref: Johnston	100
3.367	336	1807	↑↑	Ref: Kaslove	100

Copper Two Dubs 1808 to 1812

3.368

A Persian Inscription in four lines:

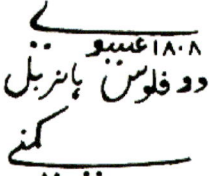

Do fulus Hanarabal Kampani isavi 1808 =
Two fulus of the honourable Company.
Christian year 1808

The value in Telugu in three lines:

కండిన
వారువేశన
రెండు దబ్బులు
2 DUBS

The value in English below. Within a
toothed rim. (Telugu = *Kampani
varuvesana renddu dabbulu* = Honourable
Company, two dubs).

Official Weight (g)	20.61
Actual Weight (g)	19.69
Actual Diameter (mm)	36.0
Metal	Copper
Edge	Plain
Axis	↑↑

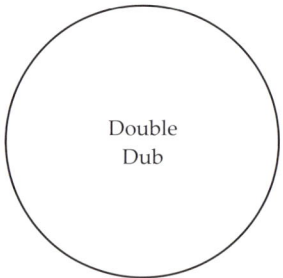

Double
Dub

Catalogue

Cat No	Pr No.	Date	Comments	Value ($)
3.368	332	1808	Not sold in last 20 years. BM has an example, as has at least one private collector. Forgeries exist	NV

Copper Dub 1808 to 1812

3.370

1 DUB

A Persian Inscription in four lines: *Fulus Hanarabal Kampani isavi 1808* (= Fulus of the honourable Company. Christian year 1808)

The value in Telugu in three lines. The value in English below. Within a toothed rim. (Telugu = *Kampini varuvesana dabbulu* = Honourable Company, dub).

Official Weight (g)	10.31
Actual Weight (g)	9.90-10.28
Actual Diameter (mm)	Varies. See table below
Metal	Copper
Edge	Plain
Axis	↑↑

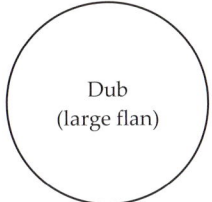

Dub
(large flan)

Catalogue

Cat No	Pr No.	Date	Actual Diam (mm)	Comments	Value ($)
3.369	333	1808	26.8	Large flan variety	200
3.370	334	″	20.9-24.3	Small flan variety. Also occurs with large and small dates (R. Weir)	150

Copper Half Dub 1808 to 1812

3.371

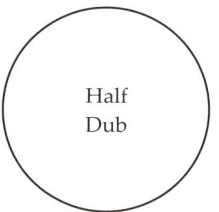

½ DUB

A Persian Inscription in four lines: *Nim fulus Hanarabal Kampani isavi 1808* (= Half fulus of the honourable Company. Christian year 1808)

The value in Telugu in three lines. The value in English below. Within a toothed rim. (Telugu = *Kampini varuvesana Ara dabbu* = Honourable Company, half dub).

Official Weight (g)	5.15
Actual Weight (g)	4.61-5.36
Actual Diameter (mm)	26.0-28.1
Metal	Copper
Edge	Plain
Axis	↑↑

Half Dub

Catalogue

Cat No	Pr No.	Date	Obverse	Comments	Value ($)
3.371	335	1808	A	Small date	100
3.372	335	"	B	Large date	100

Obverse Varieties

Date Size	The date may be large or small.

	A	B
Date Size	Small	Large

Small date   *Large date*

Copper Regulating Dub 1808 to 1812

3.373

A Persian Inscription in four lines: *In sikka Hanarabal Kampani seh fulus yek falam-i-Khurd ast. Isavi 1808* (= this coin of the Honourable Company and three fulus is one small fanam. Christian year 1808)

The value in Telugu in five lines within a plain circle. Around this is the value in Tamil. All within another plain circle. (Telugu = *idi nara mudu kadta dabbulu numera cinara ruku*, Tamil = *idu ammunu pudu dabbum oru sinna panam* = This and three new dubs are one small fanam)

Official Weight (g)	7.56
Actual Weight (g)	6.87-7.65
Actual Diameter (mm)	26.5-27.0
Metal	Copper
Edge	Plain
Axis	↑↑

Regulating Dub

Catalogue

Cat No.	Pr No.	Date	Comments	Value ($)
3.373	337	1808	Rare	1000

'The Magic of India'. An original painting by Penelope Stevens

Madras Presidency Madras Mint Later Coinages 1812 to 1835

Summary

In 1806, the Board of Directors in London, had sent a letter to their Presidencies in India expressing the desire that they should all produce a single coinage based on a rupee standard. It took several years for the Presidency authorities to comply with this, but in 1812 a new coinage based on the rupee was issued at Madras, although the amount of silver in the coins did not comply with the fineness stated by the Board of Control. Because of this, yet another coinage was begun in 1818 with the coins now fully complying with the 1806 letter. The only visible difference between these two coinages is the lotus flower on the reverse. This takes an open form on the 1812 coins and a closed form on the later issue.

Between 1823 and 1825, mintage of Arkot rupees, for use in Bengal, was undertaken at the Calcutta mint. These coins have a rose in place of the lotus.

Madras Mint – Later Coinages – Gold Mohur *et infra* – 1817

Design for Single and Half Mohurs

 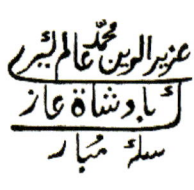

4.1

sikka mubarak badshah ghazi Aziz-ud-din Muhammad. Alamgir (= The auspicious coin of the Victorious Emperor Chosen of the faith of Muhammad. Alamgir). All within a raised toothed border. Dated 1172.

Zarb Arkot sanat 6 julus maimanat manus (= Struck at Arkot in the 6th year of tranquil prosperity). All within a raised toothed border.

Design for Quarter Mohur

4.3

sikka Badshah Alamgir (= Money of the Emperor Alamgir). Within a raised toothed border. Dated 1172

zarb arket sanat 6 (= Struck at Arkat in the 6th year). All within a raised toothed border.

	Mohur	Half Mohur	Quarter Mohur
Official Weight (g)	11.66	5.83	2.91
Actual Weight (g)	11.63-11.66	5.84	2.91
Actual Diameter (mm)	27.7-27.9	21.7-21.8	17.4
Metal	Gold		
Edge	Centre Grained Left		
Axis	↑↑		

Madras Mint – Later Coinages – Gold Mohur *et infra* – 1817 (cont)

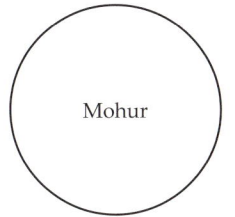
Mohur

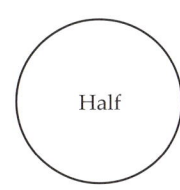
Half

Quarter

Catalogue

Cat No.	Pr. No.	Denomination	Comments	Mintage	Value ($)
4.1	238	Mohur		59,250	800
4.2	239	Half Mohur		7,500	1,500
4.3	240	Quarter Mohur		2,000	3,000

Madras Mint – Later Coinages – Gold Ashrafi *et infra* – 1819

Design for Ashrafi

4.4

The arms of the Company surrounded by the legend: ENGLISH EAST INDIA COMPANY All within a raised toothed rim.

Ashrafi Kampani Angrez Bahadur (= Ashrafi (or mohur) of the honourable English Company). Within a raised, toothed border.

Madras Mint – Later Coinages – Gold Ashrafi *et infra* – 1819 (cont)

Design for Half and Quarter Ashrafi

4.5

The crest of the Company surrounded by the legend

Nim Ashrafi Kampani Angrez Bahadur (= Half Ashrafi (or mohur) of the honourable English Company). Within a raised, toothed border.

Design for Five Rupees (1/3 Mohur)

4.7

The arms of the Company without the supporters or the motto surrounded by the legend

Panj Rupiya Kampani Angrez Bahadur (= Five rupees of the honourable English Company). Within a raised, toothed border.

	Ashrafi	Half Ashrafi	Quarter Ashrafi	Five Rupees
Official Weight (g)	11.66	5.83	2.91	3.89
Actual Weight (g)	11.67	5.80	2.92	3.86-3.89
Actual Diameter (mm)	26.6	21.2	18	19.3-19.4
Metal	Gold			
Edge	Straight Grained			
Axis	↑↑			

Madras Mint – Later Coinages – Gold Ashrafi *et infra* – 1819 (cont)

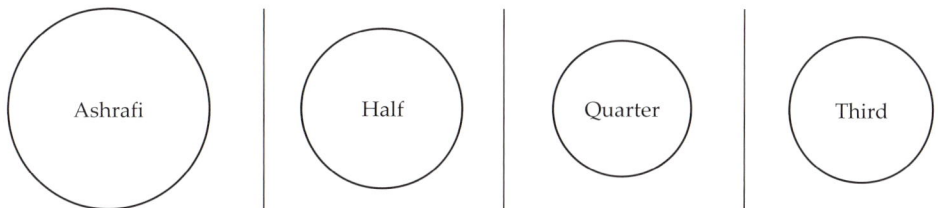

| Ashrafi | Half | Quarter | Third |

Catalogue

Cat No.	Pr. No.	Denomination	Comments	Mintage	Value ($)
4.4	241	Ashrafi		1,117,800	800
4.5	242	Half Ashrafi	Several varieties exist but more work is needed	212,690	1,500
4.6	243	Quarter Ashrafi	Several varieties exist but more work is needed	91,834	1,500
4.7	244	Five Rupees	The 5 rupees occurs with 4 rev varieties. Size of lion and placement of stop after COMPANY vary (R Weir). Also the position of the crown relative to the letters above, varies.	2,179,573	350

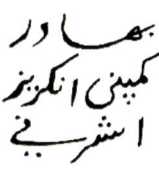

Jeweller's copy of an ashrafi

Madras Mint – Later Coinages – Silver Rupee *et infra* – 1812 to 1817

Open top to lotus flower

Design for Single and Half Rupees

4.8

1172 sikka Mubarak badshah ghazi Aziz-ud-din Muhammad. Alamgir (= 1172 the auspicious coin of the Victorious Emperor. Chosen of the faith of Muhammad. Alamgir). All within a raised toothed border.

Zarb Arcat sanat 6 julus maimanat manus (= Struck at Arkot in his 6th year of tranquil prosperity). A lotus flower occurs on the reverse. All within a raised toothed border.

Design for Quarter and Eighth Rupees

4.18

1172 sikka badshah alamgir (= 1172 Money of the Emperor. Alamgir). Within a beaded border.

zarb arkat sanat 6 (= Struck at Arkot in his 6th year). Within a beaded border.

	Rupee	Half Rupee	Quarter Rupee	Eighth Rupee
Official Weight (g)	11.66	5.83	2.91	1.46
Actual Weight (g)	11.53-11.83	5.74-5.86	2.86-2.94	1.45-1.47
Actual Diameter (mm)	26.8-28.0	21.5-22.0	17.3-17.5	13.3-13.5
Metal	Silver			
Edge	Varies. See table below			
Axis	↑↑			

Madras Mint – Later Coinages – Silver Rupee *et infra* – 1812 to 1817 (cont)

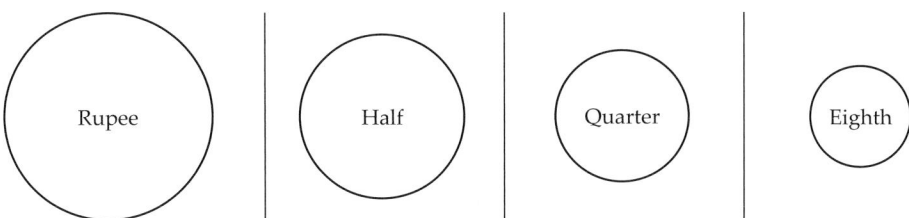

Rupee   Half   Quarter   Eighth

Catalogue

Cat No.	Pr. No.	Denom	Status	Date	Edge	Rev	Comments	Mintage	Value ($)
4.8	251	Rupee	Currency	1172	CGR	-		10,939,021	60
4.9	-	"	"	1172	CGL	-	Ref: Puddester		150
4.10	-	"	"	1172	CGL	-	Struck on thick flan. 11.83g. Ref: Stevens		200
4.11	-	"	Proof	1172	CGL	-	Ref: BM		NV
4.12	252	"	Currency	1176	CGR	-			60
4.13	253	Half Rupee	Currency	1172	CGL	-		3,392,021	50
4.14	-	"	"	1172	CGR	-	Ref: Puddester		60
4.15	254	"	"	1176	CGR	-			50
4.16	-	"	Proof	1176	CGL	-	Ref: BM.		NV
4.17	-	"	Currency	1176	CGL	-	RY 2 instead of 6. Ref: Hemanth Kumar		NV
4.18	255	Quarter Rupee	Currency	1172	CGL	I		784,021	50
4.19	-	"	"	1172	CGR	II	Ref: Puddester.		50
4.20	256	"	"	1176	CGR	II	Ref: Thompson		50
4.21	256	"	"	1176	CGR	III			50
4.22	257	Eighth Rupee	Currency	1172	GR	-	Large lotus compared to later issue	104,020	250

Madras Mint – Later Coinages – Silver Rupee *et infra* – 1812 to 1817 (cont)

Quarter Rupee Reverse Varieties

Letter *Zar*	The first part of the word *Zarb* may point below, directly at or above the first letter (*Alif*) of the mint name

	I	**II**	**III**
Letter *Zar*	Below *Alif*	Above *Alif*	At *Alif*

Below Alif	*Above Alif*	*At Alif*

Madras Mint – Later Coinages – Silver Rupee *et infra* – 1817 to 1835

Closed top to lotus

Design for Single and Half Rupees

4.23

1172 sikka Mubarak badshah ghazi Aziz-ud-din muhammad. alamgir (= 1172 the auspicious coin of the Victorious Emperor. Chosen of the faith of Muhammad. Alamgir). Within a beaded border. Dated 1172.

zarb arkat sanat 6 julus maimanat manus (= Struck at Arkot in his 6th year of tranquil prosperity). A closed lotus flower occurs on the reverse. Within a beaded border.

Madras Mint – Later Coinages – Silver Rupee *et infra* – 1817 to 1835 (cont)

Design for Quarter, Eighth & Sixteenth Rupees

4.26

1172 sikka Badshah Alamgir (= 1172 Money of the Emperor. Alamgir). Within a beaded border. Dated 1172.	*zarb arkat sanat 6* (= Struck at Arkot in his 6th year). A closed lotus occurs on the reverse. Within a beaded border.

	Rupee	Half Rupee	Quarter Rupee	Eighth Rupee	Sixteenth Rupee
Official Weight (g)	11.66	5.83	2.91	1.46	0.73
Actual Weight (g)	11.68	5.73-5.83	2.91	1.46	0.71
Actual Diameter (mm)	28.3	21.8-22.0	17.4-17.6	13.5-13.8	10.4-11.0
Metal	Silver				
Edge	Varies. See table below				

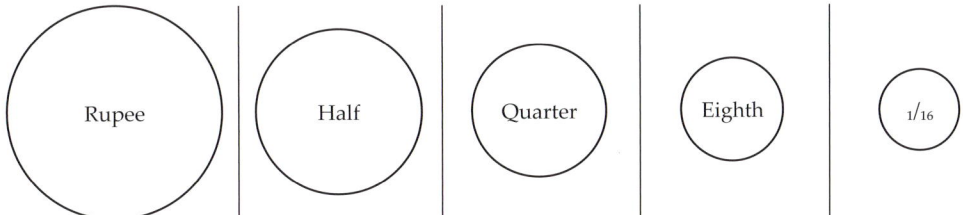

Madras Mint – Later Coinages – Silver Rupee *et infra* – 1817 to 1835 (cont)

Catalogue

Cat No.	Pr. No.	Denom	Obv	AH	RY	Edge	Comments	Mintage	Value ($)
4.23	258	Rupee	-	1172	6	CGL	Large and small date and beading close together or far apart. Also specimen in BM called proof which may be fake?? (R. Weir)	63,116,258	60
4.24	259	Half Rupee	-	1172	6	CGL	Large and small date varieties (R. Weir)	10,674,396	50
4.25	-	"	-	1172	6	CGL	Ref: Mitchiner No. 1866. No stalk to lotus		50
4.26	260	Quarter Rupee	A	1172	6	CGL		5,227,322	50
4.27	260		B	1172	6	CGL			50
4.28	261	Eighth Rupee	-	1172	6	GR	Small open lotus compared to earlier type. Large and small regnal year numeral 6 (R. Weir)	10,789,655	40
4.29	262	Sixteenth Rupee	-	1172	6	GR		8,684,254	40

See also Arkot rupees issued from the Calcutta mint (next entry)

Obverse Varieties for Quarter Rupee

Size of Date	The date may be expressed in large or small numerals

	A	B
Size of Date	Large	Small

Large Date

Small Date

Calcutta Mint – Silver Rupee *et infra* – 1823 to 1825 Mint Name: Arkot

Rose on reverse

Design for Single & Half Rupees

4.30

1172 sikka mubarak. badshah ghazi aziz-ud-din muhammad. alamgir (= 1172 the auspicious coin of the Victorious Emperor. Chosen of the faith of Muhammad. Alamgir). Within a beaded border.

zarb arkat sanat 6 julus maimanat manus (= Struck at Arkot in his 6th year of tranquil prosperity). Within a beaded border.

Design for Quarter, Eighth & Sixteenth Rupees

4.33

1172 sikka badshah alamgir (= 1172 Money of the Emperor. Alamgir). Within a toothed border.

zarb arkat sanat 6 (= Struck at Arkot in his 6th year). Within a toothed border.

	Rupee	Half Rupee	Quarter Rupee	Eighth Rupee	Sixteenth Rupee
Official Weight (g)	11.66	5.83	2.91	1.46	0.73
Actual Weight (g)	11.62-11.72	5.82-5.84	2.90-2.98	1.45-1.46	0.70-0.72
Actual Diameter (mm)	26.5-26.7	21.2-21.5	17.2-17.3	13.0-13.5	10.5-10.6
Metal	Silver				
Edge	Varies. See table below				

Calcutta Mint – Silver Rupee *et infra* – 1823 to 1825 Mint Name: Arkot (cont)

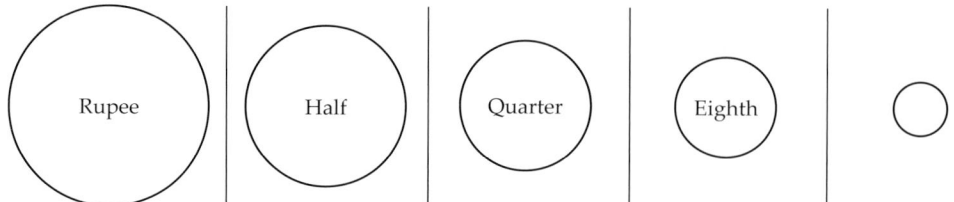

Catalogue

Cat No.	Pr. No.	Denom	Status	Edge	Comments	Value ($)
4.30	263	Rupee	Currency	SG	BM has proof specimen of Pr. 263 with high and low relief roses (R. Weir)	60
4.31	264	Half Rupee	Currency	SG		50
4.32	-	"	Proof			500
4.33	265	Quarter Rupee	Currency	SG		40
4.34	266	Eighth Rupee	Currency	GR		40
4.35	267	Sixteenth Rupee	Currency	GR		40

There are a lot of other varieties of this issue that have not yet been identified and recorded

Madras Mint – Later Coinages – Silver Pattern Rupee 1824

4.36

1172. sikka Mubarak. Badshah ghazi Aziz-ud-din Muhammad. Alamgir (= 1172. The auspicious coin of the Victorious Emperor. Chosen of the faith of Muhammad. Alamgir). All within a beaded border.

zarb arket sanat 6 julus maimanat manus (= Struck at Arkot in his 6th year of tranquil prosperity). A lotus flower occurs on the reverse. All within a beaded border.

Official Weight (g)	Varies. See table below
Actual Weight (g)	"
Actual Diameter (mm)	"
Metal	Silver
Edge	Varies. See table below

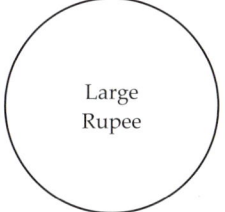
Large Rupee

Catalogue

Cat No.	Pr. No.	AH	RY	Edge	Official Wt (g)	Actual wt (g)	Actual Diam (mm)	Comments	Value ($)
4.36	339	1172	6	SG	11.40	11.42	28.5		1,500
4.37	340	1172	6	CGR	11.66	11.62	26.7	Modern restrike	1,000

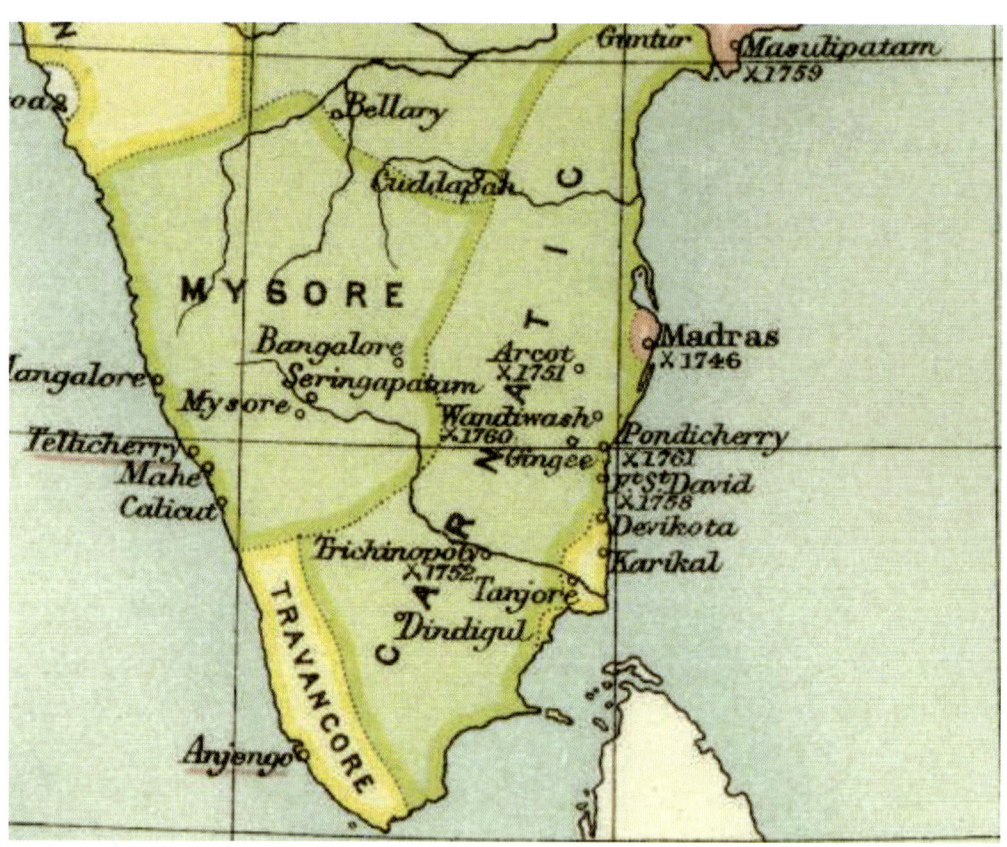

Madras Presidency Other Mints

Summary

As with the other Presidencies, the area under the control of the Madras Presidency expanded over time and many local mints either came into the possession of the EIC or were established by them. A mint was established at Fort St David early in the life of the Presidency and during the French occupation of Madras in the middle of the eighteenth century, this became the major mint of the Presidency. Other mints were acquired in the Northern Circars (the main one being at Masulipatam), in the Baramahal (e.g. Salem and Krishnagiri) or from the Dutch (Negapatam). There is a great opportunity for further research to be undertaken on these 'transitional' mints and no doubt more will be added to the list in due course.

Copper coins were produced by Boulton and sent out to India during the 1790s. These consisted of copper cash coins for use in the area of Madras itself and dubs for use in the Northern Circars and, following the sale of the contents of the Soho mint later in the nineteenth century, a number of interesting mules of these coins with various other Soho coins, were produced.

In 1824/25 copper coins were produced also at the Royal Mint in London and shipped out to Madras.

Armagon Mint – Gold Pagoda – c1628/29

The Armagon factory may have been the first English establishment in India to obtain the right to strike coins. In 1626 the local Naik agreed to strike pagodas and fanams in the British Factory for a charge of 1½ per cent[8]. Later in the year Thomas Mills at Masulipatam reported that the Armagon factory had obtained the authority to coin gold fanams and pagodas and they had been promised a stamp[9]. In 1628[10] President Kerridge reported receiving two gold coins from Armagon (though whether or not the English struck these is not clear) and in 1629[11] they definitely seem to have got the dies they needed.

Unfortunately, the coins cannot be identified separately from others struck in the area.

Design, weight etc. of coins not known

Catalogue

Cat No	Pr. No.	Comments	Value ($)
5.1	–	No coins known	NV

---

[8] Foster W. (1909). The English Factories in India 1624-1629. Clarendon Press, Oxford, p128:
[9] Foster W. (1909). The English Factories in India 1624-1629. Clarendon Press, Oxford, p135:
[10] Foster W. (1909). The English Factories in India 1624-1629. Clarendon Press, Oxford, p200:
[11] Foster W. (1909). The English Factories in India 1624-1629. Clarendon Press, Oxford, p341:

Bangalore Mint – Copper Pice – 1793 to 1793

In 1792 Tipu Sultan was forced to cede large tracts of territory to the British EIC, including Bangalore. Bangalore remained in British hands until the final defeat of Tipu in 1799 when it was re-incorporated into Mysore State. Thus, coins issued during this time fall under the EIC.

5.2

The legend in two lines: *Shah Alam Badshah* (= Shah Alam Emperor [12]06). Within a dotted circle

Legend in two lines: *sanah 33 julus zarb bangalur* (= struck at Bangalore in his 33rd regnal year) within a border.

Actual Weight (g)	15.8
Actual Diameter (mm)	~18
Metal	Copper
Edge	Plain

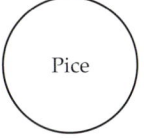

Pice

Catalogue

Cat No.	Pr. No.	AH	RY	=AD	Comments	Value ($)
5.2	-	1206?	33	1792/93	Bhandare S, (2000), ONS 164, p. 26-27	NV

Photo posted on SACG website by S. Bhandare., 13.13g

501

Fort St David (Tegnapatam) Mint – Gold Pagoda 1698

The Tegnapatam pagoda was introduced in 1698 but by 1700 it was clear that the local populace would not accept the coin and the coins began to be melted down and turned into 'Madras' pagodas. Minting appears to have been stopped in 1704.

5.3

A single standing deity with the legend around.

TEVNAPATNAM

The commencing ornament is the outline of the old Company's balemark.

Granulated

Actual Weight (g)	3.41
Actual Diameter (mm)	11.5
Metal	Gold

Catalogue

Cat No.	Pr. No.	Comments	Value ($)
5.3	288	No sales traced. Recorded from Pridmore	NV

Fort St David Mint – Copper Ten Cash (Dudu) -1748 to 1752

Coins minted at Fort St. David during the French occupation of Madras.

5.4

Balemark with GCE within a decorative stroke border

Date between wavy lines within a beaded circle

	Dudu	Half Dudu
Official Weight (g)	8.85	4,42
Actual Weight (g)	8.06-8.75	4.10
Actual Diameter (mm)	15.2-18.2	12.8-13.4
Metal	Copper	

Dudu

Catalogue

Cat No.	Pr. No.	Denomination	Date	Comments	Value ($)
5.4	41	Dudu	1748		100
5.5	42		1750	Atk. 81. Date confirmed by Johnston	200
5.6	43		1752	Atk. 82. Date confirmed	200
5.7	-	Half Dudu	1752	Ref: Craig Fernandez, Johnston	400

See also Madras mint dudus

Pridmore records a dudu dated 1753 (Pr 44) referencing a coin in the ANS collection (ANS 1919.999.129). The date is not clear and the weight (6.23) corresponds to the second issue dudu. It is probably 1755.

1752 half dudu

Fort St David Mint – Copper Cash – c1740

Pridmore attributes these cash coins to Fort St David on the grounds that:

1. The coins can be attributed to the EIC because of their inscription.
2. The cash coins issued at Madras have been identified, and these coins cannot therefore have been issued from Madras.
3. He found documentary evidence of cash being produced at Fort St David in 1740.

5.8

Tamil inscription (= *Sri* = Honourable), within a beaded border.	Tamil inscription = *KUMPINI* = Company. All within a plain square.

	Double Cash	Cash
Actual Weight (g)	2.46-2.60	1.12-1.14
Actual Diameter (mm)	10.7-11.8	8.9-9.6
Metal	Copper	
Edge	Plain	

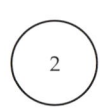

Catalogue

Cat No.	Pr. No.	Denomination	Comments	Value ($)
5.8	-	Double Cash	Ref: Johnston	250
5.9	289	Cash		50

Fort St David Mint- Copper Cash – c1741

These coins are attributed to the Fort St David mint on the basis of the reverse inscription, which is the same as that on the previous type.

5.10

| An eight pointed star within a beaded border. | Tamil inscription that translates as *KUMPINI* = Company within a plain square |

Actual Weight (g)	0.95-1.22
Actual Diameter (mm)	8.7-9.5
Metal	Copper
Edge	Plain

Catalogue

Cat No.	Pr. No.	Comments	Value ($)
5.10	290		50

Other possible EIC coins that may have been struck at local mints either by the EIC or as copies by local rulers. More research is needed.

Fort St David Mint – Copper Cash – 1748 to c1752

Coins minted at Fort St. David during the French occupation of Madras. (See comments about dudus in the section on early Coinages of the Madras Mint).

5.13

A heart shaped shield with a 4 on top. Triply divided. In each third is a letter E I C. A wavy line above. All within a beaded border?

Date within a dotted circle. All within a beaded border.

Official Weight (g)	1.20
Actual Weight (g)	1.18-1.39
Actual Diameter (mm)	7.4-10.1
Metal	Copper
Edge	Plain

Catalogue

Cat No.	Pr No.	Date	Comments	Value ($)
5.11	103	1748		100
5.12	-	1750	Ref: Johnston	100
5.13	104	1752		80

See also Madras mint cash pp. 368-369

Madapollam Mint? – Copper Cash –c1701 to 1702

A new company called the English Company Trading to the East Indies, was created in 1698 and established their main site in India at Madapollam. They appear to have obtained rights to issue coins and Pridmore attributes this style of copper cash coin to that mint although I am not entirely sure why.

5.14

A heart shaped shield with a 4 on top. Within the shield are the letters EEIC.

A group of standing deities.

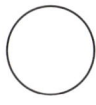

Actual Weight (g)	1.79-2.24
Actual Diameter (mm)	10.6-12.8
Metal	Copper
Edge	Plain

Catalogue

Cat No.	Pr. No.	Comments	Value ($)
5.14	287	Ref: BM..	200
5.15	-	Retrograde letters in balemark. Ref: Hemanth Chopra	250

Retrograde letters

507

Masulipatam (Machhlipatan) Mint – Silver Rupee *et infra*

An eighth rupee probably also exists but has not yet been discovered.

For both the silver and copper coins the RYs initially refer to the rule of Alamgir II but sometime between AH 1190 and 1192 they start referring to Shah Alam II.

5.18

sikka mubarak badshah ghazi Alamgir (= the auspicious coin of the Victorious Emperor Alamgir)

zarb machlipatan sanat [RY] julus maimanat manus (= Struck at Machhlipatan in the [RY] year of tranquil prosperity)

	Double Rupee	Rupee	Half Rupee	Quarter Rupee	Sixteenth Rupee
Official Weight (g)	22.52	11.26	5.64	2.82	0.70
Actual Weight (g)	22.55	11.09-11.27	5.27-5.52	2.81-2.82	0.62
Actual Diameter (mm)	32.4	19.8-23.5	18.2-18.9	12.4-13.1	~9
Metal	Silver				

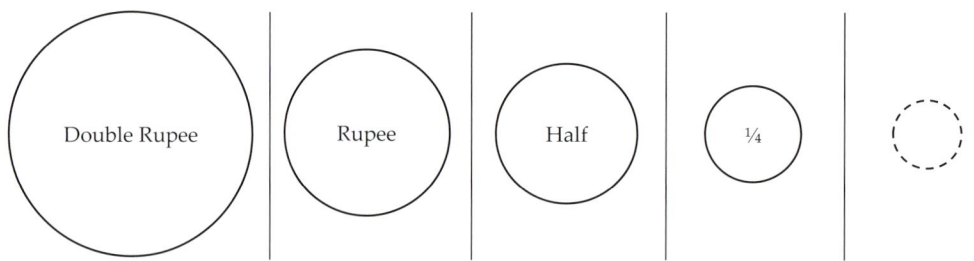

Double Rupee | Rupee | Half | ¼ |

Masulipatam (Machhlipatan) Mint – Silver Rupee *et infra* (cont)

Catalogue

Cat No.	Pr No.	Denomination	AH	RY	Comments	Value ($)
5.16	291	Double Rupee	1194	21	Three specimens known	2,000
5.17	-	Rupee	1173	5	Ref: ANS 1988.84.128	700
5.18	-	"	1174	6	Ref: Puddester. May be pre-EIC	700
5.19	-	"	1174	7	Ref: Baldwin (2004), sale 39, lot 2936	700
5.20	-	"	1176	8	Ref: Baldwin (2003), sale 35, lot 1735. Baldwin (2005), sale 40, lot 998	700
5.21	-	"	1177	9	Ref: Johnston	700
5.22	-	"	1178	5	Ref: Baldwin (2003), sale 33, lot 1031. AH 1178 & RY 5 do not fit. Could it be RY9 with the tail missing?	700
5.23	-	"	1178	9	Ref: Lingen. AH = 1764/65. RY = 1767/68.	700
5.24	-	"	1179		Ref: HK/Sing (2004), sale 38, lot 618	700
5.25	-	"	1182	x	Ref: Puddester	700
5.26	-	"	1184	15	Ref: Hemanth Chopra. AH may be 1183	700
5.27	-	"	11xx	17	Ref: Puddester	700
5.28	-	"	1189	xx	Ref: HK/Singapore (2002), Sale 34, lot 584	700
5.29	-	"	119x	21	Ref: Puddester	700
5.30	-	"	1194	xx	Ref: Baldwin (2013), New York Sale XXX, lot 519	700
5.31	-	"	1195	2x	Baldwin (2006), sale 47, lot 882	700
5.32	-	"	1197	23	Ref: Johnston	700
5.33	292	"	1197	24		700
5.34	-	"	1198	2x	Ref: Baldwin (2003), sale 35, lot 1738	700
5.35	-	"	1199	2x	Ref: Puddester	700
5.36	-	"	1200	26	Ref: Baldwin sale 84, lot 2115, also Puddester	700
5.37	-	"	1202	xx	Ref: HK/Singapore (2002), Sale 34, lot 587	700
5.38	293	"	1205	xx		700
5.40	293A	"	1211	xx		700
5.41	294	"	1212	xx		700
5.42	295	"	1213	xx		700
5.43	-	"	1214	xx	Ref: BM	NV

Listing continued on next page

Masulipatam (Machhlipatan) Mint – Silver Rupee *et infra* (cont)

Catalogue

Cat No.	Pr No.	Denomination	AH	RY	Comments	Value ($)
5.44	-	Half Rupee	1177	9	Ref: ClassNG	2,000
5.45	296	"	1198	xx		2,000
5.46	297	"	1199	2x		2,000
5.47	298	"	1204	xx	Also Hemanth Chopra	2,000
5.48	-	Quarter Rupee	11xx	xx	Ref: Baldwin (2001), sale 25 (Wiggins), lot 525	800
5.50	299	"	1200	xx		800
5.51	-	"	1202	2x	Ref: Lingen	800
5.52	-	"	1204	3x	Ref: Puddester	800
5.53	300	"	1210	3x		800
5.54	-	"	1212	xx	Ref: Howard Simmons who found it on ebay	800
5.55	-	Sixteenth Rupee	[xxxx]	5	Ref: Fitzwilliam Museum. See also Timmerman F (1985), ONSNL 94/95	NV

 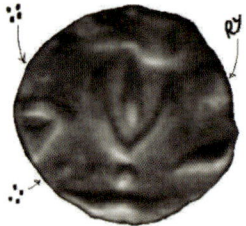

Sixteenth Rupee

This coin is identified particularly from its reverse, which has the 3 tined symbol, the two quartets of dots and the RY in positions similar to those on other denominations. The obverse is not so clear.

Rupee, 1194. Photo from Baldwin

Masulipatam (Machhlipatan) Mint – Copper Single and Half Dubs

Struck on and off for a period of about fifty years, these coins are nevertheless quite rare (see also Vizagapatam). However, similar coins were apparently struck by other European companies (see Pridmore p. 48).

5.65

sanah julus mubarak [AH] (= Auspicious year of accession [AH])
S to the left of AH date

zarb bandar machhlipatan sanah [mubarak] (= struck at the port of Machhlipatan in the auspicious year of his reign)

	Dub	Half Dub
Official Weight (g)	13.86	6.93
Actual Weight (g)	12.53-13.98	6.51-6.64
Actual Diameter (mm)	17.3-22.2	15.5-17.2
Metal	Copper	

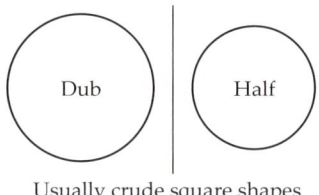

Dub   Half

Usually crude square shapes

Catalogue

Cat No.	Pr. No.	Denomination	AH	RY	Comments	Value ($)
5.56	301	Dub	1173	5	Ref: Johnston	150
5.57	"	"	1174		Ref: BM	NV
5.58	"	"	1177		Ref: BM	NV
5.59	"	"	1180		Ref: Wiggins	150
5.60	"	"	1187	18	Ref: Johnston	150
5.61	"	"	1188		Ref: BM	150
5.62	"	"	1189	21	Ref: ANS 1988.84.129	150
5.63	"	"	1190	2x	Ref: Johnston	150
5.64	"	"	1192	18	Ref: Wiggins, Johnston	150
5.65	"	"	1198	24	Ref: Wiggins, Johnston	150
5.66	"	"	1199		Ref: Wiggins	150
5.67	"	"	1201	27	Ref: Johnston	150
5.68	"	"	1211	37	Ref: Johnston	150
5.69	"	"	1212	3x	Ref: Johnston	150
5.70	"	"	1213		Ref: Lingen, BM	150

Listing continued on next page

Masulipatam (Machhlipatan) Mint – Copper Single and Half Dubs (cont)						

Catalogue

Cat No.	Pr. No.	Denomination	AH	RY	Comments	Value ($)
5.72	301	Dub	1214		Ref: Wiggins, BM	150
5.73	"	"	1217		Ref: BM	NV
5.74	"	"	1218	4x	Ref: Johnston	150
5.75	"	"	1222	47	Ref: Wiggins, BM	150
5.76	-	Half Dub	1174	5	Ref: Johnston	300
5.77	-	"	1186	18	Ref: ANS 1988.84.130	300
5.78	302	"	1212		Most specimens do not show date. Usually off flan	300

Dub dated 1171

Half dub dated 1212

Dub, 1213.

Masulipatam Mint – Copper M Dub

5.79

sanah julus mubarak [AH] (= Auspicious year of accession [AH])
S to the left of AH date

M with Persian inscription: *zarb bandar machhlipatan sanah [RY] [maimanat?]* (= struck at the port of Machhlipatan in the auspicious year of his reign)
RY next to M

	Dub	Half Dub
Official Weight (g)	13.86	6.93
Actual Weight (g)	13.37-13.72	6.04
Actual Diameter (mm)	17.5-20.6	~15
Metal	Copper	

Catalogue

Cat No.	Pr. No.	Denomination	AH	RY	Comments	Value ($)
5.79	303	Dub	[xxxx]	20		250
5.80	"	"	1218	xx	Ref: JNSI (1963) p. 117, BM. No sales traced.	NV
5.81	"	"	[xxxx]	28	M upside-down. Ref: Lingen. No sales traced.	NV
5.82	-	Half Dub	[xxxx]	25	Ref: Fitzwilliam museum. No sales traced	NV

Half M Dub

Silver Vizagapatam Rupee

The EIC records indicate that a mint was available to the authorities at Vizagapatam, at least in 1793, because they asked the Madras government for permission to recoin part of a batch of rupees they had received[12].

The mint name on the coin shown is not certain but is probably a poorly written Machhlipatam not Vizagapatam

5.83

sikka mubarak badshah ghazi Alamgir (= the auspicious coin of the Victorious Emperor Alamgir)

zarb vizagapatam? sanat [RY] julus maimanat manus (= Struck at Vizagapatam? in the [RY] year of tranquil prosperity)

Official Weight (g)	13.86
Actual Weight (g)	?
Actual Diameter (mm)	~20
Metal	Silver
Edge	Plain

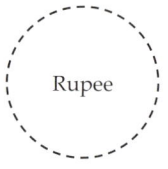

Rupee

Catalogue

Cat No.	Pr No.	AH	=AD	Comments	Value ($)
5.83	-	1206		Baldwin (2003), sale 33, lot 1032. Attribution to Vizagapatam somewhat doubtful. Probably Masulipatam.	NV

[12] Madras Consultations, 1793. IOR P/241/40, p. 2388. Letter from the Vizagapatam authorities to Madras Government, dated 19th June 1793

Copper Vizagapatam Dub

Recorded in the EIC records but no coins currently known

Official Weight (g)	13.86
Actual Weight (g)	?
Actual Diameter (mm)	?
Metal	Copper
Edge	Plain

Catalogue

Cat No.	Pr. No.	Comments	Value ($)
5.84	304	Not traced	NV

Royal Mint, London – Copper Pattern Four Pice Pattern 1824

In 1824 the Royal Mint struck a pattern for the proposed copper coinage of Madras. The currency coins have a different reverse design (see next type).

5.85

The arms of the Company with the date below. On the ribbon is the motto:
AUSP REGIS & SEN ANGLIA
All within a raised toothed rim.

The value:
IV PII
With an ornament above and below.
Surrounded by the legend:
EAST INDIA COMPANY
All within an open wreath and surrounded by a plain, raised rim.

Actual Weight (g)	8.62
Actual Diameter (mm)	26.8
Metal	Copper
Edge	Plain

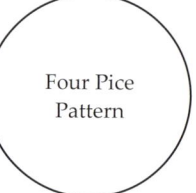

Four Pice Pattern

Catalogue

Cat No.	Pr. No.	Comments	Value ($)
5.85	343		1,000

Royal Mint, London – Copper Four Pice 1824 to 1825

A coinage consisting of 4, 2 & 1 copper pice was struck at the Royal mint for use at Madras. Pridmore traced records indicating that 100 tons of copper coins were requested. A coin dated 1823 has recently come to light (Mahapatra, internet communication) and needs some further research.

5.87

The arms of the Company with the date below. On the ribbon is the motto:
AUSP REGIS & SEN ANGLIAE
All within a raised toothed rim.

The value in Persian (= *Chahar pai*): With the numeral 4 above and the AH year, 1240, below. This is surrounded by an open wreath. All with a raised, toothed border.

Official Weight (g)	8.55
Actual Weight (g)	2.24-2.59
Actual Diameter (mm)	26.8
Metal	Copper
Edge	Plain
Axis	↑↓
Mintage	7,136,448

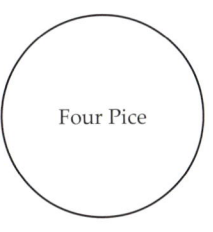

Four Pice

Catalogue

Cat No.	Pr. No.	Status	Rev	Date	Comments	Value ($)
5.86	-	Trial Striking	I	1824	Struck on a larger flan and without collar - Wiggins Sale	250
5.87	274	Currency	I	1824		80
5.88	275	Proof	I	1824		500
5.89	276	Currency	I	1825		60
5.90	277	Proof	I	1825		500
5.91	278	Currency	II	1825		60
5.92	279	Currency	III	1825		60

Royal Mint, London – Copper Four Pice 1824 to 1825 (cont)

Reverse Varieties

Right Wreath tip	The right hand tip of the wreath may point down, up, or straight. See below for further identifying features

	I	II	III
Right Wreath tip	Down	Up	Straight

I – Down

II – Up

III – Straight

Reverse I – Right wreath tip points down and is slightly to the right of the 4. Thick leaves in wreath.

Reverse II – Right wreath tip points up and is above the 4. Thick leaves in wreath

Reverse III – Right wreath tip is straight and slightly to the right of the 4. Thinner leaves in wreath

Royal Mint, London – Copper Two Pice 1824 to 1825

The two pice denomination was only issued in 1825

5.93

چارپای
سکه

The arms of the Company with the date below. All within a raised toothed rim.

The value in Persian (= *Do pai*) with a value numeral above and the AH year below. All within an open wreath surrounded by a raised, toothed rim.

Official Weight (g)	4.27
Actual Weight (g)	4.34
Actual Diameter (mm)	21.9
Metal	Copper
Edge	Plain
Axis	↑↓
Mintage	7,126,104

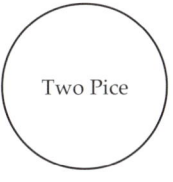

Two Pice

Catalogue

Cat No.	Pr. No.	Status	Date	Comments	Value ($)
5.93	280	Currency	1825		50
5.94	281	Proof	1825		250

Royal Mint, London – Copper One Pice 1824 to 1825

The one pice denomination was also only issued in 1825. There are a number of reverse varieties associated with the diacritical marks on the reverse of the coin, and one strange piece dated 1833 that is probably a local copy.

5.95

The arms of the Company with the date below. All within a raised toothed rim.

The value in Persian (= *Yek pai*) with a value numeral above and the AH year below. All within an open wreath surrounded by a raised, toothed rim.

Official Weight (g)	2.13
Actual Weight (g)	2.07-2.21
Actual Diameter (mm)	17.7-17.8
Metal	Copper
Edge	Plain
Axis	↑↓
Mintage	4,741,328

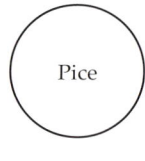

Pice

Catalogue

Cat No.	Pr. No.	Date	Status	Obv	Rev	Comments	Value ($)
5.95	282	1825	Currency	A	I		50
5.96	283	"	Proof	A	I		200
5.97	284	"	Currency	A	II		50
5.98	285	"	"	A	III		50
5.99	286	1833	"	B	IV	Local copy	50

Royal Mint, London – Copper One Pice 1824 to 1825 (cont)

Obverse Varieties

Design	May be normal or crude

	A	B
Design	Normal	Crude

Normal Design

Crude Design

Reverse Varieties

Design	May be normal or crude
Diacritical Marks	There may be 0, 1 or 2 diacritical marks below the last letter of the word pai.

	I	II	III	IV
Diacritical Marks	2	1	0	2
Design	Normal	Normal	Normal	Crude

Diacritical Marks – One

Diacritical Marks – Two

Design – Normal

Design – Crude

Negapatam Mint – Early Coinages – Hindu System – Gold 'Iskat' or 'Scott' Pagoda 1781

The coin shown below contains 62% gold, which fits with the reported fineness of the 'Scott' pagoda. The only way to distinguish these from Madras pagodas seems to be by measuring the gold content.

5.100

A standing deity.   Granulated

Actual Weight (g)	3.42
Actual Diameter (mm)	11.1-11.5
Metal	Gold
Edge	Plain

Catalogue

Cat No.	Pr No.	Comments	Value ($)
5.100	-		500

Anecdotally this style of pagoda has been call the 'Scott' (or Negapatam) pagoda However, Barbara Mears has attributed this style to Travancore and XRF analysis of one specimen shows that it contains too much gold (82%) to be the Scott pagoda

Krishnagiri Mint – 1790s

The records contain an entry about a mint established at Krishnagiri[13]. The coins struck were probably gold star pagodas[14] but it is not known if the coins have any distinguishing features. It is possible that copper coins were also struck there.

Coins not known but possibly star pagodas

Catalogue

Cat No.	Pr No.	Comments	Value ($)
5.101	–	No coins known	NV

---

[13] Paper read by the late Ken Wiggins on 12 June 1999, at the ONS study day organised at the Department of Coins and Medals, Fitzwilliam Museum, Cambridge. It was published earlier as 'Two Unsuccessful Mints of the East India Company' in The Numismatic Circular, Volume 88, No.10, pp. 349-350.

[14] Madras District Gazetteer, Salem. Madras 1918, vol. 1, part 1, p. 292.
    Madras Consultations, 1793. IOR P/241/38, p. 1277

Salem Mint – Copper Five Cash –1798

அநுசு காசு
5.102

A flower surrounded by a circle. Around this is the value in Tamil interspersed with groups of four dots. The legend reads: *Anacu kasu* (= Five cash).

Zarb Salem 1213 (= Struck at Salem AH 1213).

Actual Weight (g)	6.00
Actual Diameter (mm)	20.4-21.0
Metal	Copper
Edge	Plain

Five Cash

Catalogue

Cat No.	Pr No.	AH	=AD	Comments	Value ($)
5.102	-	1213	1798/99	Ref: Wiggins SNC Oct 1980. Also specimen in Ashmolean museum, Oxford and two in BM.	2,000

Salem Mint – Copper Cash – c1793 to 1798

5.104

A heart shaped shield, point uppermost, containing GVEI. Within a beaded border.

Double lines forming a square. An inscription in Persian: *Salem* and the hijri date.

Actual Weight (g)	0.82-1.51
Actual Diameter (mm)	8.7-11.9
Metal	Copper
Edge	Plain

Catalogue

Cat No.	Pr. No.	Obv	AH	AD	Comments	Value ($)
5.102c	-	A	-	1793?	AD date above Salem, Ref: Johnston	30
5.103	105	B	VIII = 1211?			30
5.104	106	B	1212			30
5.105	107	C	1212			50
5.106	-	B	1213		Ref: BM.	NV
5.107	-	B	1226		Ref: Lingen. Error date.	50
5.108	108	B	No date			30

The letters in the shield may be ordered differently on some specimens. See photos below (Ref: Tamil Vanan)

Salem Mint – Copper Cash – c1793 to 1798

Obverse Varieties

Shield	The shield may be present or absent.
Letters	Letters may be arranged as VEIC or CVEI

	A	B	C
Shield	Present	Present	Absent
Letters	VEIC	CVEI	?

Shield – Present

Letters arranged differently

Possibly 1793 on reverse (posted on SACG by Bob Johnston 9.5.06)

Soho Mint – Northern Circars Copper – Mule Dub

Probably a later concoction by Taylor.

5.109

Arms of the Company with the date below and the legend above. The ribbon below the arms bears an inscription. All within a raised toothed border.

An Elephant standing and facing left. Below is the date 1802. All this within a border composed of annulets.

Actual Weight (g)	13.91-14.00
Actual Diameter (mm)	30.3-30.6
Metal	Copper
Edge	Plain

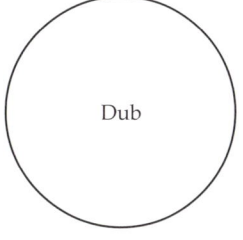

Dub

Catalogue

Cat No.	Pr. No.	Axis	Comments	Value ($)
5.109	Bengal 378		Ref: Singapore/HK (2001), sale 32, lot 632. Also BM. See Pr. Part 2, Asian Territories, Ceylon 262.	600

Soho Mint – Copper Twenty Cash 1803 & 1808

The currency coins in this series are common in lower grades but much more difficult to find in high grades.

5.111

Arms of the Company with the date below and the legend above.
EAST INDIA COMPANY
On the ribbon is the inscription:
AUSPICIO REGIS & SENATUS ANGLIAE
All within a raised toothed border.

The value in Persian: *bist kas chahar falus ast* = Twenty cash make four falus. Below this is the value in English:
XX . CASH .
All within a plain raised rim.

Official Weight (g)	Varies. See table below
Actual Weight (g)	″
Actual Diameter (mm)	30.5-30.9
Metal	Copper
Edge	Plain
Axis	Varies. See table below
Mintage	1,323,360 (Doty)

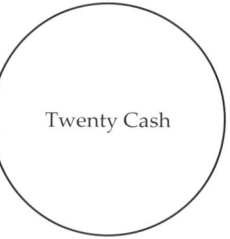

Twenty Cash

Soho Mint – Copper Twenty Cash 1803 & 1808 (cont)

Catalogue

Cat No.	Pr. No.	Date	Status	Axis	Official wt (g)	Actual wt (g)	Comments	Value ($)
5.110	190	1803	Currency	↑↓	12.95	11.90-12.35		60
5.111	191	"	Proof	↑↓	"	"		200
5.112	191	"	Proof	↑↑	"	"		200
5.113	192	"	Gilt Proof	↑↓	"	"		350
5.114	192A	1804	Mule		"	"	Very rare	1000
5.115	193	1808	Currency	↑↓	"	14.50		60
5.116	194	"	Proof			11.90-12.35		200
5.117	195	"	Gilt Proof	↑↓		"		350
5.118	196	"	Silver Proof	↑↓		"		1,000
5.119	197	"	Currency	↑↓	9.33	9.13-9.75		60
5.120	-	"	Currency		"	14.1		100
5.121	-	1808/7	Currency		"	?	Last 8 over 7	NV
5.122	198	1808	Proof	↑↓	"	8.85	Ref: Hemanth Chopra	200
5.123	198	"	Proof	↑↑	"	9.54	Ref: BM, Johnston	200
5.124	-	"	Gilt Proof	↑↓	"	"	Bombay/Madras mule. Less than half a dozen specimens known. Not in BM collection	600

Soho Mint – Copper Ten Cash 1803 & 1808

Pridmore classifies the weights of these coins as heavy issue 1803 and 1808 (6.47g) and a light issue of 1808 (4.66g). However the weights of the proofs vary in a more complicated way than this. An example of the light issue exists, dated 1803, and there are both intermediate weight coins (5.35g) and very light weight coins (3.36g) dated 1808.

5.127

Arms of the Company with the date below and the legend above.
EAST INDIA COMPANY
On the ribbon is the inscription:
AUSPICIO REGIS & SENATUS ANGLIAE
All within a raised toothed border.

The value in Persian: *dah kas do falus ast* = Ten cash make two falus. Below this is the value in English:
X . CASH .
All within a plain raised rim.

Official Weight (g)	Varies. See table below
Actual Weight (g)	″
Actual Diameter (mm)	25.6-25.7
Metal	Copper
Edge	Plain
Axis	Varies. See table below
Mintage	6,304,560 (Doty)

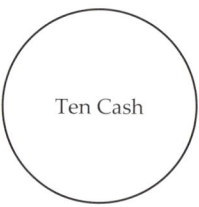

Ten Cash

Soho Mint – Copper Ten Cash 1803 & 1808 (cont)

Catalogue

Cat No.	Pr. No.	Date	Status	Axis	Official wt (g)	Actual wt (g)	Comments	Value ($)
5.125	199	1803	Currency	↑→	6.47	6.24-6.46	NB die axis.	50
5.126	199	"	Currency	↑↓	"	"		50
5.127	200	"	Proof	↑↓	"	6.63		150
5.128	201	"	Gilt Proof	↑↓	"	"	Ref: BM	250
5.129	-	"	Proof	↑↓	4.66	4.72	Ref: Johnston	150
5.130	202	1808	Currency	↑↓	6.47	6.47-6.56		50
5.131	203	"	Proof	↑↓	"	"		150
5.132	204	"	Gilt Proof	↑↓	"	"	Ref: BM	NV
5.133	205	"	Silver Proof	↑↓	-	-	Ref: BM. Also Baldwin (2013), sale 82 (Fore), lot 948.	800
5.134	-	"	Proof	↑↑	6.47	4.85-5.35	Intermediate weight. NB die axis. Ref: Stevens, Johnston	200
5.135	206	"	Currency	↑↓	4.66	4.48-4.84		50
5.136	207	"	Proof	↑↓	"	"		150
5.137	-	"	Proof		"	3.36	Ref: Peter Mitchell at Baldwin. NB Weight.	200
5.138	-	"	Gilt Proof		"	4.66-4.76	Ref: Pridmore Sale (1982), Lot 392. NB. Weight..	500

Soho Mint – Copper Five Cash 1803

The V cash proof and pattern issues differ from the V cash currency coins in that the flags are nearly vertical and point between the letters N & D. Catalogues have featured proofs with small letters on the obverse but none have been examined. The small letter currency coin is often nicely struck and could be mistaken for a proof.

5.142

The arms of the Company with the date below. Above, the legend:
EAST INDIA COMPANY
On the ribbon is the inscription:
AUSPICIO REGIS & SENATUS ANGLIAE
All within a raised toothed rim.

The value in Persian: *Panj kas yek falus ast* = Five cash make one falus. Below this is the value in English:
V . CASH .
All within a raised, toothed rim.

Official Weight (g)	3.23
Actual Weight (g)	Varies. See table below
Actual Diameter (mm)	"
Metal	Copper
Edge	Plain
Axis	Varies. See table below
Mintage	12,304,416 (Doty)

Five Cash

Soho Mint – Copper Five Cash 1803 (cont)

Catalogue

Cat No.	Pr. No.	Date	Obv	Status	Axis	Actual wt (g)	Actual Diam (mm)	Comments	Value ($)
5.139	208	1803	A	Currency	↑↓	2.99-3.17	21.0-21.1		40
5.140	208A	1803	B	Currency		"	"	Recorded from Pr.	80
5.141	-	1803	A or B	Proof		"	"	Ref: Baldwin (2013), sale 82 (Fore), lot 946	150
5.142	-	1803	C	Currency	↑↓	"	"		80
5.143	209	1803	C	Proof	↑↓	3.46-4.22	21.0-22.3	Ref: Format 9/97. Also Pridmore sale 10/82 part lot 388. Also Johnston	150
5.144	210	1803	C	Gilt Proof	↑↓	3.29	"		250
5.145	211	1803	C	Silver Proof	↑↓	4.82	"	Ref: BM	NV

Obverse Varieties

Letters	The letters may be 0.8mm or 1.2mm high.
Design	The direction that the left-hand flagstaff points, is an easily seen difference. The helmet is also a different shape. This is most often seen on proofs but also, more rarely, on currency specimens.

	A	B	C
Letters	1.2mm	0.8mm	1.2mm
Design	Normal	Normal	Differs

Spear points to N
Normal design

Spear points between N & D
Design differs

Soho Mint – Copper Pattern One Cash 1803

The one cash coin was so small that it required special production techniques, and these coins were produced last of all the denominations. Matthew Boulton had sent John Phillp to London in 1802 to consult the EIC's experts on the designs, and he returned in October. Production of the three larger denominations began almost immediately, but production of the one cash pieces caused problems until January 1803 when a new method was perfected. The pattern shown here may have been Phillp's original design that was not suitable for high throughput production. Perhaps the design was then modified to that of the currency coins to accommodate the new method of minting the coins.

Howard Simmons first drew my attention to this coin

Note the toothed border

5.146

The Company's crest of rampant lion facing left, with the date below. Stroke border

The value in Persian: (= *Kas* = cash). Underneath is the value in English. Stroke border

Actual Weight (g)	0.6
Actual Diameter (mm)	11.7
Metal	Copper
Edge	Plain
Axis	↑↓

Catalogue

Cat No.	Pr. No.	Date	Status	Comments	Value ($)
5.146	-	1803	Pattern	Only one known at present	850

Soho Mint – Copper One Cash 1803

Modern fantasy pieces are said to exist by KM. They are copper, have thick flans and weigh about 1.3g

5.149

The Company's crest of a rampant lion facing left, with the date below. Plain border

The value in Persian: (= *Kas* = cash). Underneath is the value in English:
I CASH
Plain border

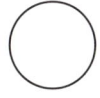

Official Weight (g)	0.64
Actual Weight (g)	Varies. See table below
Actual Diameter (mm)	11.4-11.5
Metal	Varies. See table below
Edge	Plain
Axis	Varies. See table below
Mintage	17,994,240 (Doty)

Catalogue

Cat No.	Pr. No.	Date	Status	Axis	Official wt (g)	Actual wt (g)	Comments	Value ($)
5.147	212	1803	Currency	↑↑	0.64	0.77		40
5.148	212	1803	Currency	↑↓	0.64	0.60-0.64		40
5.149	213	1803	Proof	↑↓	"	0.64-0.77		100
5.149c	213	1803	Proof	↑↑	"	0.60	Ref: Johnston	100
5.150	214	1803	Gilt Proof	↑↓	"	0.59-0.73		150
5.151	214	1803	Gold Proof	↑↑	"	1.53	Heavy weight. Solid gold confirmed by XRF analysis	500
5.152	215	1803	Silver Proof	↑↑	"	0.79-0.90		250

Soho Mint – Northern Circars – Copper Pattern Dub – Type 1

سکه کمپنی
عیسوی ۱۷۹۳

5.153

Sicca Kampani isavi 1793 (= Money of the Company Christian year 1793). All within a broad raised rim. Incuse on the rim is the English legend:
ENGLISH EAST INDIA COMPANY

Persian inscription as obverse. All within a broad raised rim. Incuse on the rim is the English legend as on the obverse

Actual Weight (g)	13.99-14.26
Actual Diameter (mm)	30.6-30.7
Metal	Copper
Edge	1. ENGLISH.UNITED.EAST.INDIA.COMPANY &.. (incuse) 2. Plain
Axis	↑↑

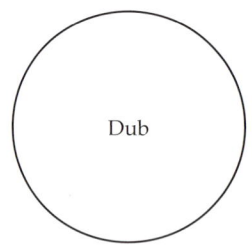

Dub

Catalogue

Cat No.	Pr. No.	Edge	Comments	Value ($)
5.153	Bengal 369	1		800
5.154	Bengal 370	2		800

Soho Mint – Northern Circars – Copper Pattern Dub – Type 2

سکه کمپنی
عیسوی ١٧٩٣

5.155

Persian inscription: *Sicca Kampani isavi 1793* (= Money of the Company Christian year 1793). All within a broad raised rim. Incuse on the rim is the English legend:
ENGLISH EAST INDIA COMPANY

The Crest of the Company over the numerals 48. On the broad, raised rim is an incuse Latin legend:
AUSPICIO REGIS ET SENATUS ANGLIAE
(= By the authority of the King and Parliament of England). In a sunken panel at the bottom of the rim is a relief inscription.

Actual Weight (g)	?
Actual Diameter (mm)	~30
Metal	Copper
Edge	Plain
Axis	?

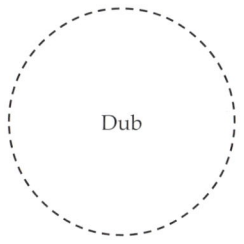

Dub

Catalogue

Cat No.	Pr. No.	Comments	Value ($)
5.155	Bengal 371		800

Soho Mint – Northern Circars – Copper Pattern Dub – Type 3

5.156

The Crest of the Company over the numerals 48. On the broad, raised rim is the incuse Latin legend:
AUSPICIO REGIS ET SENATUS ANGLIAE
(= By the authority of the King and Parliament of England). Below and in a sunken panel at the bottom of the rim is a relief inscription:
48 TO ONE RUPEE

The balemark of the Company within a broad raised rim. On the rim is the incuse legend:
ENGLISH EAST INDIA COMPANY

Actual Weight (g)	?
Actual Diameter (mm)	30.7
Metal	Copper
Edge	ENGLISH.UNITED.EAST.INDIA.COMPANY &.. (incuse)
Axis	?

Dub

Catalogue

Cat No.	Pr. No.	Comments	Value ($)
5.156	Bengal 373		800

Soho Mint – Northern Circars – Copper Pattern Dub – Type 4

This pattern is an early design for the 1802 coinage of Ceylon, the obverse being from the Madras coinage of 1794/97 except for a slight change in the legend, and the reverse being a particular, rather more elongated form of the elephant seen on other patterns (see below). This style is extremely rare, with perhaps only two specimens in existence. However, although the obverse is modified from the Madras die, it is a distinctively different design, and therefore belongs to Ceylon and not Madras. The coin is included in the catalogue for the sake of completeness.

5.157

The balemark of the Company within a broad raised rim. On the rim is the incuse legend: UNITED EAST INDIA COMPANY	An Elephant standing and facing left. On the broad, raised rim is the legend: BY WISDOM & FORCE

Actual Weight (g)	13.27
Actual Diameter (mm)	30.8
Metal	Copper
Edge	ENGLISH.UNITED.EAST.INDIA.COMPANY &.. (incuse)
Axis	

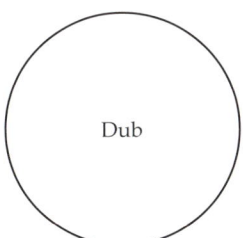

Dub

Catalogue

Cat No.	Pr. No.	Comments	Value ($)
5.157	Bengal 374	Only two specimens known. See also Pridmore, part 2, Asian Territories, Ceylon No. 258	2,000

Soho Mint – Northern Circars – Copper Pattern Dub – Type 5

Two further patterns are known for the 1802 Ceylon coinage that mix dies from the 1794/97 copper coinage with elephant designs on the reverse. The elephant on these two patterns is more upright and less elongated than that on the previous pattern.

5.158

The balemark of the Company within a broad raised rim. On the rim is the incuse inscription:
UNITED EAST INDIA COMPANY 1794

An Elephant standing and facing left. Below are the numerals 48. On the broad, raised rim is the legend:
BY WISDOM AND FORCE
Below and in a sunken panel at the bottom of the rim is a relief inscription:
48 TO ONE RUPEE

Actual Weight (g)	12.50-13.20
Actual Diameter (mm)	30.5
Metal	
Edge	1. ENGLISH.UNITED.EAST.INDIA.COMPANY &.. (incuse) 2. Plain
Axis	

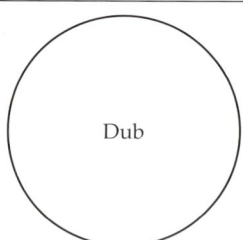

Dub

Catalogue

Cat No.	Pr. No.	Date	Edge	Comments	Value ($)
5.158	Bengal 375	1794	1	See also Pridmore, part 2, Asian Territories, Ceylon No. 259	1,500
5.159	Bengal 376	1797	2	See also Pridmore, part 2, Asian Territories, Ceylon No. 260	1,500

Soho Mint – Northern Circars Copper – Mule Dub – Type 6

Mule: Obverse as for 5.159 for Madras. Reverse is the obverse of 1/48th rix dollar (1 stiver) 1802 Ceylon. This is probably a later striking.

5.160

Arms and supporters of the Company resting on a scroll bearing the incuse inscription:
UNITED EAST INDIA COMPANY
On the broad, raised rim is the incuse inscription:
AUSPICIO REGIS ET SENATUS ANGLIAE
(= By the authority of the King and Parliament of England).
Below and in a sunken panel at the bottom of the rim is a relief inscription:
48 TO ONE RUPEE

An Elephant standing and facing left. Below is the date 1802. All this within a border composed of annulets.

Actual Weight (g)	13.05-13.6
Actual Diameter (mm)	30.6-30.7
Metal	Copper
Edge	Plain
Axis	↑↓

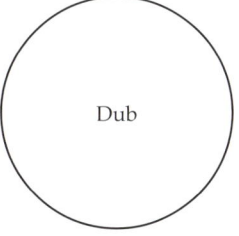

Dub

Catalogue

Cat No.	Pr. No.	Comments	Value ($)
5.160	Bengal 377	See also Pr. Part 2, Asian territories, Ceylon 261	1,000

Soho Mint – Northern Circars – Copper Mule Dub – Type 7

Mule: Obverse as 5.159 for Madras. Reverse is the Obverse of the Sierra Leone Co. penny (1791). Struck from a very worn obverse die. Vice[15] reports weights ranging from 8.94g to 14.19g.

5.161

Arms and supporters of the Company resting on a scroll bearing the incuse inscription:
UNITED EAST INDIA COMPANY
On the broad, raised rim is the incuse inscription:
AUSPICIO REGIS ET SENATUS ANGLIAE
(= By the authority of the King and Parliament of England).
Below and in a sunken panel at the bottom of the rim is a relief inscription:
48 TO ONE RUPEE

A facing lion standing on a mountaintop. Around is the inscription.

Actual Weight (g)	8.94-14.19
Actual Diameter (mm)	30.7
Metal	Copper
Edge	Plain
Axis	Varies. See table below

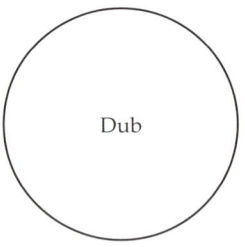

Dub

Catalogue

Cat No.	Pr. No.	Axis	Comments	Value ($)
5.161	Bengal 379	↑↑	Ref: BM	1,000
5.162	Bengal 379	↑↓	Ref: BM	1,000

---

[15] Vice D. (1983), The Coinage of British West Africa & St. Helena 1684-1958. Pub. by Peter Ireland (Format) Ltd.

Soho Mint – Northern Circars – Copper Mule Dub – Type 8

Mule: Obverse as 5.166, a Madras dub. Reverse as 5.11, a Madras twenty cash without the final 4 of the date.

5.163

Arms and supporters of the Company resting on a scroll bearing the incuse inscription:
UNITED EAST INDIA COMPANY
On the broad, raised rim is the incuse inscription:
AUSPICIO REGIS ET SENATUS ANGLIAE
(= By the authority of the King and Parliament of England).
Below and in a sunken panel at the bottom of the rim is a relief inscription:
48 TO ONE RUPEE

Arms of the Company surrounded by the legend:
EAST INDIA COMPANY
Incomplete date below (180x). All within a raised, border.

Actual Weight (g)	9.34
Actual Diameter (mm)	30.8-30.9
Metal	Copper
Edge	ENGLISH.UNITED.EAST.INDIA.COMPANY &.. (incuse)
Axis	↑↑

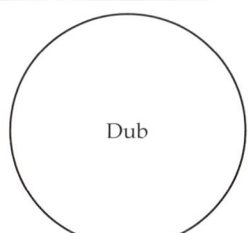

Dub

Catalogue

Cat No.	Pr. No.	Comments	Value ($)
5.163	-	Ref: SNC October 1980. Also Format 51.	800
5.164	-	Obverse Die Splash in lead	500
5.165	-	Reverse Die Splash in lead	500

Soho Mint – Northern Circars – Copper Mule Dub – Type 8 (cont)

Obverse lead die splash

Reverse lead die splash

Soho Mint – Northern Circars – Copper Pattern Dub – Type 9

5.166

Arms and supporters of the Company resting on a scroll bearing the incuse inscription:
UNITED EAST INDIA COMPANY
On the broad, raised rim is the incuse inscription:
AUSPICIO REGIS ET SENATUS ANGLIAE
(= By the authority of the King and Parliament of England).
Below and in a sunken panel at the bottom of the rim is a relief inscription:
48 TO ONE RUPEE

The balemark of the Company within a broad, raised rim. On the rim is an incuse inscription:
UNITED EAST INDIA COMPANY
1974

Actual Weight (g)	16.02
Actual Diameter (mm)	30.7
Metal	Copper
Edge	DO AS YOU WOULD BE DONE BY
Axis	↑↑

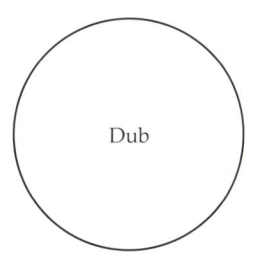

Dub

Catalogue

Cat No.	Pr. No.	Comments	Value ($)
5.166	-		800

545

Soho Mint – Northern Circars – Copper Currency Dub 1793 to 1797

5.169

Arms and supporters of the Company resting on a scroll bearing the incuse inscription:
UNITED EAST INDIA COMPANY
On the broad, raised rim is the incuse inscription:
AUSPICIO REGIS ET SENATUS ANGLIAE
(= By the authority of the King and Parliament of England).
Below and in a sunken panel at the bottom of the rim is a relief inscription:
48 TO ONE RUPEE

The balemark of the Company within a broad raised rim. On the rim is the incuse inscription:
UNITED EAST INDIA COMPANY

Official Weight (g)	13.34
Actual Weight (g)	13.33-14.19
Actual Diameter (mm)	30.7-30.8
Metal	Copper
Edge	1. ENGLISH.UNITED.EAST.INDIA.COMPANY &.. (incuse) 2. ENGLISH.UNITED.EAST INDIA.COMPANY (incuse) 3. ENGLISH.UNITED.EAST.INDIA.COMPANY (incuse) 4.Plain N.B. Different stops between words
Axis	↑↓

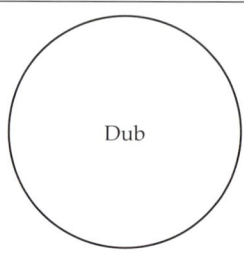

Dub

Soho Mint – Northern Circars – Copper Currency Dub 1793 to 1797

Catalogue

Cat No.	Pr. No.	Obv	Date	Status	Edge	Comment	Value ($)
5.167	310	A	1794	Currency	2		80
5.168	310	A	1794	"	3		80
5.169	311	A	1794	Proof	2		350
5.170	312	A	1794	Gilt Proof	2		500
5.171	313	A	1794	Currency	4		150
5.172	314	B	1794	Proof mule	1	Lion supporters full face	250
5.173	315	C	1794	Proof	2?	ANGLICE	250
5.174	316	B	1797	Currency	2		80
5.175	317	B	1797	Proof	2		80
5.176	318	B	1797	Gilt Proof	2		80

Obverse Varieties

Lion Supporters	Lion supporters may be side facing, or full face
Motto	The motto may be correct (SENATUS ANGLIAE), or may read SENATUS ANGLICE

	A	B	C
Lion Supporters	Side	Full	Side?
Motto	ANGLIAE	ANGLIAE	ANGLICE

Lion Supporters – Side

Lion Supporters – Full

Soho Mint – Northern Circars – Copper Pattern Half Dub 1794

Larger letters on both sides and larger arms. Ns on scroll reversed

5.177

Arms and supporters of the Company resting on a scroll bearing the incuse inscription:
UNITED EAST INDIA COMPANY
On the broad, raised rim is the incuse inscription:
AUSPICIO REGIS ET SENATUS ANGLIAE
(= By the authority of the King and Parliament of England).
Below and in a sunken panel at the bottom of the rim is a relief inscription:
96 TO ONE RUPEE

Balemark of the Company surrounded by a broad flat rim.
On the rim is the incuse legend:
UNITED EAST INDIA
COMPANY 1794

Actual Weight (g)	6.81
Actual Diameter (mm)	24.5
Metal	Copper
Edge	Plain
Axis	↑↓

Half Dub.

Catalogue

Cat No.	Pr. No.	Date	Comments	Value ($)
5.177	-	1794	May be unique. Ref: SNC October 1980. Thanks to Vikram Coins	1500

Ns on scroll reversed (but poor photo)

Soho Mint – Northern Circars – Copper Currency Half Dub 1793 to 1797

5.180

Arms and supporters of the Company resting on a scroll bearing the incuse inscription:
UNITED EAST INDIA COMPANY
On the broad, raised rim is the incuse inscription:
AUSPICIO REGIS ET SENATUS ANGLIAE
(= By the authority of the King and Parliament of England).
Below and in a sunken panel at the bottom of the rim is a relief inscription:
96 TO ONE RUPEE

Balemark of the Company surrounded by a broad flat rim. On the rim is the incuse legend:
UNITED EAST INDIA COMPANY 1794

Official Weight (g)	6.67
Actual Weight (g)	Varies. See table below
Actual Diameter (mm)	24.3-24.4
Metal	Copper
Edge	1. ENGLISH UNITED EAST INDIA COMPANY (incuse) 2. Plain
Axis	↑↓

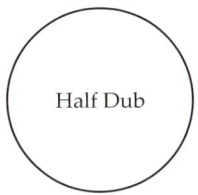

Half Dub

Soho Mint – Northern Circars – Copper Currency Half Dub 1793 to 1797 (cont)

Catalogue

Cat No.	Pr. No.	Obv	Date	Status	Edge	Actual wt (g)	Comment	Value ($)
5.179	319	A	1794	Currency	1	6.60-7.09		60
5.180	320	A	1794	Proof	1	"		150
5.181	-	A	1794	Proof	2	"	Ref: Noble Sale 48 (1995), Lot 2040	150
5.182	321	A	1794	Gilt Proof	1	"		250
5.183	-		1794	Silver Proof	?	6.96	Ref: Format 4/80	750
5.184	322	B	1794	Proof	1	"	Mule	400
5.185	-	A	1797	Currency	1		Ref: Format (1997) No.56 Cat No. Brt-2627	60
5.186	323	B	1797	Currency	1	7.18		60
5.187	-	B	1797	Proof	1	4.79	NB. Light weight.	150
5.188	324	B	1797	Proof	1			150
5.189	-	B	1797	Proof	2		Ref: Baldwin (2013), sale 82 (Fore), lot 954	250
5.190	325	B	1797	Gilt Proof	1			250
5.191	-		1797	Currency mule	1	7.04	Ref: Puddester. Mule: Obverse 5.170, Reverse 5.177	250
5.192	326	B	1797	Silver Proof	1			750

Obverse Varieties

ANGLIAE	ANGLIAE may end close to the sunken panel or away from the panel.

	A	B
ANGLIAE	Close	Away

Madras Presidency Coins for use in Sumatra

Summary

A settlement was established by the EIC at Bencoolen in Sumatra in 1687 and copper and silver coins were produced for use of the settlement between 1687 and 1695. Bencoolen formed part of the Madras Presidency and the coins were produced in the Madras mint[16].

In 1714 Fort Marlborough was built but it was not until 1783 that the first coins were produced for use there. Subsequent coins were produced by Boulton at Soho and are not included in this work.

---

[16] Pridmore (1974), SNC LXXXII pp. 429-430

Coins for use in Sumatra – Half Dollar

All the following coins were struck at Madras for use at Benculen.

6.1

2
FORT
MARLBRO'
[date]

2 *Uwang Kumpani dua Suku*

Actual Weight (g)	12.71-12.75
Actual Diameter (mm)	24.1-25.4
Metal	Silver

Half Dollar

Catalogue

Cat No.	Pr. No.	AD	AH	Comments	Value ($)
6.1	Sumatra 1	1783	1197		850
6.2	Sumatra 2	1784	1198		850

Half dollar, 1784

Coins for use in Sumatra – Fanams

6.4

Balemark of the Company

A crude Persian inscription translitered as *Angriz Kampani* (= English Company)

	3 Fanams	2 Fanams	Fanam
Official Weight (g)	3.3	2.2	1.1
Actual Weight (g)	3.25	2.02-2.19	1.04-1.14
Actual Diameter (mm)	~11.5	9.7-10.6	7.8-8.4
Metal	Silver		

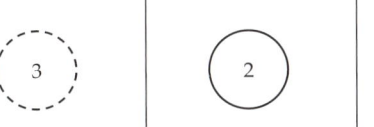

Catalogue

Cat No.	Denomination	Comments	Value ($)
6.3	3 Fanams	Extremely rare	1000
6.4	2 Fanams		300
6.5	Fanam		300

Double Fanam, a second example showing other parts of the design

Coins for use in Sumatra – Cash. First Issue

6.6

Balemark of the Company

Well written *Angriz Kampani* (=English Company)

Official Weight (g)	3.54
Actual Weight (g)	3.16-3.37
Actual Diameter (mm)	?
Metal	Copper

Catalogue

Cat No.	Comments	Value ($)
6.6	Extremely rare	500

Coins for use in Sumatra – Cash, Second Issue

6.7

Balemark of the Company

A crude Persian inscription translitered as *Angriz Kampani* (= English Company)

Official Weight	3.54
Actual Weight (g)	3.18-3.39
Actual Diameter (mm)	10.9-13.5
Metal	Copper

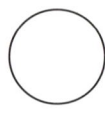

Catalogue

Cat No.	Comments	Value ($)
6.7	Issued 1695? See Wiggins (1989), ONSNL 116	200